Singapore

written and researched by

Mark Lewis

**ROUGH
GUIDES**

NEW YORK • LONDON • DELHI

www.roughguides.com

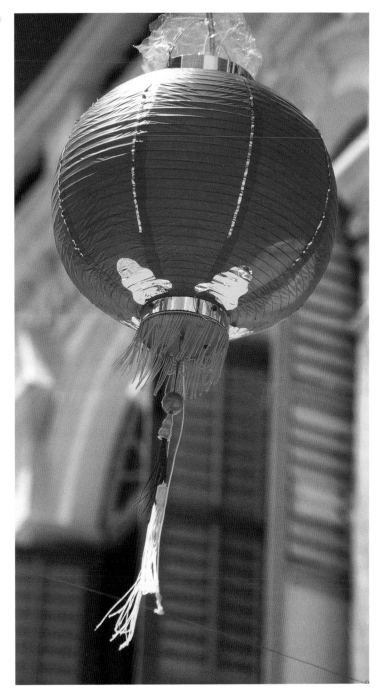

Introduction to
Singapore

Singapore is certainly the handiest and most marvellous city I ever saw, as well planned and carefully executed as though built entirely by one man. It is like a big desk, full of drawers and pigeon-holes, where everything has its place, and can always be found in it.

W. Hornaday, 1885

Despite the immense changes that the twentieth century has imposed upon the tiny island of **Singapore**, natural historian William Hornaday's succinct appraisal is as valid today as it was in 1885. Since gaining full independence from Malaysia in 1965, this absorbing city-state has been transformed from a sleepy colonial backwater into a pristine, futuristic shrine to consumerism. Yet visitors prepared to peer beneath the state's squeaky-clean surface will discover a profusion of age-old buildings, and values and traditions that have survived the profound social and geographical change.

The island has not been overwhelmed by development – even as you make your way in from the airport, you'll be struck immediately by Singapore's abundance of parks, nature reserves, and lush, tropical greenery.

Singapore's **progress** over the past three decades has been remarkable. Lacking any noteworthy natural resources, its early prosperity was based on a vigorous free trade policy, in place since 1819 when Sir Stamford Raffles first set up a British trading post here. Later, mass industrialization bolstered the economy, and today the state boasts the world's second-busiest port after Rotterdam, minimal unemployment, and a super-efficient infrastructure. Almost the entire population has been moved from unsanitary kampungs (villages) into new apartments, and the average per capita income is over S$37,000 (US$21,500). Yet none of this was achieved without considerable compromise – indeed, the state's detractors claim it has sold its soul in return for prosperity.

Put simply, at the core of the Singapore success story is an unwritten bargain between its **government** and population that critics describe as soft **authoritarianism**. The loss of a certain amount of personal freedom has been accepted in return for levels of affluence and comfort that would have seemed unimaginable thirty years ago. But as the nation's youth (who don't remember a time before the improvements they take for granted) begin to find a voice, public life should become increasingly, if gradually, more liberal and democratic.

Whatever the political ramifications of the state's economic success, of more relevance to its millions of annual visitors (7.56 million in 2002) is that improvements in living conditions have resulted in a steady loss of the state's **heritage**, with historic buildings and streets bulldozed to make way for shopping centres. Singapore undoubtedly lacks the personality of some Southeast Asian cities, but its reputation for being sterile and sanitized is unfair. Shopping on state-of-the-art Orchard Road is undoubtedly a major draw for many tourists, but elsewhere can still be found the dusty temples, fragrant medicinal shops, and colonial buildings of old Singapore, neatly divided into historical enclaves.

> **Much of the city's fascination springs from its multicultural population**

Much of the city's fascination springs from its **multicultural population**: of the 3.32

million permanent residents, 77 percent are Chinese, whose shops, restaurants and temples are found across the island, fourteen percent are Malays, and eight percent are Indians, with the remainder made up of other ethnic groups. This diverse ethnic mix textures the whole island, and often turns a ten-minute walk into what seems like a hop from one country to another. One intriguing by-product of this ethnic melting pot is **Singlish**, or Singaporean English, a patois that blends English with the speech patterns, exclamations and vocabulary of Chinese and Malay. Another is the amazing range of mouth-watering **cuisines** on offer in the city. Inevitably, the greatest emphasis is on Chinese, Malay and Indian foods, but your trip to Singapore will give you the opportunity to sample Thai, Vietnamese, and any number of other Asian specialities.

Singlish

Upon first hearing the machine-gun rattle of Singaporean English, or Singlish, you could easily be forgiven for thinking you're listening to a language other than English. Pronunciation is so staccato that many words are rendered almost unrecognizable – especially monosyllabic words such as "cheque" and "book", which together would be spoken "che-boo". In contrast, in two-syllable words the second syllable is lengthened, and stressed by a rise in tone: ask a Singaporean what they've been doing, and you'll variously be told "wor-king", "shop-ping", and "slee-ping".

But it's the unorthodox rhythms of phrasing that make Singlish so memorable. Conventional English syntax is twisted and wrung, and tenses and pronouns discarded. If you ask a Singaporean if they've ever seen Michael Jackson, you might be answered "I ever see him", while enquiring whether they've just been shopping might yield "go come back already".

Responses are almost invariably reduced to their bare bones, with single-word replies often repeated for stress. Request something in a shop and you'll hear "have, have", or "got, got". Suffixes and exclamations drawn from Malay, Hokkien and English complete this patois, the most distinctive being "lah", as in "okay lah", and "so cheap one lah" (which translates as "this is really inexpensive, isn't it?").

If Singlish still has you totally baffled, you might try raising your eyes to the heavens, and crying either "ay yor" (with a drop of tone on "yor") or "Allama" – both expressions of annoyance or exasperation.

What to see

The diamond-shaped island of Singapore is 42km from east to west at its widest points, 23km from north to south, making it compact enough to be explored exhaustively in just a few days. The state's central or downtown districts lie within a three-kilometre radius of the mouth of the river. Although MRT lines and buses do run between these districts (see p.00), you might prefer to explore the whole central region on foot. You'll need at least two days to do justice to the downtown area. You should also bear in mind that you are in the tropics: apply sunscreen and stay out of the midday sun. And beware, strolling through the remaining pockets of old Singapore entails negotiating uneven five-foot ways (the covered pavements that front Singapore's old shophouses) and yawning storm drains.

Ever since Sir Stamford Raffles first landed on its northern bank in 1819, the area around the **Singapore River**, which strikes into the heart of the island from the south coast, has formed the hub of the city.

Historical roots: the layout of Singapore

The basic skeleton plan of Singapore's central streets and districts has changed little since the British assembled it in the first half of the nineteenth century. Modern Singapore's founder, Sir Stamford Raffles, established the Padang as the nucleus of European life as early as 1819, and the trappings of colonial rule – government building, court house, church – were constructed around it in subsequent decades. Elsewhere, "native divisions or campongs" were established. An 1823 map of Singapore shows Chinatown and the Arab quarter in the positions they occupy now. By the late 1820s, Indian immigrants were starting to gravitate towards the brick kiln and livestock industries that were developing along Serangoon Road – the spine of today's Little India.

The south bank of the Singapore River was clawed back from the swamp that covered it in 1823, to form the site of modern-day Raffles Place. This was the earliest example of a trend towards land reclamation that has substantially remoulded the coastline and contours of Singapore, and which still continues. To appreciate just how much of modern Singapore lay underwater a century ago, turn to the map of Central Singapore at the back and check out how far from the sea Beach Road and Telok Ayer ("Watery Bay") Street are, today.

North of the river, and forming the core of downtown Singapore is the **Colonial District**, around whose public buildings and lofty cathedral the island's British residents used to promenade. The Colonial District has a cluster of buildings that recall the days of early British rule: Parliament House, the Cathedral, the Supreme Court, the Cricket Club and, most famously, **Raffles Hotel**. Further west, **Fort Canning**

Park provides a welcome splash of green to the high-rise landscape. The park has several attractions, including the **Singapore History Museum**. From here, it's a five-minute stroll to the eastern end of **Orchard Road**, the main shopping area in the city, and a metropolis of retails malls and shopping centres. South, across the river, the monolithic towers of the **Financial District** cast their long shadows over the city.

Each of Singapore's three **ethnic enclaves** has its own distinct flavour, ranging from the aromatic spice stores and mind-expanding Hindu temples of **Little India**, to the tumbledown back streets of **Chinatown**, where it's still possible to happen upon calligraphers and fortune-tellers. Visitors to the **Arab Quarter** can browse stores stacked with fine cloths and silks, to the accompaniment of the otherworldly wail of the Muezzin's call to prayer at the **Sultan Mosque**.

Downtown Singapore is probably where you'll spend most of your time, but the rest of the island has its attractions too. The super-efficient bus and underground train networks link the city centre with the suburbs to the north, east and west, and there's even the chance to take a ride on a **cable car**.

The area **north** of downtown Singapore is the island's suburban heartland, and home to a grid of vast new towns; but it's here that you'll also find the state's last remaining pocket of primary rainforest, the **Bukit Timah Nature Reserve**, and the splendid **Singapore Zoological Gardens**. In addition to Singapore's industrial zone and port, the **west** of the island boasts a clutch of good theme parks, most notably **Jurong BirdPark**, and **Haw Par Villas** – a mind-boggling hybrid of eastern mythology and Disneyland kitsch.

Aside from the infamous jail near **Changi** Village, where so many soldiers lost their lives in World War II, the **east** of Singapore features some of Singapore's best **seafood restaurants**, set behind long stretches of sandy beach.

Over fifty **islands and islets** lie within Singaporean waters, all of which can be reached

> Shopping on state-of-the-art Orchard Road is undoubtedly a major draw for many tourists, but elsewhere can still be found the dusty temples, fragrant medicinal shops, and colonial buildings of old Singapore

with varying degrees of ease. The best day-trips, however, are to **Sentosa**, the island amusement arcade linked to the south coast by causeway and cable car; and to **Pulau Ubin**, off the east coast, whose inhabitants continue to live a kampung life long since eradicated from the mainland.

When to go

Singapore is just 136km north of the equator, which means that you should be prepared for a hot and sticky time whenever you go. Temperatures are uniformly high throughout the year, but it's the region's humidity levels that make the heat really uncomfortable – a good downpour is the only thing that really clears the air. Be prepared for rain during your stay – November and December are usually the coolest, and the wettest, months, but rain can fall all year round. On average, June,

July and August record the lowest annual rainfall. Otherwise, the only other consideration is the possibility of coinciding with one of the island's many festivals (see p.00), of which the liveliest and most extensive is Chinese New Year.

	Jan	Feb	Mar	Apr	May	Jun	Jul	Aug	Sep	Oct	Nov	Dec
Average daily temperatures												
max. temp. (°C)	31	32	32	32	32	32	31	31	31	31	31	30
min. temp. (°C)	21	22	23	23	23	23	22	22	22	22	22	22
Average monthly rainfall												
rainfall (mm)	146	155	182	223	228	151	170	163	200	199	255	258

20

things not to miss

Though roughly the same size as the Isle of Wight, Singapore is rich in adventures and attractions, so unless you're in town for a while, it won't be possible to see everything it has to offer in one trip. What follows is a selective taste of the city-state's highlights: its best museums, most charismatic restaurants, most memorable experiences and vibrant neighbourhoods. They're arranged in five colour-coded categories, which you can browse through to find the very best things to see and do. All highlights have a page reference to take you straight into the guide, where you can find out more.

01 **The view from the Swissôtel's City Space** Page **47** • From the City Space bar at the top of the Swissôtel, pictured here, you can see as far as Malaysia to the north, and Indonesia to the south, while enjoying a well-mixed cocktail and nibbling on warmed chilli cashews.

02 A trip to the Theatres on the Bay

Page **47** • Singapore's spectacular new arts centre offers a full range of Western and Oriental cultural treats.

03 Chilli crab on the East Coast

Page **98** • Fresh crabs tossed in a fiery and lip-smackingly tasty chilli sauce, eaten overlooking the South China Sea. Roll your sleeves up and get stuck in – but don't wear a white shirt.

04 Satay

Page **144** • Satay is a staple of Malay cooking, just one of the amazing range of mouth-watering cuisines on offer in the city.

05 Bukit Timah Reserve Page **85** • An incongruous but pristine pocket of primary rainforest, slap bang in the middle of twenty-first century Singapore.

06 An Orchard Road shopping spree Page **54** •
Think Oxford Street, think 5th Avenue, think Champs-Elysées: shopping centres and famous brands enough to test even the most confirmed shopaholic.

07 A cable car to Sentosa
Page **111** • Never mind bussing it across the causeway – this is the most fun approach to Singapore's pleasure island.

08 Night-time on Boat Quay Page **71** • Alfresco dining at its best: bars and restaurants galore, whose reflected lights dance on the waters of the Singapore River.

09 The Thian Hock Keng temple Page **60** • Gilt altars, Eastern deities, chanting monks, praying worshippers and incense smoke – stroll into the courtyard and drink in the atmosphere.

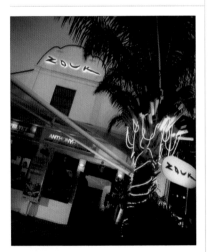

11 Clubbing at Zouk Page **153** • Some of the world's most happening DJs guest at Singapore's hippest nightspot, set in a converted warehouse beside the river.

10 Renting bikes Page **31** • Renting a bike is the perfect way to explore some of Singapore's outlying areas, such as the East Coast Parkway or sleepy Pulau Ubin.

12 Timithi at Sri Mariamman temple Page **64** • No surprise in multicultural Singapore, a Hindu temple in Chinatown and the venue for the annual fire-walking festival.

13 A Singapore Sling at Raffles Hotel Page
118 • No trip is complete without an obligatory glass of 1920's bartender, Ngiam Tong Boon's famous cherry brandy cocktail, best sipped in the Bar & Billiards Room.

14 Geylang Serai Page 93 • The
vibrant market and hawker centre of Geylang Serai frame a perfect snapshot of Malay life and culture; best visited during the month of Ramadan.

15 Changi Prison Museum
Page **95** • A hushed and moving memorial to the horrors perpetrated in Singapore during the Second World War.

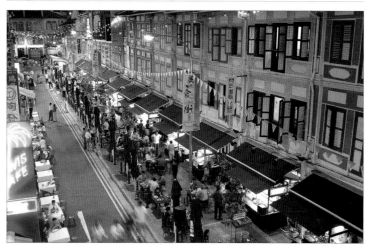

16 Chinatown Page 57 • Chinatown has been extensively redeveloped in recent
years and its once characterful shophouses rendered improbably perfect, but if you venture into the tumbledown back streets it's still possible to happen upon calligraphers and fortune-tellers.

17 A walk down Serangoon Road Page 75 •
Sensual overload: colourful sarees, aromatic spice-grinding shops, fortune-telling parrots and jasmine garlands.

18 Evening prayer at the Sultan Mosque
Page 83 • The muezzin's wailing call to prayer floats hauntingly on the warm evening air.

19 Breakfast with the animals
Page 90 • You've heard of a chimp's tea party – now try orange juice with an orang utan.

20 Standing in Raffles Place looking up at the skyline Page 41 •
Ground-level vertigo: look up for long, and you'll swear Singapore's immaculate skyscrapers are bowing towards one another to form a roof above you.

Contents

Using this Rough Guide

We've tried to make this Rough Guide a good read and easy to use. The book is divided into six main sections, and you should be able to find whatever you want in one of them.

Colour section

The front colour section offers a quick tour of Singapore. The **introduction** aims to give you a feel for the place, with suggestions on where to go and information on what the weather is like. Next, our author rounds up his favourite aspects of Singapore in the **things not to miss** section – whether it's great food, amazing sights or a special hotel. Right after this comes a full **contents** list.

Basics

You've decided to go and the basics section covers all the pre-departure nitty-gritty to help you plan your trip. This is where to find out which airlines fly to your destination, what to do about money and insurance, about Internet access, food, security, public transport, car rental – in fact just about every piece of **general practical information** you might need.

Guide

This is the heart of the Rough Guide, divided into user-friendly chapters, each of which covers a specific district. Each chapter starts with an **introduction**

that helps you to decide where to go, followed by a tour of the sights.

Listings

Listings contain all the consumer information you need to make the most of your stay, with chapters on **accommodation**, **eating**, **nightlife**, **entertainment** and the arts, **festivals**, **shopping** and **sports**.

Contexts

Read Contexts to get a deeper understanding of what makes Singapore tick. We include a brief history, religion and Chinese astrology, and a detailed further reading section that reviews dozens of **books** relating to the city.

Index + small print

Apart from a full index, which includes maps as well as places, this section covers publishing information, credits and acknowledgements, and also has our contact details in case you want to send in updates and corrections to the book – or suggestions as to how we might improve it.

Map and chapter list

- Colour section
- Contents
- **B** Basics
- **1** The Colonial District
- **2** Orchard Road
- **3** Chinatown and the Financial District
- **4** Little India and the Arab Quarter
- **5** Nothern Singapore
- **6** Eastern Singapore
- **7** Western Singapore
- **8** Sentosa and the southern isles
- **9** Accommodation
- **10** Eating
- **11** Nightlife
- **12** Entertainment and the arts
- **13** Festivals
- **14** Shopping
- **15** Sports
- **16** Kids' Singapore
- **17** Directory
- **C** Contexts
- **I** Index

Contents

Colour section   i–xvi

Introduction iii
What to see vi

When to go..ix
Things not to miss..................................x

Basics   7–38

Getting there 9
Red tape and visas 18
Information, websites and maps..........19
Money, banks and costs..................,.......20
Insurance 23
Health 24
Arrival 26

Departure 28
Getting around 29
Opening hours, holidays and festivals ..32
Communications..................................33
The media 35
Trouble and the police 36
Travellers with disabilities 37

The City   39–112

1 The Colonial District.........................41
2 Orchard Road 54
3 Chinatown and the Financial District ..57
4 Little India and the Arab Quarter 74

5 Nothern Singapore...........................85
6 Eastern Singapore 93
7 Western Singapore 99
8 Sentosa and the southern isles 107

Listings

115–179

⑨ Accommodation 115
⑩ Eating...123
⑪ Nightlife 148
⑫ Entertainment and the arts 155
⑬ Festivals..159

⑭ Shopping 163
⑮ Sports 171
⑯ Kids' Singapore 175
⑰ Directory 178

Contexts

182–214

A brief history of Singapore 183
Religion 190
Chinese astrology 194
Singaporean recipes 198

Singapore in literature........................202
Books 210
Glossary 214

Index + small print

215–222

Full index..216
A rough guide to Rough Guides 219
Rough Guide credits...........................220
Publishing information 220

Help us update 220
Acknowledgements 221
Readers' letters..................................221
Photo credits......................................222

Colour maps

Central Singapore
Singapore

The MRT system

Map symbols

Maps are listed in the full index using coloured text.

⎯⎯	Railway
▬▬	Expressway
══	Main road
══	Minor road
▬▬	Pedestrianized road
-----	Footpath
---	Ferry route
•---•	Cable car
○⎯○	Tramway/monorail
══	Waterway
----	Chapter division boundary
·-··-·	International border
✈	Airport
)(	Bridge/tunnel
▲	Peak
⍦	Public gardens
◉	Accommodation
▣	Restaurant/café/bar
♦	General point of interest

♥	Museum
ⓘ	Tourist office
⊠	Post office
①	Telephone office
@	Internet access
⊞	Hospital/clinic
⊖	MRT station
▮	Building
▨	Underground mall
⬭	Stadium
⊹	Church
✡	Synagogue
☪	Mosque
♠	Buddhist temple
♣	Hindu temple
⊞ ♱	Christian cemetery
⊔	Muslim cemetery
▦	Park

Basics

Basics

Getting there 9

Red tape and visas 18

Information, websites and maps 19

Money, banks and costs..20

Insurance...23

Health..24

Arrival 26

Departure 28

Getting around 29

Opening hours, holidays and festivals...................................32

Communications 33

The media 35

Trouble and the police 36

Travellers with disabilities 37

Getting there

The easiest and quickest way to get to Singapore is to fly, and with Singapore being one of the world's main air hubs finding a flight should be relatively straightforward.

Generally speaking, booking a scheduled ticket direct with the airline is the most expensive way to fly. You can usually cut costs considerably by booking through a specialist flight agent – either a consolidator or a **discount agent**. **Consolidators** buy up large blocks of tickets to sell on at a discount. They don't normally impose advance purchase requirements (although in busy periods you'll want to book ahead to be sure of getting a seat), but they often charge very stiff fees for date changes; note also that airlines generally won't alter tickets after they've gone to a consolidator, so you can make changes only through the consolidator. **Discount agents** also deal in blocks of tickets off-loaded by the airlines, and may in addition offer special student and youth fares and a range of other travel-related services such as travel insurance, rail passes, car rentals, tours and the like.

Reliable flight agents are listed on the pages that follow. Alternatively, consult the ads in the Sunday newspaper travel sections. Occasionally you'll turn up better deals by calling the **airlines** direct (be sure to ask about seasonal promotions).

Discount **travel clubs**, offering money off air tickets, car rental and the like, are an option if you travel a lot. Most charge annual membership fees.

A further possibility is to see if you can arrange a **courier flight**, although you'll need a flexible schedule, and preferably be travelling alone with very little luggage. In return for shepherding a parcel through customs, you can expect to get a deeply discounted ticket, though you'll probably also be restricted in the duration of your stay.

If you want to see more of Southeast Asia on your trip to Singapore you could consider buying an **open-jaw** ticket which allows you, for example, to fly into Bangkok, travel over-land to Singapore and then fly home from there. There's also the option of a **round-the-world ticket** (RTW), if Singapore is just one stop on a longer itinerary. Some travel agents can sell you an "off-the-shelf" RTW ticket that will have you touching down in about half a dozen cities (Singapore is on many itineraries); these tickets can also be tailored to your needs, though this is apt to be more expensive. If you're not too pushed for time you could also consider flying to another **Southeast Asian gateway**, such as Bangkok, and travelling by air or overland from there.

Additionally, an increasing number of **package holidays** are available, including fly-drive deals and city breaks. Although usually not the cheapest way of travelling, these can be worthwhile if your time is limited.

Online travel agents

Many airlines and discount travel websites offer you the opportunity to book your tickets **online**, cutting the cost of agents and middlemen. Good deals can often be found through discount or auction sites, as well as through the airlines' own websites.

Online booking agents and general travel sites

Ⓦ **travel.yahoo.com** Incorporates a lot of Rough Guide material in its coverage of destination countries and cities across the world, with information about places to eat, sleep, etc.

Ⓦ **www.cheapflights.com** Flight deals, travel agents, plus links to other travel sites.

Ⓦ **www.cheaptickets.com** Discount flight specialists.

Ⓦ **www.etn.nl/discount.htm** A hub of consolidator and discount agent Web links, maintained by the non-profit European Travel Network.

Ⓦ **www.expedia.com** Discount air fares, all-airline search engine and daily deals.

ⓦ www.flyaow.com Online air travel info and reservations site.

ⓦ www.gaytravel.com Gay online travel agent, offering accommodation, cruises, tours and more.

ⓦ www.hotwire.com Bookings from the US only. Last-minute savings of up to forty percent on regular published fares. Travellers must be at least 18 and there are no refunds, transfers or changes allowed. Log-in required.

ⓦ www.lastminute.com Offers good last-minute holiday package and flight-only deals.

ⓦ www.priceline.com Name-your-own-price website that has deals at around forty percent off standard fares. You cannot specify flight times (although you do specify dates) and the tickets are non-refundable, non-transferable and non-changeable.

ⓦ www.skyauction.com Bookings from the US only. Auctions tickets and travel packages using a "second bid" scheme. The best strategy is to bid the maximum you're willing to pay, since if you win you'll pay just enough to beat the runner-up regardless of your maximum bid.

ⓦ www.smilinjack.com/airlines.htm Lists an up-to-date compilation of airline website addresses.

ⓦ www.travelocity.com Destination guides, hot Web fares and best deals for car rental, accommodation and lodging as well as fares. Provides access to the travel agent system SABRE, the most comprehensive central reservations system in the US.

ⓦ www.travelshop.com.au Australian website offering discounted flights, packages, insurance, and online bookings.

Flights from the UK and Ireland

There are regular daily flights to Singapore from Britain and connecting flights from Ireland to all major British airports. Singapore Airlines, British Airways, Qantas and Virgin Atlantic all offer **direct** flights out of London, a journey time of twelve to thirteen hours. Many other scheduled airlines offer **indirect** flights, which typically touch down at their own national hubs, and maybe elsewhere, en route to the final destination. These flights take longer (16–22 hours), but work out cheaper. Add-on costs from other British airports are around £60 return to London.

There are no non-stop flights from **Ireland** to Singapore; airlines will quote you through-fares via British airports. Alternatively, you could take advantage of the cheap air fares between Ireland and Britain and pick up an onward flight from London with another airline.

Discounted return **fares** start from around £380 for non-stop flights and £280 for indirect in low season, but you should be prepared to add to that a couple of hundred pounds in the high-season months of July, August and December. The cheapest tickets will be with airlines such as KLM (via Amsterdam), Finnair (via Helsinki), Pakistan International Airlines (via Karachi), Turkish Airlines (via Istanbul), Thai International (via Bangkok), Gulf Air (via Bahrain), Kuwait Airways, or Aeroflot (via Moscow and Dubai).

The cheapest **round-the-world tickets** start from around £700 in low season (departing Jan–June & Sept to early Dec). A typical one-year open ticket could depart from and return to London, taking in, say, Singapore, Bangkok, Bali, Sydney, Auckland, Tahiti, Los Angeles and New York, allowing you to cover the Singapore–Bangkok and Los Angeles–New York legs overland. STA, usit Now and Trailfinders all specialize in RTW tickets.

Open-jaw tickets, which allow you to fly into one airport and out of another without having to retrace your steps, are calculated in different ways by different airlines, but you can expect to pay at least the highest of the two return fares you are combining. Flying into Bangkok and out of Singapore, reckon on around £500, although it's well worth shopping around for deals on these tickets. For details of the overland sector see "Getting there from Southeast Asia", p.16.

If you're considering a **courier flight**, contact the International Association of Air Travel Couriers UK (☎0800/0746 481, ⓦwww.aircourier.co.uk) which acts as a courier agent for lots of companies.

Airlines in the UK and Ireland

Aer Lingus ☎0845/08 44444, Rep Ireland ☎0818/365 000; ⓦwww.aerlingus.ie.
Aeroflot ☎020/7355 2233, ⓦwww.aeroflot.co.uk.
bmibaby ☎0870/264 2229, Rep Ireland ☎01/236 6130; ⓦwww.bmibaby.com.
British Airways ☎0845/773 3377, Rep Ireland ☎1800/626 747; ⓦwww.ba.com.
British Midland ☎0870/607 0555, Rep Ireland ☎01/4073036; ⓦwww.flybmi.com.
EasyJet ☎0870/600 0000, ⓦwww.easyjet.com.
Finnair ☎0870/241 4411, Rep Ireland ☎01/844 6565; ⓦwww.finnair.com.

Go ☎0870/607 6543, ⊛www.go-fly.com.
Gulf Air ☎0870/777 1717, ⊛www.gulfairco.com.
KLM ☎0870/507 4074, ⊛www.klmuk.com.
Kuwait Airways ☎020/7412 0006,
⊛www.kuwait-airways.com.
Lufthansa ☎0845/7737747, Rep Ireland
☎01/844 5544; ⊛www.lufthansa.co.uk.
Malaysia Airlines (MAS) ☎0870/607 9090, Rep
Ireland ☎01/676 1561;
⊛www.malaysiaairlineseurope.com.
Pakistan International Airlines ☎020/7499
5500, ⊛www.fly-pia.com.
Qantas ☎0845/774 7767, ⊛www.qantas.co.uk.
Royal Brunei Airlines ☎020/7584 6660,
⊛www.bruneiair.com.
Ryanair ☎0871/246 0000, Rep Ireland
☎0818/303 030; ⊛www.ryanair.com.
SAS Scandinavian Airlines ☎0845/607 2772,
Rep Ireland ☎01/844 5440;
⊛www.scandinavian.net.
Singapore Airlines ☎0870/608 8886, Rep
Ireland ☎01/671 0722; ⊛www.singaporeair.com.
SriLankan Airlines ☎020/8538 2000,
⊛www.srilankan.lk.
Thai International ☎0870/606 0911,
⊛www.thaiair.com.
Turkish Airlines ☎020/7766 9300,
⊛www.turkishairlines.com.
Virgin Atlantic Airways ☎01293/747 747,
⊛www.virgin-atlantic.com.

Discount flight and travel agents in the UK and Ireland

Apex Travel Rep Ireland ☎01/241 8000,
⊛www.apextravel.ie. Specialists in flights to Far
East and other long-haul destinations.
Bridge the World ☎0870/444 7474,
⊛www.bridgetheworld.com. Specializing in round-
the-world tickets, with good deals aimed at the
backpacker market.
Flightbookers ☎0870/010 7000,
⊛www.ebookers.com. Low fares on an extensive
selection of scheduled flights.
Joe Walsh Tours Rep Ireland ☎01/676 0991,
⊛www.joewalshtours.ie. General budget fares agent.
North South Travel ☎01245/608 291,
⊛www.northsouthtravel.co.uk. Friendly, competitive
travel agency, offering discounted fares worldwide –
profits are used to support projects in the developing
world, especially the promotion of sustainable tourism.
STA Travel ☎0870/1600 599,
⊛www.statravel.co.uk. Worldwide specialists in
low-cost flights and tours for students and under-
26s, though other customers welcome.
Trailfinders London ☎020/7628 7628,

⊛www.trailfinders.co.uk; Rep Ireland ☎01/677
7888, ⊛www.trailfinders.ie. One of the best-
informed and most efficient agents for independent
travellers.
Travel Bag ☎0870/890 1456, ⊛www.travelbag
.co.uk. Discount flights to the Far East.
usit Now Rep Ireland ☎01/602 1600, Northern
Ireland ☎028/9032 7111; ⊛www.usitnow.ie.
Student and youth specialists.

Packages and organized tours

There is a range of **package holidays** and
organized tours available to Singapore, and
the main operators are listed below; all also
offer trips further afield into Malaysia and
beyond. For **city breaks**, five nights in
Singapore, including flights but with room-
only accommodation in a three-star hotel,
cost around £650 (£850 in high season),
rising to £900–1100 for two weeks.

Specialist operators can also arrange itineraries which include a ride on the extremely
swish **Eastern and Oriental Express** train
between Singapore and Bangkok (see p.17
for more details).

Several companies offer **multi-centre packages** to Singapore and other Southeast Asian
destinations. For example, a ten-night stay in
Singapore and Thailand's Phuket Island
should cost around £750, including return
flight and accommodation in three-star hotels.

Specialist tour operators in the UK and Ireland

Abercrombie & Kent Travel ☎020/7730 9600,
⊛www.abercrombiekent.com. Top-of-the-range,
tailor-made cruises and tours.
AsiaWorld ☎08700/799788,
⊛www.asiaworld.co.uk. Short breaks in Singapore
out of various UK cities.
Bales Worldwide ☎0870/241 3208,
⊛www.balesworldwide.com. Tailor-made trips
incorporating the Eastern and Oriental train journey
from Singapore to Bangkok.
British Airways Holidays ☎0870/442 3820,
⊛www.baholidays.co.uk. Five-night city breaks
starting from £700.
Eastern and Oriental Express ☎020/7805
5100, ⊛www.orient-express.com. Tours based
around one of the most exclusive train journeys in
the world.
Hayes and Jarvis ☎0870/898 9890,
⊛www.hayes-jarvis.com. Specialists in long-haul

holidays; five-night city breaks, flying with Singapore Airlines, offer good value.

Kuoni Travel ☎01306/742888, ⓦwww.kuoni.co.uk. Tailor-made tours in Southeast Asia, plus Singapore city breaks.

Magic of the Orient ☎01293/537700, ⓦwww.magic-of-the-orient.com. Offers a two-week Singapore & Vietnam Highlights tour for £1500, plus swish seven-night stays at the Fullerton.

Qantas Holidays ☎0870/5673 464, ⓦwww.qantas-holidays.co.uk. Stylish Singapore holidays flying business class and staying at Raffles.

Silverbird Travel ☎020/8875 9090, ⓦwww.silverbird.co.uk. Tours pair Singapore up with Malaysian and Thai islands.

Thomas Cook Holidays ☎0173/3417 100, ⓦwww.thomascook.com. Good selection of flight-and-board holidays and city breaks.

Tradewinds Worldwide Holidays ☎0870/751 0003, ⓦwww.tradewinds.co.uk. Lush multi-centre trips to Singapore plus the Maldives, or Thailand.

Flights from the US and Canada

With strong competition between a large number of carriers, Singapore is one of the cheapest Southeast Asian destinations to reach **from North America**.

Singapore is roughly halfway around the world from the **east coast** of the USA, which means that whether you plan on flying east or west you're going to have a long flight with at least one stopover. The eastbound (transatlantic) route is more direct and a bit faster – about 21 hours' total travel time – which makes it cheaper than flying west. From the **west coast**, it's faster and cheaper to head west (over the Pacific) – Los Angeles to Singapore takes as little as nineteen hours – although flying via Europe may suit your itinerary better and doesn't cost much more.

Air fares from North America to Southeast Asia are highest from around early June to late August, and again from early December to early January. All other times are considered low season. The price difference between high season and low season is about $200–300 on a typical round-trip fare, but bear in mind that you will have to make your reservation further in advance during the high season. Remember that flying on weekends ordinarily adds about $100 to the round-trip fare; price ranges quoted below assume midweek travel.

Singapore Airlines offers the most frequent departures, with **direct flights** originating in New York (eastbound via Frankfurt or Amsterdam), Los Angeles/San Francisco (westbound via Tokyo, Taipei or Hong Kong) and Vancouver (westbound via Seoul). However, **indirect flights** on other airlines – or a combination of airlines – might not actually add much time to your journey, and if you go through a consolidator you might be able to get a free stopover each way. The airlines that fly to Singapore are too numerous to list here: see below for some of the major carriers.

If you're planning to **travel in several Asian countries**, consider making Hong Kong or Bangkok your first stop; you'll save about $200 over the fare to Singapore and from Bangkok you can travel overland by train to Singapore – see "Getting there from Southeast Asia" (p.16).

From **New York**, you'll pay $750 direct round-trip in the low season, but as much as $11000 in the high season; from **Los Angeles**, **San Francisco** or **Seattle**, $800/$11000; from **Toronto** or **Montréal**, CDN$2200/$2500; and from **Vancouver**, CDN$2000/$2400.

If Singapore is only one stop on a longer journey, you might want to consider buying a **round-the-world ticket (RTW)**. Plan for between $1300 and $1500 for a RTW ticket travelling for example New York–Hong Kong–Singapore–(overland on your own)–Bangkok–Delhi–London–New York.

Most airlines operating in this part of the world offer so-called **Circle Pacific** fares, allowing four (or sometimes more) stopovers in the course of a round trip between North America and Asia or Australasia. However, fares for these deals can approach $2000 – not very economical unless you have some really obscure stopovers in mind, and plan to travel right across Australia as well. Otherwise, you'll probably find it's cheaper to have a discount travel agent put together a ticket with your intended stops.

A further possibility is a **courier flight**. Courier flights to Singapore come up regularly, but most departures are from Los Angeles – figure on paying around $300, maybe less if it's a last-minute deal. Contact the Air Courier Association (☎1-800/282-1202, ⓦwww.aircourier.org) or the International Association of Air Travel Couriers (☎308/632-3273, ⊛www.courier.org), both of which levy a modest membership fee before they'll arrange flights for you.

Airlines in the US and Canada

Air Canada ☎1-888/247-2262, ⊛www.aircanada.ca.
Air France US ☎1-800/237-2747, ⊛www.airfrance.com; Canada ☎1-800/667-2747, ⊛www.airfrance.ca.
British Airways ☎1-800/247-9297, ⊛www.british-airways.com.
British Midland ☎1-800/788-0555, ⊛www.flybmi.com.
Cathay Pacific ☎1-800/233-2742, ⊛www.cathay-usa.com.
EVA Airways ☎1-800/695-1188, ⊛www.evaair.com.
Finnair ☎1-800/950-5000, ⊛www.finnair.com.
Gulf Air ☎1-800/FLY-GULF, ⊛www.gulfairco.com.
Japan Air Lines ☎1-800/525-3663, ⊛www.japanair.com.
Korean Airlines ☎1-800/438-5000, ⊛www.koreanair.com.
Lufthansa US ☎1-800/645-3880 Canada ☎1-800/563-5954; ⊛www.lufthansa-usa.com.
Malaysia Airlines ☎1-800/552-9264, ⊛www.mas.com.my.
Northwest/KLM Airlines domestic ☎1-800/225-2525, international ☎1-800/447-4747, ⊛www.nwa.com, ⊛www.klm.com.
Pakistan International Airlines ☎1-800/221-2552 or 212/760-8484, ⊛www.piac.com.pk.
Philippine Airlines ☎1-800/435-9725, ⊛www.philippineairlines.com.
Singapore Airlines ☎1-800/742-3333, ⊛www.singaporeair.com.
SriLankan Airlines ☎1-877/915-2652, ⊛www.srilankan.lk.
Thai Airways International ☎1-800/426-5204, ⊛www.thaiairways.com.
United Airlines domestic ☎1-800/241-6522, international ☎1-800/538-2929, ⊛www.ual.com.

Agents, consolidators and travel clubs in the US and Canada

Air Brokers International ☎1-800/883-3273, ⊛www.airbrokers.com. Consolidator and specialist in round-the-world and Circle Pacific tickets.
Airtreks.com ☎1-877-AIRTREKS or 415/912-5600, ⊛www.airtreks.com. Round-the-world and Circle Pacific tickets. The website features an interactive database that lets you build and price

your own round-the-world itinerary. Also does Asian overland connections.
Council Travel ☎1-800/2COUNCIL, ⊛www.counciltravel.com. Nationwide organization that mostly specializes in student/budget travel.
Educational Travel Center ☎1-800/747-5551 or 608/256-5551, ⊛www.edtrav.com. Student/youth discount agent.
SkyLink US ☎1-800/AIR-ONLY or 212/573-8980, Canada ☎1-800/SKY-LINK, ⊛www.skylinkus.com. Consolidator.
STA Travel US ☎1-800/781-4040, Canada ☎1-888/427-5639, ⊛www.sta-travel.com. Worldwide specialists in independent travel; also student IDs, travel insurance, car rental, rail passes, etc.
TFI Tours ☎1-800/745-8000 or 212/736-1140, ⊛www.lowestairprice.com. Consolidator.
Travel Avenue ☎1-800/333-3335, ⊛www.travelavenue.com. Full-service travel agent that offers discounts in the form of rebates.
Travel Cuts Canada ☎1-800/667-2887, US ☎1-866/246-9762; ⊛www.travelcuts.com. Canadian student-travel organization.
Worldtek Travel ☎1-800/243-1723, ⊛www.worldtek.com. Discount travel agency for worldwide travel.

Packages and organized tours

Packages to Singapore can include five-star city breaks, sightseeing excursions and opulent splendour aboard the Eastern and Oriental Express train. Inevitably, these packaged journeys are more expensive and less spontaneous than they would be if done independently, but for the traveller with more money than time they offer a convenient and hassle-free experience.

The **Eastern and Oriental train journey** between Bangkok and Singapore (see p.17 for more information) is the ultimate in luxury: tours start at $600 and invariably throw in several days' worth of side trips along with the two-night train journey.

Note that your local travel agent should be able to book any tour for you at no additional cost. For a list of North American tour companies, see below.

Tour operators in the US and Canada

Abercrombie & Kent ☎1-800/323-7308 or 630/954-2944, ⊛www.abercrombiekent.com. De luxe tours built around the Eastern and Oriental Express.
Absolute Asia ☎1-800/736-8187,

● www.absoluteasia.com. Luxury, multi-centre trips to Southeast Asia, including Singapore.

Adventure Center ☎1-800/228-8747 or 510/654-1879, ● www.adventurecenter.com. Hiking and "soft adventure" specialists that include Singapore in Southeast Asian itineraries.

Adventures Abroad ☎1-800/665-3998 or 360/775-9926, ● www.adventures-abroad.com. Small-group adventure tours taking in Singapore and other spots in Southeast Asia.

Cox & Kings ☎1-800/999-1758, ● www .coxandkingsusa.com. Top-notch company offering Singapore stopovers in its Southeast Asian schedules.

Eastern and Oriental Express ☎1-866/674-3689, ● www.orient-express.com. Tours based around one of the most exclusive train journeys in the world.

Globus ☎1-866/755-8581, ● www.globusjourneys.com. Features Singapore in its Asia Medley and Asia Selection schedules.

Pacific Bestours ☎1-800/272-1149, ● www.bestour.com. Custom-built city breaks with city tours.

Pleasant Holidays ☎1-800/742-9244, ● www .pleasantholidays.com. City breaks and fly-drives.

Vacationland ☎1-800/245-0050, ● www.vacation-land.com. Extensive range of city breaks, fly-drives, regional tours, sightseeing add-ons, plus golf itineraries.

Flights from Australia and New Zealand

Singapore is one of the main stops on the way from Australasia to Europe, so there are plenty of airlines and routes to choose from. Direct flights are not always the cheapest and it's well worth taking advantage of a **stopover** en route – Asian airlines fly via their home base giving you a perfect opportunity to explore a bit more of the area. If you want to visit Singapore as part of a wider trip there are several good-value options worth considering such as: an **open-jaw ticket** that allows you to fly you into one country and out of another, and travel overland in between; multi-stop **Circle Asia** fares; **round-the-world** (RTW) tickets; or flying somewhere else first – such as Thailand, Malaysia or Indonesia – and continuing **overland** from there. For example, you could take the train from Malaysia (Kuala Lumpur to Singapore takes only six hours – see "Getting there from Southeast Asia", p.16 for details).

Fares to Southeast Asian destinations are very competitive, so whatever kind of ticket you're after it's best to shop around. The flight agents listed on p.15 can fill you in on all the latest deals and any special limited offers. If you're a student or under 26, you may be able to get a discounted fare; STA is a good place to start.

Fares are seasonally rated, with prices for flights usually higher during Christmas and New Year and mid-year periods; generally high season is mid-May to end-Aug and Dec to mid-Jan, shoulder March to mid-May and Sept to mid-October and low the rest of the year – with a difference of around A/NZ$200– 300 between each. Air fares from east coast Australian gateways are all pretty much the same (common rated on most airlines, with Qantas providing a shuttle service to the point of departure); Perth and Darwin are A$100–200 cheaper. From New Zealand you can expect to pay NZ$150–300 more from Christchurch and Wellington than from Auckland.

Malaysian Airlines (MAS), Singapore Airlines, Royal Brunei, Qantas and Garuda all have regular services **from Australia** to Singapore. On the whole, fares to Singapore from Brisbane, Sydney or Melbourne and Cairns are roughly between A$600 low season and A$800 high season for a single and A$900–1200 for a return depending on which airline you choose. But the real bargains are often with Middle Eastern airlines keen to fill flights for the leg to Singapore before they head for home.

From New Zealand, Air New Zealand, British Airways, Garuda, Qantas, Singapore Airlines and Malaysian, among others, fly to Singapore and Kuala Lumpur, with fares starting at NZ$750 low season and NZ$1000 high season for a single and NZ$1200–1500 for a return.

Airlines in Australia and New Zealand

Air New Zealand Australia ☎13 24 76, ● www.airnz.com.au; New Zealand ☎0800/737 000, ● www.airnz.co.nz.

British Airways Australia ☎1300/767 177, New Zealand ☎0800/274 847 or 09/356 8690; ● www.britishairways.com.

Egypt Air Australia ☎02/9232 6677, ● www.egyptair.com.eg.

Finnair Australia ℡02/9244 2299, New Zealand ℡09/308 3365; ⊛www.finnair.com.
Garuda Indonesia Australia ℡02/9334 9970, New Zealand ℡09/366 1862; ⊛www.garuda-indonesia.com.
Gulf Air Australia ℡02/9244 2199, New Zealand ℡09/308 3366; ⊛www.gulfairco.com.
Lufthansa Australia ℡1300/655 727, ⊛www.lufthansa-australia.com; New Zealand ℡09/303 1529, ⊛www.lufthansa.com/index_en.html.
Malaysia Airlines Australia ℡13 26 27, New Zealand ℡0800/777 747; ⊛www.malaysiaairlines.com.my.
Qantas Australia ℡13 13 13, ⊛www.qantas.com.au; New Zealand ℡0800/808 767, ⊛www.qantas.co.nz.
Royal Brunei Airlines Australia ℡07/3017 5000, ⊛www.bruneiair.com; no NZ office.
Scandinavian Airlines (SAS) Australia ℡1300/727 707, New Zealand agent: Air New Zealand ℡09/357 3000; ⊛www.scandinavian.net.
Singapore Airlines Australia ℡13 10 11, New Zealand ℡0800/808 909; ⊛www.singaporeair.com.
Thai Airways Australia ℡1300/651 960, New Zealand ℡09/377 0268; ⊛www.thaiair.com.

Discount flight agents in Australia and New Zealand

Flight Centre Australia ℡13 31 33 or 02/9235 3522, ⊛www.flightcentre.com.au; New Zealand ℡0800 243 544 or 09/358 4310, ⊛www.flightcentre.co.nz. Large chain of discount flight specialists.
Holiday Shoppe New Zealand ℡0800/808 480, ⊛www.holidayshoppe.co.nz. Cheap flight agent.
STA Travel Australia ℡1300/733 035, ⊛www.statravel.com.au; New Zealand ℡0508/782 872, ⊛www.statravel.co.nz. Worldwide specialists in "learning travel", with low-cost flights for students and under-26s; other customers also welcome.
Student Uni Travel Australia ℡02/9232 8444, ⊛www.sut.com.au; New Zealand ℡09/379 4224, ⊛www.sut.co.nz. Specialists in student and backpacker deals.
Trailfinders Australia ℡02/9247 7666, ⊛www.trailfinders.com.au. Australian branch of large UK-based independent travel specialists.

Packages and organized tours

Package holidays to Singapore are numerous and good value, especially if you just want a relaxing break around the pool. As well as flights and accommodation, most compa-

nies also offer a range of itineraries that take in the major sights and activities. Bookings are usually made through travel agents who carry a wide selection of brochures for you to choose from. An organized tour is worth considering if you're after a more energetic holiday, have ambitious sightseeing plans and limited time, are uneasy with the language and customs or just don't like travelling alone.

City stays, fly-drive options and **coach tours** are offered by a whole host of operators through your travel agent; most of these can also arrange add-on trips to resort islands, cruises from Singapore, air passes, rail travel and can book accommodation in regional Malaysia. Extended journeys from Singapore cater to all tastes – from those in search of thrills and adventure to those who simply prefer to tour in a group. Most of the specialists listed below can organize activities that may be difficult to arrange yourself such as whitewater rafting, diving, cycling and trekking.

Most organized tours don't include air fares from Australasia.

Specialist tour operators in Australia and New Zealand

Abercrombie & Kent Australia ℡03/9536 1800, New Zealand ℡0800/441 638; ⊛www.abercrombiekent.com.au. Upmarket tours of Southeast Asia including travel on the Eastern and Oriental Express (see p.17).
Adventure World Australia ℡02/8913 0755, ⊛www.adventureworld.com.au; New Zealand ℡09/524 5118, ⊛www.adventureworld.co.nz. Agents for a vast array of international adventure travel companies.
Eastern & Orient Express Australia ℡1800/000 395, New Zealand ℡09/379 3708; ⊛www.orient-express.com. Tours on the Eastern and Orient Express.
Intrepid Travel Australia ℡03/9473 2626, ⊛www.intrepidtravel.com.au. Small-group tours with the emphasis on cross-cultural contact and low-impact tourism.
San Michele Travel Australia ℡02/9299 1111 or 1800/22 22 44, ⊛www.asiatravel.com.au. Long-running Southeast Asia specialist, with customized rail tours throughout the region, as well as city breaks, sightseeing trips and cruises out of Singapore.
Silke's Travel Australia ℡1800 807 860, or 02/8347 2000, ⊛www.silkes.com.au. Specially tailored packages for gay and lesbian travellers.

15

Getting there from Southeast Asia

If you are not too restricted by time, it can work out cheaper to get a flight to another Southeast Asian city and then continue your journey from there. Flights to **Bangkok** can often be particularly good value, and from there, as well as from **Jakarta** and **Hong Kong**, there are frequent daily flights to Singapore. It's obviously longer, but cheaper, to travel overland by train from Bangkok – the main line runs down the west coast of Malaysia and ends in Singapore.

From Thailand

The cheapest way of getting to Singapore from Thailand is to catch the bus from Bangkok, though taking a train is a more comfortable option. Trains depart from Bangkok's Hualamphong station (book at least a day in advance at the station ticket office, or check out ⓦwww.thailandrailway .com) five times a day for Hat Yai, where the line divides. One daily train goes south via the Malaysian border town of Padang Besar to Butterworth, Kuala Lumpur and Singapore in 28 hours (£35/US$55 one-way).

There are five or six daily non-stop flights from Bangkok on Thai Airways to Singapore. From Phuket, there's one direct flight daily, and also one daily from Hat Yai. All these flights cost around £100/US$160.

Tickets are available from travel agents in Bangkok; students and under-26s will probably be able to undercut these prices by booking through STA, 14th floor, Wall Street

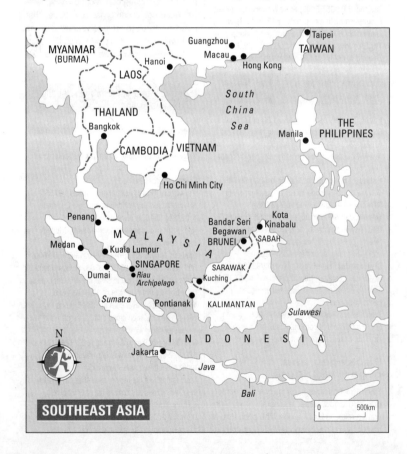

Tower, 33 Suriwong Rd (☎2/237 6005, ⓦwww.statravel.co.th).

Jakarta) to Singapore – a thirty-minute trip; £10/US$16).

From Indonesia

There are daily Garuda flights from Jakarta to Singapore (£120/US$190 one-way; 3hr). From other Indonesian regions you'll need to take an internal flight to Jakarta first. In addition, ferries run through the day from Pulau Batam in the Riau archipelago (accessible by plane or boat from Sumatra or

From Malaysia

Regular flights connect the major Malaysian airports with Singapore (£50/US$80 from KL with MAS), and there are four trains a day from Kuala Lumpur. Buses link Singapore with all large towns and cities in peninsular Malaysia and represent the most affordable means of reaching the city-state. From KL expect to pay the equivalent of £9/US$14.

Eastern and Oriental Express

If you've got money to burn, there's no more luxurious way to cover the 1900km between Bangkok and Singapore than on the sumptuous **Eastern and Oriental Express**, a fairy-tale trip that unashamedly re-creates the pampered days of the region's colonial past. Departing once or twice weekly from Bangkok (and Singapore), the Express takes 41 hours to wend its unhurried way between the two cities, stopping at Butterworth, Ipoh and KL en route. At Butterworth, passengers disembark for a whistle-stop tour of Penang by bus and trishaw. On board, guests enjoy breakfast in bed, lunch, tea and dinner, all served by attentive Thai and Malaysian staff in traditional or period garb. There are two bars (one in the observation carriage at the rear of the train), as well as two luxurious restaurant cars serving Western and Oriental cuisine of a high standard; fortune-tellers, Chinese opera singers and musicians keep you entertained. Many guests dress up lavishly for the occasion so be sure to have smart clothes with you or you'll feel decidedly uncomfortable.

The two-night trip costs from £960/US$1500 per person. Bookings can be made in Bangkok through Sea Tours Co. Ltd, 8th Floor, Payatai Plaza, 128 Phyathai Road (☎2/2165783); in Singapore at E&O Services, 32-01/3 Shaw Towers, 100 Beach Road (☎63923500); or contact the specialist tour operators on p.11, p.13 and p.15 before leaving home.

Red tape and visas

British citizens, and those of the Republic of Ireland, the United States, Canada, Australia and New Zealand, don't need a visa to enter Singapore. Regulations change from time to time, though, so check with the embassy before departure. You'll normally be stamped in for fourteen days, although you can be given one month on request.

Extending your stay for up to three months is perfectly possible, at the discretion of the Immigration Department (see p.179); extensions beyond three months are not unknown, but are less common. If you have any problems with extending your stay, there's always the option of taking a bus up to Johor Bahru, across the border in Malaysia, and then coming back in again.

Singaporean embassies and consulates abroad

Australia 17 Forster Crescent, Yarralumla, Canberra, ACT 2600 ☎02/6273 3944.
Canada Suite 1305, 999 Hastings St, Vancouver, BC V6C 2W2 ☎604/669-5115.
Indonesia Block X/4 Kav No. 2, Jalan H.R. Rasuna Said Kuningan, Jakarta 12950 ☎021/520 1489.
Ireland Contact UK embassy.
Malaysia 209 Jalan Tun Razak, Kuala Lumpur 50400 ☎03/2161 6277.

New Zealand 17 Kabul St, Khandallah, Wellington, PO Box 13-140 ☎04/470 0850.
UK 9 Wilton Crescent, London SW1X 8SP ☎020/7235 8315.
USA 3501 International Place NW, Washington, DC 20008 ☎202/537-3100; 231 East 51st St, New York, NY 10022 ☎212/223-3331.

Customs

Upon entry from anywhere other than Malaysia you can bring into Singapore one litre each of spirits, wine and beer duty-free; duty is payable on all tobacco. There are no restrictions if you're coming from Malaysia. For up-to-the-minute customs information, go to ⊛www.customs.gov.sg.

Many goods for sale in Singapore are duty-free, including electronic and electrical items, cosmetics, cameras, clocks, watches, jewellery, and precious stones and metals, but you should bear in mind how much you are allowed to import into your own country with you free of charge.

Information, websites and maps

The Singapore Tourism Board (STB) maintains five Tourist Information Centres. The main one is at Tourism Court, 1 Orchard Spring Lane (Mon–Fri 8.30am–5pm, Sat 8.30am–midnight; toll-free ☏1-800/736 2000). The others are at Liang Court Shopping Centre, Level 1, 177 River Valley Road (daily 10.30am–9.30pm; ☏63362888); 01-35 Suntec City Mall, 3 Temasek Boulevard (Mon–Sat 8am–6.30pm, Sun 9am–6.30pm; toll-free ☏1-800/332 5066); 01-01 Prinsep Place, 44 Prinsep Street (Sun–Thurs 11am–11pm, Fri & Sat 11am–2am; ☏63363660); and 01-20a CHIJMES, 30 Victoria Street (Mon–Sat 10am–6pm; ☏63382529).

A number of publications offer **"what's on"** listings and recommendations. Two of these – *Where Singapore* and *This Week Singapore* – are available free at hotels all over the island. The "Life!" section of the *Singapore Straits Times* has a decent listings section, but best of all are *8 Days* magazine, which is published weekly and costs $1.50, and the newer *IS*, a free paper published fortnightly.

Singapore tourist offices abroad

Australia c/o Glasson Marketing & Representation, Level One, 235 Queen St, Melbourne, VIC 3000 ☏3/9606 0222; c/o Sandra Devahasdin PR & Promotions, 15 Lawrence Avenue, West Perth, WA 6005 ☏8/9226 5666.
New Zealand c/o Vivaldi World Limited, 85B Hebron Rd, Waiake, Auckland 1311, PO Box 89203 Torbay – Auckland ☏9/473 8658.
UK lst floor, Carrington House 126–130 Regent St, London W1B 5JX ☏0207/437 0033.
USA 590 Fifth Avenue, 12th floor New York, NY 10036 ☏212/302-4861; 4929 Wilshire Blvd, Suite 510, Los Angeles CA 90010 ☏323/677-0808.

Useful websites

🌐 **afterdark.hotspots.com** Ratings and reviews of Singapore's latest nightspots.
🌐 **www.ehotelsingapore.com** Good hotel reservation service with lots of travel information.
🌐 **www.expatsingapore.com** A definitive guide to life in Singapore.
🌐 **www.getforme.com** An excellent portal to all things Singaporean, from local cuisine to info for backpackers.
🌐 **www.gov.sg** The offical website of the Singapore government.

🌐 **www.happening.com.sg** Online arts and entertainments guide.
🌐 **www.visitsingapore.com** The Singapore Tourism Board's official site, featuring tour planner, attractions, current events, a virtual "tour" of the island and an accommodation search by price range.
🌐 **www.makansutra.com** Quirky website maintained by the foodies who annually publish the *makansutra* food guide to Singapore; fascinating essays about cultural and culinary facets of eating out in Singapore.
🌐 **www.sg** Maintained by the Ministry of Information, a mine of useful practical and cultural information.
🌐 **straitstimes.asia1.com.sg** The *Singapore Straits Times* on the Internet.
🌐 **www.talkingcock.com** The best (and only?) satirical website out of Singapore.

Maps

The best available **map** of Singapore Island is the 1:22,500 Nelles *Singapore*, though the *Singapore Street Directory*, from all Singapore bookshops, is essential if you have to rent a car.

Map outlets

In the UK and Ireland

Blackwell's Map and Travel Shop 50 Broad St, Oxford OX1 3BQ ☏01865/793 550, 🌐 maps.blackwell.co.uk.
Easons Bookshop 40 O'Connell St, Dublin 1 ☏01/858 3881, 🌐 www.eason.ie.
Heffers Map and Travel 20 Trinity St, Cambridge CB2 1TJ ☏01865/333 536, 🌐 www.heffers.co.uk.
Hodges Figgis Bookshop 56–58 Dawson St, Dublin 2 ☏01/677 4754.

The Map Shop 30a Belvoir St, Leicester LE1 6QH ☎0116/247 1400, ⊛www.mapshopleicester.co.uk.
National Map Centre 22–24 Caxton St, London SW1H 0QU ☎020/7222 2466, ⊛www.mapsnmc.co.uk.
Newcastle Map Centre 55 Grey St, Newcastle-upon-Tyne NE1 6EF ☎0191/261 5622.
Ordnance Survey Ireland Phoenix Park, Dublin 8 ☎01/802 5300, ⊛www.osi.ie.
Ordnance Survey of Northern Ireland Colby House, Stranmillis Ct, Belfast BT9 5BJ ☎028/9025 5755, ⊛www.osni.gov.uk.
Stanfords 12–14 Long Acre, London WC2E 9LP ☎020/7836 1321, ⊛www.stanfords.co.uk.
The Travel Bookshop 13–15 Blenheim Crescent, London W11 2EE ☎020/7229 5260, ⊛www.thetravelbookshop.co.uk.

In the US and Canada

Adventurous Traveler.com US ☎1-800/282-3963, ⊛adventuroustraveler.com.
Book Passage 51 Tamal Vista Blvd, Corte Madera, CA 94925 ☎1-800/999-7909, ⊛www.bookpassage.com.
Distant Lands 56 S Raymond Ave, Pasadena, CA 91105 ☎1-800/310-3220, ⊛www.distantlands.com.
Elliot Bay Book Company 101 S Main St, Seattle, WA 98104 ☎1-800/962-5311,

⊛www.elliotbaybook.com.
Globe Corner Bookstore 28 Church St, Cambridge, MA 02138 ☎1-800/358-6013, ⊛www.globercorner.com.
Map Link 30 S La Patera Lane, Unit 5, Santa Barbara, CA 93117 ☎1-800/962-1394, ⊛www.maplink.com.
Rand McNally US ☎1-800/333-0136, ⊛www.randmcnally.com. Around thirty stores across the US; dial ext 2111 or check the website for the nearest location.
The Travel Bug Bookstore 2667 W Broadway, Vancouver V6K 2G2 ☎604/737-1122, ⊛www.swifty.com/tbug.
World of Maps 1235 Wellington St, Ottawa, Ontario K1Y 3A3 ☎1-800/214-8524, ⊛www.worldofmaps.com.

In Australia and New Zealand

The Map Shop 6–10 Peel St, Adelaide, SA 5000 ☎08/8231 2033, ⊛www.mapshop.net.au.
Specialty Maps 46 Albert St, Auckland 1001 ☎09/307 2217, ⊛www.specialtymaps.co.nz.
MapWorld 173 Gloucester St, Christchurch ☎0800/627 967 or 03/374 5399, ⊛www.mapworld.co.nz.
Mapland 372 Little Bourke St, Melbourne, Victoria 3000 ☎03/9670 4383, ⊛www.mapland.com.au.
Perth Map Centre 900 Hay St, Perth, WA 6000 ☎08/9322 5733, ⊛www.perthmap.com.au.

Money, banks and costs

Singapore is one of the more expensive Asian cities, especially for accommodation. The city affords few savings for special groups – senior citizens do not get reductions, although an ISIC card might occasionally pay dividends for students. However, you will find that bargaining is a way of life throughout Singapore, especially when shopping or renting a room for the night – it's always worth trying to haggle, though note that you don't bargain for meals. Most tourist attractions offer discounted entrance fees for children.

Currency

The currency is the Singapore dollar, written simply as $ and divided into 100 cents. Notes are issued in denominations of $1, $2, $5, $10, $20, $50, $100, $500, $1000 and $10,000; coins are in denominations of 1, 5, 10, 20 and 50 cents, and $1. The current exchange rate is around $2.80 to £1 and $1.80 to US$1. All prices given in the guide are in Singapore dollars, unless otherwise stated.

Costs

If money is no object, you'll be able to take advantage of hotels, restaurants and shops as sumptuous as any in the world. On the other hand, with budget dormitory accommodation in plentiful supply, and both food and internal travel cheap in the extreme, you could survive on less than £10/US$16 a day. Upgrading your lodgings to a private room in a guesthouse, eating in a restaurant and having a beer or two gives a more realistic daily budget of £25/US$40 a day.

Banks

Singapore **banking hours** are generally Monday to Friday 9.30am–3pm and Saturday 9.30am–12.30pm, outside of which you'll have to go to a moneychanger in a shopping centre, or to a hotel. Major banks represented include the Overseas Union Bank, the United Overseas Bank, the OCBC, the Development Bank of Singapore, Standard Chartered Bank, Hong Kong Bank and Citibank. No black market operates in Singapore, nor are there any restrictions on carrying currency in or out of the state. This means that rates at moneychangers are as good as you'll find in the banks.

Travellers' cheques and cards

Although they are the traditional way to carry funds, **travellers' cheques** are no longer the cheapest nor the most convenient option – bank cards are better (see below). That said, they do offer safety against loss or theft, and can be cashed at Singaporean banks, licensed moneychangers and some hotels, upon presentation of a passport. Some shops will even accept travellers' cheques as cash. Either sterling or US dollar cheques are acceptable in Singapore; but check with your bank for the latest advice before you buy.

The usual fee for travellers' cheque sales is one or two percent, though this fee may be waived if you buy the cheques through a bank where you have an account. It pays to get a selection of denominations. Make sure you keep the purchase agreement and a record of cheque serial numbers safe and separate from the cheques themselves. In the event that cheques are lost or stolen, the issuing company will expect you to report the loss forthwith to their office in Singapore; most companies claim to replace lost or stolen cheques within 24 hours.

Credit cards are a very convenient way of carrying funds. They are widely accepted in mid-range and upmarket hotels, shops and restaurants throughout the region, but beware of the illegal surcharges levied by some establishments – check before you buy something with a card that there's no surcharge; if there is, contact your card company and tell them about it.

Cards can be used either in ATMs or over the counter. Mastercard, Visa and American Express are accepted just about everywhere, but other, lesser known cards may not be recognized, so check with your card issuer before you travel. Remember that all cash advances are treated as loans, with interest accruing daily from the date of withdrawal; there may be a transaction fee on top of this. However, you may be able to make withdrawals from ATMs in Singapore using your debit card, which is not liable to interest payments, and the flat transaction fee is usually quite small – your bank will be able to advise on this. Make sure you have a personal identification number (PIN) that's designed to work overseas.

A compromise between travellers' cheques and plastic is **Visa TravelMoney**, a disposable pre-paid debit card with a PIN that works in all ATMs that take Visa cards. You load up your account with funds before leaving home, and when they run out, you simply throw the card away. You can buy up to nine cards to access the same funds – useful for couples or families travelling together – and it's a good idea to buy at least one extra as a back-up in case of loss or theft. There is also a 24-hour toll-free customer assistance number (☎800-110-0344). The card is available in most countries from branches of Thomas Cook and Citicorp. For more information, check the Visa TravelMoney website at ⊛usa.visa.com /personal/cards/visa_travel_money.html.

Youth and student discounts

Once obtained, various official and quasi-official **youth/student ID cards** soon pay for themselves in savings. Full-time students are eligible for the International Student ID Card (ISIC, Ⓦ www.isiccard.com), which entitles the bearer to special air, rail and bus fares and discounts at museums, theatres and other attractions. For Americans there's also a health benefit, providing up to $3000 in emergency medical coverage and $100 a day for sixty days in the hospital, plus a 24-hour hotline to call in the event of a medical, legal or financial emergency. The card costs $22 in the USA; CDN$16 in Canada; A$16.50 in Australia; NZ$21 in New Zealand; £6 in the UK; and €12.70 in the Republic of Ireland.

You only have to be 26 or younger to qualify for the **International Youth Travel Card**, which costs US$22/£7 and carries the same benefits. Teachers qualify for the **International Teacher Card**, offering similar discounts and costing £7, US$22, CDN$16, A$16.50 and NZ$21. All these cards are available in the US from Council Travel, STA, Travel CUTS (see p.13); in Australia and New Zealand from STA (see p.15) or Campus Travel; and in the UK from CTS Travel (Ⓦwww.ctstravel.co.uk).

Several other travel organizations and accommodation groups also sell their own cards, good for various discounts. A university photo ID might open some doors, but is not as easily recognizable as the ISIC cards. However, the latter are often not accepted as valid proof of age, for example in bars or liquor stores.

Wiring money

Having money wired from home using one of the companies listed below is never convenient or cheap, and should be considered a last resort. It's also possible to have money wired directly from a bank in your home country to a bank in Singapore, although this is somewhat less reliable because it involves two separate institutions. If you go this route, your home bank will need the address of the branch bank where you want to pick up the money and the address and telex number of the Singapore head office, which will act as the clearing house; money wired this way normally takes two working days to arrive, and costs around £25/$40 per transaction.

Money-wiring companies

Thomas Cook US ☎ 1-800/287-7362, Canada ☎ 1-888/823-4732, Great Britain ☎ 01733/318 922, Northern Ireland ☎ 028/9055 0030, Republic of Ireland ☎ 01/677 1721;
Ⓦ www.thomascook.com.
Travelers Express MoneyGram
US ☎ 1-800/955-7777, Canada ☎ 1-800/933-3278, UK ☎ 0800/018 0104, Republic of Ireland ☎ 1850/205 800, Australia ☎ 1800/230 100, New Zealand ☎ 0800/262 263;
Ⓦ www.moneygram.com.
Western Union US and Canada ☎ 1-800/325-6000, Australia ☎ 1800/501 500, New Zealand ☎ 0800/270 000, UK ☎ 0800/833 833, Republic of Ireland ☎ 1800/395 395;
Ⓦ www.westernunion.com.

Insurance

Since there are no reciprocal agreements between Singapore and any other country, the cost of medical services must be borne by the visitor. Consequently, it's essential to arrange travel insurance before you leave home, which will cover you for medical expenses incurred, as well as for loss of luggage, cancellation of flights and so on.

Before paying for a new policy, however, it's worth checking whether you are already covered: some all-risks home insurance policies may cover your possessions when overseas, and many private medical schemes include cover when abroad. In Canada, provincial health plans usually provide partial cover for medical mishaps overseas, while holders of official student/teacher/youth cards in Canada and the US are entitled to meagre accident coverage and hospital in-patient benefits. Students will often find that their student health coverage extends during the vacations and for one term beyond the date of last enrolment.

After exhausting the possibilities above, you might want to contact a specialist travel insurance company, or consider the travel insurance deal we offer (see box). A typical travel insurance policy usually provides cover for the loss of baggage, tickets and – up to a certain limit – cash or cheques, as well as cancellation or curtailment of your journey. Most of them exclude so-called dangerous sports unless an extra premium is paid. Many policies can be chopped and changed to exclude coverage you don't need – for example, sickness and accident benefits can often be excluded or included at will. If you do take medical coverage, ascertain whether benefits will be paid as treatment proceeds or only after return home, and whether there is a 24-hour medical emergency number. When securing baggage cover, make sure that the per-article limit – typically under £500 – will cover your most valuable possession. If you need to make a claim, you should keep receipts for medicines and medical treatment, and in the event you have anything stolen, you must obtain an official statement from the police.

Rough Guides travel insurance

Rough Guides offers its own travel insurance, customized for our readers by a leading UK broker and backed by a Lloyd's underwriter. It's available for anyone, of any nationality and any age, travelling anywhere in the world.

There are four main Rough Guide insurance plans: **No Frills** for the bare minimum for secure travel; **Essential**, which provides decent all-round cover; **Premier** for comprehensive cover with a wide range of benefits; and **Annual multi-trip**, a cost-effective way of getting premier cover if you travel more than once a year. Unlike many policies, the Rough Guides schemes are calculated by the day, so if you're travelling for 27 days rather than a month, that's all you pay for. If you intend to be away for the whole year, the Adventurer policy will cover you for 365 days. Each plan can be supplemented with a "Hazardous Activities Premium" if you plan to indulge in sports considered dangerous, such as skiing, scuba-diving or trekking.

For a policy quote, call the Rough Guide Insurance Line on UK freephone ☎0800/015 0906; or, if you're calling from elsewhere ☎+44 1392 314 665. Alternatively, get an online quote at ⊛www.roughguidesinsurance.com.

Health

The levels of hygiene and medical care in Singapore are higher than in much of the rest of Southeast Asia, and with any luck, the most serious thing you'll go down with is a cold or an upset stomach. Tap water is drinkable throughout the island and all food for public consumption is prepared to exacting standards. Drinking excessive amounts of alcohol is a more likely cause of diarrhoea than the food you may eat, as in a tropical climate your tolerance level is likely to be much lower than it would be at home.

Travellers unused to tropical climates periodically suffer from **sunburn** and **dehydration**. The easiest way to avoid this is to restrict your exposure to the sun, use high-factor sun screens, wear dark glasses to protect your eyes and wear a hat. You should also drink plenty of water and, if you do become dehydrated, keep up a regular intake of fluids; weak black tea and clear soups are useful for mineral salts, and rehydration preparations such as Dioralyte, available from pharmacies, also do the trick. The DIY version is a handful of sugar with a good pinch of salt added to a litre of water, which creates roughly the right mineral balance. Even if you aren't suffering, it's worth supplementing your daily water intake with the odd can of isotonic drink,

which replaces the minerals lost through perspiration.

Heat stroke is more serious: it is indicated by a high temperature, dry red skin and a fast pulse and can require hospitalization. To prevent **heat rashes**, **prickly heat** and **fungal infections**, use a mild antiseptic soap and dust yourself with medicated talcum powder, which you can buy throughout Singapore.

Medical services are excellent, with staff almost everywhere speaking good English and using up-to-date techniques. **Pharmacies** are well stocked with familiar brand-name drugs; pharmacists can also recommend products for skin complaints or simple stomach problems, though if you're in any doubt, it always pays to get a proper

The threat of SARS

The spectre of SARS, or Severe Acute Respiratory Syndrome, visited Singapore in early March 2003. A serious respiratory infection whose symptoms are a high fever, coughing and shortness of breath, SARS is spread through close contact with an infected person, and can lead to death.

As this guide went to press, in early June 2003, the World Health Organization had just removed Singapore from its official list of areas with recent local transmission of SARS. By then, 206 cases had come to light, of which 31 had proved fatal. The WHO's executive director for communicable diseases praised Singapore for its "exemplary" handling of its SARS outbreak. Even so, you can be sure, should a fresh outbreak have arisen since this book went to press, that complacency on the part of Singapore's medical authorities will not have been the cause.

For up-to-the-minute advice on the global status of SARS, check out the WHO's advisory site at ⊛www.who.int/csr/sars/en, go to your own ministry of health's website, or visit Singapore's own site, ⊛www.sars.gov.sg, which pools information on SARS from local and international sources, for the consumption of locals and visitors to the island.

diagnosis. Opening hours are usually Monday to Saturday 9.30am–7pm. **Private clinics** are found throughout the city – your hotel or the local tourist office will be able to recommend a good English-speaking doctor. A visit costs around $25, not including the cost of any prescribed medication. Don't forget to keep any receipts for insurance claim purposes.

Inoculations

There are no inoculations required for visiting Singapore, although the immigration authorities may require proof of a yellow fever vaccination (administered within the last ten years) if you're arriving from an endemic country.

However, it's a wise precaution to visit your doctor or local immunization clinic no later than four weeks before you leave to check that you are up to date with your polio, typhoid, tetanus and hepatitis A inoculations.

If you are travelling on from Singapore to other destinations in Southeast Asia, it is likely that you will require further protection, particularly against malaria. Singapore is malaria-free, but you must start taking any course of tablets one week before you plan to move on.

Medical resources for travellers

Websites

⊛ **health.yahoo.com** Information on specific diseases and conditions, drugs and herbal remedies, as well as advice from health experts.
⊛ **www.fitfortravel.scot.nhs.uk** UK NHS website carrying information about travel-related diseases and how to avoid them.
⊛ **www.istm.org** The website of the International Society for Travel Medicine, with a full list of clinics specializing in international travel health.
⊛ **www.tmvc.com.au** Contains a list of all Travellers Medical and Vaccination Centres throughout Australia, New Zealand and Southeast Asia, plus general information on travel health.
⊛ **www.tripprep.com** Travel Health Online provides an online-only comprehensive database of necessary vaccinations for most countries, as well as destination and medical service provider information.

In the US and Canada

Canadian Society for International Health 1 Nicholas St, Suite 1105, Ottawa, ON K1N 7B7 ☏613/241-5785, ⊛www.csih.org. Distributes a

free pamphlet, "Health Information for Canadian Travellers", containing an extensive list of travel health centres in Canada.
International Association for Medical Assistance to Travellers (IAMAT) 417 Center St, Lewiston, NY 14092 ☏716/754-4883, ⊛www.iamat.org, and 40 Regal Rd, Guelph, ON N1K 1B5 ☏519/836-0102. A non-profit organization supported by donations, it can provide climate charts and leaflets on various diseases and inoculations.
MEDJET Assistance ☏1-800/9MEDJET, www.medjetassistance.com. Annual membership program for travellers ($175 for individuals, $275 for families) that, in the event of illness or injury, will fly members home or to the hospital of their choice in a medically equipped and staffed jet.
Travelers Medical Center 31 Washington Square West, New York, NY 10011 ☏212/982-1600. Consultation service on immunizations and treatment of diseases for people travelling to developing countries.

In the UK and Ireland

British Airways Travel Clinics 156 Regent St, London W1 (Mon–Fri 9.30am–5.15pm, Sat 10am–4pm, no appointment necessary; ☏020/7439 9584); 101 Cheapside, London EC2 (hours as above, appointment required; ☏020/7606 2977);
⊛www.britishairways.com/travel/healthclinintro. Vaccinations, tailored advice from an online database and a complete range of travel healthcare products.
Hospital for Tropical Diseases Travel Clinic 2nd floor, Mortimer Market Centre, off Capper St, London WC1E 6AU (Mon–Fri 9am–5pm by appointment only; ☏020/7388 9600,
⊛www.masta.org; a consultation costs £15 which is waived if you have your injections here). A recorded Health Line (☏0906/133 7733; 50p per min) gives hints on hygiene and illness prevention as well as listing appropriate immunizations.
MASTA (Medical Advisory Service for Travellers Abroad) 40 regional clinics (call ☏0870/6062782 for the nearest). Also operates a pre-recorded 24-hour Travellers' Health Line (UK ☏0906/822 4100, 60p per min), giving written information tailored to your journey by return of post.
Travel Health Centre Department of International Health and Tropical Medicine, Royal College of Surgeons in Ireland, Mercers Medical Centre,

For a list of hospitals, clinics and pharmacies in Singapore, turn to the "Directory", pp.178–179. In a medical emergency, dial ☏995.

Stephen's St Lower, Dublin 2 ☎01/402 2337. Expert pre-trip advice and inoculations.
Travel Medicine Services PO Box 254, 16 College St, Belfast BT1 6BT ☎028/9031 5220. Offers medical advice before a trip and help afterwards in the event of a tropical disease.

In Australia and New Zealand

Travellers' Medical and Vaccination Centres 27–29 Gilbert Place, Adelaide, SA 5000 ☎08/8212 7522, ✉adelaide@traveldoctor.com.au; 1/170 Queen St, Auckland ☎09/373 3531, ✉auckland@traveldoctor.co.nz; 5/247 Adelaide St, Brisbane, Qld 4000 ☎07/3221 9066, ✉brisbane@traveldoctor.com.au; 5/8–10 Hobart Place, Canberra, ACT 2600 ☎02/6257 7156, ✉canberra@traveldoctor.com.au; Moorhouse Medical Centre 9 Washington Way, Christchurch ☎03/379 4000, ✉christchurch@traveldoctor .co.nz; 270 Sandy Bay Rd, Sandy Bay Tas, Hobart 7005 ☎03/6223 7577, ✉hobart@traveldoctor .com.au; 2/393 Little Bourke St, Melbourne, Vic 3000 ☎03/9602 5788, ✉melbourne@traveldoctor .com.au; Level 7, Dymocks Bldg, 428 George St, Sydney, NSW 2000 ☎02/9221 7133, ✉sydney@traveldoctor.com.au; Shop 15, Grand Arcade, 14–16 Willis St, Wellington ☎04/473 0991, ✉wellington@traveldoctor.co.nz.

Arrival

Most people's first glimpse of Singapore is of Changi International airport, and a telling glimpse it is. Its two terminals, connected by the Skytrain monorail, are modern, efficient and air-conditioned – Singapore in microcosm. A third terminal is scheduled to open in 2006. Flights from the Malaysian resort island of Tioman set down at smaller Seletar airport, up in the north of the island.

You might also arrive via one of the two causeways connecting Singapore to the southernmost Malaysian state Johor; or by boat from the Indonesian archipelago. Wherever you arrive, Singapore's well-oiled infrastructure means that you'll have no problem getting into the centre.

By air

Changi airport is at the far eastern end of Singapore, 16km from the city centre. As well as duty-free shops, moneychanging and left-luggage facilities, the airport boasts a 24-hour post office and telephone service, hotel reservations counters, day rooms, saunas, and business and Internet centres. There are also several fast-food outlets and, in Terminal One's basement, a food centre – the cheapest and most authentically Singaporean option. But the likelihood is that you'll barely get the chance to take in Changi – baggage comes through so quickly that you can be on a bus or in a taxi within fifteen minutes of arrival. Be sure to pick up one of the free maps and weekly *This Week Singapore* guides that the Singapore Tourism Board (STB) leaves at the airport, plus a copy of the excellent what's on magazine, *Where Singapore*.

Getting into the city from the airports

Singapore's **underground train** system (MRT – Mass Rapid Transit) now extends as far as Terminal Two of **Changi airport,** and is the most affordable means of getting into the city centre. A single to downtown City Hall is $1.40, and shouldn't take more than half an hour. From City Hall interchange, you can move on to any part of the island.

The **bus** departure points in the basements of both terminals are well signposted, but make sure you've got the right money before you leave the concourse, as Singapore bus drivers don't give change; take the #36 (every 10min, 6am–midnight; $1.50). The bus heads west to Stamford Road before skirting the southern side of Orchard Road. Ask the driver to give you a shout at the

Finding an address

With so many of Singapore's shops, restaurants and offices located in vast high-rise buildings and shopping malls, deciphering addresses can sometimes be tricky. The numbering system generally adhered to is as follows: 02-15 means room number 15 on the second floor; 10-08 is room 8 on the 10th floor. Bear in mind that in Singapore, ground level is referred to as 01, or the first floor.

Capitol Building stop for Beach Road, or at the YMCA stop, where you need to cross over Bras Basah Park if you are staying in Bencoolen Street. Another option is to take a **MaxiCab** shuttle into town. These six-seater taxis depart every fifteen minutes, or when full, and will take you to any hotel in the city for a flat fare of $7 (children $5). MaxiCabs are equipped to take wheelchairs.

Taxis from the airport levy a $3 surcharge on top of the fare, rising to $5 at the weekend. Again, the taxi rank is well signposted, and a trip into downtown Singapore costs around $15 and takes twenty minutes. There are also **car-rental** agencies at the airport (see p.178), though you'd be advised not to travel around Singapore by car (see "Getting around", p.31). From **Seletar airport**, a taxi into town will cost around $15, plus $3 airport surcharge, but be prepared to have to make a phone booking upon landing (see telephone numbers on p.179).

By bus

Buses stop at one of three terminals in Singapore. Local buses from **Johor Bahru (JB)** in **Malaysia** arrive at Ban San Terminal at the junction of Queen and Arab streets, from where a two-minute walk along Queen Street and a left turn along Rochor Road takes you to Bugis MRT station. Buses from elsewhere in Malaysia and from **Thailand** terminate at one of two sites, Lavender Street Terminal and the Golden Mile Complex. Lavender Street Terminal, at the corner of Lavender Street and Kallang Bahru, is around five minutes' walk from Lavender MRT. Bus #145 passes the Lavender Street Terminal on its way down North Bridge and South Bridge roads. From the Golden Mile, take any bus along Beach Road to Raffles City to connect with the MRT system. You'll have no trouble hailing a cab at any terminal.

By train

Trains from Malaysia end their journey at the **Singapore Railway Station** on Keppel Road, southwest of Chinatown. You haven't officially arrived in Singapore until you step out of the station – which is owned by Malaysia – as the "Welcome to Malaysia" sign above the main entrance testifies. The grounds of Singapore's rail system were sold lock, stock and barrel to the Federal Malay States in 1918, though recently the Singapore government has been buying back segments of it piecemeal. From Keppel Road, bus #97 travels past Tanjong Pagar, Raffles Place and City Hall MRT stations and on to Selegie and Serangoon roads, or you can usually find a cab in the forecourt.

By sea

Boats from the **Indonesian island of Batam** dock at the World Trade Centre, off Telok Blangah Road, roughly 5km east of the centre. From adjacent HarbourFront MRT, the city centre is just a few stops away. Otherwise, from Telok Blangah Road, bus #97 runs to Tanjong Pagar MRT. Bus #65 goes to Selegie and Serangoon roads, via Orchard Road, or take #166 for Chinatown. Boats from Indonesian **Bintam** dock at the Tanah Merah Ferry Terminal, linked by bus #35 to Bedok MRT station.

It's also possible to reach Singapore by **boat from Malaysia**. Bumboats from Kampung Pengerang on the southeastern coast of Johor moor at Changi Village, beyond the airport, from where bus #2 travels into the centre, via Geylang, Victoria and New Bridge roads. Swisher ferries from Tanjung Belungkor, also in Johor, dock at the Changi Ferry Terminal a little way east of Changi Village, from where you'll have to take a taxi – either all the way into town, or into Changi Village to connect with bus #2. Finally, ferries from Tioman Island dock at the Tanah Merah Ferry Terminal.

Departure

All International flights take off from Changi airport in the far east of the island – excepting flights to Malaysia's Tioman Island, which depart from Seletar airport. Boats to Malaysia and Indonesia push off from one of three points along the southern coast, and buses and trains access Malaysia via the causeway in the far north of the island. The recently completed second causeway links Tuas in the west of the island with Geylang Patah, 20km west of Johor Bahru, but trains and most buses still use the original link.

By air

There are good deals on plane tickets from Singapore to **Australia**, **Bali**, **Bangkok** and **Hong Kong**. However, if you're planning to head for either **Malaysia** or **Indonesia** by air, it might be worth going to JB (see below), across the causeway, or Batam, the nearest Indonesian island (see information on boats below), and buying a flight from there.

Allow plenty of time for getting out to the airport (45–60min), especially during the morning and evening rush hours. The MRT runs right up to Terminal Two; and bus #36 (daily 6am–midnight; $1.50) runs frequently down Orchard Road and Bras Basah Road en route to Changi. Taxis cost $12–15.

Flights for Tioman Island in Malaysia depart from Seletar airport, for which the best approach is to take a taxi.

By road

The easiest way across the causeway to **Johor Bahru** is to get the #170 JB-bound **bus** from the Ban San Terminal (every 10min; 5.30am–midnight; $1.20) or the plusher air-con Singapore–Johor Express (every 10min; 6.30am–midnight; $2.40), both of which take around an hour (including border formalities) and stop at JB bus terminal. From the **taxi** rank next to the terminal, a car to JB (seating four) costs $28, or $7 a head if you share. The Singapore–KL (Kuala Lumpur) Express leaves from the Ban San Terminal daily at 9am, 1pm, 5pm and 10pm (6hr; $23). For other destinations, go to either the Lavender Street Terminal or the Golden Mile Complex.

At peak hours (6.30–9.30am and 5.30–7.30pm) and at weekends, the roads leading to the causeway seethe with cars and trucks – all full of petrol, after a law passed in the early 1990s banned Singaporeans from driving out of the country on an empty tank. Previously, people crossed into Malaysia, filled up with cut-price fuel and then headed home; now, signs line the roads approaching the causeway requesting that Singaporean cars top up to three-quarters of a tank or risk a $500 fine.

By train

You can make free seat reservations up to one month in advance of departure at the information kiosk (daily 8.30am–2.30pm & 3–7pm; ☎62225165) in the train station. There are air-conditioned trains to KL at 8am, 10.30am, 3.05pm and 10pm. These trains all stop at JB. For more up-to-the-minute schedule information, go to ⓦwww.ktmb.com.my. For information on the **Eastern and Oriental Express** to Bangkok, see p.17.

By boat to Malaysia

From Changi Point bumboats run to **Kampung Pengerang** in Johor. Boats leave when they're full (daily 7am–4pm; $6 one-way) and the trip takes 45 minutes. A newer, more reliable service departs three times daily for **Tanjung Belungkor**, also in Johor, from the new Changi Ferry Terminal. Run by Cruise Ferries (☎65468518), the service takes 45 minutes and costs $22 return; check in one hour before departure. Finally, from the Tanah Merah Ferry Terminal, there's an 8.35am service (March–Oct daily except Tues & Thurs; Sun–Thurs $154 return, Fri &

Sat $190 return) to **Tioman Island**. Information and tickets from Penguin Ferry Services (☎62714866). Again, check in one hour before departure.

By boat to Indonesia

Boats to **Batam** in the Riau archipelago depart at least half-hourly throughout the day from the World Trade Centre (7.30am–7.30pm; $17 one-way), docking at Sekupang, from where you take a taxi to Hangnadim airport for internal Indonesian

flights. There are also several boats a day ($49 one-way) from the Tanah Merah Ferry Terminal to **Tanjung Pinang** on Pulau Bintan, from where cargo boats leave three times a week for Pekanbaru in Sumatra. Information and tickets are available from either Dino Shipping (☎62760668), Bintan Resort Ferries (☎65424369, ⊛www.brf .com.sg) or Penguin Ferry Services (☎62714866). From Kijang Port, south of Tanjung Pinang, there are boat services to Jakarta.

Getting around

All parts of the island are accessible by MRT (the underground rail network) or bus, and fares are reasonable, so that there's little to be gained by renting a car. However you travel, it's best to avoid the rush hour (roughly 8–9.30am and 5–7pm) if at all possible; outside these times, things are relatively uncongested. The annually updated *Transitlink Guide* ($1.50), available from bus interchanges, MRT stations and major bookshops, outlines every bus and MRT route on the island in exhaustive detail. Singapore also has thousands of easily available and affordable taxis.

You're unlikely to have cause to make use of the LRT (Light Rail Transit) loop-line that links Bukit Panjang New Town to Choa Chu Kang MRT. It's a suburban feeder line, and doesn't serve any of Singapore's tourist attractions.

The MRT (Mass Rapid Transport System)

Singapore's **MRT** system was officially opened on March 12, 1988, and has been expanding ever since. A third line opened in 2003; and a new Circle Line is under construction. In terms of cleanliness, efficiency and value for money, the system is second to none – compared to London's tubes or New York's subways, a trip on the MRT is a joy. Nor is there any possibility of delays owing to a passenger falling onto the line – the automatic doors dividing the platform from the track open only when trains are stationary.

The system has **three main lines**: the

north–south line, which runs a vaguely horseshoe-shaped route from Marina Bay up to the north of the island and then southwest to Jurong; the east–west line, connecting Boon Lay to Changi in the east; and the new north–east line, linking the World Trade Centre on the south coast, to Punggol in the northeast of the island. Trains run every four to five minutes on average, daily from 6am until midnight. For **information**, pick up the free *MRT Handy Guide* from any station, or call the MRT Information Centre on ☎1-800/3368900 (toll-free).

A no-smoking rule applies on all trains, and eating and drinking are also outlawed. Signs in the ticket concourse seem to indicate that there is a ban on hedgehogs as well. In fact, they mean "no durians" – not an unreasonable request if you've ever spent any length of time in a confined space with one of these pungent fruits.

Tickets and fares

Tickets cost between 60c and $1.80 for a one-way journey. Change machines will break $1 and $2 notes; larger notes can be changed at the information counter. The easiest way of getting about is to buy an **ez-link Farecard**, a stored-value card that's valid on all MRT and bus journeys in Singapore, is sold at MRT stations and bus interchanges, and shaves a few cents off the cost of each journey. There's a minimum purchase of $10 credit, and a maximum of $100; a $5 deposit is also collected. Hold the card over a reader when you pass through an MRT barrier, and the cost of each journey you make will be automatically deducted from the card; any credit on the card when you leave Singapore will be reimbursed at a Farecard outlet. The **Tourist Day Ticket** is also available for $10 from most MRT stations. The ticket allows you to take up to twelve bus or MRT rides a day, regardless of distance travelled.

Buses

Singapore's **bus network** is slightly cheaper to use than the MRT system, and far more comprehensive – there are several routes that are particularly useful for sightseeing (see box). Two bus companies operate on the roads of Singapore: the **Singapore Bus Service (SBS Transit)** and **Trans-Island Bus Services (TIBS)**. Most buses charge distance-related **fares** ranging from 60c to $1.20 (70c–$1.50 for air-con buses). Change isn't given, so make sure you have the correct fare. For bus-route information, call toll-free ☏1-800/2872727 (SBS) or ☏1-800/4825433 (TIBS). There are now **night buses** running along a few major routes across the island; call the hotlines above for more information.

If you are in town for a while, buy an **ez-link Farecard** (see above), which you hold against an electronic reader as you board and alight; your fare is automatically deducted from the stored value. Another ticket option is the **Tourist Day Ticket** (see

Useful bus routes

Below is a selection of handy bus routes; note that many of the services from the Orchard Road area actually leave from Penang Road or Somerset Road:

#2 passes along Eu Tong Sen Street (in Chinatown) and Victoria Street (past the Arab Quarter) en route to Changi Prison and Changi Village.

#7 runs along Orchard Road, Bras Basah Road and Victoria Street; its return journey takes in North Bridge Road, Stamford Road, Penang Road and Somerset Road en route to Holland Village.

#36 loops between Orchard Road and Changi airport.

#65 terminates at the World Trade Centre, after passing down Jalan Besar, Bencoolen Street, Penang Road and Somerset Road.

#97 runs along Stamford Road to Little India, then on to Upper Serangoon Road; returns via Bencoolen Street and Collyer Quay.

#103 runs between New Bridge Road Terminal (Chinatown) and Serangoon Road (Little India).

#124 connects Scotts Road, Orchard Road and North Bridge Road with South Bridge Road and New Bridge Road in Chinatown; in the opposite direction, travels along Eu Tong Sen Street, Hill Street, Stamford Road and Somerset Road.

#139 heads past Tai Gin Road, via Dhoby Ghaut, Selegie Road, Serangoon Road and Balestier Road.

#167 passes down Scotts Road, Orchard Road and Bras Basah Road, Collyer Quay, Shenton Way and Neil Road (for Chinatown).

#170 starts at the Ban San Terminal at the northern end of Queen Street, passing Bukit Timah Nature Reserve and Kranji War Cemetery on its way to JB in Malaysia.

above), though this is not a very cost-effective means of travel. Neither is the **Singapore Explorer**, a red tourist tram bus that plies a route between Orchard Road and the Colonial District. One day's unlimited travel is $14.90 (children $9.90), which includes a riverboat tour; call ☎63396833 for more details.

One final option – and one kids will love – is to board the **Wacky Duck**, an amphibious craft dating from the Vietnam War, which provides hour-long, land- and sea-based tours (daily 10am–6pm; $33, children $17) of the civic district and harbour. Tours start at Suntec City Mall; call ☎63333825.

Taxis

There are over eighteen thousand **taxis** on the streets of Singapore, so you shouldn't have any trouble hailing a cab, day or night; they come in various colours, but are clearly marked "TAXI". All cabs are **metered**, the fare starting at $2.40 for the first kilometre and rising 10c for every 240 metres. However, there are **surcharges** to bear in mind, notably the fifty percent charged on journeys between midnight and 6am. Journeys from Changi airport incur a $3 surcharge ($5 at the weekend), and there's a $5 surcharge for taxis booked over the phone. More confusingly still, the Singaporean government maintains an Electronic Road Pricing programme (ERP) in order to relieve congestion within the city's Central Business District (CBD) at peak times, and these electronic tolls will be reflected in your bill, depending upon the time of day.

Singapore's taxis have in-built **speed monitors**. If you hear a persistent chiming noise your driver is breaking the 80kph expressway speed limit.

On the whole, Singaporean taxi drivers are friendly, but their English isn't always good, so it's worth having your **destination written down** (in English) if you are heading off the beaten track. If a taxi displays a red destination sign on its dashboard, it means the driver is changing shift and will accept customers only if they are going in his direction. Finally, **tourists with wheelchairs** should note that TIBS Taxis (☎65558888) has wheelchair-accessible cabs in its fleet.

Renting cars and bikes

The Singapore government has introduced huge disincentives to driving in order to combat traffic congestion. If you want to drive into the CBD (see above) you'll have to buy a stored value **CashCard** to cover the electronic tolls that are now automatically levied. What's more, **parking** is expensive: you need to purchase coupons from a licence booth, post office or store. In fact, the only real reason for renting a car in Singapore is to travel up into Malaysia, and even then it's far cheaper to rent from a company based over the causeway (in JB), as Singaporean firms levy a $25 Malaysia surcharge. If you're still keen on driving in Singapore itself, rental companies are listed on p.178.

Bike rental is offered by Wheelpower, #01-09 Sunshine Plaza, 91 Bencoolen Street (daily 9.30am–7pm, $28 per day; ☎1800-238 2388). There are also rental firms along the East Coast Parkway, where the cycle track that skirts the seashore is always crowded with Singaporeans in full cycling gear. Expect to pay around $4–8 an hour for a mountain bike, and bring some form of ID to leave at the office. There are cycling trails at Bukit Timah Nature Reserve; Biker & Hike at 382 Upper Bukit Timah Road (☎67638382) rent out mountain bikes at $6 an hour. The dirt tracks that crisscross Pulau Ubin, off Changi Point at the eastern tip of the island, are ideal for cycling – a day's rental at one of the cluster of shops near the jetty again costs $4–8, though the price doubles during the school holidays (June, Nov & Dec). Finally, there's a range of bikes – including tandems – available for rent next to the ferry terminal on Sentosa Island ($2–5 an hour), which provide by far the best way to see the island.

Organized tours

If you're pushed for time, there are several reputable companies in Singapore offering **sightseeing tours**. The main operators are listed on p.179, or ask at your hotel or the tourist office. Tours vary according to the operator, but four-hour city tours typically take in Orchard Road, Chinatown and Little India, and cost around $30. Specialist tours are also available – on such subjects as

Singapore by night, World War II sights, Chinese opera, Asian cuisines, even feng shui – costing $30–80 per person. For more details, contact the STB. Members of the Registered Tourist Guides Association (☎63392114) charge $25–50 an hour (minimum 4hr) for a personalized tour – as can the guides of Geraldene's Tours (☎67375250).

Trishaws – three-wheeled bicycles with a carriage on the back – were once a common form of transport in Singapore, though they're a bit of an anachronism these days. You'll still see a few trishaws providing a genuine service around Little India and Chinatown, but most drivers now congregate on the open land opposite the Summer View Hotel on Bencoolen Street, from where they'll give you a 45-minute sightseeing ride for $40.

Boat cruises

Fleets of **cruise boats** ply Singapore's southern waters day and night. Singapore River Cruise boats (9am–11pm;

☎63366111) cast off from Boat Quay and Raffles' landing site for a $12 cruise (children $6) on a traditional bumboat, passing the old **godowns** where traders once stored their merchandise. Singapore Explorer (9am–11am; ☎63396833) offers pretty much the same tour, starting from Clarke Quay, Merlion Park and Raffles Place. The two companies also run river taxis ($3) between Merlion Park and Robertson Quay.

In addition, several cruise companies operate out of Clifford Pier, offering everything from luxury catamaran trips around Singapore's southern isles to dinner on a Chinese sailing boat. A straightforward cruise will set you back around $20, and a dinner special $35–50. Cruise companies include Eastwind (☎63333432), Singapore Riverboat (☎63389205), Singapore River Cruises (☎63366111) and Watertours (☎65339811). If you don't relish the idea of an organized cruise, you can haggle with a **bumboat** man on Clifford Pier: if you're lucky, he'll take a group around the southern isles for $25 an hour.

Opening hours, holidays and festivals

Shopping centres are open daily 10am–9.30pm, while offices generally work Monday to Friday 8.30am–5pm and sometimes on Saturday mornings (see p.21 for banking hours). In general, Chinese temples open daily from 7am to around 6pm, Hindu temples 6am–noon and 5–9pm, and mosques 8.30am–noon and 2.30–4pm; specific opening hours for all temples and museums are given in the text.

As there are so many ethnic groups and religions in Singapore, your visit could easily coincide with a **festival**. Bear in mind that the major festival periods will make traffic on the island heavier and crossing into Malaysia much slower. Over Ramadan in particular, transport networks and hotel capacity are stretched to their limits, as countless Muslims engage in *balik kampung* – the return to one's home village. Chinese New Year causes similar problems. Some, but by no means all, festivals are also public holidays (when everything closes); check the list below for those. For full details on Singapore's festivals see p.159.

Most of the festivals have **no fixed dates**, but change annually according to the lunar calendar; the Islamic calendar shifts forward relative to the Gregorian calendar by about ten days each year, so that, for example, a Muslim festival which happens in mid-April one year will be nearer the beginning of April the following year. We've listed rough timings, but for specific dates each year it's a good idea to check with the local tourist office.

Public holidays

January 1 New Year's Day
January/February Chinese New Year (2 days)
January/February Hari Raya Haji
March/April Good Friday
May 1 Labour Day
May Vesak Day
August 9 National Day
November Deepavali
October/November Hari Raya Puasa
December 25 Christmas Day

Communications

The communications network in high-tech Singapore is fast and efficient, and you can bank on easy access to the Internet. You can send mail to Singapore care of the poste restante section of the General Post Office (see below); when picking up mail, be sure to have the staff check under first names as well as family names – misfiling is common.

Postal services

In Singapore, the GPO (Mon–Fri 8am–6pm, Sat 8am–2pm), housing the **Poste Restante**, is beside Paya Lebar MRT station.

There are more than 1300 other post offices across the state, with usual opening hours of Monday to Friday 8.30am–5pm and Saturday 8.30am–1pm. In addition, postal services are available until 9pm at the Comcentre on Killiney Road. Call ☎1605 to find your nearest post office.

Singapore's **postal system** is predictably efficient, with letters and cards often reaching their destination within three days. Stamps are available at post offices (some have vending machines operating out of hours), and some stationers and hotels. Airmail letters to Europe and the USA rise from $1, aerogrammes to all destinations cost 50c and postcards cost 50c to send. You'll find **fax and telex** facilities at all major post offices, too.

Telephones

Local calls from private phones in Singapore cost next to nothing; calls from public phones cost 10c for three minutes, with the exception of the free courtesy phones at Changi airport.

Singapore has no area codes. The only time you'll punch more than eight digits for a local number is if you are dialling a toll-free number (☎1800-) or a pager. Bear in mind that Singapore recently added a prefix of 6- to all landline numbers; if you are trying a number and having no luck, adding an extra 6 might do the trick.

Payphones accept 10c, 20c and 50c coins. That said, **cardphones** are taking over from payphones in Singapore.

It's possible to make **IDD calls** from all public phone-card and **credit-card** phones. Cards are available from post offices, stationery shops, bookshops, 7-Elevens and money-changers, and come in $3–50 denominations. International cards come in $10–50 denominations. You can also use the **booths** at the 24-hour Comcentre, on Killiney Road.

IDD calls made from hotel rooms in Singapore carry no surcharge.

Calling home from abroad

One of the most convenient ways of phoning home from abroad is via a **telephone charge card** from your phone company back home. Using a PIN number, you can make calls from most hotels, public and private phones that will be charged to your account. Since most major charge cards are free to obtain, it's certainly worth getting one at least for emergencies; enquire first though whether your destination is covered, and bear in mind that rates aren't necessarily cheaper than calling from a public phone.

In **the UK and Ireland**, British Telecom (℡0800/345 144, ⊛www.chargecard.bt.com) will issue free to all BT customers the BT Charge Card, which can be used in 116 countries; AT&T (dial ℡0800/890 011, then 888/641-6123 when you hear the AT&T prompt to be transferred to the Florida Call Centre, free 24 hours) has the Global Calling Card; while NTL (℡0500/100 505) issues its own Global Calling Card, which can be used in more than sixty countries abroad, though the fees cannot be charged to a normal phone bill.

In the **US and Canada**, AT&T, MCI, Sprint, Canada Direct and other North American long-distance companies all enable their customers to make credit-card calls while overseas, billed to your home number. Call your company's customer service line to find out if they provide service from Singapore, and if so, what the toll-free access code is.

To call **Australia and New Zealand** from overseas, telephone charge cards such as Telstra Telecard or Optus Calling Card in Australia, and Telecom NZ's Calling Card can be used to make calls abroad, which are charged back to a domestic account or credit card. Apply to Telstra (℡1800/038 000), Optus (℡1300/300 937), or Telecom NZ (℡04/801 9000).

Mobile phones

If you want to use your **mobile phone** abroad, you'll need to check with your phone provider if it will work abroad, and what the call charges are. **In the UK**, for all but the top-of-the-range packages, you'll have to inform your phone provider before going abroad to get international access switched on. You may get charged extra for this depending on your existing package and where you are travelling. You are also likely to be charged extra for incoming calls when abroad, as the people calling you will be paying the usual rate. If you want to retrieve messages while you're away, you'll have to ask your provider for a new access code, as your home one is unlikely to work abroad. Most UK mobiles use GSM too, which gives access to most places worldwide, except the US. For further information about using your phone abroad, check out ⊛www.telecomsadvice.org.uk/features/using_your_mobile_abroad.htm.

Unless you have a tri-band phone, it is unlikely that a mobile bought for use outside **the US** will work inside the States and vice versa. For details of which mobiles will work outside the US, contact your mobile service provider.

Most mobiles **in Australia and New Zealand** use GSM, which works well in Southeast Asia – check with your provider.

Email and the Internet

One of the best ways to keep in touch while travelling is to sign up for a free Internet email address that can be accessed from anywhere, for example YahooMail or Hotmail – accessible through ⊛www.yahoo.com and

Dialling codes

To call home **from Singapore**, dial ℡00 plus the country code. Note that the initial zero is omitted from the area code when dialling the UK, Ireland, Australia and New Zealand from abroad.

UK international access code + 44 + city code.

Republic of Ireland international access code + 353 + city code.

USA and Canada international access code + 1 + area code.

Australia international access code + 61 + city code.

New Zealand international access code + 64 + city code.

@www.hotmail.com. Once you've set up an account, you can use these sites to pick up and send mail from any Internet café, or hotel with Internet access.

You can get online at numerous **cafés** in Singapore; some of the more central ones are listed on p.146. In addition, hotels increasingly offer in-room modems, or Web access through the TV.

For details of how to plug your **laptop** in when abroad, plus information on country codes around the world, and electrical systems in different countries, check out the useful website, @www.kropla.com.

The media

As well as dailies in Chinese, Malay and Tamil, Singapore has two English-language newspapers, the *Straits Times*, a decent broadsheet, with good coverage of international events, and the *Business Times,* dealing mainly with commercial and financial news. In addition, an amusingly tame tabloid, the *New Paper*, hits the streets every afternoon, though there's little of real interest in it for non-Singaporeans. All three are owned by Singapore Press Holdings, which is careful to steer well clear of any criticism of the government.

International publications include the ubiquitous *Time* and *Newsweek*, as well as a widening range of glossy consumer magazines. Those titles that do reach the stands are effectively sold on remand – one word of criticism and they are pulled, as *FHM* and the *Far Eastern Economic Review* discovered to their cost in recent years.

The Media Corporation of Singapore screens **TV programmes** in English, Chinese, Malay and Tamil. Channel 5, NewsAsia and Channel i feature the most English-language programmes, while Channel 8 specializes in Chinese soap operas. Most Singaporean TV sets also receive a handful of Malaysian channels.

MediaCorp also broadcasts four English-language **radio** shows daily: Gold (90.5FM), an information and classic hits channel; Symphony (92.4FM) featuring classical music; NewsRadion (93.8FM); Class (95FM) playing middle-of-the-road hits; and Perfect (98.7FM), playing contemporary hits. Another channel that's good for current chart-toppers is SAFRA Radio's Power 98FM. There's also a decent pirate radio station operating from Indonesia's Batam Island. For locals, there are daily shows in Chinese (95.8FM), Malay (94.2FM) and Tamil (96.8FM). For listings, check in the daily newspapers, or in *8 Days* magazine.

With a shortwave radio you can pick up the **BBC World Service** (@www.bbc.co.uk /worldservice), **Radio Canada** (@www.rcinet .ca) and **Voice of America** (@www.voa.gov). Most stations post an up-to-date schedule on their websites.

Trouble and the police

If you lose something in Singapore, you're more likely to have someone running after you with it than running away. Nevertheless, you shouldn't become complacent – muggings have been known to occur and theft from dormitories by other tourists is a common complaint. Guesthouses and hotels will often have a safety deposit box. Always keep a separate record of the numbers of your travellers' cheques, together with a note of which ones you've cashed. It's a good idea to take a photocopy of the relevant pages of your passport, too, in case it's lost or stolen.

It's very unwise to have anything to do with **drugs** of any description in Singapore. The penalties for trafficking drugs in or out of the country are severe in the extreme – foreigners have been executed in the past – and if you are arrested for drugs offences you can expect no mercy and little help from your consular representatives.

Singapore's **police**, who wear dark blue, keep a fairly low profile, but are polite and helpful when approached. For details of the main police station, and other emergency information, check "Directory", pp.178–179.

Singapore is known locally as **fine city**. There's a fine of $500 for smoking in public places such as cinemas, trains, lifts, air-conditioned restaurants and shopping malls, and a one-off $50 fine for "jaywalking" – crossing a main road within 50m of a pedestrian crossing or bridge. Littering carries a $1000 fine, with offenders now issued Corrective Work Orders and forced to do litter-picking duty; eating and drinking on the MRT could cost you $500.

Other fines include those for urinating in lifts (legend has it that some lifts are fitted with urine detectors), not flushing a public toilet and chewing gum (which is outlawed in Singapore).

For Singapore's legal position on **homosexuality**, see p.153.

Emergencies

In an emergency, dial the following numbers:
Police ☎999
Fire brigade/Ambulance ☎995.

Travellers with disabilities

Singapore is an accessible city for travellers with disabilities, as hefty tax incentives are provided for developers who include access features for the disabled in new buildings. However, life is made a lot easier if you can afford to pay for more upmarket hotels and to shell out for taxis. Similarly, the more expensive international airlines tend to be better equipped to get you there in the first place: MAS, British Airways, KLM and Qantas all carry aisle wheelchairs and have at least one toilet adapted for disabled passengers. However, few, if any, tour operators offering holidays in the region accommodate the needs of those with disabilities.

The best resource for pre-trip advice is the **Disabled People's Association of Singapore**, #02-00 Day Care Centre, 150a Pandan Gardens (☎68991220; ⊛www.dpa .org.sg). Their informative website links to *Access Singapore*, a Singapore Council of Social Service publication, which, while in need of updating, is still a thorough and informative brochure detailing amenities for the disabled in Singapore's hotels, hospitals, shopping centres, cinemas and banks. You'll find Access Singapore at ⊛www.dpa.org .sg/DPA/access/contents.htm.

Access is improving all the time, and most **hotels** now make some provision for disabled guests, though often there will be only one specially designed bedroom in an establishment – always call first for information, and book in plenty of time. **Getting around** the city is less straightforward: buses are not accessible to wheelchairs and there are no elevators in the MRT system. However, two taxi companies, TIBS (☎65558888) and CityCab (☎65522222), have cabs big enough to take a wheelchair. There are acoustic signals at most street crossings.

Contacts for travellers with disabilities

In the UK and Ireland

Holiday Care 2nd floor, Imperial Building, Victoria Rd, Horley, Surrey RH6 7PZ ☎0845/124 9971, minicom ☎0845/124 9976, ⊛www.holidaycare.org.uk. Provides free lists of accessible accommodation abroad – European,

American and long-haul destinations – plus a list of accessible attractions in the UK. Information on financial help for holidays available.
Irish Wheelchair Association Blackheath Drive, Clontarf, Dublin 3 ☎01/818 6400, ⊛www.iwa.ie. Useful information provided about travelling abroad with a wheelchair.
Tripscope Alexandra House, Albany Rd, Brentford, Middlesex TW8 0NE ☎0845/7585 641, ⊛www.tripscope.org.uk. This registered charity provides a national telephone information service offering free advice on UK and international transport for those with a mobility problem.

In the US and Canada

Access-Able ⊛www.access-able.com. Online resource for travellers with disabilities.
Directions Unlimited 123 Green Lane, Bedford Hills, NY 10507 ☎1-800/533-5343 or 914/241-1700. Travel agency specializing in bookings for people with disabilities.
Mobility International USA 451 Broadway, Eugene, OR 97401 ☎541/343-1284, ⊛www.miusa.org. Information and referral services, access guides, tours and exchange programmes. Annual membership $35 (includes quarterly newsletter).
Society for the Advancement of Travelers with Handicaps (SATH) 347 5th Ave, New York, NY 10016 ☎212/447-7284, ⊛www.sath.org. Non-profit educational organization that has actively represented travelers with disabilities since 1976.
Wheels Up! ☎1-888/38-WHEELS, ⊛www.wheelsup.com. Provides discounted airfare, tour and cruise prices for disabled travellers, also publishes a free monthly newsletter and has a comprehensive website.

In Australia and New Zealand

ACROD (Australian Council for Rehabilitation of the Disabled) PO Box 60, Curtin ACT 2605; Suite 103, 1st floor, 1–5 Commercial Rd, Kings Grove 2208; ☎02/6282 4333, TTY ☎02/6282 4333, ✉www.acrod.org.au.

Provides lists of travel agencies and tour operators for people with disabilities.

Disabled Persons Assembly 4/173–175 Victoria St, Wellington, New Zealand ☎04/801 9100 (also TTY), ✉www.dpa.org.nz. Resource centre with lists of travel agencies and tour operators for people with disabilities.

The City

The City

1. The Colonial District..41

2. Orchard Road..54

3. Chinatown and the Financial District.................57

4. Little India and the Arab Quarter.......................74

5. Northern Singapore..85

6. Eastern Singapore..93

7. Western Singapore..99

8. Sentosa and the southern isles 107

The Colonial District

The British left Singapore an impressive legacy in the stately nineteenth-century piles of the **COLONIAL DISTRICT**. From the Bencoolen Street/Beach Road area, it's an easy jaunt on foot to survey the fruits of grandiose empire building; if you're coming from further afield, you'll need to take the MRT to either Raffles Place or City Hall MRT stations.

As the colony's trade grew in the nineteenth century, the Singapore River became its main artery, clogged with the traditional cargo boats known as bumboats, with painted eyes, as though they could see where they were going. The boats ferried coffee, sugar and rice to the riverbank warehouses (godowns), where coolies loaded and unloaded sacks. These days, with the bumboats all but gone, the river is quieter, cleaner and inevitably less fascinating, though both banks are undergoing a profound commercial revitalization, as new restaurants and bars move into formerly abandoned buildings.

The heart of the Colonial District is the immaculately groomed grass of the **Padang** ("field" in Malay), which stretches out below **St Andrew's Cathedral** towards the river. To the south of the Padang are the **Empress Place Building** (now home to the second wing of the Asian Civilizations Museum), **Parliament House** and the **Singapore Cricket Club** – the epitome of the colonizers' stubborn refusal to adapt to their surroundings. To the north is grand old **Raffles Hotel**, beyond which a string of nineteenth- and twentieth-century churches leads to Singapore's famous entertainment centre, **Bugis Village**. Also in the north of the district are the **Singapore Art Museum**, **Singapore History Museum**, and the shops and restaurants of the **CHIJMES** complex. Heading west from the Padang, you pass **City Hall** and the **Supreme Court** before climbing the slopes of **Fort Canning Hill**, ten minutes' walk from the Padang, and one of the few hills in Singapore not lost to land reclamation. Dominating the newly reclaimed land to the east of the Padang, the bug's-eye beauty of the **Theatres on the Bay** project hauls the Colonial District into the twenty-first century.

Along the north riverbank

From Raffles Place MRT it's just a couple of minutes' walk, past Singapore's former GPO (now the splendid Fullerton Hotel), to the elegant suspension struts of **Cavenagh Bridge** – a good place to start a tour of the colonial centre. Named after Major General Orfeur Cavenagh, governor of the Straits Settlements from 1859 to 1867, the bridge was constructed in 1869 by Indian convict labourers using imported Glasgow steel. Times change, but not necessarily here, where a police sign maintains: "The use of this bridge is prohibited to any vehicle of which the laden weight exceeds 3cwt and to all cattle and horses."

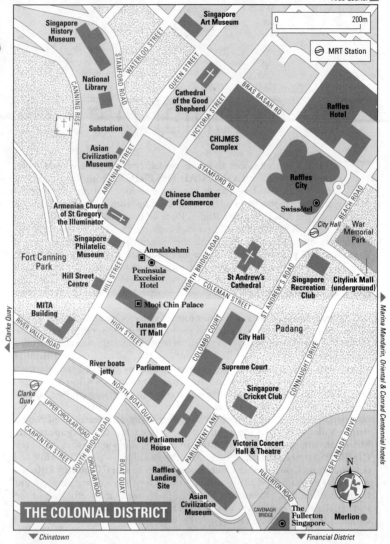

Arab Quarter ▲

Singapore
History
Museum

Singapore
Art Museum

| 0 | 200m |

⊖ MRT Station

WATERLOO STREET

STAMFORD ROAD

National
Library

QUEEN STREET

Cathedral
of the Good
Shepherd

BRAS BASAH RD

Raffles
Hotel

CANNING RISE

VICTORIA STREET

Substation

CHIJMES
Complex

Asian
Civilization
Museum

STAMFORD RD

Raffles
City

ARMENIAN STREET

Armenian Church
of St Gregory
the Illuminator

Chinese Chamber
of Commerce

BEACH ROAD

Swissôtel ⊙

Fort Canning
Park

Singapore
Philatelic
Museum

NORTH BRIDGE ROAD

City Hall ⊖

War
Memorial
Park

Hill Street
Centre

Annalakshmi

HILL STREET

Peninsula
Excelsior
Hotel

COLEMAN STREET

St Andrew's
Cathedral

ST ANDREW'S ROAD

Singapore
Recreation
Club

Citylink Mall
(underground)

MITA
Building

RIVER VALLEY ROAD

Clarke Quay ◄

Mooi Chin Palace

HIGH STREET

Funan the
IT Mall

COLOMBO COURT

City Hall

Padang

Marina Mandarin, Oriental & Conrad Centennial hotels ►

River boats
jetty

Parliament

NORTH BOAT QUAY

Supreme Court

CONNAUGHT DRIVE

Clarke ⊖
Quay

UPPER CIRCULAR ROAD

CARPENTER STREET

SOUTH BRIDGE ROAD

CIRCULAR ROAD

BOAT QUAY

Singapore
Cricket Club

Old Parliament
House

PARLIAMENT LANE

Victoria Concert
Hall & Theatre

ESPLANADE DRIVE

Raffles
Landing
Site

FULLERTON ROAD

N

THE COLONIAL DISTRICT

Asian
Civilization
Museum

CAVENAGH
BRIDGE

The
Fullerton
Singapore

⊙

Merlion ■

▼ Chinatown

▼ Financial District

Stepping off the bridge, you're confronted by **Empress Place Building**, a robust Neoclassical structure named after Queen Victoria and completed in 1865. It served for ten years as a courthouse before the Registry of Births and Deaths and the Immigration Department moved in. Today it houses one of the two "wings" of the **Asian Civilization Museum** (Mon noon–6pm, Tues–Thurs 9am–6pm, Fri 9am–9pm; $3 including free guided tour Mon–Fri 11am & 2pm, Sat & Sun 11am, 2pm & 3.30pm; ☎63327798, ⓦwww.nhb.gov.sg); the other is nearby on Armenian Street (see p.50). Together, the ACM's two branches trace the origins and growth of Asia's many and varied cultures. While its sister museum concentrates specifically on Singapore's Chinese and Peranakan communities, Empress Place focuses more broadly on western, southern and Southeast Asian and Chinese religions, history and cultures. Its ten themed galleries hold approaching 2000 artefacts bringing to life every corner of Asia. There is also an engaging Singapore River Interpretive Gallery, featuring oral history accounts of the river delivered by individuals from generations that lived beside and worked it all their lives. The pyramid-shaped time capsule in the grounds in front of the building was sealed in 1990 as part of Singapore's silver jubilee celebrations. It contains "significant items" from Singapore's first 25 years of independence: the clever money says that when opened it will yield a Lee Kuan Yew speech or two. The southern flank of the Empress Place Building has been appropriated by the all-conquering *Indochine* bar and restaurant chain. Its string of Khmer-influenced outlets afford peerless views of the Singapore River.

Next to the Empress Place Building stand two fine examples of colonial architecture, the **Victoria Concert Hall** and adjoining **Victoria Theatre**, still the venues for some of Singapore's most prestigious cultural events. The theatre was completed in 1862 as Singapore's town hall, while the concert hall was added in 1905 as a tribute to the monarch's reign. During the Japanese occupation, the clock tower was altered to Tokyo time, while the statue of Raffles that once stood in front of the tower narrowly escaped being melted down. The newly installed Japanese curator of the National Museum (where the statue was sent) hid the statue and reported it destroyed. A copy can be seen by the river at **Raffles' landing site**, where, in January 1819, the great man apparently took his first steps on Singaporean soil. Sir Stamford now stares contemplatively across the river towards the business district. Singapore River cruise boats (see p.32) depart from a tiny jetty, a few steps along from Raffles' statue.

North of the statue, up Parliament Lane, the dignified white Victorian building ringed by fencing is the **Old Parliament House**, built as a private dwelling for a rich merchant by Singapore's pre-eminent colonial architect, the Irishman George Drumgould Coleman. The bronze elephant in front of Old Parliament House was a gift to Singapore from King Rama V of Thailand (whose father was the king upon whom *The King and I* was based) after his trip to the island in 1871 – the first foreign visit ever made by a Thai monarch. It is sometimes possible to watch Singapore's parliament in session in the **new Parliament House**, across Parliament Lane from its predecessor; call ☎63368811 or 63326666 for details, or check out Ⓦwww.gov.sg/parliament.

The Padang

The **Padang** is the very essence of colonial Singapore. Earmarked by Raffles as a recreation ground shortly after his arrival, such is its symbolic significance that its borders have never been encroached upon by speculators and it remains much as it was in 1907, when G.M. Reith wrote in his *Handbook to Singapore*: "Cricket, tennis, hockey, football and bowls are played on the plain . . . beyond the carriage drive on the other side, is a strip of green along the sea wall, with a footpath, which affords a cool and pleasant walk in the early morning and afternoon." Once the last over of the day had been bowled, the Padang assumed a more social role: the image of Singapore's European community hastening to the corner once known as Scandal Point to catch up on the latest gossip is pure Somerset Maugham. Today the Padang is kept as pristine as ever by a bevy of gardeners mounted on state-of-the-art lawnmowers. As an April

Sir Stamford Raffles

Let it still be the boast of Britain
to write her name in characters of light;
let her not be remembered as the tempest
whose course was desolation,
but as the gale of spring reviving
the slumbering seeds of mind and
calling them to life
from the winter of ignorance and oppression.
If the time shall come
when her empire shall have passed away,
these monuments will endure when her triumphs
shall have become an empty name.

This verse, written by Sir Stamford Raffles himself, speaks volumes about the man whom history remembers as the founder of modern Singapore. Despite living and working in a period of imperial arrogance and self-motivated land-grabbing, Raffles maintained an unfailing concern for the welfare of the people under his governorship, and a conviction that British colonial expansion was for the general good. He believed Britain to be, as Jan Morris says in her introduction to Maurice Collis's biography of Raffles, "the chief agent of human progress . . . the example of fair Government".

Fittingly for a man who was to spend his life roaming the globe, Thomas Stamford Raffles was born at sea on July 6, 1781 on the *Ann*, whose master was his father Captain Benjamin Raffles. By his fourteenth birthday, the young Raffles was working as a clerk for the **East India Company** in London, his schooling curtailed because of his father's debts. Even at this early age, Raffles' ambition and self-motivation was evident as, faced with a lifetime as a clerk, he resolved to educate himself, staying up through the night to study and developing a hunger for knowledge which would later spur him to learn Malay, amass a vast treasure-trove of natural history artefacts and write his two-volume *History of Java*.

Abdullah bin Kadir, Raffles' clerk while in Southeast Asia, describes him in his autobiography, *The Hikayat Abdullah*: "He was broad of brow, a sign of his care and thoroughness; round-headed with a projecting forehead, showing his intelligence. He had light brown hair, indicative of bravery; large ears, the mark of a ready listener . . . He was solicitous of the feelings of others, and open-handed with the poor. He spoke in smiles. He took the most active interest in historical research. Whatever he found to do he adopted no half-measures, but saw it through to the finish."

Raffles' diligence and hard work showed through in 1805, when he was chosen to join a team going out to Penang, then being developed as a British entrepôt; overnight, his annual salary leapt from £70 to £1500. Once in Southeast Asia, Raffles' rise was meteoric. By 1807 he was named **chief secretary to the governor in Penang** and soon Lord Minto, the governor-general of the East India Company in India, was alerted to his Oriental expertise. Meeting Minto on a trip to Calcutta in 1810, Raffles was appointed **secretary to the governor-general in Malaya**, a

Fool's Day joke, the *Straits Times* reported in 1982 that the Padang was to be sold off for development; the ensuing public outcry jammed the newspaper's switchboard.

The brown-tiled roof, whitewashed walls and dark-green blinds of the **Singapore Cricket Club**, at the southwestern end of the Padang, have a nostalgic charm. Founded in the 1850s, the club was the hub of colonial British society and still operates a "members only" rule, though there's nothing to stop promotion quickly followed by the **governorship of Java** in 1811. Raffles' rule of Java was wise, libertarian and compassionate, his economic, judicial and social reforms transforming an island bowed by Dutch rule.

Post-Waterloo European rebuilding saw the East Indies returned to the Dutch in 1816 – to the chagrin of Raffles, who foresaw problems for British trade should the Dutch regain their hold on the area. From Java, Raffles transferred to the **governorship of Bencoolen**, on the southern coast of Sumatra, but not before he had returned home for a break, stopping at St Helena en route to meet Napoleon ("a monster"). While in England he met his second wife, Sophia Hull (his first, Olivia, had died in 1814), and was knighted.

Raffles and Sophia sailed to Bencoolen in early 1818, Sophia reporting that her husband spent the four-month journey deep in study. Once in Sumatra, Raffles found the time to study the region's flora and fauna as tirelessly as ever, discovering the **rafflesia arnoldii** – "perhaps the largest and most magnificent flower in the world" – on a jungle field trip. By now, Raffles felt strongly that Britain should establish a base in the Straits of Melaka. Meeting Hastings (Minto's successor) in late 1818, he was given leave to pursue this possibility and in 1819 duly sailed to the southern tip of the Malay Peninsula, where his securing of **Singapore** early that year was a daring masterstroke of diplomacy.

For a man whose name is inextricably linked with Singapore, Raffles spent a remarkably short time on the island. His first stay was for one week, and the second for three weeks, during which time he helped delineate the new settlement (see p.183): "Looking a century or two ahead so as to provide for what Singapore may one day become," as Raffles himself later put it. Subsequent sojourns in Bencoolen ended tragically with the loss of four of his five children to tropical illnesses, while his own health also began to deteriorate. Raffles visited Singapore one last time in late 1822; his final public duty there was to lay the foundation stone of the Singapore Institution (later the **Raffles Institution**), an establishment created to educate local Malays, albeit upper-class ones. From Singapore, Raffles and Sophia travelled back to Bencoolen to pick up their personal effects, and from there journeyed home to Europe. The *Fame*, on which they set sail on February 2, 1824, caught fire 80km out to sea, claiming no lives but destroying Raffles' vast collection of natural history specimens and notes.

By August 1824, Raffles was back in England. Awaiting news of a possible pension award from the East India Company, he spent his free time founding the London Zoo and setting up a farm in Hendon. But the new life Raffles had planned for Sophia and himself never materialized. Days after hearing that a Calcutta bank holding £16,000 of his capital had folded, his pension application was refused; worse still, the Company was demanding £22,000 for overpayment. Three months later, the brain tumour that had caused Raffles headaches for several years took his life on July 4, 1826. Buried at Hendon, he was honoured by no memorial stone – the vicar had investments in slave plantations in the West Indies and was unimpressed by his friendship with William Wilberforce. Only in 1832 was Raffles commemorated, with a statue in Westminster Abbey.

you watching the action from outside on the Padang itself. The Singapore Rugby Sevens are played here, as well as a plethora of other big sporting events and parades; a timetable of forthcoming events is available at the club's reception. Eurasians, who were formerly ineligible for membership of the Cricket Club, founded their own establishment in 1883, the **Singapore Recreation Club**, which lies across on the north side of the Padang. The current grandiose, colonnaded clubhouse dates back to a $65m overhaul completed in 1997.

The Sepoy Mutiny

Plaques on the west wall of St Andrew's Cathedral commemorate the victims of one of Singapore's bloodiest episodes, the **Sepoy Mutiny** of 1915. The mutiny began when a German warship, *Emden*, was sunk by an Australian ship off the Cocos Islands: its survivors were brought to Singapore and imprisoned at Tanglin Barracks, at the western end of Orchard Road. With almost all of Singapore's troop contingent away in Europe fighting the Kaiser, the Muslim Punjabi soldiers of the **Fifth Light Infantry**, known as sepoys, were sent to guard the prisoners. Unfortunately, these men's allegiance to the British had recently been strained by the news that Turkey had come out against the Allies in Europe. A rumour that they were soon to be sent to Turkey to fight fellow Muslims upset them still further, and the German prisoners were able to incite the sepoys to mutiny. In the ensuing rampage through the city on February 15, 1915, the sepoys killed forty other soldiers and civilians before they were finally rounded up by some remaining European sailors and a band of men led by the Sultan of Johor. All were court-martialled and the resultant executions saw 36 sepoys shot before huge crowds. As for the Germans, they took the opportunity to effect an escape. Nine of them finally got back to Germany via Jakarta and one, Julius Lauterbach, received an Iron Cross in recognition of his daring and rather convoluted flight home through China and North America.

Just to the west of the Cricket Club, Singapore's Neoclassical **Supreme Court** (formerly the site of the exclusive Hotel de L'Europe, whose drawing rooms allegedly provided Somerset Maugham with inspiration for many of his Southeast Asia short stories) was built between 1937 and 1939, and sports a domed roof of green lead and a splendid, wood-panelled entrance hall – which is as far as you'll get unless you're appearing in front of a judge, as it's not open to the public. Next door is the older **City Hall**, whose uniform rows of grandiose Corinthian columns lend it the austere air of a mausoleum. Wartime photographs show Lord Louis Mountbatten (then Supreme Allied Commander in Southeast Asia) on the steps announcing Japan's surrender to the British in 1945. Fourteen years later, Lee Kuan Yew chose the same spot from which to address his electorate at a victory rally celebrating self-government for Singapore. Nowadays, rather less dramatic photographs are taken on the steps as newlyweds line up to have their big day captured in front of one of Singapore's most imposing buildings.

The final building of note on the west side of the Padang, **St Andrew's Cathedral**, on Coleman Street, gleams even brighter than the rest. The third church to be built on this site, the cathedral was constructed in high-vaulted, Neo-Gothic style, using Indian convict labour, and was consecrated by Bishop Cotton of Calcutta on January 25, 1862. Its exterior walls were plastered using Madras *chunam* – an unlikely composite of eggs, lime, sugar and shredded coconut husks which shines brightly when smoothed – while the small cross behind the pulpit was crafted from two fourteenth-century nails salvaged from the ruins of Coventry Cathedral in England, which was destroyed during World War II.

During the Japanese invasion of Singapore, the cathedral became a makeshift hospital; the vestry was an operating theatre and the nave a ward. Closed-circuit TVs have been installed, which allow the whole congregation to view proceedings up at the altar – a reflection of the Chinese fascination with all things high-tech, since the cathedral's size hardly requires it.

Esplanade – Theatres on the Bay

Singapore's skyline seems to change almost by the day, but rarely has a building caused such ripples as the new, $600-million **Esplanade – Theatres on the Bay** project (@www.esplanade.com), which occupies six hectares of waterfront land to the east of the Padang. Esplanade boasts a concert hall, theatre, recital studio, theatre studio, gallery space and outdoor theatre. Esplanade Mall threads round these various auditoria, offering shopping, eating and drinking and making the complex as much a social hub as a cultural landmark. From the waterfront restaurants and bars on the south side of the complex, there are unbeatable views across the bay. On the third floor is library@esplanade, a performing arts library with a wide range of arts-related resources.

Opinion is split over whether the two huge, spiked shells that roof the complex are peerless modernistic architecture or plain indulgent kitsch. They have variously been compared to hedgehogs, kitchen sieves, golf balls, huge microphones, even mating aardvarks; locals have taken to calling them "the durians", though they are perhaps best described as resembling two giant insects' eyes.

The idea for an integrated national arts centre was first mooted in the 1970s. The project's radical architecture was unveiled to the Singaporean public in 1994, and work began officially in 1996. The gala opening night, in October 2002, saw thousands of Singaporeans turn out for a spectacular fireworks display. In giving this ambitious project a green light, the government has upped the ante in its attempts to nurture a unified Singaporean culture. The authorities are viewing Esplanade as an iconic statement of Singapore's developing nationhood.

Should you decide to investigate Esplanade's monthly schedule, you'll find a varied programme of **events** spanning jazz, Asian dance, pipe-organ recitals, classical ballet, musicals such as *Singin' in the Rain* and contemporary drama. Real theatre buffs might enjoy the 45-minute **guided tours** (Mon–Fri 11am & 2pm, Sat & Sun 11am; $8; ☎68288377) of the area that start from the Concourse Information Counter.

Raffles City and Raffles Hotel

Northwest of the Theatres on the Bay is **Raffles City**, a huge development that sits beside the intersection of Bras Basah and North Bridge roads and comprises two enormous hotels – one of which is the 73-storey **Swissôtel** – a multi-level shopping centre and floor upon floor of offices. Completed in 1985, the complex was designed by Chinese-American architect I.M. Pei (the man behind the Louvre's glass pyramid) and required the highly contentious demolition of the venerable Raffles Institution, established by Raffles himself and built in 1835 by George Drumgould Coleman. The Swissôtel holds an annual vertical marathon, in which hardy athletes attempt to run up to the top floor in as short a time as possible: the current record stands at under seven minutes. Lifts transport lesser mortals to admire the view from the sumptuous bars and restaurants on the top floors. The imposing **Singapore War Memorial** stands on the open land east of Raffles City; comprising four seventy-metre-high white columns, it's known locally as the "chopsticks".

If the Swissôtel is the tallest hotel in the world, across the way is perhaps the most famous. The lofty halls, restaurants, bars, and peaceful gardens of the legendary **Raffles Hotel**, almost a byword for colonialism, prompted Somerset Maugham to remark that it "stood for all the fables of the exotic East". Oddly, though, this most inherently British of hotels started life as a modest seafront bungalow belonging to an Arab trader, Mohamed Alsagoff. After a spell as a tiffin house, the property was bought in 1886 by the enterprising Armenian Sarkies brothers, who eventually controlled a triumvirate of quintessentially colonial lodgings: the *Raffles*, the (still extant) *Eastern and Oriental* in Penang, and the *Strand* in Rangoon.

Raffles Hotel opened for business on December 1, 1887 and quickly attracted some impressive guests. It is thought that Joseph Conrad stayed in the late 1880s; certainly Rudyard Kipling visited soon after this, though the hotel was far from sumptuous. "Let the traveller take note," wrote Kipling, "feed at Raffles and stay at the Hotel de l'Europe". The hotel enjoyed its real heyday during the first three decades of the new century, when it established its reputation for luxury and elegance – it was the first building in Singapore with electric lights and fans.

In 1902, a little piece of Singaporean history was made at the hotel, according to a (probably apocryphal) tale, when the last tiger to be killed on the island was shot inside the building. Thirteen years later another *Raffles* legend, the Singapore Sling cocktail, was created by bartender Ngiam Tong Boon.

The rich, famous and influential have always patronized the hotel, but it is its literary connections of which the hotel is proudest. Herman Hesse, Somerset Maugham, Noël Coward and Günter Grass all stayed at *Raffles* at some time – Maugham is said to have written many of his Asian tales under a frangipani tree in the garden.

During World War II, when the Japanese swept through the island, the hotel became the invading officers' quarters. After the Japanese surrender in 1945, *Raffles* was a transit camp for liberated Allied prisoners. Postwar deterioration earned it the affectionate but melancholy soubriquet "grand old lady of the East" and the hotel was little more than a shabby tourist diversion when the government finally declared it a national monument in 1987. A $160-million facelift followed and the hotel reopened on September 16, 1991.

The new-look *Raffles* gets a very mixed reception. Though it retains much of its colonial grace, the shopping arcade that now curves around the back of the hotel lacks finesse, selling *Raffles*-related souvenirs, exclusive garments, leatherware and perfume. Still, if you're in Singapore, there's no missing *Raffles* and, if you can't afford to stay here, there are other ways to soak up the atmosphere. A free **museum** (daily 10am–9pm), located upstairs, at the back of the hotel complex, is crammed with memorabilia, much of which was recovered in a nationwide heritage search that encouraged Singaporeans to turn in souvenirs that had found their way up sleeves and into handbags over the years. Otherwise, a Singapore Sling in *The Bar and Billiards Room* – one of thirteen food and beverage outlets in the hotel – will cost you around $17.

Along Bras Basah Road

Bras Basah Road cuts west from *Raffles*, crossing North Bridge Road and then passing one of Singapore's most aesthetically pleasing eating venues, the **CHIJMES** complex. Based around the Neo-Gothic husk of the former Convent of the Holy Infant Jesus (from whose name the complex's acronymic title is derived), CHIJMES is a rustic version of London's Covent Garden, whose lawns, courtyards, waterfalls, fountains and sunken forecourt give a sense of spatial dynamics that is rare indeed in Singapore. A relic from CHIJMES' convent days survives on its Victoria Street flank, where local families left unwanted babies at the **Gate of Hope**, to be taken in by the convent. Many were "Tiger girls", so called because they were born in the year of the tiger and were therefore thought to bring bad luck to their families. CHIJMES' shops and boutiques open from 9am to 10pm, the restaurants and bars from 11am to 1am.

Beyond CHIJMES, Bras Basah crosses Victoria and Queen streets, where elderly trishaw drivers in yellow T-shirts tout for custom, before arriving at the **Singapore Art Museum** at 71 Bras Basah Road (Mon noon–6pm, Tues–Thurs 9am–6pm, Fri 9am–9pm, Sat & Sun 9am–6pm; $3 including free tour, Mon–Fri 11am & 2pm, Sat & Sun 11am, 2pm & 3pm; ☎63323222, ⓦwww.nhb.gov.sg). A long-overdue replacement for the tired art wing of the National Museum, the art museum has a peerless location in the venerable St Joseph's Institution, Singapore's first Catholic school, whose silvery dome rang to the sounds of school bells and rote learning until 1987. Though extensions have been necessary, many of the original rooms survive, among them the school chapel (now an auditorium), whose Stations of the Cross and mosaic floor remain intact. The school quad, the former gymnasium, periodically displays statues and sculptures such as the glassworks of American designer Dale Chihuly.

The Art Museum's rolling schedule of visiting collections brings work by such acclaimed artists as Marc Chagall and the sculptor Carl Milles to Singapore. But greater emphasis is placed on contemporary local and Southeast Asian artists and art work. Indeed, the museum's real strength lies in its permanent collection's mapping of the Asian experience. Only a selection from the collection is displayed at any one time, but works you may be lucky enough to catch are Bui Xian Phai's *Coalmine*, an unremittingly desolate memory of his labour in a Vietnamese re-education camp, and Srihadi Sudarsono's *Horizon Dan Prahu*, in which traditional Indonesian fishing boats ply a Mark Rothko-esque canvas. Look out, too, for local artist, Liu Kang's sketches and paintings of post-war kampung life in Singapore.

Outside the museum, the souvenir shop stocks prints and postcards, and there's a classy branch of *Dôme*, where you can have a coffee under the watchful gaze of a statue of the seventeenth-century saint, John Baptist de la Salle, which stands over the museum's porch.

Waterloo Street to Bugis Village

Semi-pedestrianized **Waterloo Street** is at its best on Sundays, springing to life as worshippers throng to its temples and churches. The modern **Kuan Yim Temple**, named after the Buddhist goddess of mercy, may not have the cluttered altars, dusty old rafters and elaborate roofs of Chinatown's temples, but is still extremely popular; all along the pavement outside, old ladies in floppy, wide-brimmed hats sell fresh flowers from baskets. Religious artefact shops on the ground floor of the apartment buildings opposite are well placed to catch worshippers on their way out – one shop specializes in small **shrines** for the house: the de luxe model boasts flashing lights and an extractor fan to expel unwanted incense smoke. **Fortune-tellers** and street traders operate along this stretch of the road, too, and look out for the cage containing turtles and a sleepy old snake: make a donation, touch one of the creatures inside, and it's said that good luck will come your way.

One block east of Waterloo Street's shops and temples, at the junction of Rochor Road and Victoria Street, sits **Bugis Village**, a rather tame manifestation of infamous Bugis Street. Until it was demolished to make way for an MRT station, Bugis Street embodied old Singapore: after dark it was a chaotic place, crawling with rowdy sailors, preening transvestites and prostitutes – and as such it was anathema to the Singapore government, keen to clean up the country's reputation. Singaporean public opinion demanded a replacement, though when Bugis Village opened in 1991 it was revealed as a shadow of its former self. Beer gardens, seafood restaurants, pubs and stalls line its streets, and while local reaction has been largely negative, a steady stream of tourists passes through nightly. The transvestites are noticeable only by their absence, and even the weak cabaret shows of the *Boom Boom Room* nightclub have decamped to Chinatown.

Along Hill Street to Fort Canning Park

From Stamford Road, Hill Street heads south to the river, flanking the eastern side of Fort Canning Park. The **Singapore Chinese Chamber of Commerce**, at 47 Hill Street, a brash, Chinese-style building from 1964 featuring a striking pagoda roof, lies 30m down on the left. Along its facade are two large panels, depicting nine intricately crafted porcelain dragons. By way of contrast, the tiny **Armenian Church** of St Gregory the Illuminator, across the road and next to the former American Embassy, was designed by George Drumgould Coleman in 1835 (which makes it one of the oldest buildings in Singapore). Inside is a single, circular chamber, fronted by a marble altar and a painting of the Last Supper. Among the white gravestones and statues in the church's grounds is the tombstone of Agnes Joaquim, a nineteenth-century Armenian resident of Singapore, after whom the national flower, the delicate, purple Vanda Miss Joaquim Orchid, is named; she discovered the orchid in her garden, and had it registered at the Botanic Gardens.

Given its past, it seems appropriate that the spectacular colonial-era mansion, fronted by two black eagles, around the corner on Armenian Street, should house so worthy a tenant as the second branch of the **Asian Civilization Museum** (Mon noon–6pm, Tues–Thurs 9am–6pm, Fri 9am–9pm, Sat & Sun 9am–6pm; $3 including free guided tours Mon–Fri 11am & 2pm, Sat & Sun 11am, 2pm & 3.30pm; ☎63323015, ⓦwww.nhb.gov.sg). Dating from 1910, the building was once home to the Tao Nan School, the first school in Singapore to cater for new arrivals from the Hokkien region of China. The old school gates are displayed upstairs.

The museum's ten galleries provide a cultural and historical context to Singapore's Chinese and Peranakan communities. (The other "wing" of the Asian Civilization Museum, in the Empress Place Building, covered on p.42, focuses on the broader historical and cultural aspects of Asia in general.) After kicking off with a breakdown of the Middle Kingdom's various imperial dynasties, the museum walks visitors through the architecture, religions, arts and crafts of the Chinese. Best of all is the Peranakan collection, which features some finely embroidered and beaded bridal dresses, and a fantastically ornate Peranakan wedding four-poster. There's also the ancestral altar of wealthy nineteenth-century Singaporean businessman, Tan Kim Seng: amid the silver offering-bowls and plates, and wooden plaques recognizing the importance of honouring ancestors, there's a silver washbasin for the gods to wash their hands after feasting.

Adjacent to the museum, the **Substation**, a disused power station, has been converted into a multimedia arts centre. Even if you don't have the time to check out its classes, discussions and performances (see p.158 for more details), the coffee shop is a pleasant place to hang out for a while. A market takes place in the courtyard every Sunday afternoon, with stalls selling anything from local crafts to secondhand Russian watches.

Singapore History Museum

Turning left at the end of Armenian Street, you'll see the eye-catching dome of stained glass that tops the entrance to the **Singapore History Museum** on Stamford Road (Mon noon–6pm, Tues–Thurs 9am–6pm, Fri 9am–9pm, Sat & Sun 9am–6pm; $3 including free tour Tues–Fri 11am & 2pm, Sat & Sun 11am, 2pm & 3pm; ☏63323659, ⊛www.nhb.gov.sg). The museum's forerunner, the Raffles Museum and Library, was opened in 1887 and soon acquired a reputation for the excellence of its natural history collection. In 1969, the place was renamed the National Museum in recognition of Singapore's independence, and subsequently altered its bias towards local history and culture – a bias that it maintained after it adopted its current name, in 1993. Out front, a stack of silver triangles marks the site of the "Singapore at the turn of the millennium" capsule, to be opened in January 2050; near it stands a chunky slate statue of Tai chi boxers by Taiwanese sculptor, Ju Ming.

The museum houses a fairly low-key collection. Following a recent shake-up, the only permanent exhibitions are the **History of Singapore Gallery**, which features twenty dioramas depicting significant historical events, from the arrival of Raffles in 1819 to the first session of parliament in 1965; the **Rumah Baba**, or **Peranakan** house, where the lifestyle and culture of the Straits Chinese is brought to life; and the Haw Par jade collection. There's also a theatrette, showing **Singapore Story: Overcoming the Odds** (Mon 1.30pm, 2.30pm & 3.30pm, Tues–Sun hourly 10.30am–3.30pm; $2, children $1), a half-hour 3D show that traces five centuries of Singaporean history. Kids are likely to find the show's political history lessons hard to swallow, but they'll love the 3D effects, and the outsized glasses that must be worn to appreciate them.

Recent visiting exhibitions have focused on the Hakka people, Chinese secret societies in Singapore, and the nineteenth-century botanical prints of durians, whipsnakes, flying foxes, orchids and jackfruit commissioned by William Farquhar, Commandant and Resident of Singapore from 1819 to 1833; check the local press for details.

Fort Canning Park and around

When Raffles first caught sight of Singapore, **Fort Canning Park** was known locally as Bukit Larangan (Forbidden Hill). Malay annals tell of the five ancient kings of Singapura, said to have ruled the island from this point six hundred years ago – and archeological digs have unearthed artefacts which prove it was inhabited as early as the fourteenth century. The last of the kings, Sultan Iskandar Shah, reputedly lies here, and a *keramat*, or auspicious place, on the eastern slope of the hill marks the supposed site of his grave. It was out of respect for and fear of his spirit that the Malays decreed the hill forbidden, and these days the *keramat* still attracts a trickle of Singaporean Muslims, as well as childless couples who offer prayers here for fertility.

However, when the British arrived, Singapore's first British resident, William Farquhar, displayed typical colonial tact by promptly having the hill cleared and building a bungalow on the summit; named Government House, it stood on what was then called Government Hill. The bungalow was replaced in 1859 by a fort named after Viscount George Canning, governor-general of India, but of this only a gateway, guardhouse and adjoining wall remain. An early European **cemetery** survives, however, upon whose stones are engraved intriguing epitaphs to nineteenth-century sailors, traders and residents, among them the pioneering colonial architect, George Coleman. In colonial times, the report of a

68-pound artillery gun fired at Fort Canning Hill marked the hours of 5am, noon and 7pm.

History apart, Fort Canning Park is spacious and breezy, and offers respite from, as well as fine views of, Singapore's crowded streets. There's a "back entrance" to the park that involves climbing the exhausting flight of steps that runs between the Hill Street Building and Food Centre, on Hill Street. Once you reach the top, there's a brilliant view along High Street towards the Merlion. The hill, which houses two theatres, is ringed by two walks, signs along which illuminate aspects of the park's fourteenth- and nineteenth-century history. There's also a nod to more recent wartime history.

The Battle Box

On the northwest flank of Fort Canning Hill lies the **Battle Box** (Tues–Sun 10am–6pm; adults $8, children $5), the underground operations complex from which the Allied war effort in Singapore was masterminded. The complex uses audio and video effects and animatronics to bring to life the events leading up to the decision by British officers to surrender Singapore to Japanese occupation, on February 15, 1942. Authentic, if a little clunky, it provides an engaging enough context to Singapore's darkest hour.

Conceived as a gas- and bombproof operations chamber, the Battle Box was completed in October 1939, after which it became a part of the Malaya Command World War II Headquarters. So well protected was it against gas attack, that its residents were forced to hack the tops off internal doors, in order to increase circulation and combat the stifling heat. Following faithful restoration of its 26 rooms, the complex now conveys a palpable sense of the claustrophobia and tension suffered by the British as the Japanese bore down upon Singapore.

The experience gets off to a low-key start, with a history lesson on a small TV set whose muddy sound is barely audible over the buzzing air-con unit. Thankfully, things look up once you proceed to the chambers themselves. First stop is the switchboard and exchange room, where an animatronic signalman is hard at work patching through messages from bases at Changi, Pulau Bukum and Pulau Blakang Mati (modern-day Sentosa). Next door, in the cipher rooms, the air crackles with the rat-tat-tat of Morse sets and the furious tapping of typewriters, cipher machines and coding machines. Meanwhile, soldiers shift Jap fighter planes around a huge map of Malaya in the operations room, like croupiers raking up chips in a casino.

The Battle Box reaches a theatrical climax in the conference room, where more life-sized figures act out the debate that convinced Lieutenant-General Arthur Percival that surrender was the only option open to him.

River Valley Road

Fort Canning Park's southern boundary is defined by **River Valley Road**, which skirts below the park from Hill Street. At its eastern end is the **MITA Building** – formerly the Hill Street Police Station, but now home to the Ministry of Information, Communications and the Arts. The MITA Building's rows of shuttered windows are painted a rainbow of colours, making it a vibrant addition to the riverfront area; its central atrium houses several galleries majoring in Asian artworks. Further west, **River Valley** sweeps past **Clarke Quay**, a chain of nineteenth-century godowns renovated into an attractive shopping and eating complex. If Boat Quay is a better bet for evening drinks and fine dining, Clarke Quay has the greater family appeal. Its street performers, souvenir stalls and arcades make it a reasonably buzzy, if slightly gimmicky, place. River taxis for Clarke Quay (daily 11am–11pm; $3) depart every five minutes from several quays further down the river (see p.32).

The **Chettiar Hindu Temple** (daily 8am–noon & 5.30–8.30pm), to the west of Fort Canning Park, is the goal of every participant in Singapore's annual Thaipusam Festival (see p.160). This large temple, dwarfed by the pink shell of the erstwhile *Imperial Hotel*, is dedicated to Lord Subramaniam and boasts a wonderful *gopuram*, or bank of sculpted gods and goddesses. Erected in 1984, it replaced a nineteenth-century temple built by Indian chettiars (moneylenders); inside, 48 glass panels etched with Hindu deities line the roof.

Orchard Road

t would be hard to conjure an image more opposed to the reality of modern-day **ORCHARD ROAD** than C.M. Turnbull's description of it during early colonial times as "a country lane lined with bamboo hedges and shrubbery, with trees meeting overhead for its whole length". One hundred years ago, a stroll down Orchard Road would have passed row upon row of nutmeg trees and would have been enjoyed in the company of strolling merchants taking their daily constitutionals, followed at a discreet distance by their trusty manservants. Today, Orchard Road is synonymous with **shopping** – indeed, tourist brochures refer to it as the "Fifth Avenue, the Regent Street, the Champs Elysées, the Via Veneto and the Ginza of Singapore". Huge malls, selling everything you can imagine, line the road, but don't expect shopping to be relaxing; hordes of dawdling tourists from the numerous hotels along the road make browsing difficult. The road runs northwest from Fort Canning Hill and is served by three MRT stations – Orchard, Somerset and Dhoby Ghaut – of which Orchard is the most convenient for shopping expeditions.

Orchard Road does have one or two other diversions if you get tired of staring at CDs, watches and clothes. Near its eastern extent, the president of

ACCOMMODATION		Lloyds Inn	16	Singapore Marriott	9	RESTAURANTS		Cuppage Thai	G
Elizabeth Hotel	7	Meritus Mandarin	12	Sloane Court Hotel	5	Akashi	J	Dan Ryan's	S
Garden Hotel	2	Metro Y Lodge	3	Hotel Supreme	11	Bengawan Solo	P	Delifrance	F
Goodwood Park Hotel	6	Regent Singapore	14	YMCA	13	Blu	A	Don Noodle Bistro	V
Hilton Hotel	10	New Sandy's Place	4	YWCA	15	Bombay Woodlands	J	The Dubliner	T
Holiday Inn Park View	8	Shangri-La	1			Café Espresso	C	Famous Amos	R

Singapore's abode – the **Istana Negara Singapura** – is open to the public a few times a year, and rows of houses that hark back to old Singapore flank Cuppage Road and Emerald Hill Road. And, way up beyond the westernmost point of the road, the **Singapore Botanic Gardens** make for a relaxing stroll in beautiful surroundings. On the whole, though, you really only come to Orchard Road in the daytime to shop and at night for a whole host of clubs and bars (see pp.163–170 & pp.150–152 for details).

Dhoby Ghaut to Emerald Hill

In the **Dhoby Ghaut** area, at the eastern tip of Orchard Road, Indian *dhobies*, or laundrymen, used to wash clothes in the Stamford Canal, which once ran along Orchard and Stamford roads. Those days are long gone, and today the area is ringed by shopping centres, though there is a remnant of old Singapore in the **Hotel Rendezvous**, on the corner of Selegie and Bras Basah roads, where the venerable *Rendezvous Restaurant* is once again cooking up its famous curries (see p.142). Three minutes' walk west along Orchard Road from Dhoby Ghaut MRT takes you past Plaza Singapura, beyond which stern-looking soldiers guard the gate of the **Istana Negara Singapura**. Built in 1869, the istana, with its ornate cornices, elegant louvred shutters and high mansard roof, was originally the official residence of Singapore's British governors, though on independence it became the residence of the president of Singapore – currently S.R. Nathan, whose portrait you'll see in banks, post offices and shops across the state. The shuttered palace is only open to visitors on public holidays; the president goes walkabout at some point during every open day as thousands of Singaporeans flock to picnic on the well-landscaped lawns, and local brass bands belt out jaunty tunes. The changing of the guard ceremony at the Istana takes place at 5.45pm on the first Sunday of the month.

Food Life Food Court	N	Lao Beijing	M	Min Jiang	C	Picnic Food Court	F	Steeple's Deli	J
The Gapz	D	Lawry's The Prime Ribs	L	Nooch	K	Pine Court	Q	Supernature	K
Gordon Grill	C	Li Bai	B	Orchard Emerald		Rose Verandah	A	Tambuah Mas	J
Kabayan	H	Lingzhi	E	Food Chain	O	Sakae Sushi	K	Teochow	
Korean Restaurant	R	Magic of		Orchard Maharajah	G	Sanur	P	City Seafood	P
Kublai Khan	U	Chongqing Hotpot	J	Patara	V	Snackworld	I	Top of the M	Q

The **Tan Yeok Nee Mansion**, across Orchard Road from the Istana Negara Singapura at 207 Clemenceau Avenue, is now home to the Chicago Graduate School of Business. Built in traditional South Chinese style for a wealthy Teochew pepper and gambier (a resin used in tanning) merchant, and featuring ornate roofs and massive granite pillars, the mid-1880s mansion served as headquarters to the Singapore Salvation Army from 1940 until 1991.

Further west, in the **Emerald Hill** area of Orchard Road, most of Cuppage Road has been pedestrianized, making it a great place to sit out and have a beer or a meal. **Cuppage Terrace**, halfway along Cuppage Road on the left, is an unusually (for Orchard Road) old row of shophouses, where a burgeoning restaurant and bar scene has developed. A number of even more architecturally notable houses have also survived the developers' bulldozers in Emerald Hill Road, parallel to Cuppage Road. Emerald Hill was granted to Englishman William Cuppage in 1845 and for some years afterwards was the site of a large nutmeg plantation. After Cuppage's death in 1872, the land was subdivided and sold off, much of it bought by members of the **Peranakan** community, which evolved in Malaya as a result of the intermarriage between early Chinese settlers and Malay women. A walk up Emerald Hill Road takes you past a number of exquisitely crafted houses dating from this period, built in a decorative architectural style known as Chinese Baroque, typified by highly coloured ceramic tiles, carved swing doors, shuttered windows and pastel-shaded walls with fine plaster mouldings.

West to the Botanic Gardens

West of Emerald Hill Road, the shopping centres of Orchard Road come thick and fast. A couple of minutes north of Orchard Road along Scotts Road, the impressive **Goodwood Park Hotel** started life in 1900 as the *Teutonia Club* for German expats. With the start of war across Europe in 1914, the club was commandeered by the British Custodian of Enemy Property, and it didn't open again until 1918, after which it served for several years as a function hall. In 1929, it became a hotel, though by 1942 the Goodwood – like *Raffles* – was lodging Japanese officers. So it was fitting that after the war, the hotel was chosen as one of the venues for a war crimes court.

After a few hours' shopping you'll be glad of the open space afforded by the **Singapore Botanic Gardens**, a ten-minute walk beyond the western end of Orchard Road on Cluny Road. Founded in 1859, it was here, in 1877, that the Brazilian seeds from which grew the great **rubber plantations** of Malaysia were first nurtured. No one had taken much notice of them by the time Henry Ridley was named director of the Botanic Gardens the following year, but he recognized their financial potential and spent the next twenty years of his life persuading Malayan plantation-owners to convert to this new crop, an occupation which earned him the nickname "Mad" Ridley. The fifty-odd hectares of land feature a mini-jungle rose garden, topiary, fernery, palm valley and lakes that are home to turtles and swans. There's also the **National Orchid Garden** (daily 8.30am–7pm; $2) with sixty thousand plants; orchid jewellery, made by plating real flowers with gold, is on sale here – pieces start from around $30. At dawn and dusk, joggers and students of t'ai chi haunt the lawns and paths of the gardens, while at the weekend, newlyweds bundle down from church for their photos to be taken – a ritual recalled in Lee Tzu Pheng's poem *Bridal Party at the Botanics*, whose bride's "two hundred dollar face/is melting in the sun", while beside her is her groom, "black-stuffed, oil-slicked, fainting/in his finery, by the shrubbery". You can pick up a free **map** of the grounds at the ranger's office, a little to the right of the main gate.

Chinatown and the Financial District

T he two square kilometres of **Chinatown** once constituted the focal point of Chinese life and culture in Singapore. Nowadays, the area is on its last traditional legs, scarred by demolition and dwarfed by the sky-scrapers of the **Financial District**, where the island's yuppies oversee the machinations of one of Asia's most dynamic money markets. Even so, a wander through the surviving nineteenth-century streets still unearths musty and atmospheric temples, traditional craft shops, clan associations and old-style coffee shops and restaurants. Provision stores crammed with birds' nests, dried cuttlefish, ginger, chillies, mushrooms and salted fish do a brisk trade, and you might hear the rattle of a game of mahjong being played. Chinatown is bounded by New Bridge Road to the west, Neil and Maxwell roads to the south and Cecil Street to the east, while to the north, the Singapore River snakes west and inland passing the last few surviving godowns from Singapore's original trade boom.

Chinatown

The area now known as **CHINATOWN** was earmarked for settlement by the Chinese community by Sir Stamford Raffles himself, who decided in June 1819 that the ethnic communities should live separately. As increasing numbers of **immigrants** poured into Singapore, Chinatown became just that – a Chinese town, where new arrivals from the mainland, mostly from the Canton and Fujian provinces, would have been pleased to find temples, shops and, most importantly, clan associations (*kongsi*), which helped them to find food, lodgings and work, mainly as small traders and coolies. The prevalent architectural form was the **shophouse**, a shuttered building with a moulded facade fronting living rooms upstairs and a shop on the ground floor. The three-day Verandah Riots of 1888 erupted when colonial administrators ordered Chinatown's merchants to clear their five-foot ways of stalls and produce to enable pedestrians to pass by.

By the mid-twentieth century, the area southwest of the Singapore River was rich with the imported cultural heritage of China, but with independence came ambition. The government regarded the tumbledown slums of Chinatown

◀ Chettiar Hindu Temple

◀ 1 & 2

Suntec City

Marina Square

BRAS BASAH ROAD

RAFFLES AVENUE

Theatres on the Bay **G**

Citylink Mall

BEACH ROAD

Raffles City

ESPLANADE DRIVE

Merlion •

River boats jetty

One Fullerton

Clifford Pier

St Andrew's Cathedral

City Hall

STAMFORD ROAD

Singapore Recreation Club

Padang

CONNAUGHT DRIVE

ST ANDREWS ROAD

CITY HALL

FULLERTON ROAD

The Fullerton Singapore **4**

Standard Chartered Bank Road

BATTERY ROAD

COLLYER QUAY

Singapore Land Tower

Caltex House

Chinese Chamber of Commerce

Armenian Church of St Gregory the Illuminator

HILL ST

COLEMAN ST

COLOMBO COURT

Singapore Cricket Club

Victoria Concert Hall & Theatre

Asian Civilization Museum

CAVENAGH BRIDGE

River boats jetty

RAFFLES PLACE

MARKET ST

MALACCA ST

Clifford Centre

OUB Centre

CANNING

ARMENIAN ST

CANNING RISE

Singapore Philatelic Museum

Fort Canning Park

HIGH STREET

Supreme Court

NORTH BRIDGE ROAD

Parliament

Old Parliament House

Raffles Landing Site

PARLIAMENT LANE

NORTH BOAT QUAY

ELGIN BRIDGE

BOAT QUAY

CHULIA ST

UOB Plaza & Plaza 2

Wak Hai Cheng Bio Temple

CHURCH ST

PHILIP ST

River Valley Swimming Complex

MITA Building

RIVER VALLEY ROAD

HILL ST

River boats jetty

UPPER CIRCULAR ROAD

CIRCULAR ROAD

CARPENTER ST

SOUTH BRIDGE ROAD

NORTH CANAL RD

HONGKONG ST

GEORGE ST

PICKERING ST

CHINA ST

NANKIN ST

PEKIN ST

CLARKE QUAY

Singapore River

The River Walk

Clarke Quay **F**

CLARKE QUAY

READ ST

B

C

D

E

River boats jetty

TEW CHEW ST

NEW BRIDGE ROAD

MERCHANT RD

UPPER PICKERING ST

UPPER HOKKIEN ST

SOUTH BRIDGE ROAD

UPPER CHIN CHEW ST

HOKKIEN ST

CHIN CHEW ST

Riverside Point

Thong Chai Medical Institute

CLARKE QUAY

HAVELOCK ROAD

CUMMING ST

People's Park Centre

CROSS ST

MOSQUE ST

Chinatown **5**

6

UE Square

Robertson Walk

A

1

UNITY STREET

CLEMENCEAU AVENUE

QUAY PROMENADE

MOHAMAD

SULTAN ROAD

MAGAZINE ROAD

UPPER CROSS ST

People's Park Complex

Chinatown Heritage Centre

NEW BRIDGE ROAD

PEARLS HILL TERRACE

HAVELOCK ROAD

Pearl's Hill Park

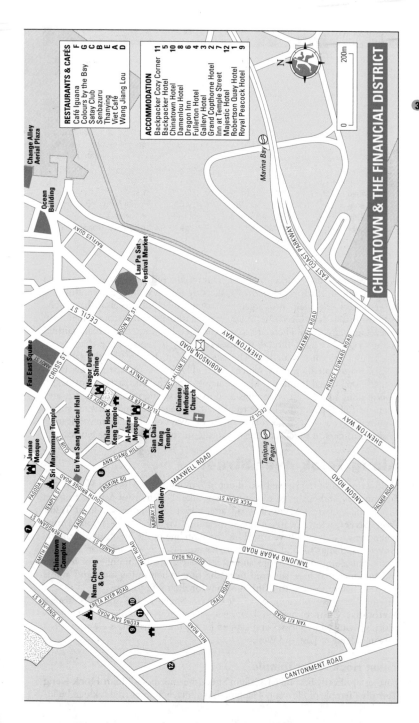

CHINATOWN & THE FINANCIAL DISTRICT

RESTAURANTS & CAFÉS

Café Iguana	F
Colours by the Bay	G
Satay Club	C
Senbazuru	B
Thanying	E
Viet Café	A
Wang Jiang Lou	D

ACCOMMODATION

Backpacker Cozy Corner	11
Backpacker Hotel	5
Chinatown Hotel	10
Damenlou Hotel	8
Dragon Inn	6
Fullerton Hotel	4
Gallery Hotel	3
Grand Copthorne Hotel	2
Inn at Temple Street	7
Majestic Hotel	12
Robertson Quay Hotel	1
Royal Peacock Hotel	9

Songbirds

One of the most enduringly popular of Singaporean hobbies is the keeping and training of **songbirds**. Every Sunday morning scores of enthusiasts and their birds congregate at an unnamed nondescript coffee shop on the corner of Tiong Bahru and Seng Poh roads, just west of Chinatown. Songbird competitions are commonplace in Singapore, but this gathering is an informal affair with bird owners coming to show off their pets and admire those of fellow collectors. The **exquisite cages** that house the birds are hung on a metal frame that fronts the coffee shop. Birds are grouped according to their breed, lest they pick up the distinctive songs of other breeds. The various breeds of bird you'll see include the delicate green mata puteh, or "white eye bird", the jambul, with its showy black crest and red eye patches, and the sharma, with beautiful long tail feathers. You can have toast and coffee at the café while watching and listening to the proceedings, which start around 6am – a good early morning start to a tour around nearby Chinatown. Take bus #851 from North Bridge Road which passes along Tiong Bahru Road, or hop in a cab.

Another central Sunday songbird venue is Sturdee Road, off Petain Road, which lies between Serangoon Road and Jalan Besar in Little India.

as an eyesore and embarked upon a catastrophic **redevelopment** campaign that saw whole roads bulldozed to make way for new shopping centres, and street traders relocated into organized complexes. Only recently has public opinion finally convinced the Singaporean authorities to restore rather than redevelop Chinatown. There are some renovated buildings that remain faithful to the original designs, though there's a tendency to render once characterful shophouses improbably perfect. The latest problem to threaten the fabric of Chinatown is spiralling rents, which are steadily driving out the last few families, and traditional businesses like medicine shops, bakers, *popiah* skin makers (*popiah* skins are the soft wrappings used to make spring rolls), leaving the area open for full exploitation by bistros, advertising agencies and souvenir shops. Ironically, if you want to get a taste of the old ways of Chinatown, you'll need to spurn its central streets and head into the surrounding housing blocks.

Along Telok Ayer Street

Follow the signs for Maxwell Road out of Tanjong Pagar MRT and you'll surface on the southern edge of Chinatown. Take the left-hand path in front of the station and cross Maxwell Road; after about fifty metres you'll hit **Telok Ayer Street**, whose Malay name – meaning "Watery Bay" – recalls a time when the street would have run along the shoreline of the Straits of Singapore. Nowadays, thanks to land reclamation, it's no closer to a beach than is Beach Road, but alongside the shops and stores there are still a number of temples and mosques that have survived from the time when immigrants and sailors stepping ashore wanted to thank the gods for their safe passage.

Facing you as you approach Telok Ayer Street is the square **Chinese Methodist Church**, built in 1889, whose design – portholes and windows adorned with white crosses and capped by a Chinese pagoda-style roof – is a pleasing blend of East and West.

Thian Hock Keng Temple

Further up, shortly beyond McCallum Street, the enormous **Thian Hock Keng Temple** (Temple of Heavenly Happiness) is a hugely impressive Hokkien build-

CHINATOWN RESTAURANTS

0 _____ 200m

RESTAURANTS

X	Ann Siang 5
A	Ban Seng
V	Beaujolais
Z	Bee Heong
R	Belachan
C	Beng Thin Hoong Kee
N	Beng Hiang
H	Beppu Menkan
	Capital
aa	China Square Food Centre
L	Chinese Opera Teahouse
U	Da Paolo
S	De Boa
G	Gorkha Grill
T	Happy Realm
W	Hillman
bb	House of Mao
	Hunan Hotpot
K	Indochine
Q	Jing
B	Mouth
D	New Flavour Gourmet
F	Old Shanghai
J	Soup
P	Spinelli
K	Spizza
O	Starbucks
C	Swee Kee
	Tan Hock Seng Cake Shop
M	Ya Kun Kaya Toast
E	Yum Cha
I	

ing, and sprucer than ever after a recent makeover. Built on the site of a small joss house where immigrants made offerings to Ma Chu Por (or Tian Hou), the queen of heaven, the temple was started in 1839 using materials imported from China. By the time the temple was finished in 1842 a statue of the goddess had been shipped in from southern China, and this still stands in the centre of the temple's main hall, flanked by the god of war on the right and the protector of life on the left. From the street, the temple looks spectacular: dragons stalk its broad roofs, while the entrance to the temple compound bristles with ceramic flowers, foliage and figures. Two stone lions stand guard at the entrance, and door gods, painted on the front doors, prevent evil spirits from entering. Look out for the huge ovens, always lit, in which offerings to gods and ancestors are burnt.

It's a testament to Singapore's multicultural nature that Thian Hock Keng's next-door neighbour should be the **Nagore Durgha shrine**, built in the 1820s by Chulias from southern India as a shrine to the ascetic, Shahul Hamid of Nagore. Sadly, the shrine's tiered minarets, onion domes and Islamic facades are currently in a state of some disrepair. **Telok Ayer Green**, a tranquil, paved garden dotted with life-sized metal statues depicting the area's earliest settlers, separates temple and shrine.

Amoy Street

A block west of Telok Ayer Street is **Amoy Street**, which – together with China and Telok Ayer streets – was designated as a Hokkien enclave in the colony's early days. Long terraces of shophouses flank the street, all featuring characteristic **five-foot ways**, or covered verandahs, so called simply because they jut five feet out from the house. A few of the shophouses are in a ramshackle state, but most have been marvellously renovated and bought up by companies in need of some fancy office space. It's worth walking down to the **Sian Chai Kang Temple**, at 66 Amoy Street, painted a shade of red as fiery as the dragons on its roof – it's a musty, open-fronted place dominated by huge urns, full to the brim with ash from untold numbers of burned incense sticks.

Far East Square and around

North of Cross Street, Amoy Street strikes into the heart of **Far East Square**, a new shopping-cum-dining centre which taps Chinatown's heritage for its inspiration, and which boasts the **Fuk Tak Ch'i Street Museum** as its party piece. It's the surest sign yet of the gentrification of Chinatown that one of its oldest temples has had to suffer the ignominy of being turned into a tourist attraction – and a fairly dull one at that. The Fuk Tak Ch'i Temple was established by Singapore's Hakka and Cantonese communities in 1824. The temple has scrubbed up nicely – too nicely, in fact: none of the musty ambience that once made it such an interesting and atmospheric place has survived its $200,000 renovation. A model junk of the kind that would have brought across Singapore's earliest Chinese settlers sits on what used to be the temple's main altar. Elsewhere, you'll see odds and sods – opium pillows and pipes, Peranakan jewellery, an instrument once used by food hawkers to drum up trade – from old Singapore, though the most arresting exhibit is a diorama depicting how Telok Ayer would have appeared when it was still a waterfront street in the nineteenth century.

Wak Hai Cheng Bio Temple

Just north of Far East Square, an ugly concrete courtyard, crisscrossed by a web of ropes supporting numerous spiralled incense sticks, fronts the **Wak Hai**

Cheng Bio Temple on Philip Street. Its name means "Temple of the Calm Sea", which made it a logical choice for early worshippers who had arrived safely in Singapore; an effigy of Tian Hou, the queen of heaven and protector of seafarers, is housed in the temple's right-hand chamber. This temple, too, has an incredibly ornate roof, crammed with tiny models of Chinese village scenes. The temple cat meanders across here sometimes, dwarfing the tableaux like a creature from a Godzilla movie.

China Street and Club Street

Far East Square has subsumed **China Street** and its offshoots, meaning another slice of residential Chinatown has been lost forever. To get a flavour of the old ways that survived in these streets until the turn of the millennium you'll have to push on across South Bridge Road into the **Hong Lim Complex**, a modern housing estate where old men in white T-shirts and striped pyjama trousers sit chewing the cud in walkways lined with medical halls, chop makers, and stores selling birds' nests, pork floss, dried mushrooms and gold jewellery.

At the southern end of China Street is steep **Club Street**, once noted for its temple-carving shops, though these too have now fallen to the demolition ball and been replaced by swish apartment blocks and swanky bars and restaurants. An impromptu **flea market** still takes place on the far side of the car park opposite, where traders squat on their haunches surrounded by catalogues, old coins, sleeveless records and phone cards.

Even the **clan associations** and **guilds** that gave Club Street its name are fast disappearing, though there are still a few to be seen, higher up the hill. These are easy to spot; black-and-white photos of old members cover the walls, and behind the screens that almost invariably span the doorway, old men sit and chat. From upstairs, the clacking sound of mahjong tiles reaches the street.

Along South Bridge Road

South Bridge Road, stretching all the way from the Elgin Bridge to Tanjong Pagar, is Chinatown's backbone. During the Japanese occupation roadblocks were set up at the point where South Bridge meets Cross Street, and Singaporeans were vetted at an interrogation post for signs of anti-Japanese feeling. Those whose answers failed to satisfy the guards either ended up as POWs or were never seen again. Today, South Bridge Road is fast becoming antiques-central, as more and more of the numerous dingy shops that line it are spruced up and turned into Asian arts curiosity shops.

Eu Yan Sang Medical Hall

The beautifully renovated **Eu Yan Sang Medical Hall** (Mon–Sat 8.30am–6pm), at 267–271 South Bridge Road, offers a great introduction to traditional Chinese medicines. First opened in 1910, the shop is partially geared to the tourist trade – some of the staff speak good English. It smells a little like a compost heap on a hot day and there is a weird assortment of ingredients on the shelves, which to the uninitiated look more likely to kill than cure. Besides the usual herbs and roots favoured by the Chinese are various dubious remedies derived from exotic and endangered species. Blood circulation problems and external injuries are eased with centipedes and insects crushed into a "rubbing liquor", the ground-up gall bladders of snakes or bears apparently work wonders on pimples, monkey's gallstones aid asthmatics, and deer penis is supposed to provide a lift to any sexual problem. Antlers, sea horses, scorpions and turtle shells also feature regularly in Chinese prescriptions, though the greatest cure-all of Oriental medicine is said to be **ginseng**, a clever little root that will combat anything from weakness of the heart to acne and jet lag. If you need a pick-me-up, or are just curious, the shop administers free cups of ginseng tea.

Sri Mariamman Hindu Temple

Opposite the Eu Yan Sang Medical Hall on South Bridge Road, the compound of the **Sri Mariamman Hindu Temple** bursts with primary-coloured, wild-looking statues of deities and animals. There's always some ritual or other being attended to by one of the temple's priests, drafted in from the subcontinent and dressed in simple loincloths. A wood-and-atap hut was erected on this site in 1827, on land belonging to Naraina Pillay – a government clerk who arrived in Singapore on the same ship as Stamford Raffles. The present temple was completed in 1843 and boasts a superb *gopuram* over the front entrance. Once inside the temple, look up at the roof and you'll see splendidly vivid friezes depicting a host of Hindu deities, including the three manifestations of the supreme being: Brahma the Creator (with three of his four heads showing), Vishnu the Preserver, and Shiva the Destroyer (holding one of his sons). The main sanctum, facing you as you walk inside, is devoted to Goddess Mariamman, who's worshipped for her power to cure disease. Smaller sanctums dotted about the open walkway which runs round the temple honour a host of other deities. In the one dedicated to Goddess Periachi Amman, a sculpture portrays her with a queen lying on her lap, whose evil child she has ripped from her womb. Odd, then, that the Periachi Amman should be the protector of children, to whom one-month-old babies are brought. Sri Aravan, with his bushy moustache and big ears, is far less intimidating. His sanctum is at the back on the right-hand side of the complex.

To the left of the main sanctum there's a patch of sand which, once a year during the festival of **Thimithi** (see p.161), is covered in red-hot coals, across which male Hindus run to prove the strength of their faith. The participants, who line up all the way along South Bridge Road waiting their turn, are supposedly protected from the heat of the coals by the power of prayer, though the ambulance parked round the back of the temple suggests that some aren't praying quite hard enough.

The URA Gallery

A skip around the **URA Gallery** (Mon–Fri 9am–4.30pm, Sat 9am–12.30pm, free; ☎63218321, ⓦwww.ura.gov.sg) at the URA Centre, set back from South Bridge Road at 45 Maxwell Road, offers a fascinating insight into the grand designs of Singapore's Urban Redevelopment Authority. Town planning may not sound the most inspiring premise for a gallery; but, then again, no other nation plans with such extravagant ambition as Singapore, whose land architects continue to remould their island like a ball of putty, erasing roads here and reclaiming land there. You need only consider the distance between downtown Beach Road and the shoreline it used to abut, to appreciate the extent of change that Singapore has undergone up to now. At the URA Gallery, you can view the blueprint for the island's future.

Interactive exhibits, touch-screen terminals and scale models trace Singapore's progress from sleepy backwater to modern metropolis and chart ongoing efforts to reshape and redefine specific regions of the island. The URA has rightly been criticized in the past for its disregard for Singapore's architectural heritage, so it is heartening to see displays making such reassuring noises

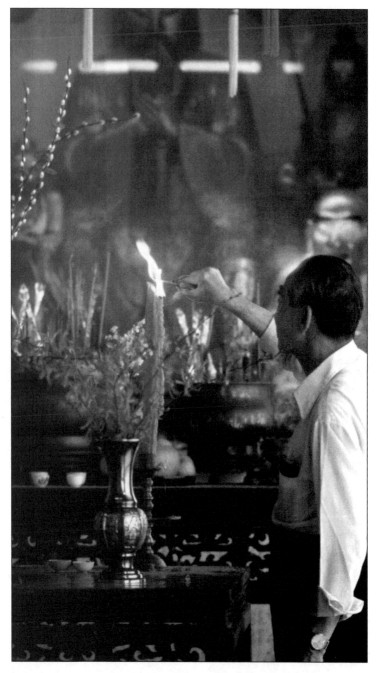

△ A temple in Chinatown

about the future of the venerable shophouses and colonial villas that remain in such districts as Balestier Road, Tanjong Katong and Joo Chiat. But the gallery's emphasis is more upon the future than the past. A vast model of the downtown area of Singapore – which highlights districts currently under development and offers new arrivals to the island the chance to get their bearings – is best scrutinized through one of the telescopes set up on the floor above. Elsewhere on the upper floor, there is the chance to control a sky cam high above the city, try your hand at a little municipal planning and learn more about Singapore's state-of-the-art MRT system.

Tanjong Pagar

The district of **Tanjong Pagar** at the southern tip of South Bridge Road, between Neil and Keong Saik roads, has changed beyond recognition in recent years. Once a veritable sewer of brothels and opium dens, it was earmarked as a conservation area, following which over two hundred shophouses were painstakingly restored, painted in sickly pastel hues and converted into bars catering to the Financial District crowd, or restaurants and shops which prey on passing tourists.

While touring Tanjong Pagar, it's worth making time for a stop at one of the traditional **teahouses** along Neil Road. At *Tea Chapter* at no. 9a–11a (daily 11am–11pm), you can have tea in the very chair in which Queen Elizabeth sat when she visited in 1989; the shop is plastered with photographs of the occasion. The Chinese take tea drinking very seriously. Buy a bag of tea here and one of the staff will teach you all the attached rituals (see box); 100g bags cost from $5 to over $65 and tea sets are also on sale, though they don't come cheap.

Taking Chinese Tea

If you're in need of a quick, thirst-quenching drink, avoid **Chinese teahouses**: the art of tea-making is heavily bound up with **ritual**, and unhurried preparation time is crucial to the production of a pleasing brew. What's more, when you do get a cup, it's barely more than a mouthful and then the whole process kicks off again.

Tea-drinking in China traces its origins back thousands of years. Legend has it that the first cuppa was drunk by Emperor Shen Nong, who was pleasantly surprised by the aroma produced by some dried tea leaves falling into the water he was boiling. He was even more pleased when he tasted the brew. By the eighth century, the art form was so complex that Chinese scholar Lu Yu produced a three-volume tome on the processes involved.

Teashops normally have conventional tables and chairs but the authentic experience involves kneeling at a much lower traditional table. The basic procedure is as follows: the server places a towel in front of himself and his guest, with the folded edge facing the guest, and stuffs leaves into the pot with a bamboo scoop. Water, boiled over a flame, has to reach an optimum temperature, depending on which type of tea is being made; experts can tell its heat by the size of the bubbles rising, which are described, rather confusingly, as "sand eyes", "prawn eyes" and "fish eyes". Once the pot has been warmed inside and out, the first pot of tea is made, transferred into the pouring jar and then, frustratingly, poured back *over* the pot – the thinking being that over a period of time, the porous clay of the pot becomes infused with the fragrance of the tea. Once a second pot is ready, a draught is poured into the **sniffing cup**, from which the aroma of the brew is savoured. Only now is it time actually to drink the tea and, if you want a second cup, the whole procedure has to start again.

Sago Street to Mosque Street

Today, the tight knot of streets west of South Bridge Road between Sago Street and Mosque Street is tour-bus Chinatown, heaving with gangs of holiday-makers plundering souvenir shops. But in days gone by these streets formed Chinatown's nucleus, their shophouses harbouring opium dens and brothels, their streets teeming with trishaw drivers, peddlers and food hawkers. From the upper windows of tumbledown shophouses, wizened old men in white T-shirts and striped pyjama trousers would stare out from behind wooden gates, flanked by songbird cages and laundry poles hung with washing.

Until as recently as the 1950s, **Sago Street** was home to several death houses – rudimentary hospices where skeletal citizens saw out their final hours on rattan camp beds. These houses were finally deemed indecent and have all now gone, replaced by lifeless restaurants and shops stacked to the rafters with cheap Chinese vases, teapots, cups and saucers. Sago, Smith, Temple and Pagoda streets only really recapture their youth around the time of Chinese New Year, when they're crammed to bursting with stalls selling festive branches of blossom, oranges, sausages and waxed chickens – which look as if they have melted to reveal a handful of bones inside.

Sago Street skirts to the right of the Chinatown Complex, and its name changes to Trengganu Street. Despite the hordes of tourists, and the shops selling Singapore Airlines uniforms, presentation chopstick sets and silk hats with false pigtails, there are occasional glimpses of Chinatown's **old trades** and industries, such as Nam's Supplies at 22 Smith Street, which offers shirts, Rolex watches, Nokia mobile phones, money and passports – all made out of paper – which the Chinese burn to ensure their ancestors don't want for creature comforts in the next life. They even have "Otherworld Bank" credit cards, "Hell Airlines" air tickets and "Hell City" cigarettes. Nam Cheong and Co, off nearby Kreta Ayer Street, takes this industry to its logical conclusion, producing huge paper houses and near life-sized paper safes, servants and Mercedes for the self-respecting ghost about town; the shop is at 01-04 Block, 334 Keong Saik Road, between Chinatown Complex and New Bridge Road. Meanwhile, back on Smith Street, you'll smell Chan Lai Kee, down the road at no. 52, from afar – it specializes in pungent soy sauces.

The Chinatown Complex

The hideous concrete exterior of the **Chinatown Complex**, at the end of Sago Street, belies the charm of the teeming market it houses. Walk up the front steps, past the garlic, fruit and nut hawkers, and once you're inside, the market's many twists and turns reveal stalls selling silk, kimonos, rattan, leather, jade, tea, Buddhist paraphernalia and clothes. There are no fixed prices, so you'll need to haggle. Deep in the market's belly is Yun Shi Services Agency (shop 01-K3) – where a **calligrapher** can quickly draw an Oriental ink sign for you – while the Capitol Plastics stall (01-16) specializes in **mahjong sets**. There's a food centre on the second floor, and the wet market within the complex gets pretty packed early in the morning, when locals come to buy fresh fish or meat. Here, abacuses are still used to tally bills, and sugar canes lean like spears against the wall.

The Chinatown Heritage Centre

Many of Chinatown's links with its cultural and mercantile history have been erased, but at least the excellent **Chinatown Heritage Centre** (daily

SPRING STREET

NEIL ROAD

Maxwell Food Centre

MAXWELL ROAD

MURRAY STREET

Tea Chapter

Shima Yakiniku

Moti Mahal Restaurant

Goldleaf Taiwan Restaurant

Moi Kong Restaurant

Haebok's

Mitzi's Restaurant

Cumi Bali

COOK STREET

TANJONG PAGAR ROAD

DUXTON ROAD

NEIL ROAD

Heritage Exhibition

Broth

Blue Ginger Restaurant

CRAIG ROAD

DUXTON HILL

0   100m

10am–7pm; adults $8, children $4.80), at 48 Pagoda Street, offers a window on the district's past. If you go to just one museum in Singapore, this should be it. Housed in three superbly restored shophouses, the centre is an invaluable social document, where the history, culture, pastimes and employments of Singapore's Chinese settlers spring vividly to life. The museum is crammed to bursting with displays, artefacts and information boards; but its masterstroke is to give voice to former local residents, whose first-hand accounts of Chinatown life, projected onto walls at every turn, form a unique oral history of the Chinese in Singapore.

A model junk, like those on which early immigrants ("singkehs") came in search of work, sets the scene at the start of the tour. Accounts on the wall tell the story of their perilous journeys across the South China Sea. Once ashore at Bullock Cart Water (the name they gave the area that would become Chinatown), settlers quickly formed clan associations, or less savoury secret societies, and looked for employment. As you move through the centre's narrow shophouse corridors, these associations and societies, and every other facet of Chinatown life, work and leisure, are made flesh. All the while, you progress to a soundtrack of crashing gongs and cymbals, age-old songs of mourning and Fifties' crooners on scratchy 78s.

The genius of the centre lies in its detail, from the mock-up of the shabby flourishes of a prostitute's boudoir, and the marble table of a traditional coffee shop, to the pictures and footage of thin and haunted addicts seeking escape from the pain of their backbreaking work through opium, their "devastating master". Among the many artefacts, look out for an example of an original hawker stall – a charcoal burner and a collection of ingredients yoked over the shoulders and carried from street to street, and a million miles away from the air-con luxury of today's incarnations. Look out, too, for the section focusing upon the death houses of Sago Street, where the sick and old went to die. Trishaws riders collecting the dead would, one Chinatown veteran recounts, "put a hat on the corpse, put it onto the trishaw, and cycle all the way back to the coffin shop".

The tour climaxes with a superb re-creation of the unbearable living quarters that settlers endured in the shophouses of Chinatown. Landlords were known to shoehorn as many as forty tenants into a single floor, and their cramped cubicles, cooking and bathing facilities are reproduced in all their grisly squalor. (Plumbing was non-existent in these times. One former resident tells of an occasion when a tenant knocked a full bucket of human waste down a staircase, and was forced to burn incense for ages afterwards, to mask the

Shopping in Chinatown

As well as the markets and stores covered in the text, look out for the following, all either on or near to New Bridge Road and Eu Tong Sen Street. Opening hours are generally 10am–9.30pm.

Chinatown Point 133 New Bridge Rd. One of its two buildings houses bright, fashionable, Orchard Road-style shop units; the other is a handicraft centre, with scores of tourist-oriented businesses.

Hong Lim Complex 531–531a Upper Cross St. Several Chinese provisions stores, fronted by sackfuls of dried mushrooms, cuttlefish, chillies, garlic cloves, onions, fritters and crackers. Other shops sell products ranging from acupuncture accessories to birds' nests.

Lucky Chinatown Complex 11 New Bridge Rd. Fairly upmarket place with lots of jewellery shops, and even an Oriental-style *McDonald's*.

New Bridge Centre 336 Smith St. The Da You Department Store (second floor) sells Chinese religious artefacts, tea sets and crockery.

Pearl's Centre 100 Eu Tong Sen St. A centre for Chinese medicine. The Chinese Patent Medicines and Medicated Liquors Centre at 03-19 and TCM Chinese Medicines at 02-21 both have a Chinese clinic, where a consultation will cost you $5.

People's Park Centre 101 Upper Cross St. Stall-like shop units selling cheap shoes, cassettes, electronics and gold. Look into Nison Department Store, on the first and second floors, which has some beautiful statues and rosewood screens.

People's Park Complex 1 Park Rd. The Overseas Emporium is at 02-70 and sells Chinese instruments, calligraphy pens, lacquer work and jade. Cobblers set up stall in the courtyard beside the complex, behind which is a market and food centre.

stench.) The absence of the cooling effect of any air-con goes some way towards conveying the stifling heat that residents daily suffered.

Back on the ground floor is a tailor's shop, the mercantile element of the shophouse. Beside that, a traditional *kopi tiam*, featuring old metal signs advertising Horlicks, Brylcreem, and huge biscuit boxes on the counter, is a good place to grab a coffee and reflect on what you've seen. There are sometimes walking tours of Chinatown based out of the centre; call ☎63252878 for more details.

New Bridge Road and Eu Tong Sen Street

Chinatown's main shopping drag comprises southbound **New Bridge Road** and northbound **Eu Tong Sen Street**, along which are found a handful of large malls (see box). Try to pop into one of the barbecue pork vendors around the intersection of Smith, Temple and Pagoda streets with New Bridge Road – the squares of red, fatty, delicious meat that they cook on wire meshes over fires produce an odour that is pure Chinatown.

The **Thong Chai Medical Institute** has been sited at the top of Eu Tong Sen Street since 1892, when it first opened its doors with the avowed intention of dispensing free medical help regardless of race, colour or creed. Listed as a national monument, this beautiful southern Chinese-style building has recently been transformed into a bar-restaurant complex (see p.151) whose decor is thankfully sympathetic to the wonderful serpentine gables and wooden inscribed pillars.

The Financial District

Until an early exercise in land reclamation in the mid-1820s rendered the zone fit for building, the patch of land south of the river where Raffles Place now stands was a swampland. However, within just a few years, Commercial Square (later renamed Raffles Place) was the colony's busiest business address, boasting the banks, ship's chandlers and warehouses of a burgeoning trading port. The square now forms the nucleus of the **FINANCIAL DISTRICT** – the commercial heart of the state, home to many of its banks and financial institutions. Cutting through the district is **Battery Road**, whose name recalls the days when Fort Fullerton (named after Robert Fullerton, first governor of the Straits Settlements) and its attendant battery of guns used to stand on the site of the Fullerton Building.

Raffles Place and the south riverbank

Raffles Place was Singapore's central shopping area until Orchard Road superseded it in the late 1960s. Two department stores, Robinsons and John Little, dominated the area then, but subsequent development turned it into the centre of Singapore's financial epicentre, ringed by buildings so tall that pedestrians crossing the square feel like ants in a canyon. The most striking way to experience the giddy heights of the Financial District is by surfacing from Raffles Place MRT, following the signs for Raffles Place itself out of the station, and looking up to gleaming towers, blue skies and racing clouds. To your left is the soaring metallic triangle of the **OUB Centre** (Overseas Union Bank), and to its right, the rocket-shaped **UOB Plaza 2** (United Overseas Bank); in front of you are the rich brown walls of the **Standard Chartered Bank**, and to your

The Barings Bank scandal

Singapore hit the international headlines early in 1995, when the City of London's oldest merchant bank, **Barings**, collapsed as a result of what the London *Evening Standard* called "massive unauthorized dealings" in derivatives on the Japanese stock market. The supposed culprit – "the man who broke the bank", as the press dubbed him – was named as Nick Leeson, an Englishman dealing out of the bank's offices in the Financial District of Singapore. Leeson, it was alleged, had gambled huge funds in the hope of recouping losses made through ill-judged trading, only calling it a day when the bank's losses were approaching one billion pounds. One of his colleagues claimed that Leeson made "other fraudsters look like Walt Disney", although many have questioned the quality of Barings' management and financial controls, which allowed such a catastrophe to happen.

By the time the scandal broke, Leeson was missing, and a pan-Southeast Asian search was in full swing when he finally turned up – and was promptly arrested – six days later in Frankfurt. News of his capture was greeted with cheers from dealers in the Singapore Stock Exchange when it flashed across their screens. In the weeks that followed, Dutch bank ING bought out Barings for one pound sterling, while Nick Leeson languished in a Frankfurt jail. In time, Singapore's application for extradition was duly granted, and less than two weeks after being passed into Singaporean custody, on December 2, 1995, the rogue trader pleaded guilty to two charges of deceit, and received a six-and-a-half-year sentence, three and a half years of which he served out in Tamah Merah Prison. While inside, Leeson was divorced from his wife, and diagnosed with cancer of the colon. In 1999, the movie *Rogue Trader* was released with Ewan McGregor playing the part of Leeson.

right rise sturdy **Singapore Land Tower** and the almost Art Deco **Caltex House**. A smallish statue, entitled *Progress and Advancement*, stands at the northern end of Raffles Place. Erected in 1988, it's a miniature version of what was then the skyline of central Singapore. Inevitably, the very progress and advancement it celebrates has already rendered it out of date – not featured, for instance, is the **UOB Plaza**, a vast monolith of a building only recently built beside its twin, the UOB Plaza 2. The three roads that run southwest from Raffles Place – Cecil Street, Robinson Road and Shenton Way – are all chock-a-block with more high-rise banks and financial houses; to the west is Chinatown.

Boat Quay

Just north of Raffles Place, and beneath the "elephant's trunk" curve of the Singapore River, the pedestrianized row of shophouses known as **Boat Quay** has enjoyed an upturn in fortunes. Derelict until the early Nineties, it's currently one of Singapore's most fashionable hangouts, sporting a huge collection of thriving restaurants and bars, and is an excellent spot for an alfresco meal or drink. There are those around the Singapore restaurant scene that think that the authorities aren't vetting tenants of Boat Quay's units rigorously enough, and that the area's charm is becoming diluted as a result. Certainly, some stretches of the quay are noisier than others, so it's worth taking a stroll before you pick a spot for dinner.

Around Raffles Place

Branching off the second floor of the Clifford Centre, on the eastern side of Raffles Place, is **Change Alley Aerial Plaza**. The original Change Alley was a cheap, bustling, street-level bazaar, which redevelopment wiped off the face of Singapore; all that remains is a sanitized, modern-day version, housed on a covered footbridge across Collyer Quay. The tailors here have a persuasive line in patter – you'll have to be very determined not to waste half an hour being convinced that you need a new suit. But if you want to have a suit made, there are better places to make for (see p.169).

Walking through Change Alley Aerial Plaza deposits you at **Clifford Pier**, long the departure point for trips on the Singapore River and to the southern islands (see p.32). There are still a few bumboats tied up here, though these days they're rented out as cruise boats rather than earning a living as cargo boats. Just north of Clifford Pier, **One Fullerton** is a new entertainments venue that has been constructed on land reclaimed from Marina Bay. Its bars, restaurants and nightclub share peerless views out over the bay. Just above One Fullerton a statue of Singapore's national symbol, the **Merlion**, guards the mouth of the Singapore River. Half-lion, half-fish, and wholly ugly, the creature reflects Singapore's name (*Singapura* means "Lion City" in Sanskrit) and its historical links with the sea.

Across the road stands the elegant **Fullerton Building**, fronted by sturdy pillars. Built in 1928 as the headquarters for the General Post Office – a role it fulfilled until the mid-1990s – remarkably, this was once one of Singapore's tallest buildings. Old photographs of Singapore depict Japanese soldiers marching past the building after the surrender of the Allied forces during World War II. These days, the building is a luxury hotel, and the lighthouse that used to flash up on the roof is a swanky restaurant.

Back at Clifford Pier, it's a short walk south along Raffles Quay to Telok Ayer Market, now called **Lau Pa Sat Festival Market**. Built in 1884 on land reclaimed from the sea, its octagonal cast-iron frame has been turned into

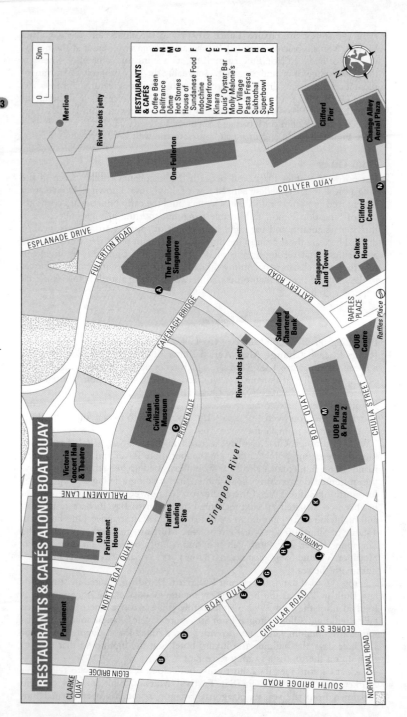

RESTAURANTS & CAFÉS ALONG BOAT QUAY

RESTAURANTS & CAFÉS

Coffee Bean B
Delifrance N
Dôme M
Hot Stones G
House of F
Sundanese Food
Indochine C
Waterfront E
Kinara J
Louis' Oyster Bar L
Molly Malone's I
Our Village K
Pasta Fresca H
Sukhothai D
Superbowl A
Town

Singapore's most tasteful food centre (daily 24hr), which offers a range of Southeast Asian cuisine, as well as laying on free entertainment such as local bands and Chinese opera. After 7pm, the portion of Boon Tat Street between Robinson Road and Shenton Way is closed to traffic, and traditional hawker stalls take over the street.

Marina South and the Port of Singapore

One of Singapore's most ambitious land reclamation projects, **Marina South**, is plainly visible from Raffles Quay and Shenton Way to the south of the Financial District. For years, the project has shown all the makings of a splendid folly – the entertainment and recreation park that was built on it during the 1980s has gone bankrupt, and the large patch of land now seems to serve no other purpose than to carry the East Coast Parkway on its journey west. For now, Marina South is a ghost town, its only real asset an imaginative children's playground within a pleasant park. But plans are afoot to extend Singapore's downtown area into this space.

Below Marina South, Singapore's **port** begins its sprawl westwards. Singapore is the world's busiest container port (the second busiest port overall after Rotterdam), and hundreds of ships are at anchor south of the island at any one time, waiting for permission from the Port of Singapore Authority to enter one of the state's seven terminals.

Little India and the Arab Quarter

aces, temples and sights suddenly change from Oriental to Indian when you head north of the Colonial District to Serangoon Road and **Little India**. The new Little India MRT station deposits you a minute's walk from all the action. The **Arab Quarter**, the focal point of Singapore's Muslim population, is no more than a ten-minute stroll from Little India across the Rochor Canal – take Syed Alwi Road if you're at the top of Serangoon; it's more convenient to loop around Rochor Canal Road if you're down by the Zhujiao Centre. From elsewhere, hop on the MRT and alight at Bugis station.

Little India

A tour around Singapore's answer to Bombay amounts to an all-out assault on the senses. Indian pop music blares from gargantuan speakers outside cassette shops, the air is perfumed with incense, spices and jasmine garlands, Hindu women promenade in bright sarees, and a wealth of "hole-in-the-wall" restaurants serve up superior curries.

Indians did not always dominate this convenient central niche of Singapore; its original occupants were Europeans and Eurasians who established country houses here, and for whom a racecourse was built (on the site of modern-day Farrer Park) in the 1840s. Only when Indian-run **brick kilns** began to operate here did a pronouncedly Indian community start to evolve. The enclave grew when a number of **cattle** and **buffalo yards** opened in the area in the latter half of the nineteenth century, and more Hindus were drawn in in search of work. Street names hark back to this trade: side by side off the western reach of Serangoon Road are Buffalo Road and Kerbau ("buffalo" in Malay, confusingly) Road, along both of which cattle were kept in slaughter pens. Singapore's largest maternity hospital, nearby on Bukit Timah Road, is called Kandang Kerbau (Buffalo Pen) Hospital. Indians featured prominently in the development of Singapore, though not always out of choice: from 1825 onwards, convicts were transported from the subcontinent and by the 1840s there were over a thousand Indian prisoners labouring on buildings such as St Andrew's Cathedral and the istana.

The district's backbone is the north–south **Serangoon Road**, whose southern end is alive with shops, restaurants and fortune-tellers; to the east, stretching as far as Jalan Besar, is a tight knot of roads that's good for exploration. Parallel to Serangoon Road, **Race Course Road** boasts a clutch of fine restaurants (for details of Indian restaurants, see p.139) and some noteworthy temples.

Along Serangoon Road

Dating from 1822 and hence one of the island's oldest roadways, Serangoon Road is a kaleidoscopic whirl of Indian life, its shops selling everything from nose studs and ankle bracelets to incense sticks and kum kum powder (used to make the red dot Hindus wear on their foreheads). Little stalls, set up in doorways and under "five-foot ways", sell garlands, gaudy posters of Hindu gods and gurus, movie soundtracks and newspapers such as *The Hindu* and *India Today*. Look out for parrot-wielding **fortune-tellers** – you tell the man your name, he passes your name onto his feathered partner, and the bird then picks out a card with your fortune on it.

The Zhujiao Centre and around

At the southwestern end of Serangoon Road, the **Zhujiao Centre** combines many of Little India's ventures under one roof. Beyond its ground-floor food centre is a wet market that's not for the faint-hearted – traders push around trolleys piled high with goats' heads, while the halal butchers go to work in full view of the customers. Elsewhere, live crabs shuffle busily in buckets, their claws tied together, and there's a mouthwatering range of fruits on sale, including mangoes and whole branches of bananas. Upstairs, on the second floor, you'll find Indian fabrics, leatherware, footwear, watches, and cheap electronic goods. On Sunday, the forecourt of the centre becomes an ad hoc social club for immigrant labourers working in Singapore, most of whom are Bangladeshi. Along the northern side of the Zhujiao Centre, **Buffalo Road** has a cluster of provisions stores with sacks of spices and fresh coconut, ground using a primitive machine out on the road.

Little India's remaining shophouses are fast being touched up from the same pastel paintbox that has "restored" Chinatown to its present doll's house tweeness. Fortunately, the colours work far better in an Indian context, and the results are really quite pleasing. In particular, check out **Kerbau Road**, one block north of Buffalo Road, where shophouses have been meticulously renovated and now harbour a proliferation of Indian produce stores and a pleasant beer garden. (A right turn from Kerbau Road takes you onto Race Course Road, whose fine restaurants serve both north and south Indian food; several specialize in fish-head curry.)

Little India Conservation Area and around

Bounded by Serangoon Road to the west, Campbell Lane to the north, and Hastings Road to the south, the lovingly restored block of shophouses comprising the **Little India Conservation Area** was opened recently as a sort of Little India in microcosm: behind its cream walls and green shutters you'll find the Hastings Road Food Court and the Little India Arcade, where you can purchase textiles and tapestries, bangles, religious statuary, Indian tapes and CDs, and even traditional Ayurvedic medicines. At the time of Deepavali, the arcade's narrow ways are choked with locals hastening to buy decorations, garlands, traditional confectionery and fine clothes.

The roads nearby are also worth exploring. Campbell Lane is a good place for buying Indian sandals, while walking along Clive Street towards Upper Dickson

LITTLE INDIA & THE ARAB QUARTER

RESTAURANTS & CAFÉS		
Bayview Café	Q	
Billy Bombers	I	
Bobby Rubino's	Y	
Bumbu	D	
Cherry Garden	X	
Doc Cheng's	V	
Food Junction	I	
Fut Sai Kai	A	
Grand City	aa	
Hai Tien Lo	W	
Imperial Herbal	O	
Islamic	B	
Kopitiam	aa	
Kwan Yim	U	
Lei Garden	F	
Madam Saigon	H	
Mr Bean's Café	M	
Noorul Ameen	K	
Ocho	Y	
Pacific Coffee Company	bb	
Paulaner Bräuhaus	Y	
Ponderosa	aa	
Rendezvous	T	
Rumah Makan Minang	C	
Seah Street Deli	P	
Seoul Garden	Z	
Shinghtai Palace	L	
Sim Lim Square Food Court	E	
Singapura Seafood	G	
Starbucks	aa	
Tatsu Sushi	Y	
Tiffin Room	V	
Victoria Street Food Court	S	
Viet Lang	Y	
Warung M Nasir	J	
Yet Con	N	

ACCOMMODATION	
Ali's Nest	2
Boon Wah Hotel	8
Broadway Hotel	4
Dickson Court Hotel	7
Fortuna Hotel	1
Haising Hotel	9
Inn Crowd	10
Julia's Guesthouse	3
Kerbau Hotel	6
Little India Guesthouse	5
Perak Lodge	11

Road you'll find on your right a batch of junk dealers patiently tinkering with ancient cookers, air-con units and TVs. Left along Upper Dickson Road – past an old barber's shop where a short back and sides is followed by a crunching head yank to "relieve tension" – are the *Madras New Woodlands Restaurant*, at no. 12–14 and, around the corner, *Komala Vilas*, 76 Serangoon Road, two of Little India's best southern Indian restaurants (see p.141 for full details). Dunlop Street's **Abdul Gaffoor Mosque** (at no. 41; daily 8.30am–noon & 2.30–4pm) is a little-known, crumbling beauty, bristling with small spires.

The Sri Veeramakaliamman Temple and Pink Street

In the heart of Little India on Serangoon Road, opposite the turning to Veerasamy Road, the **Sri Veeramakaliamman Temple** (6am–noon & 5–9pm) – dedicated to the ferocious Hindu goddess, Kali – features a fanciful *gopuram* that's flanked by majestic lions on the temple walls. Inside the temple, the *mandapam*, or worship hall, holds an image of Kali, the darkest manifestation of the Great Goddess, depicted with a club in hand. Each year during Deepavali (see box), a pulsating market takes place on the open land above the temple.

North from the temple, and off to the right, lies **Pink Street**, one of the most incongruous and sordid spots in the whole of clean, shiny Singapore – but you won't find it on any city map. The entire length of the "street" (in fact it's merely an alley between the backs of Rowell and Desker roads) is punctuated by open doorways, inside which gaggles of bored-looking prostitutes sit knitting or watching TV, oblivious to the gawping local men who accumulate outside. Stalls along the alley sell distinctly un-Singaporean merchandise such as sex toys, blue videos and potency pills, while con men work the "three cups and a ball" routine on unwary passers-by.

North of Desker Road

Beyond Desker Road, a five-minute walk north takes you to the edge of Little India, a diversion worth making to see two very different temples. Each year,

HOTELS AROUND BENCOOLEN STREET

ACCOMMODATION									
Ah Chew	8	City Bayview	19	Lee Home Stay	10	Plaza Park Royal	3		
Albert Court Hotel	4	Golden Landmark Hotel	2	Lee Traveller's Club	12	Raffles	20		
Aliwal Park Hotel	1	Hawaii Hostel	7	Metropole	14	Southeast Asia Hotel	6		
Beach Hotel	9	Intercontinental	11	New 7th Storey Hotel	5	Strand Hotel	18		
Bencoolen Hotel	15	Lee Boarding House	16	Oxford Hotel	13	Waterloo Hostel	17		

on the day of the Thaipusam festival (see p.160), the courtyard of the **Sri Srinivasa Perumal Temple** (daily 6am–noon & 5–9pm), at 397 Serangoon Road, witnesses a gruesome melee of activity, as Hindu devotees don huge metal frames (*kavadis*) topped with peacock feathers, which are fastened to their flesh with hooks and prongs. The devotees then leave the temple, stopping only while a coconut is smashed at their feet for good luck, and parade all the way to the Chettiar Temple on Tank Road, off Orchard Road. Even if you miss the festival, it's worth a trip to see the five-tiered *gopuram* with its sculptures of the various manifestations of Lord Vishnu the Preserver. On the wall to the right of the front gate is a sculpted elephant, its leg caught in a crocodile's mouth.

The Sakaya Muni Buddha Gaya Temple

Just beyond the Sri Srinivasa temple complex, a small path leads northwest to Race Course Road, where the **Sakaya Muni Buddha Gaya Temple** (or Temple of the Thousand Lights; daily 7am–6pm) is on the right at no. 366. It's a slightly kitsch building that betrays a strong Thai influence – not surprising, since it was built entirely by a Thai monk, Vutthisasala. On the left of the temple as you enter is a huge replica of the Buddha's footprint, inlaid with mother-of-pearl, and beyond is a great Buddha ringed by the thousand electric lights from which the temple takes its alternative name. Twenty-five scenes from the Buddha's life decorate the pedestal on which he sits. It is pos-

RESTAURANTS
Azmi Muslim Food Stall	C
Banana Leaf Apolo	D
Fatty's Wing Seong	K
Gandhi Eating House	E
Hastings Road Food Court	H
Komala Vilas	G
Madras New Woodlands	F
Muthu's Curry	A
New Generation Eating House	B
Roshni	J
Selera	J
Sri Vijayah	I

LITTLE INDIA RESTAURANTS

sible to walk inside the statue, through a door in its back; inside is a smaller representation of the Buddha, this time reclining. The left wall of the temple features a sort of wheel of fortune – spin it (for 30c) and take the numbered sheet of paper that corresponds to the number at which the wheel stops, to discover your fortune. Further along the left wall, a small donation entitles you to a shake of a tin full of numbered sticks, after which, again, you get a corresponding sheet of forecasts.

Double back onto Serangoon Road and a five-minute walk southeast along Petain Road leads to Jalan Besar, a route that takes in some immaculate examples of **Peranakan** (Straits Chinese) shophouses, their facades covered with elegant ceramic tiles reminiscent of Portuguese *azulejos*. There's more Peranakan architecture on display on Jalan Besar itself – turn right at the end of Petain Road – and along Sam Leong Road, where the shophouse facades are decorated with depictions of stags, lotuses and egrets. Further south a daily **flea market** takes place around Pitt Street, Weld Road, Kelantan Lane and Pasar Lane – secondhand tools, odd shoes and foreign currency are all laid out for sale on plastic sheets at the side of the road by citizens whom Singapore's economic miracle has passed by.

The Arab Quarter

Before the arrival of Raffles, the area of Singapore west of the Rochor River housed a Malay village known as Kampong Glam, after the *Gelam* tribe of sea gypsies who lived there. After signing a dubious treaty with the newly installed "Sultan" Hussein Mohammed Shah, Raffles allotted the area to the sultan and designated the land around it as a Muslim settlement, and soon the zone was attracting Arab traders, as the road names in today's **ARAB QUARTER** – Baghdad Street, Muscat Street and Haji Lane – suggest. Even now, descendants of Sultan Hussein live in the grounds of the Istana Kampong Glam, a palace right in the centre of the district, bounded by Arab Street, Beach Road, Jalan Sultan and Rochor Canal Road. Just outside the quarter, **Beach Road** still maintains shops which betray its former proximity to the sea – ships' chandlers and fishing tackle specialists – and you should also take the time to walk southeast from Arab Street to see the two logic-defying office buildings that together comprise **The Gateway**. Designed by I.M. Pei, they rise magnificently into the air like vast razor blades and appear two-dimensional when viewed from certain angles.

Arab Street

While Little India is memorable for its fragrances, it's the vibrant colours of the shops of **Arab Street** and its environs that stick in the memory. The street boasts the highest concentration of shops in the Arab Quarter; its pavements are an obstacle course of carpets, cloths, baskets and bags. Most of the shops have been renovated, though one or two (such as C. Rashiwala Bros at no. 97 and Aik Bee at no. 73) still retain their original dark-wood and glass cabinets, and wide wooden benches where the shopkeepers sit. Textile stores are most prominent, their walls, ceilings and doorways draped with cloths and batiks. Elsewhere you'll see leather, basketware, gold, gemstones and jewellery for sale, while the most impressive range of basketware and rattan work – fans, hats and walking sticks – is found at Rishi Handicrafts, at no. 58. It's easy to spend a couple of hours weaving in and out of the stores, but don't expect a quiet window-shopping session – the traders here are masters of the forced sale, and will have you loaded with sarongs, baskets and leather bags before you know it.

Around North Bridge Road

The Arab Quarter's most evocative patch is the stretch of **North Bridge Road** between Arab Street and Jalan Sultan. Here, the men sport long sarongs and Abe Lincoln beards, the women fantastically colourful shawls and robes, while the shops and restaurants are geared more towards locals than tourists: Jamal Kazura Aromatics, at 728 North Bridge Road, for instance, sells alcohol-free perfumes, while neighbouring shops stock rosaries, prayer mats and the *songkok* hats worn by Muslim males in mosques, and *miswak* sticks – twigs the width of a finger used by some locals to clean their teeth. A gaggle of superb Muslim Indian restaurants operates along this stretch of North Bridge Road: see pp.139–142 for details.

Several roads run off the western side of North Bridge Road, including Jalan Pisang (Banana Street), on which a street barber works under a tarpaulin. A walk up Jalan Kubor (Grave Street) and across Victoria Street takes you to an

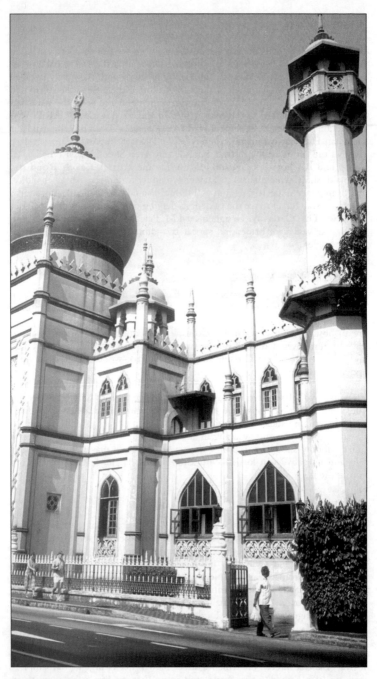

△ Sultan Mosque

unkempt Muslim **cemetery** where, it is said, Malay royalty are buried. On Sundays, Victoria Street throngs with children in full Muslim garb on their way to study scripture at the Arabic school, **Madrasah Al Junied Al-Islamiah**.

Istana Kampong Glam

Squatting between Kandahar and Aliwal streets, the **Istana Kampong Glam** was built as the royal palace of Sultan Ali Iskandar Shah, son of Sultan Hussein who negotiated with Raffles to hand over Singapore to the British; the sultan's descendants live here to this day, and continue to share an annual government allowance. Despite its royal provenance, the istana is a modest, colonial-style building, run-down and dingy, its grounds dotted with huts. This should soon change, as long-held plans to turn the property into a Malay heritage museum are finally set to reach fruition. Until the museum's completion, you have to make do with glimpsing the building from outside the front gates.

Approaching the palace, you'll see a **stonemason's** shop on the corner of Baghdad Street and Sultan Gate, which chips out the lions that stand outside Chinese temples, and Muslim gravestones – uniformly shaped stones that look remarkably like chess pawns.

The Sultan Mosque

Looking down pedestrianized Bussorah Street from Baghdad Street, you get the best initial views of the golden domes of the **Sultan Mosque** or Masjid Sultan (daily 9am–1pm), the beating heart of the Muslim faith in Singapore. An earlier mosque stood on this site, finished in 1825 and constructed with the help of a $3000 donation from the East India Company. The present building was completed a century later, according to a design by colonial architects Swan and MacLaren: if you look carefully at the glistening necks of the domes, you can see that the effect is created by the bases of thousands of ordinary glass bottles, an incongruity which sets the tone for the rest of the building. Steps at the top of Bussorah Street lead into a wide lobby, where a digital display lists current prayer times. Beyond, and out of bounds to non-Muslims, is the main prayer hall, a large, bare chamber that's fronted by two more digital clocks. An exhaustive set of rules applies to visitors wishing to enter the lobby: shoes must be taken off and shoulders and legs covered, no video cameras are allowed inside the mosque, and entry is not permitted during the Friday mass congregation (11.30am–2.30pm). The best time to come is in the Muslim fasting month of Ramadan – the faithful can eat only after dusk, and Muskat Street and Kandahar Street are awash with stalls selling *biriyani*, barbecued chicken and cakes.

Hajjah Fatimah Mosque and around

From the Sultan Mosque, it's only a five-minute walk on to the **Hajjah Fatimah Mosque** (daily 8.30am–noon & 2.30–4pm) on Beach Road, where a collection of photographs in the entrance porch show the mosque through the years following its construction in 1846 – first surrounded by shophouses, then by open land, and finally by huge housing projects. The mosque is named after a wealthy Malaccan businesswoman who amassed a fortune through her mercantile vessels, and whose family home formerly stood here. After two break-ins and an arson attack on her home, Hajjah Fatimah decided to move elsewhere, then underwrote the construction of a mosque on the site. The minaret looks strangely like a church steeple (perhaps because its architect was a European) and is beautifully illuminated at night. Its 6-degree list – locals call the mosque Singapore's Leaning Tower of Pisa – is barely noticeable.

Across from the mosque, the Golden Mile Complex at 5001 Beach Road attracts so many Thai nationals that locals refer to it as "**Thai Village**". Numerous bus firms selling tickets to Thailand operate out of here, while inside, the shops vend Thai foodstuffs, cafés sell Singha beer and Mekong whisky, and authentic restaurants serve up old favourites. On Sundays, Thais come down here in hordes to meet up with their compatriots, listen to Thai pop music and have a few drinks.

5

Northern Singapore

W hile land reclamation has radically altered the east coast, and indus-
trialization the west, the **northern** expanses of the island up to the
Straits of Johor still retain pockets of the **rainforest** and mangrove
swamp which blanketed Singapore until the British arrival in 1819.
These are interspersed today with sprawling, maze-like **new towns** such as Toa
Payoh, Bishan and Ang Mo Kio, built in the 1970s. The name of the last, meaning "red-haired devil's bridge", refers to the nineteenth-century British surveyor,
John Turnbull Thomson, under whose supervision the transport network of
Singapore began to penetrate the interior of the island. Man-eating tigers
roamed these parts well into the twentieth century, and it was here that Allied
forces confronted the invading Japanese army in 1942, a period of Singaporean
history movingly recalled by the **Kranji War Memorial** on Woodlands Road.
Still visible at the far northern sweep of the island are the remnants of
Singapore's agricultural past: you'll see prawn and poultry farms, orchards and
vegetable gardens when travelling in these parts.

Dominating the central northern region are two nature reserves, divided by
the main road route to Malaysia, the Bukit Timah Expressway. West of the
expressway is **Bukit Timah Nature Reserve**, an accessible slice of primary
rainforest, while to the east, the four reservoirs of the Central Catchment Area
are one of Singapore's main sources of water. North of here, the principal
tourist attractions are the excellent **Singapore Zoological Gardens** and the
adjacent **Night Safari**, sited on a finger of land pointing into the Seletar
Reservoir. To the east are two of Singapore's most eye-catching Buddhist temples – **Lian Shan Shuang Lin Temple** and the **Kong Meng San Phor
Kark See** complex – as well as tiny Tai Gin Road, where the sometime residence of Chinese nationalist leader Dr **Sun Yat Sen** and Singapore's **Burmese
Temple** are found.

Travel between the attractions in northern Singapore is decidedly tricky
unless you are driving, or in a cab, so don't expect to take in everything in a
day. However, Lian Shan Shuang Lin Temple, Sun Yat Sen Villa and the
Burmese Temple all nestle around the outskirts of Toa Payoh new town and
could be incorporated into a single expedition; as could the zoo, Mandai
Orchid Gardens and the Kranji War Cemetery and Memorial. The Kong Meng
San Phor Kark See temple complex really requires a separate journey.

Bukit Timah Nature Reserve and
Bukit Batok

Bukit Timah Road runs northwest from the junction of Selegie and Serangoon
roads, to the faceless town of **Bukit Timah**, 8km further on. Bukit Timah

NORTHERN SINGAPORE

boasts Singapore's last remaining pocket of primary rainforest, which now comprises **Bukit Timah Nature Reserve** (daily 7am–7pm; free; ☎1800-4685736, ⓦwww.nparks.gov.sg). Visiting this area of Singapore in the mid-eighteenth century, natural historian Alfred Russel Wallace reported seeing "tiger pits, carefully covered with sticks and leaves and so well concealed, that in several cases I had a narrow escape from falling into them … Formerly a sharp stake was stuck erect in the bottom," he continued, "but after an unfortunate traveller had been killed by falling into one, its use was forbidden."

Today the reserve, established in 1883 by Nathaniel Cantley, who was superintendent of the Botanic Gardens, yields no such hazards and is a refuge for the dwindling numbers of species still extant in Singapore – only 25 types of mammal now inhabit the island. Creatures you're most likely to see in Bukit Timah are long-tailed macaques, butterflies and other insects, and birds like the dark-necked tailorbird, which builds its nest by sewing together leaves. Scorpions, snakes, flying lemurs and pangolins (anteaters, whose name is derived from the Malay word *peng-goling*, meaning "roller", a reference to the animal's habit of rolling into a ball when threatened) still roam here too.

Alterations over the last few years have vastly improved the reserve, which now has an informative **visitor centre** (daily 8.30am–6pm) full of displays, specimens and photos relating to the wildlife. Several paths from the centre twist and turn through the forest around and to the top of **Bukit Timah Hill**, which, at a paltry 163m, is actually Singapore's highest hill. These paths are all well signposted, colour-coded and dotted with rest points, and they're clearly mapped on the free leaflet handed out to all visitors. Two bike tracks have also been added recently (see p.31 for bike rental details).

Bus #171 passes along Somerset and Scotts roads en route to Bukit Timah Reserve; a second option is to take bus #170 from the Ban San Terminal on Queen Street. Both buses drop you beside a row of shops on Upper Bukit Timah Road, where you can pick up light snacks and bottled water to take into the reserve. You'd do best to visit in the cool of early morning and midweek, when there are fewer visitors.

Bukit Batok and the former Ford Factory

Across Upper Bukit Timah Road from the reserve, another forested hill, **Bukit Batok**, is where British and Australian POWs were forced to erect a fifteen-metre-high wooden shrine, the Syonan Tyureito, for their Japanese captors. Only the steps at its base now remain. Legend has it that termites, which the prisoners secretly introduced to the structure, destroyed the shrine itself. Gone, too, is the wooden cross erected by the POWs to honour their dead. The hill is located at the end of Lorong Sesuai, a left turn opposite Bukit Timah fire station, 500m further up the road from the entrance to Bukit Timah reserve. Lorong Sesuai was laid by the same prisoners who built the shrine. The surrender that consigned them to such labours took place 400m further up Upper Bukit Timah Road, at the now disused Art Deco **Ford Factory**, the first car assembly plant in Southeast Asia. It was here that Lieutenant General Percival, head of the Allied forces in Singapore, surrendered to Japan's General Yamashita on February 15, 1942.

Tai Gin Road: the Sun Yat Sen Villa and Burmese Temple

Between Jalan Toa Payoh to the north, and Balestier Road to the south, is the **Sun Yat Sen Villa** (Tues–Sun 9am–5pm; $2; ☎62567377,

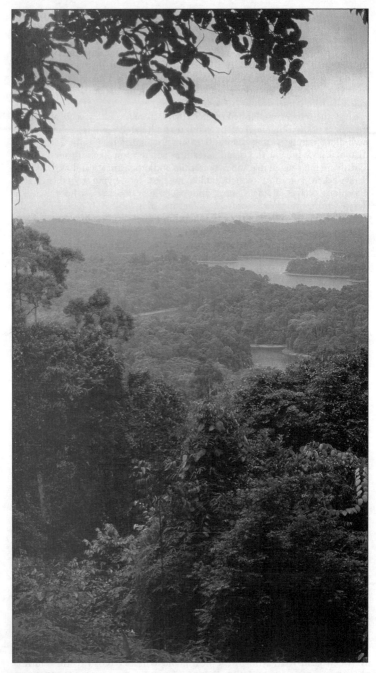

△ Bukit Timah Nature Reserve

@wanqingyuan.zaobao.com/english) on tiny Tai Gin Road, reached by bus #139 from outside Dhoby Ghaut MRT station. Built to house the mistress of a wealthy Chinese businessman, this attractive Palladian-style bungalow changed hands in 1905, when one Teo Eng Hock bought it for his mother. Chinese nationalist leader Dr Sun Yat Sen paid the first of several visits to Singapore the following year, and was invited by Teo to stay at Tai Gin Road, where he quickly established a Singapore branch of the Tong Meng Hui – a society dedicated to replacing the Manchu dynasty in China with a modern republic. After serving as a communications camp for the Japanese during World War II, the villa fell into disrepair until 1966, when it was done up and opened to the public. A recent renovation has added an extra wing to the building, allowing space for six **galleries**, whose displays, artefacts and visuals variously focus upon the villa's history, the life of Dr Sun, and the historical context to the Chinese revolution in which he played such a substantial part. There's also a gallery celebrating the role of Southeast Asia's overseas Chinese in supporting the revolution – a huge painting of Dr Sun rallying support from the tin miners and rubber tappers in Malaya dominates it. There's enough to engage the mind for a while, but, realistically, this is best left to visitors with an active interest in Chinese history.

Next door to the Sun Yat Sen Villa is the **Sasanaramsi Burmese Buddhist Temple** (daily 6am–10pm; ☎62511717, @www.bbt.org.sg) reconstructed in just two years after being forced to move from its previous site at Kinta Road because of redevelopment. Craftsmen from Burma decorated the temple, and its ground floor is dominated by a large, white marble statue of the Buddha brought over from Burma in 1932; upstairs is another Buddha statue, this time standing, and ringed by blue skies painted on the wall behind. Tiny Buddha images are presently being "bought" by worshippers at $1000 a throw in order to raise funds; when they're all sold they'll be mounted on the painted sky. There are meditation classes for free – but call ahead.

The Lian Shan Shuang Lin and Phor Kark See temples

Two of Singapore's largest Chinese temples are situated in the island's central region, east of the Central Catchment Area. Both are rather isolated, but buzz with activity at festival times and have plenty to interest temple enthusiasts.

The name of the popular **Lian Shan Shuang Lin Temple** (daily 7am–6pm), at 184e Jalan Toa Payoh, means "Twin Groves of the Lotus Mountain" – a reference to the Buddha's birth in a grove of trees and his death under a Bodhi tree. The Chinese abbot Sek Hean Wei established the temple at the turn of the twentieth century when, passing through Singapore on his way home after a pilgrimage to Sri Lanka, he was waylaid by wealthy Hokkien merchant and philanthropist Low Kim Pong, who supplied both land and finances for the venture. Several renovations have failed to rob the temple of its grandeur: set behind a rock garden that combines a water cascade, ponds, streams and bridges, it is guarded by statues of the **Four Kings of Heaven**, each posted to repel evil, symbolized by the demons on which they are treading. The highly regarded collection of carved and sculpted gods inside the temple's several halls includes a **Laughing Buddha**, believed to grant good luck if you rub his stomach, a shrine to Kuan Yin, goddess of mercy (in the rear hall), and a number of Thai-style Buddha figures. To **get here**, take the MRT to Toa Payoh station, from where the temple is a ten-minute walk.

The largest temple complex in Singapore – and one of the largest in Southeast Asia – lies north of MacRitchie Reservoir, right in the middle of the island. **Phor Kark See Temple** (known in full as the Kong Meng San Phor Kark See Temple Complex; daily 7am–6pm), at 88 Bright Hill Drive, spreads over nineteen acres and combines temples, pagodas, pavilions, a Buddhist library and a vast crematorium so impressive that it has been used several times as a backdrop to Chinese kung fu movies. More modern than Lian Shan Shuang Lin, Phor Kark See boasts none of the faded charm of Singapore's older temples, but relies instead on its sheer magnitude and exuberant decor for effect. Multi-tiered roofs bristle with ceramic dragons, phoenixes, birds and human figures, while around the complex are statues of various deities, including a nine-metre-high marble statue of Kuan Yin, goddess of mercy. A soaring pagoda capped by a golden *chedi* (reliquary tower) renders the complex even more striking. Even the **crematorium** – conveniently placed for the nearby Evergreen Home for the elderly – doesn't do things by half. Housed below a Thai-style facade of elaborately carved gilt wood, it can cope with five ceremonies at a time.

Below the crematorium is a pair of ponds, where thousands of turtles sunbathe precariously on wooden planks that slant into the waters. A nearby sign prohibits worshippers from putting new turtles into the ponds, a practice supposed to bring good luck. Old ladies beside the viewing gallery sell bunches of vegetables for "one dolla, one dolla", which purchasers then throw to the lucky turtles.

To **reach the complex** take bus #130 up Victoria Street, alighting at the far end of Sin Ming Drive.

Singapore Zoological Gardens and Night Safari

The **Singapore Zoological Gardens** (daily 8.30am–6pm; $12, children $5; Ⓦwww.zoo.com.sg) on Mandai Lake Road are spread over a promontory jutting into peaceful Seletar Reservoir. The gardens attract over a million visitors a year – a fact perhaps explained by their status as one of the world's few open zoos, where moats are preferred to cages. Spacious exhibits manage to approximate the natural habitats of the animals, and though leopards, pumas and jaguars still have to be kept behind bars, this is a thoughtful, humane environment, described as "one of the really beautiful zoos" by no less an authority than conservationist Sir Peter Scott.

There are some 2700 animals here, representing more than 200 species, so it's best to allow a whole day for your visit. A **tram** ($2.50, children $1.50) circles the grounds on a one-way circuit, but be prepared for a lot of footwork. Highlights include the Komodo dragons, the polar bears, which you view underwater from a gallery, and the primate kingdom. Also worth checking out is the **special loan enclosure** that has recently played host to a giant panda, an Indian white tiger and a golden monkey. Various **animal** and **feeding shows** run throughout the day from 10am until 5pm, featuring sea lions, elephants, polar bears and other exotic creatures. There are also elephant and pony rides ($3, children $2) and, in the **Children's World**, there's the chance to hold young chicks and watch a milking demonstration. At 9am and 4pm daily, you can even share breakfast or afternoon tea with a selection of the zoo's residents.

Upon **arrival**, pick up the leaflet with details of riding and feeding times and the helpful map, which suggests itineraries taking in all the major shows and attractions. At the other end of your trip, you might care to drop by the **gift shop** next to the exit, which stocks the usual cuddly toys, key rings and pencil cases. Several food and drink kiosks are dotted around the zoo, or you can head for the reasonable *Makan Terrace*, bang in the centre of the grounds, where there are one or two hawker stalls.

The opening of the **Night Safari** (daily 7.30pm–midnight; $15.60, children $10.40; Ⓦ www.nightsafari.com.sg) a few years back substantially increased the grounds of the zoo. Here, a thousand animals representing a hundred species – elephants, rhinos, giraffes and leopards, hyenas and otters – play out their nocturnal routines under a forest of standard lamps. Three **walking trails**, geared around forest giants, leopards, and the incredibly cute fishing cats, respectively, wind through the safari. However, only five of the safari's eight zones are walkable – to see the rest you'll need to take a 45-minute *Jurassic Park*-style tram ride ($5.05, children $3), and tolerate the intrusive chattering of its taped guide. A meal at one of two restaurants outside the entrance will pass the time between the zoo's closing and the safari's opening.

To **get to** the zoo and the Night Safari, take bus #171 to Mandai Road, then #138, or Ang Mo Kio MRT and then bus #138.

Mandai Orchid Gardens

It's only a ten-minute walk from the Singapore Zoological Gardens down Mandai Lake Road to the **Mandai Orchid Gardens** (daily 8.30am–5.30pm; $2; Ⓦ singaporeorchids.com.sg) or you can take the #138 bus from the zoo, which stops right outside. Orchids are big business in tropical Singapore. Here, the flowers are cultivated on a gentle slope, tended by old ladies in wide-brimmed hats. Unless you are a keen horticulturist, the place will be of limited interest, as little effort has been taken to make it instructive. Still, if you've been to the zoo, the gardens make a colourful detour on the way home, and the price of a gift box of orchids (starting from $15) compares favourably with more central flower shops.

Woodlands: Kranji War Cemetery and around

Five kilometres north of the zoo is the bustling town of **Woodlands**, from where a **causeway** spanning the Straits of Johor links Singapore to Johor Bahru in Malaysia. At peak hours (6.30–9.30am & 5.50–7.30pm) and at weekends, the roads leading to the causeway seethe with cars and trucks – all full of petrol, after a law passed in the early 1990s banned Singaporeans from driving out of the country on an empty tank. Previously, people crossed into Malaysia, filled up with cut-price fuel and then headed home; now, signs line the roads approaching the causeway requesting that "Singapore cars please top up to_tank" – or risk a $500 fine.

Bus #170 from Ban San Terminal on Queen Street heads towards Woodlands on its way to Johor Bahru, passing the **Kranji War Cemetery and Memorial** (daily 7am–6pm) on Woodlands Road, where only the sound of birds and insects breaks the silence in the immaculately kept grounds. (You can also get here by alighting at Kranji MRT station, from where it's a five-hundred-metre walk.) The cemetery is the resting place of the many Allied troops who died in the defence of Singapore. As you enter, row upon row of graves slope up the landscaped hill in front of you, some identified only as "known unto God".

The graves are bare: flowers are banned, as still water encourages mosquitoes to breed. A simple stone cross stands over the cemetery and above is the **memorial**, around which are recorded all the names of more than twenty thousand soldiers (from Britain, Canada, Sri Lanka, India, Malaysia, the Netherlands, New Zealand and Singapore) who died in this region during World War II. Two unassuming **tombs** stand on the wide lawns below the cemetery, belonging to Yusof Bin Ishak and Dr Benjamin Henry Sheares, independent Singapore's first two presidents.

Singapore Turf Club

Singapore's only racecourse is at the **Singapore Turf Club**, adjacent to Kranji MRT station and also reachable by bus #170. As legal gambling outside the course is restricted, the annual racing calendar here is very popular. The course typically holds twenty or so race meets annually, spaced throughout the year. The most prestigious events include the Lion City Cup, the Singapore Gold Cup and the Singapore Derby. Race dates change from year to year, so it's worth calling the information hotline or checking the website (☎68791000, ⓦwww.turfclub.com.sg) if you want to time your visit to coincide with a big race day. When there's no racing in Singapore, a giant video screen links the racecourse to various courses across the causeway in Malaysia. There's a fairly strict dress code – strapless sandals, jeans, shorts and T-shirts are out – and foreign visitors have to take their passports with them. Friday cards begin at 6.30pm, Saturday's and Sunday's after lunch, and tickets cost from $3 to $20. A day's racing viewed from the grandstand's posher upper tiers can be booked in advance, but you'd do far better just to turn up, eat at the lower grandstand's decent food court and soak up the atmosphere in the stands.

Sungei Buloh Wetland Reserve

The 130-hectare swathe of **Sungei Buloh Wetland Reserve** (Mon–Sat 7.30am–7pm, Sun 7am–7pm; $1, children 50c; ☎67941401, ⓦwww.sbwr.org.sg), 4–5km northwest of Kranji cemetery on the north coast of Singapore, is the island's only protected wetland nature park. Beyond its visitor centre, café and video theatre (shows Mon–Sat 9am, 11am, 1pm, 3pm & 5pm, Sun hourly 9am–5pm), walking routes and boardwalks thread through and over a vast expanse of mangrove, mud flats, orchards and grassland, home to kingfishers, mudskippers, herons, sandpipers and sea eagles. Visit between September and March and you're likely to catch sight of migratory birds from around Asia roosting and feeding. Come on a Saturday and you can join a free guided tour (9am, 10am, 3pm & 4pm); at other times you'll need to pre-book a tour ($50 per group).

To **get to** Sungei Buloh, take the MRT to Kranji MRT station, then transfer to bus #925, which stops at Kranji Reservoir car park from Monday to Saturday, and at the reserve's entrance on Sundays.

6

Eastern Singapore

Thirty years ago, **eastern Singapore** was largely rural, dotted with Malay kampung villages that perched on stilts over the shoreline, harbouring the odd weekend retreat owned by Europeans or monied locals. Massive **land reclamation** and development programmes have altered the region beyond recognition, wiping out all traces of the kampungs and throwing up huge housing projects in their place. Today, former seafront suburbs like Bedok are separated from the Straits of Singapore by a broad crescent of man-made land, much of which constitutes the **East Coast Park**, a five-kilometre strip with leisure and watersports facilities, imported sand beaches and seafood restaurants. Despite the massive upheavals that have ruptured the communities of the east coast, parts of it, including the suburbs of **Geylang** and **Katong**, have managed to retain a strong Malay identity.

Dominating the eastern tip of the island is Changi airport, and beyond that **Changi Village**, where the Japanese interned Allied troops and civilians during World War II – a period of history commemorated at the thought-provoking **Changi Museum**. From Changi Point, it's possible to take a boat to **Pulau Ubin**, a small island that has echoes of pre-development Singapore.

Geylang and Katong

Malay culture has held sway in and around the adjoining suburbs of **Geylang** and **Katong** since the mid-nineteenth century, when Malays and Indonesians first arrived to work in the local *copra* (coconut husk) processing factory and later on its *serai* (lemon grass) farms. Many of its shophouses, restaurants and food centres are Malay-influenced, less so the thriving trade in prostitution that carries on here, unchecked by the local authorities. **Geylang Road** itself runs east from the Kallang River; off the road are 42 lorongs, or lanes, down which clusters of brothels are decked out with fairy lights. At its far eastern end, Geylang Road meets **Joo Chiat Road**, which – after the restrictions of downtown Singapore – has a refreshingly laid-back and shambolic air.

The Malay Village

Before striking off down Joo Chiat Road, cross Changi Road, to the north, where, east of a side street called Geylang Serai, a hawker centre and wet market of the same name provide more Malay atmosphere, from the clove cigarettes to the line of sarong sellers beyond the food stalls. The contrast between this authentic slice of life and the **Malay Village** (daily 10am–10pm; $5, children $3 for attractions, otherwise free) on the other side of Geylang Serai, and a short walk from Paya Lebar MRT, is huge. Opened in 1990, and conceived as a celebration of the cuisine, music, dance, arts and crafts of the

Bumboats to Malaysia ▲   ▲ Boats to Malaysia

EASTERN SINGAPORE

Boats to Malaysia ▼

Boats to Indonesia ▼

Straits of Singapore

Changi Ferry Terminal

Changi International Airport

CHANGI VILLAGE

Pulau Ubin

Bumboats

Pasir Ris Park

Escape Theme Park

Pasir Ris

Changi Prison

Tanah Merah Ferry Terminal

CHANGI COAST ROAD

TAMPINES EXPRESSWAY

LOYANG AVE.

Tampines

Simei

Expo

NEW UPPER CHANGI ROAD

Tanah Merah

Bedok Reservoir

Bedok

UPPER EAST COAST RD

EAST COAST PARKWAY

PAN ISLAND EXPRESSWAY

Kembangan

SIGLAP RD

Pasta Fresca Seasports Centre

East Coast Park

Eunos

Joo Chiat Complex

Malay Village

KATONG

EAST COAST RD

MARINE PARK ROAD

CHANGI RD

STILL RD

JOO CHIAT RD

TANJONG KATONG RD

MEYER RD

HAIG ROAD

DUNMAN RD

Paya Lebar

GPO

GEYLANG

GEYLANG RD

Aljunied

Kallang

Lavender

Bugis

National Stadium

Kallang Theatre

Indoor Stadium

Little India

Farrer Park

Novena

Boon Keng

Potong Pasir

Woodleigh

Serangoon

Kovan

Hougang

Bishan

Toa Payoh

Braddell

CENTRAL EXPRESSWAY

0   2km

RESTAURANTS
Chilli Padi   B
Geylang Serai Food Centre   B
Guan Hoe Soon   D
Mum's Kitchen   C
Peranakan Inn   E
Tekong Seafood   A

Malay people, the village has conspicuously failed either to woo tourists or to rent out its replica wooden kampung-style shops to locals, and seems to be dying a slow but certain death. Its tourist lures pack very little punch: the **Cultural Museum** features a humdrum array of household instruments, cloths, kites and *kris*, and a mock-up of a Malay wedding scene; the dismal **Kampung Days** exhibition reproduces a traditional Malay kampung homestead, complete with fishing and rice-pounding scenes, a *wayang kulit* stage, an open-air cinema, and another (seemingly obligatory) wedding scene; and the **Cultural Demonstration Corner** hosts half-hearted exhibitions of Malay games and crafts. If you give these attractions a miss, you're left with the village's **shops**, selling batik,

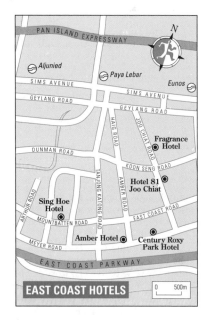

kites, spinning tops, bird cages and textiles, and the evening **food court** with free cultural performances on Saturday and Sunday nights.

Joo Chiat Road

As you walk south down Joo Chiat Road from Geylang Road, you'll have to negotiate the piles of merchandise that spill out of shophouses and onto the pavement. Cane and wood furniture clutters the Phoon Fang Cheong shop at no. 175, while the store at no. 86 specializes in Chinese religious paraphernalia. Of the buildings, none is as magnificent as the immaculate **Peranakan shophouse** on Koon Seng Road (on your left about halfway down Joo Chiat Road), where painstaking work has restored the multicoloured facades, eaves and mouldings. In the **Joo Chiat Complex** at the northern end of the road, textile merchants drape their wares on any available floor and wall space, transforming the drab interior. More market than shopping centre, it's a prime destination for anyone interested in buying cheap silk, batik, rugs or muslin.

Changi Prison

Infamous **Changi Prison** was the site of a World War II POW camp in which Japanese jailers subjected Allied prisoners to the harshest of treatment. The prison itself is still in use (drug offenders are periodically executed here), and its terrible past is marked in the hugely moving **Changi Museum** (daily 9.30am–4pm; free; ☎62142451, ⓦwww.changimuseum.com), just up the road.

A recent appeal for artefacts by the Singapore Tourist Board to Australian veterans' associations mustered a Samurai sword, a prisoner's chipped enamel mug, ration cards, a Nippon-Go primer and assorted other relics. In truth, though, the museum's power lies more in the many cruelties it portrays, than in the miscellanies it has amassed. Sketches, photographs and information boards plot the Japanese occupation of Singapore and the fate of the soldiers and civilians subsequently incarcerated in camps around the Changi area. Most movingly of all, though, is the board of remembrance, where children, wives and compatriots have pinned messages to the dead.

Novelist James Clavell was a young British artillery officer in Singapore at the time of the Japanese invasion; later he drew on his own experience of the "obscene forbidding prison" at Changi in writing *King Rat*, never forgetting that in the cells of the prison camp, " ... the stench was nauseating. Stench from rotten bodies. Stench from a generation of confined human bodies." You can get the merest sense of what Clavell means by entering the Changi Cell, a dark, stuffy alleyway that approximates the cramped confinement suffered by POWs, and in which the voices of former POWs recall enduring the "howling, crying, shouting" of fellow inmates being tortured in the middle of the night.

Clavell's recollections are borne out by the selection of photos by **George Aspinall**, in a cabinet at the entrance to the museum. Aspinall, then a young Australian trooper, recorded the appalling living conditions and illnesses suffered by POWs in Malaya and Thailand during the occupation using a folding Kodak 2 camera, later developing his shots with a stock of processing materials which he found while working on a labour gang in Singapore's docks.

The museum's **gallery** section showcases the work of various prison artists, among them W.R.M. Haxworth, who produced over 400 paintings and sketches during his internment. Haxworth's tongue-in-cheek sketches of daily Changi life reveal the dry sense of humour and stiff upper lips that sustained internees in the face of adversity. One, entitled "Changi Comforts", depicts a variety of rickety stools, some fruit and a battered biscuit tin. Another sketch, in which a character holds up two shirts, one white and one black, is entitled "White and Changi white". Elsewhere, there are full-scale reproductions of the murals of Stanley Warren, who used camouflage paint, crushed snooker chalk and aircraft paints smuggled in by fellow POWs to paint Bible scenes on a Changi chapel wall.

Outside in a courtyard is a replica of a simple wooden chapel, typical of those erected in Singapore's wartime camps; the brass cross on its altar was crafted from spent ammunition casings, while its walls carry more poignant messages of remembrance penned by visiting former POWs and relatives.

Journey's end is at the **museum shop**, where a video screen plays footage of the Japanese attack and the living conditions in Changi. On a lighter note, among the war-related books stocked in the shop is *The Happiness Box*, the first copy of which was written, illustrated and bound by POWs in Changi in 1942 as a Christmas present for children in the prison. The Japanese became suspicious of the POWs' motives when they noticed one of the book's central characters was called Winston, but it was buried in the prison grounds before it could be confiscated, and only recovered after the war had ended.

To **get to** the museum, take bus #2 from Chinatown or Victoria Street; alternatively, you could take the MRT to Tanah Merah station, and pick up the #2 there.

Changi Village

There's little to bring you out to sleepy **CHANGI VILLAGE**, ten minutes further on from the prison on bus #2, save to catch a boat from **Changi Point**, behind the bus terminal, for Pulau Ubin (see p.97) or for the coast of Johor in Malaysia (see "Departure", p.28). The left-hand jetty is for Ubin, the right-hand one for bumboats to Johor.

A stroll over the footbridge to the right of the two jetties takes you to **Changi Beach**, the execution site of many thousands of Singaporean civilians by Japanese soldiers during World War II. As a beach it wins few prizes – apart from its casuarinas and palms. Its most pleasant aspect is its view: to your left as you look out to sea is Pulau Ubin, while slightly to the right is the island of Tekong (a military zone), behind which you can see a hill on mainland Malaysia. In the water you'll see *kelongs* (large fish traps), and boats galore, from bumboats to supertankers. Changi Village Road, the village's main drag, has a growing number of decent restaurants and a few bars, or try the hawker centre near the bus terminal.

Pulau Ubin

PULAU UBIN, 2km offshore, gives visitors a pretty good idea of what Singapore would have been like fifty years ago. A lazy backwater tucked into the Straits of Johor, it's a great place to come if you're tired of shops, high-rises and traffic. It's almost worth coming for the ten-minute boat trip alone, made in an old, oil-stained bumboat ($2 each way) that chugs noisily across Serangoon Harbour, belching fumes all the way. Boats depart from Changi Point throughout the day from 6am onwards, leaving whenever they are full. The last boat back to Changi leaves as late as 10pm, if there's a demand, but plan to be at the jetty by 8.30pm at the latest, just in case.

Boats dock at the pier in **Ubin Village**, where palm trees slope and Malay stilt houses teeter over a sludgy mangrove beach that's stippled with the remains of collapsed, rotting jetties. Bear left from the jetty, and you'll soon hit the village square – but before that, swing by the **information kiosk** (daily 8.30am–5pm) to the right of the jetty for an island map.

The main road into the village is lined with scores of battered old mopeds, locals sit around, watching the day take its course, roosters run free in the dirt and dogs bask under the hot sun. The best, and most enjoyable, way to explore the dirt tracks of Ubin is by mountain bike. A cluster of **bike rental shops** operates along the jetty road, charging $6–15 for a day's rental, depending upon the bike and the season (it's most expensive during school holidays). A labyrinthine network of tracks veins Ubin, but it's only a small island (just 7km by 2km) and all roads are well signposted, so you won't get lost. As you go, look out for the monitor lizards, long-tailed macaques, lizards, butterflies, kites and eagles that inhabit Ubin, and listen for the distinctive rattle-buzz of cicadas.

The **hall** on the left flank of the square is used periodically for Chinese opera, ceremonial occasions and other Ubin functions. Opposite it is a tiny, fiery-red Chinese temple. Bear left past the hall until you come to a basketball court, where a left turn takes you to the west of the island and a right turn to the east.

Taking the left turn **west**, after about five minutes you'll come to an impressively deep quarry, from which granite was taken to build the causeway linking Singapore to Johor Bahru – Ubin is the Malay word for granite. Don't swim in this or any other Ubin quarry, however tempting it might be: the government has erected signs warning of hefty fines for doing so. A right turn after the first bridge you cross brings you to a peaceful lean-to **Chinese temple** fronted by wind chimes, a shrine holding three colourful figurines of tigers and a pool of carp, and shielded from the surrounding mangrove by a pretty lily-pad pond.

Further north along the track, over a second bridge and down a right turn marked Jalan Wat Siam, is a rather incongruous **Thai Buddhist Temple** fronted by two big, polished wooden elephants, complete with portraits of the king and queen of Thailand, and a bookcase full of Thai books. Pictures telling the story of the life of Buddha ring the inner walls of the temple, along with images of various Buddhists hells – the most disturbing of which depicts demons pouring boiling liquid down the mouths of "those who always drink liquor". Boonrai, the temple's head monk, holds free **meditation classes** every Saturday and Sunday; call ☎65423468 to book yourself into a class.

En route to the Thai Temple you'll pass the *Ubin Lagoon Resort* (see p.122), whose myriad outward-bound facilities can be used by non-guests, upon payment of a day rate. The Outward Bound Singapore centre beyond the Thai temple is, however, out of bounds.

Biking **east** from the basketball court takes you past the prawn and fish farms, rubber trees and raised kampung houses of the centre and eastern side of Ubin. **Noordin Beach**, at the top of the island, offers an unprepossessing but smart enough patch of sand, with good views across the Johor Straits to southern Malaysia. Further east, towards **Kampong Melayu**, are some beautifully maintained and brightly painted examples of kampung-style stilt houses. Beyond the village, **Tanjong Chek Jawa**, the far eastern tip of the island, constitutes Ubin's most pristine patch of mangrove; call the information kiosk on ☎65024108 to pre-arrange a customized guided tour of the mudskippers, crabs, seabirds and other wildlife here; reckon on paying around $60 for a three-hour tour.

You'll happen upon the odd drinks stop as you bike around Ubin. For **food**, there's a restaurant (daily 8am–10pm) at *Ubin Lagoon Resort*. Otherwise, of the several eating options in the village, the best bets are the *Sin Lam Huat* for its chilli crab and kampung chicken dishes, or the Malay coffee shop beside the jetty, which knocks out curries, noodles and *rendangs*.

Escape Theme Park

With kids in tow, you'll be glad of the **Escape Theme Park** (Mon & Wed–Fri 4–10pm, Sat & Sun 10am–10pm; adults $16, children $8 – includes all rides and one go-kart ride), west of Changi Village at 1 Pasir Ris Close. Singapore's largest theme park, it boasts fifteen fairground-style rides, among them the Cadbury Inverter, the Daytona Multi-tier Go Kart and Asia's highest flume ride, Wet & Wild. Clowns wander the park's byways, offering light relief while you queue for rides; and in the central pavilion there are oodles of games, galleries and food outlets. From Pasir Ris, you'll need to hop on bus #354.

Western Singapore

Since the government's industrialization programme began in the late 1960s, far **western Singapore** has become the manufacturing heart of the state, and today thousands of companies occupy units within the towns of Jurong and Tuas. Manufacturing is the backbone of Singapore's economic success – the state currently produces more than half the world's hard disk drives, for example. Despite this saturation, much of the western region – developed from former swampland and wasteland – remains remarkably verdant. Surprisingly, given the industrial surroundings, several major tourist attractions are located here, including **Haw Par Villa**, as garish a theme park as you'll ever set eyes on, and – the pick of the bunch – fascinating **Jurong BirdPark**. Slightly further east, the **Singapore Science Centre** is packed with imaginative and informative exhibitions, and is not to be missed if you've got kids to entertain, while further west – and not to be missed if you've got adults to entertain – is the **Tiger Brewery**. Just west of Chinatown is the district of **Telok Blangah**, once the seat of Singapore's *temenggong* or chieftain, and still dominated by Mount Faber, as well as the **World Trade Centre**, from where cable cars, boats and buses make for Sentosa (see p.106). All of these places are easily reached from the city centre, using either buses or the MRT.

The World Trade Centre and Mount Faber

A twenty-minute walk west of Chinatown is the district of **Telok Blangah**, home to Singapore's **World Trade Centre**, a shopping centre-cum-marine terminal from where boats depart for Indonesia's Riau Archipelago, and from which cable cars rock across the skyline, on their way to and from **Mount Faber** and across to Sentosa Island (see p.106). The WTC, the adjacent cruise centre, Cable Car Towers and surrounding Maritime Square are currently undergoing a major revamp. Upon completion in 2006, **The HarbourFront** will boast world-class cruise ship facilities, restaurants, office space and the largest single shopping centre in Singapore – in local parlance, it will be a "business and lifestyle hub".

Mount Faber (hillock would be a better word), 600m north of the WTC, commands fine views of Keppel Harbour and central Singapore to the northeast, which are even more impressive at night when the city is lit up. Originally called Telok Blangah, the mount was renamed in 1845 after government engineer Captain Charles Edward Faber. It's a long, steep walk from Telok Blangah Road up to the top of Mount Faber, and it's better to take the **cable car** from the World Trade Centre complex (daily 8.30am–9pm; $6.90 return, children $3.90 for up to 4 stations; $15, children $8 for glass cabin). As well as the WTC,

WESTERN SINGAPORE

RESTAURANTS			
Alkaff Mansion	D	Samy's	B
Cha Cha Cha	C	Sushi Tei	C
Original Sin	C	Telok Blangah	E
Pho Hoa	A	Union Farm	C

Boats to Indonesia

Singapore Discovery Centre & Tiger Brewery

the cable car has two more stations, at the top of Mount Faber and across the water on Sentosa. A four-station ticket lets you ride from the MTC to Mount Faber, back down to the WTC, over to Sentosa and then back again. An accident in 1983, when a ship's mast clipped the cables on which the cars are suspended, cost seven passengers their lives, but today laser eyes ensure that history won't repeat itself. There's a strong souvenir shop presence at the top, though you can escape this by moving away from the area immediately around the cable car station and up into the palms, bougainvilleas and rhododendrons of **Mount Faber Park**.

In the early days of colonial rule, Temenggong Abdul Rahman played prime minister to Sultan Hussein Shah's president, and his signature graced the treaty authorizing the East India Company to operate out of Singapore. All that's left of his settlement on the southern slopes of Mount Faber is its pillared mosque – the **State of Johor Mosque** – and, behind that, a small Malay cemetery and a portion of the brickwork that once housed the *temenggong*'s baths.

Haw Par Villa

As an entertaining exercise in bad taste, **Haw Par Villa** (daily 9am–7pm; free) has few equals. Located 7km from the downtown area at 262 Pasir Panjang Road, it describes itself as a "historical theme park founded on Chinese legends and values", for which read a gaudy, gory parade of over a thousand grotesque statues. Previously known as Tiger Balm Gardens, the park now takes its name from its original owners, the Aw brothers, Boon Haw and Boon Par, who made a fortune early last century selling Tiger Balm – a cure-all unction created by their father. When the British government introduced licensing requirements for the possession of large animals, the private zoo that the brothers maintained on their estate here was closed down and replaced by statues.

The rides, theatre shows and multimedia attractions that were added a few years back to broaden the appeal of the place actually did no such thing. All have now been closed, leaving only the statues for which the park is famous. These statues feature characters and creatures from Chinese legend and religion, Fu Lu Shou, Confucius and the Laughing Buddha among them, as well as a fantastical menagerie of snakes, dragons, elephants, kissing locusts, monkeys and crabs with women's heads.

The best – and most gruesome – series of statues lies in the **Ten Courts of Hell** exhibit, whose explanation of the Buddhist belief in punishment for sins and reincarnation is not for the faint-hearted. Accessed through the open mouth of a huge "walk-in" dragon, the statues depict sinners undergoing a ghastly range of tortures meted out by hideous, leering demons, before being wiped of all memory in the Pavilion of Forgetfulness and sent back to earth to have another stab at Godliness. Prostitutes are shown drowned in pools of blood, drug addicts tied to a red-hot copper pillar, thieves and gamblers frozen into blocks of ice and moneylenders who charge exorbitant interest rates thrown onto a hill of knives. If you are thinking of cracking the spine on this guidebook, bear in mind that being sawn in two is the penalty for the misuse of books.

Elsewhere, another series of statues retells the classic Chinese legend of the monk Xuanzang's **Journey into the West** in search of Buddhist scriptures. The trials and tribulations that beset the monk and his disciples, featuring such characters as the Spider Women, the Monkey Goad and the Scarlet Child, are all colourfully depicted.

It's a shame that much of the explanatory signage in front of Haw Par Villa's statues has weathered away to illegibility. Until these signs are renovated,

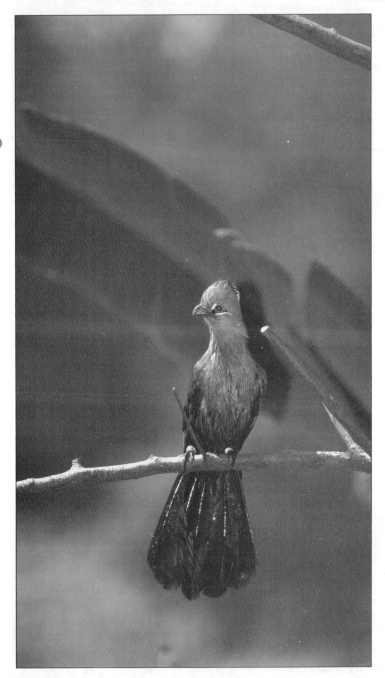

△ Jurong BirdPark

Spirits (Fri & Sat 7.30pm, $12; T68722003), a torch-lit, "polterguided" tour of the park's more chilling tales, offers the best way to familiarize yourself with the basics of Chinese legend.

To **get to** Haw Par Villa, travel to Buona Vista MRT, then hop on bus #200; or take bus #51 or #143.

Reflections at Bukit Chandu

The 1st and 2nd Battalion of the Malay Regiment's defence of Pasir Panjang against the Japanese, in 1942, is remembered at **Reflections at Bukit Chandu** (Tues–Sun 9am–5pm; free), a low-key attraction 3km west of Telok Blangah, at 31K Pepys Road. Facing some 13,000 advancing Japanese soldiers, the battalions chose to fight to the death rather than retreat. Wordily billed as a "World War II interpretive centre", Reflections uses exhibits and photographs to tell their story, and to track the unsuccessful defence of Malaya. Visitors experience the sounds of battle, the cold weight of a cast-iron helmet and a rifle, and the fear and claustrophobia of watch duty in a pillbox. However, this is no celebration of war. Rather, the emphasis is upon sombre meditation, with elements such as the Well of Reflections and the Pool of Reflections encouraging visitors to ponder the purpose of war and to muse over the terrible loss of life that occurred in this part of Singapore.

Holland Village

Holland Village was previously home to some of the British soldiers based in Singapore and has now developed into an expat stronghold, with a whole row of Western restaurants and shops. The **Holland Road Shopping Centre** at 211 Holland Avenue is the place to head for if you want to purchase Asian art, crafts or textiles: there are shops on two levels where you can buy anything from an Indian pram to a Chinese opium pipe, while newsagents, cobblers and key-cutters ply their trade outside. The small road alongside the shopping centre is called Lorong Liput, and off it is Lorong Mambong, home to a thriving restaurant scene and to **craft shops** that specialize in ceramic elephants, dragon pots, porcelain, rattan and bamboo products. **Pasar Holland**, opposite the shops, is a small, tumbledown market selling fruit, flowers, fish and meat, as well as housing a handful of hawker stalls. Details of arts and crafts outlets are given on pp.164–167. The nearest **MRT station** to Holland Village is Buona Vista, just a short walk away; bus #7 from Orchard Boulevard also stops here.

Jurong Lake and around

Several tourist destinations are dotted around the environs of tranquil **Jurong Lake**, about 4km northwest of the new town of Clementi. You're far likelier to want to come out this way if you've got children in tow.

Singapore Science Centre

At the **Singapore Science Centre** (Tues–Sun 10am–6pm; $6, children $3; T64252500, W www.science.edu.sg), situated southwest of tranquil Jurong Lake, a broad range of exhibition galleries hold over 850 hands-on exhibits designed to inject interest into even the most impenetrable scientific principles. The majority of the centre's visitors are local schoolchildren, who sweep around the galleries in vast, deafening waves, frantically trying out each interactive display. Exhibitions focusing on aviation, space science, ecology, IT, biotechnology and other disciplines allow you to experience sight through an insect's eyes, to write in Braille, and to see a thermal heat reflection of yourself. The **Omni-Theatre** (shows hourly, Tues–Sun 10am–8pm; $10, children $5; call ☎64252500 for details of current movie), within the centre's grounds, features heart-stopping movies about science, space, history and adventure sports shown, planetarium-style, on a huge dome screen. To **get out here** take the MRT to Jurong East station, then transfer to bus #335, or brave the ten-minute walk.

Snow City

High-tech machines at **Snow City** (Tues–Sun 9am–8.30pm, $8, Sat & Sun $12, including loan of jackets and boots; ☎63371511, ⓦwww.snowcity.com.sg) let it snow twelve months a year in one corner of equatorial Singapore. Don't come expecting an Alpine piste, though: the slope at this indoor centre, one stop north of the Science Centre on bus #335, on 21 Jurong Town Hall Road, is just 60m long and less than three storeys high, meaning that there's little scope for meaningful skiing or snowboarding – though there is provision for each. Nevertheless, the complex offers an invigorating alternative to the hot sun, its constant temperature of -5 degrees centigrade setting it on a par with most Singaporean cinemas. Snow City is an offshoot of the Singapore Science Centre, and as such has an educational, as well as a recreational slant, in the shape of a very worthy cold-temperature science exhibition. However, faced with the chance to explore an igloo, make snowmen, engage in snow-gun combat and even come face to face with the Abominable Snowman, kids are likely to eschew extracurricular studies.

The Chinese and Japanese gardens

The **Chinese and Japanese gardens** (daily 6am–7pm; free), by Jurong Lake, just a hop and a skip from Chinese Garden MRT, defy categorization – too far out to visit for just a sit down in the park and too dull to be a fully fledged tourist attraction. In the **Chinese Garden**, pagodas, pavilions, bridges, arches and weeping willows attempt to capture the style of Beijing's Summer Palace – and fail. That said, if you're out this way, the **Bonzai Garden** ($5, children $3), with its 1000-plus miniature trees, is worth a look. Come at the weekend, and you should be prepared to be confronted by hordes of newlyweds scouring the garden for a decent photo opportunity. The Chinese Garden is best explored on the day of the annual **Moon Cake Festival** (see p.161), when it stays open late so that children can parade with their lanterns after dark.

Walking across the impressive, 65-metre Bridge of Double Beauty takes you to the **Japanese Garden** (or Seiwaen, meaning "Garden of Tranquillity"), whose wooden bridges, carp ponds, pebble footpaths and stone lanterns do much to help you forget the awful Formica chairs and tables in the central pavilion.

Jurong BirdPark

The **Jurong BirdPark** (daily 8am–6pm; $12.10, children $5.05; ☎62650022, ⓦwww.birdpark.com.sg) on Jalan Ahmad Ibrahim contains more than eight thousand birds from over six hundred species, ranging from Antarctic penguins to New Zealand kiwis, making it one of the world's largest bird collections, and the biggest in Southeast Asia. A ride on the **Panorail** (9am–5.30pm; $2.50, children $1) is a good way to get your bearings; the bullet-shaped monorail skims over, past or through all the main exhibits, with a running commentary pointing out the attractions.

Be sure at least to catch the **Waterfall Aviary**, which allows visitors to walk amongst 1500 free-flying birds in a specially created tropical rainforest, dominated by a thirty-metre-high waterfall. Other exhibits to seek out are the colourful **Southeast Asian Birds** (a tropical thunderstorm is simulated daily at noon), featuring the Luzon Bleeding Heart Pigeon, which looks like it's just walked off the set of *Reservoir Dogs*; the **Penguin Parade** (feeding times 10.30am & 3.30pm); and the **World of Darkness**, a fascinating exhibit which swaps day for night with the aid of a system of reversed lighting, in order that its cute collection of nocturnal residents doesn't snooze throughout the park's opening hours. There are **bird shows** throughout the day, the best of which is undoubtedly the "Kings of the Skies" show (4pm) – a *tour de force* of speed flying by trained eagles, hawks and falcons. Entrance to this, and to the similar "World of Hawks" show (10am) and "All Star Bird Show" (11am & 3pm) is free. Back at the entrance complex you'll find snacks and drinks for sale. **Getting to** the park involves MRT-ing to Boon Lay station, then transferring to bus #194 or #251.

The Singapore Discovery Centre and Tiger Brewery

The hands-on **Singapore Discovery Centre** (Tues–Fri 9am–7pm; $9, children $5; ☎67926188, ⓦwww.sdc.com.sg), at 510 Upper Jurong Road, is mainly geared towards local school parties. The emphasis is on Singapore's history, technological achievements and national defences, but there are exhibits with broader appeal, such as **motion simulator** rides that let you experience flying a jet or driving a tank, and a clutch of virtual reality games. In the grounds outside the centre are a cluster of military vehicles of varying vintages, and an imaginative playground complete with its own maze. To reach the Singapore Discovery Centre, travel to Boon Lay MRT station and then transfer to bus #193.

Three kilometres due west of the Discovery Centre, on the approach road that links with Malaysia, is the home of one of Singapore's best-liked exports. **Tiger Beer**, now the flagship brew of the Asia Pacific Breweries Limited, has been brewed in Singapore since 1931, though back then its home was the Malayan Breweries on Alexandra Road, where it was developed with help from Heineken. A few years later, the establishment of Archipelago Brewery by German giants Beck's seemed to set the scene for a Singaporean **beer war**, especially when Tiger's new rival, Anchor Beer, was priced slightly lower. But in 1941, Archipelago was bought out by Malayan Breweries, since when the organization has gone from strength to strength, moving in May 1990 into new holdings in Tuas, and changing its name to reflect "the new international role the company has assumed", although it's still commonly known as the Tiger Brewery.

Today, the tiger beneath a palm tree that adorns the label on every bottle of Tiger Beer can be seen in ads across the state. Anthony Burgess borrowed *Time for a Tiger*, the original slogan for the beer, for the title of his debut novel. As the embattled, debt-ridden police-lieutenant, Nabby Adams, gulps down another beer, " . . . fresh blood flowed through his arteries, the electric light seemed brighter, what were a few bills anyway?"

A **tour** of the brewery (Mon–Fri 9.30am, 11am, 2.30pm & 5.30pm, free; ☎68603007, ⓦwww.tigerbeer.com) is made up of three component parts, arranged in rising order of appeal: first comes a film show which fills visitors in on the history of the setup; next a walk through the space-age brewing, bottling and canning halls; and finally an hour or two's free drinking in the company's own bar – Nabby would have approved. You need at least ten people in the party, though all is not lost if you are travelling alone – phone up, and if there's a tour already arranged, ask to tag along. To get to the brewery get off at Boon Lay MRT, then take bus #192.

8

Sentosa and the southern isles

M any little **islands** stud the waters immediately south of Singapore. Some, like Pulau Bukom, are owned by petrochemical companies and are off-limits to tourists. Three others, **Sentosa**, **St John's** and **Kusu**, are served by ferries and can be visited without difficulty, though their accessibility has geared them very much to tourism. If you crave a more secluded spot, you'll have to charter a bumboat to one of the **more remote islands** from the World Trade Centre or Clifford Pier (see p.32 for details) or head for Pulau Ubin, off Singapore's east coast (see p.97).

Sentosa

Given the rampant development that over the past two decades has transformed **Sentosa** (tourist info line: ☎1800-736 8672, ⓦwww.sentosa.com.sg) into the most developed of Singapore's southern islands, it's ironic that its name means "tranquillity" in Malay. Sentosa has come a long way since World War II, when it was a British military base known as Pulau Blakang Mati, or the "Island of Death Behind". Today, promoted for its beaches, sports facilities, hotels and attractions, and ringed by a speeding monorail, it's a contrived but enjoyable experience. The island is linked to the mainland by a five-hundred-metre causeway and a necklace of cable cars.

Sentosa is big business: millions of visitors descend upon this tiny island, which measures just 3km by 1km, every year. Nevertheless you'll hear mixed reports of the place around Singapore. Ultimately, it's as enjoyable as you make it; there's certainly plenty to do (though few of the attractions would make the grade at Disneyland), so much so that it's a good idea to arrive early, with a clear plan of action. Taking a round trip on the trans-island monorail on arrival helps you get your bearings. **Admission** to several attractions is included in the Sentosa entry ticket (see "Practicalities" below), though for the more popular attractions a further charge is levied. It's wise to avoid coming at the weekend, or on public holidays.

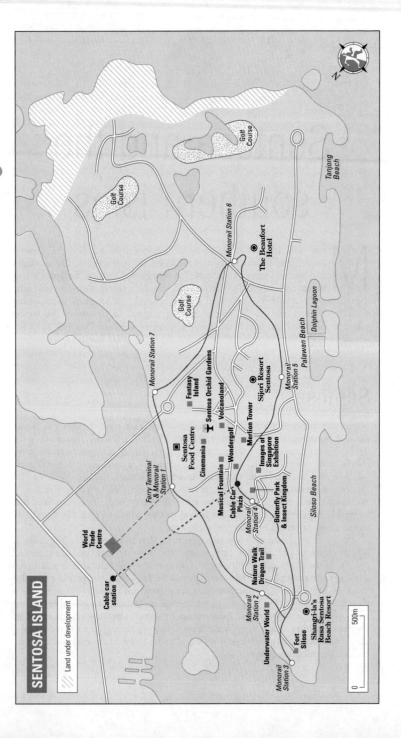

SENTOSA ISLAND

Land under development

N

World Trade Centre

Cable car station

Ferry Terminal & Monorail Station 1

Monorail Station 7

Monorail Station 2

Underwater World

Fort Siloso

Shangri-la's Rasa Sentosa Beach Resort

Monorail Station 3

Nature Walk
Dragon Trail

Monorail Station 4

Musical Fountain

Cable Car Plaza

Butterfly Park & Insect Kingdom

Images of Singapore Exhibition

Sentosa Food Centre

Cinemania

Wondergolf

Fantasy Island

Sentosa Orchid Gardens

Volcanoland

Merlion Tower

Sijori Resort Sentosa

Monorail Station 6

The Beaufort Hotel

Monorail Station 5

Siloso Beach

Palawan Beach

Dolphin Lagoon

Tanjong Beach

Golf Course

Golf Course

Golf Course

0   500m

Sentosa's main attractions

Two attractions outshine all others on Sentosa. At the **Underwater World** (daily 9am–9pm; $17, children $11), near monorail station #2, a moving walk-way carries you the length of a hundred-metre acrylic tunnel that snakes through two large tanks: sharks lurk menacingly on all sides, huge stingrays drape themselves languidly above you, and immense shoals of gaily coloured fish dart to and fro. This may not sound all that exciting, but the sensation of being engulfed by sea life – there are more than 2500 fishes here – is a breath-taking one, and the nearest you'll get to the ocean floor without a wet suit. Of particular interest is the Deadly Corridor, which is home to electric eels, pira-nha and stonefish. If that isn't enough to get the adrenaline pumping, there's even the chance to dive with the sharks by pre-arrangement; call ☎62750030 for more details. A **touchpool** beside the entrance allows you to pick up starfish and sea cucumbers – the latter rather like socks filled with wet sand – while beyond that is the **Marine Theatre** which screens educational films throughout the day.

The **Dolphin Lagoon** (daily 10.30am–6pm) is free with the Underwater World ticket, though located away on Sentosa's Central Beach; the marine acrobatics of its resident school of Indo-Pacific humpback dolphins are best viewed during one of the daily Meet the Dolphins sessions (Mon–Fri 11am, 1.30pm, 3.30pm & 5.30pm).

The other major-league attraction is the **Images of Singapore Exhibition** (daily 9am–9pm; $8, children $5), near monorail station #2. Here life-sized dioramas present the history and heritage of Singapore from its early days as a fourteenth-century trading post through to the surrender of the Japanese in 1945. Though some of the wax dummies look as if they've been pinched from clothes shop windows, the effect is fascinating. The highlight of the exhibition is the Surrender Chambers, where audiovisuals, videos, dioramas and artefacts combine to recount the events of World War II in Singapore. There are more wax dummies in the Festivals of Singapore gallery, this time dolled up in fes-tive costumes to represent Singapore's various ethnic celebrations.

A trip up to **Fort Siloso** (daily 9am–7pm; $5, children $3; monorail station #3) at the far western tip of the island, ties in nicely with a visit to the Surrender Chambers. The fort – actually a cluster of buildings and gun emplacements above a series of tunnels bored into the island – guarded Singapore's western approaches from the 1880s until 1956, but was rendered obsolete in 1942, when the Japanese moved down into Singapore from Malaysia. Today, the recorded voice of Battery Sergeant Major (BSM) Cooper talks you through a mock-up of a nineteenth-century barracks, complete with living quarters, laundry and assault course. After that, you can explore the com-plex's hefty gun emplacements and tunnels, and sit in on the Battle for Singapore, when British soldiers were forced to surrender to the Japanese.

Other attractions on Sentosa

The rest of Sentosa has lots of less interesting options. You might consider one of Sentosa's three newer attractions: **Cinemania** (daily 11am–8pm; $12.50 for two rides, children $8), whose state-of-the-art audiovisual systems and synchro-nized-motion seats combine to give the hair-raising feeling that you are moving through the film playing in front of you; **Volcanoland** (daily 11am–7pm; $12, children $6) with a half-hourly, simulated eruption and trip to the earth's core; or **Sijori WonderGolf** (daily 9am–9pm; $10, children $6), with 54 crazy holes.

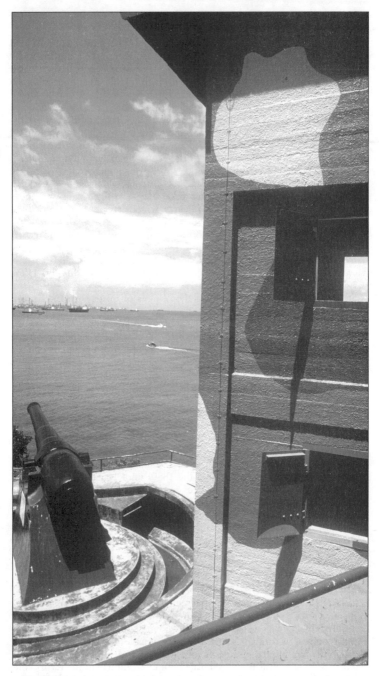

△ Fort at Sentosa

Otherwise, you could do worse than strolling in the elegant, scented grounds of the **Sentosa Orchid Gardens** (Mon–Fri 11am–7.30pm, Sat & Sun 11am–10pm; free), near monorail station #1. For something slightly more exciting head for the **Butterfly Park and Insect Kingdom Museum** (daily 9am–6.30pm; $10, children $6), near monorail station #5, which is stuffed with all sorts of creepy-crawlies, of which only the butterflies are alive; the beetles, bugs and scorpions are all mounted in display cases.

Musical Fountain

By 7pm, many of Sentosa's attractions are closed, but not so the **Musical Fountain** (shows at 5pm, 5.30pm, 7.40pm, 8.40pm, Sat & Sun also 9.30pm), which is either cute or appalling, depending on your point of view. The fountain dances along to such classics as the *1812 Overture*, with colourful lights, lasers and pyrotechnics adding to the effect. Overlooking the display is the **Merlion**, a 37-metre-high statue of Singapore's tourism totem that takes centre-stage in the shows. It's possible to walk up to the viewing decks at the top of the Merlion (9am–10pm; $3, children $2), from where there are great views of Singapore's harbour, skyline and surrounding islands.

Beaches on Sentosa

Probably the best option on Sentosa, after a trip on the monorail and a visit to one or two attractions, is to head for the three beaches, **Siloso**, **Palawan** and **Tanjong** on the southwestern coast. Created with thousands of cubic metres of imported white sand and scores of coconut palms, they offer canoes, surfboards and aqua-bikes for rent, as well as plain old deckchairs. The water here is great for swimming and Singapore does not demand the same modesty on its beaches as Malaysia, although topless and nude bathing are out. From Palawan Beach, a suspended rope bridge connects Sentosa with a tiny islet that's the southernmost part of continental Asia. In recent years, Singapore's annual Dragon Boat Festival (see p.160) has been held off Siloso Beach. There are also beach raves, Singapore-style, from time to time, which are advertised in the local press way in advance.

Sentosa Practicalities

Basic **admission** to Sentosa costs $2, though this doesn't include the cost of actually reaching the island. From the **World Trade Centre** at 1 Maritime Square (HarbourFront MRT station), **ferries** depart every twenty to thirty minutes (9.30am–10pm; $4.30 return including admission fee). However, the most spectacular route is by the **cable cars** (daily 8.30am–9pm) that travel on a loop between mainland Mount Faber (see p.99) and Sentosa. For the round trip from the WTC up to Mount Faber, across to Sentosa and back to the WTC, you'll pay $10.50 (children $5.90), including the admission fee.

Crossing the **bridge** to Sentosa costs nothing if you walk, though you still have to pay the admission fee to the island. Buses (Sun–Thurs 7am–11pm, Fri & Sat 7am–12.30am; $3, including admission fee), bound for Sentosa, depart from the WTC bus terminal and Tiong Bahru MRT station every ten to fifteen minutes.

Sentosa's basic admission fee gives unlimited rides on the **monorail** and the island's four **bus routes**. But the best way to get about is to **rent a bike** for the day ($5–10 an hour depending on the machine) from the kiosk beside the ferry terminal; tandems are also available.

The *Sentosa Food Centre* beside the ferry terminal is the cheapest of Sentosa's many **eating** options; otherwise, try the nearby *Steword's Riverboat* for Tex-Mex and Cajun dishes, or the **Tanjong Beach Muslim Café**, situated on the patch of land that divides Tanjong Beach from Palawan Beach. At the *SEA Village Restaurant*, near monorail station 7, there are reasonably priced Asian buffet lunches and dinners. Sentosa has three international-class **hotels**, cheaper chalets and limited camping possibilities (see p.122 for more details).

Kusu and St John's islands

Well kept and clean as they are, Sentosa's beaches do tend to get overcrowded and you may do better to head for either **St John's** or **Kusu** islands, which are 6km south of Singapore and connected to the mainland by a **ferry** from the WTC. Both islands have decent sand beaches, though the more interesting of the two is Kusu, also known as **Turtle Island**. Singaporean legend tells of a Chinese and a Malay sailor who were saved from drowning by a turtle that transformed itself into an island; a pool of turtles is still kept on Kusu. Another legend describes how an epidemic afflicting a ship moored off Kusu was banished by the god Tua Pek Kong. Whatever the truth in these tales, once a year during the ninth lunar month (usually in October or November), tens of thousands of Singaporean pilgrims descend upon the **Chinese temple** and **Malay shrine** a few minutes' walk from the jetty on Kusu, to pray for prosperity. The island is impossibly crowded during this time, but the rest of the year it offers a tranquil escape from the mainland. There is a modest cafeteria on St John's, but if you're going to Kusu it's wise to take a picnic.

Ferries (Mon–Sat 10am & 1.30pm, Sun 9am, 11am, 1, 3 & 5pm; $9, children $6) for Kusu and St John's depart from the WTC. Check the return times with the boatmen – or call ☎62750388 for current ferry times.

Other islands

Since no regular ferries run to any of Singapore's other southern islands, you'll have to **charter** a bumboat from Jardine Steps (beside the World Trade Centre) or from Clifford Pier. Boats take up to twelve passengers, and cost at least $40 an hour. Unless you rent a boat for the whole day, you must arrange to be picked up again. **Lazarus Island** and the attractive **Sister's Island**, which lie in the same cluster of isles as St John's and Kusu, are popular snorkelling and fishing haunts, as is **Pulau Hantu** ("Ghost Island" in Malay), 12km further west and under the shadow of Shell-owned Pulau Bukum. Most interesting of all, though, is **Pulau Seking**, 3 or 4km east of Hantu; here a handful of Malays continue to live in traditional stilt houses that teeter over the sea, their lifestyle almost untouched by the progress that has transformed the mainland. These islands are all very basic, so take a picnic and a day's supply of bottled water with you.

Listings

Listings

9 Accommodation 115

10 Eating 123

11 Nightlife 148

12 Entertainment and the arts................................155

13 Festivals...159

14 Shopping 163

15 Sports...171

16 Kids' Singapore 175

17 Directory 178

Accommodation

Accommodation in Singapore needn't take too big a bite out of your holiday budget; good deals abound if your expectations aren't too lofty or – at the budget end of the scale – if you don't mind sharing. Singapore's status as one of the main gateways to Southeast Asia means that occupancy rates at all levels of accommodation are permanently high. Even so, you shouldn't encounter too many difficulties in finding a room, and advance booking isn't really necessary unless your visit coincides with Chinese New Year or Hari Raya (see p.159).

The **Singapore Hotel Association** (Ⓦwww.sha.org.sg) has a booking counter at each of Changi airport's two terminals (Terminal One counter daily 7am–6am, except Fri 7am–11.30pm, ☎65426966; Terminal Two counter daily 7am–3am, except Mon 7am–11.30pm, ☎65459789) and will find you a room in the city for a $10 deposit that's deducted from your bill at the end of your stay, though they represent only Singapore's official hotels, all of which are listed in two free STB booklets, *Hotels Singapore* and *Budget Hotels Singapore*. Touts at the airport also hand out flyers advertising rooms in guesthouses and hostels. If you prefer to plan ahead, you might wish to book online through Ⓦwww.stayinsingapore.com or Ⓦwww.singaporehotelbooking.com.

The cheapest beds are in the communal **dormitories** of many of Singapore's resthouses, where you'll pay $10 or less a night. The next best deals are at **guesthouses**, most of which are situated in the Beach Road and Little India areas, with some south of the river, in Chinatown. Until recently, Singapore's classic guesthouse address was Bencoolen Street's Peony Mansion, where a cluster of establishments was shoehorned into several floors of a decrepit apartment building. A recent makeover of the Bencoolen area has seen most of its guesthouses closed down to make way for new hotels and commercial premises.

Guesthouses aren't nearly as cosy as their name suggests; at the $20–30 mark, rooms are tiny, bare, and divided by paper-thin partitions, toilets are shared and showers are cold. However, paying another $10–20 secures a bigger, air-con room, often including TV, laundry and cooking facilities, lockers and breakfast. Always check that everything works before you hand over any money. It's always worth asking for a discount, too, especially if you are staying a few days.

The appeal of Singapore's **Chinese-owned hotels**, similar in price to guesthouses, is their air of faded grandeur – some haven't changed in forty years. Sadly, faded grandeur is something the government frowns upon, with the result that there are precious few left. In more modern, **mid-range hotels**, a room for two with air-con, private bathroom and TV will set you back around $60–90 a night. From there, prices rise steadily, and at the top end of the scale Singapore boasts some extraordinarily opulent hotels, ranging from the colonial splendour of *Raffles* to the awesome spectacle of the *Swissôtel The Stamford*

Accommodation price codes

We've used the following **price codes** to denote the cheapest available room for two people. Prices are in Singapore dollars. Single occupancy should cost less than double, though this is not always the case. Some guesthouses provide dormitory beds, for which the individual price is given.

❶ under $25	❹ $60–100	❼ $200–300
❷ $25–40	❺ $100–150	❽ $300–400
❸ $40–60	❻ $150–200	❾ $400 and over

– until recently the world's tallest hotel. Though you'll find the greatest concentration of **upmarket hotels** around Orchard Road, most of the new breed of **boutique hotels** – which use antique furniture and fittings to create an air of Oriental nostalgia – are based in Chinatown.

Most mid-range and upmarket hotels in Singapore make no charge for **children** under 12 if they are occupying existing spare beds in rooms. However, if you require an extra bed to be put in your room, ten to fifteen percent of the room rate is usually charged. Cots are provided free.

Bencoolen Street and around

Central **Bencoolen Street** has long been the mainstay of Singapore's backpacker industry. Times are changing, though, and many of the decrepit buildings that once housed the lion's share of Singapore's budget guesthouses have already fallen to the demolition ball and been replaced by posher hotels. Peony Mansion, the classic Singapore crash pad, has survived up to now, but its days are surely numbered and guesthouse owners are fast deserting its warren of seedy halls and stairways.

Despite the changing nature of the area, however, you'll still find dorm beds and rooms as cheap as any in Singapore – at least for the time being. Bencoolen Street is a five-minute walk from **Dhoby Ghaut MRT station**. All the hotels in this section are keyed on the **map** on p.79.

Albert Court Hotel 180 Albert St ☎3393939, ☏63393252, ☻www.albertcourt.com.sg. This charmingly conceived boutique hotel, designed around the restaurants of lively Albert Court Mall, is just a short walk from both Bugis Village and Little India; rooms have all the standard embellishments. ❼

Bencoolen Hotel 47 Bencoolen St ☎63360822, ☻www.hotelbencoolen.com. With business facilities, laundry service, air-ticketing facilities, a modest rooftop spa pool and smart rooms with all mod cons, the friendly *Bencoolen* represents great value. ❹

City Bayview 30 Bencoolen St ☎63372882, ☏63382880, ☻www.bayviewintl.com.sg. A pleasing, recently renovated, mid-range hotel, with comfortable rooms, a compact rooftop swimming pool and a friendly, modern café. ❺

Hawaii Hostel 2nd floor, 171b Bencoolen St ☎63384187. Small, tidy enough, air-con rooms with breakfast included, as well as dorm beds for $10. ❷

Lee Boarding House 7th floor, Peony Mansion, 46–52 Bencoolen St ☎63383149. Peony Mansion's last remaining guesthouse, with bare but clean enough rooms, a breakfast area and laundry facilities. If you want a dorm you'll need to go to the *Hawaii Hostel* or one of the *Lee* branches on Beach Road (see opposite). ❷

South East Asia Hotel 190 Waterloo St ☎3382394, ☻www.seahotel.com.sg. Behind a jolly, yellow-and-white Fifties facade, spotless doubles with air-con, TV and phone for those yearning for a few creature comforts. Downstairs is a vegetarian restaurant (see p.137) serving Western breakfasts, and right next door is Singapore's liveliest Buddhist temple. ❹

Strand Hotel 25 Bencoolen St ☎63381866, ℱ63381330, ⩊www.strandhotel.com.sg. Excellent-value hotel with clean, welcoming rooms, a café serving Western and local dishes, and a variety of services. ❹

Waterloo Hostel 4th Floor, Catholic Centre Building, 55 Waterloo St ☎63366555, ℱ63362160, ⩊www.waterloohostel.com.sg. Catholic-run hostel, centrally located, spick and span, and boasting rooms with air-con, TV and phone. Complimentary breakfast thrown in. The mixed and single-sex dorms ($20) are as welcoming as any in Singapore. ❹

Beach Road to Victoria Street

A few blocks east of Bencoolen Street, **Beach Road** boasts a full range of accommodation options, from charismatic old Chinese hotels to swish, new, five-star affairs. What's more, you can brag about having stayed down the road from *Raffles Hotel* – or even in it – when you get home. All the hotels in this section are keyed on the **map** on p.79.

Ah Chew Hotel 496 North Bridge Rd ☎68370356. Simple but charismatic rooms with "Wild West" swing doors, crammed with period furniture, and run by T-shirted old men lounging on antique opium couches. There are also fan and air-con dorms ($8–12), and baggage storage and self-service laundry facilities. Try and get a room at the front of the building – despite its address, the *Ah Chew* is just around the corner from North Bridge Road, on buzzing Liang Seah Street. ❷

Aliwal Park Hotel 77 Aliwal St ☎62939022, ℱ62949022, ✉aliwal@starhub.net.sg. One of the few hotels in the Arab Street district, the *Aliwal* has spruce doubles with TV, air-con and attached bathrooms, at competitive prices. ❸

Beach Hotel 95 Beach Rd ☎63367712, ℱ63367713, ⩊www.beachhotel.com.sg. The Lee Empire's most salubrious address is professionally run and very tidy, though you'd expect a few more amenities for the price. ❹

Golden Landmark Hotel 390 Victoria St ☎62972828, ℱ62982038, ⩊www.goldenlandmark.com.sg. Very pleasant and well appointed, once you get past the dated shopping centre downstairs, and handy for Bugis MRT station and Arab Street. ❺

Intercontinental 80 Middle Rd ☎63387600, ℱ63387366, ⩊www.intercontinental.com. Smashing hotel within the thriving Bugis Junction development, convenient and sumptuously furnished, with business centre, swimming pool, health club and an array of excellent restaurants including *Pimai Thai* and *Olive Tree*. ❽

Lee Home Stay 3rd floor, 490a North Bridge Rd ☎63341608. Bare but adequate rooms and dorms ($10), whose rates include free flow of hot drinks – but no breakfast or hot showers. All rooms share common facilities. The rooftop terrace makes a pleasant place to relax. To enter, walk to the back of the curry house below, and up the stairs to your left. ❷

Lee Traveller's Club 6th floor, Fu Yuen Building, 75 Beach Rd ☎63395490. A bright and breezy common room overlooking Middle Road sets this place a cut above the other Lee addresses in the area. All rooms have air-con, but private facilities cost an extra $10. Laundry service is available. Dorm beds are $12. ❷

Metropole Hotel 41 Seah St ☎63363611, ℱ63393610, ⩊www.metrohotel.com. Friendly, great-value establishment, just across the road from *Raffles Hotel* and home to the recommended *Imperial Herbal Restaurant* (see p.136). ❺

New 7th Storey Hotel 229 Rochor Rd ☎63370251, ℱ63343550, ⩊www.nsshotel.com. Despite its rather old-fashioned exterior, this is a clean and characterful hotel with perfectly respectable rooms, all with TV. Rooms with bathrooms en suite are available, though the communal ones are fine. Booking online saves a few dollars; dorm beds are $17. ❹

Oxford Hotel 218 Queen St ☎63322222, ℱ63349633, ⩊www.oxfordhotel.com.sg. Terrific new 135-room hotel, centrally sited, well serviced, friendly and affordable; prices are inclusive of breakfast, Recommended. ❹

Plaza Parkroyal 7500 Beach Rd ☎62980011,

℗ 62963600, ⒲ www.plazapacifichotels.com.
Luxurious, eye-catching hotel whose
amenities include restaurants, and a business centre. Slightly off the beaten track,
though there is a free shuttle service into
town. ❼

Raffles Hotel 1 Beach Rd ⓣ 63371886,
℗ 63397650, ⒲ www.raffleshotel.com. The
flagship of Singapore's tourism industry,

Raffles takes shameless advantage of its
reputation: $25 buys you a Singapore Sling
and a glass to take home, while the souvenir shop stocks *Raffles* golf balls, socks
and cuddly tigers. Still, it's a beautiful
place, dotted with frangipani trees and
palms, and the suites (there are no rooms)
are as tasteful as you would expect at
these prices. See p.47 for more details. ❾

The Colonial District

There is a clutch of expensive hotels at the edges of the **Padang**, just north of
the Singapore River. Several of them, including the *Marina Mandarin* and
Oriental, stand on the reclaimed land that robbed Beach Road of its beach. All
the hotels in this section are keyed on the map on p.42.

Conrad Centennial Singapore 2 Temasek
Blvd ⓣ 63348888, ℗ 63339166, ⒲ www
.conradhotels.com. This relatively recent
arrival has elbowed its way into the very
top ranks of the island's hotels; all imagi-
nable comfort can be found within its
monolithic structure. ❽

Fullerton Hotel 1 Fullerton Sq, ⓣ 67338388,
℗ 67358388, ⒲ www.fullertonhotel.com. Chic,
harmonious rooms that show an awareness of the *Fullerton's* heritage. Luxury
extras include in-room Playstations, Bulgari
smellies, and Net access on the TVs. An
expensive treat. ❾

Marina Mandarin Hotel 6 Raffles Blvd
ⓣ 63383388, ℗ 68451001, ⒲ www.marina
-mandarin.com.sg. Top-flight hotel, architecturally interesting and affording great harbour
views; the atrium is particularly impressive. ❽

Oriental Singapore 5 Raffles Ave ⓣ 63380066,
℗ 63399537, ⒲ www.mandarinoriental.com.
Housed, like the *Marina Mandarin,* in
Marina Square (claimed to be Southeast
Asia's largest shopping centre and hotel
complex), the *Oriental* is one of

Singapore's priciest hotels, but with very
good reason. Rooms are exquisitely furnished, views out over Marina Bay and the
Theatres Project are breathtaking, and all
the luxuries you could want are on hand. ❾

Peninsular Excelsior Hotel 5 Coleman St
ⓣ 63372200, ℗ 63393847,
⒲ www.ytchotels.com.sg/peninsulasxcelsior.
Really two hotels merged together – hence
the name – this place is as handy for the
Financial District as for Orchard Road's
shopping centres. There are several food
outlets (best is the excellent *Annalakshmi*
Indian vegetarian restaurant), and a swimming pool whose glass walls abut the
Lobby Lounge. ❼

Swissôtel The Stamford 2 Stamford Rd
ⓣ 63388585, ℗ 63382862, ⒲ www.swissotel-
thestamford.com. Upper-floor rooms aren't
for those with vertigo, though the views are
as splendid as you'd expect from the
second-tallest hotel in the world. There are
1253 classy rooms here, oodles of restaurants and bars, and an MRT station downstairs. ❽

Orchard Road and around

Sumptuous hotels abound in and around **Orchard Road**; at all except a handful, you should be prepared to spend at least $80 a double. You can multiply
that figure by five or six, if you decide to treat yourself. All the hotels in this
section are keyed on the map on pp.54–55.

The Elizabeth 24 Mount Elizabeth ⓣ 67381188,
℗ 67323866, ⒲ www.theelizabeth.com. Within
its toy-town exterior, this boutique hotel
oozes panache; delightful and well-

appointed rooms. ❼

Garden Hotel 14 Balmoral Rd ⓣ 62353344,
℗ 62359730, Ⓔ garden@pacific.net.sg. A standard hotel with attractive rooms, a ten-

minute walk north of Orchard Road. **6**

Goodwood Park Hotel 22 Scotts Rd
☎67377411, ☏67328558, ⓦwww.goodwood-parkhotel.com.sg. This opulent hotel may
remind you of *Raffles* – both were designed
by the same architect. The building has a
long history (see p.56), but it's still a study
in elegance, its arching facades fronting
exquisitely appointed rooms. **9**

Hilton Singapore 581 Orchard Rd ☎67372233,
☏67322917, ⓦwww.hilton.com. Situated in
the middle of Orchard Road, a gargantuan
slab of a hotel with every conceivable
facility. **8**

Holiday Inn Park View 11 Cavenagh Rd
☎67338333, ☏67344593, ⓦwww.singapore
.holiday-inn.com. Guests of this smart hotel with
all the trimmings are next-door neighbours of
Singapore's president for the duration of their
stay – the palace is just across the road. **7**

Lloyd's Inn 2 Lloyd Rd ☎67377309,
☏67377847, ⓦwww.lloydinn.com. Motel-style
building boasting attractive rooms and a
fine location, just five minutes from Orchard
Road. **4**

Meritus Mandarin Hotel 333 Orchard Rd
☎67374411 ☏67322361, ⓦwww.mandarin-singapore.com.sg. Every luxury you could
hope for; even if you don't stay, it's worth
taking a trip up to the top-floor bar-restaurant for its magnificent view of central
Singapore. **8**

Metropolitan Y 60 Stevens Rd ☎67377755
☏62355528, ⓦwww.mymca.org.sg. Not as
central as the *Y* on Orchard Road, but perfectly adequate rooms with air-con, bathroom, TV and minibar, and suitable for travellers in wheelchairs. **4**

New Sandy's Place 3c Sarkies Rd
☎67341431, ☏67388580,
ⓦwww.geocities.com/sandysplacesingapore/index/htm. Rooms are all very tidy, if a touch
overpriced in this friendly, laid-back place,
set across a field from Newton MRT.
Expect to pay $15 above the basic rate for
air-con. Prices include a tropical fruit
breakfast and free flow of hot drinks. It's
best to phone ahead. **3**

The Regent Singapore 1 Cuscaden Rd
☎67338888, ☏67328838, ⓦwww

.regenthotels.com. At the western end of
Orchard Road, the elegant rooms of this
sumptuous hotel are a short stroll from the
Botanic Gardens. **8**

Shangri-La Hotel 22 Orange Grove Rd
☎67373644, ☏67373257, ⓦwww.shangri-la.com. Top-flight hotel whose 700-plus
rooms are set in six hectares of land-scaped greenery, only five minutes from
Orchard Road. Choose from the business
wing, or the more holidaymaker
-oriented wing, which overlooks the free-form pool. **9**

Singapore Marriott Hotel 320 Orchard Rd
☎67355800, ☏67359800, ⓦwww.marriotthotels.com/SINDT. A superior hotel and a
Singapore landmark, housed in a 33-storey, pagoda-style building next door to
C.K. Tangs Department Store. **8**

Sloane Court Hotel 17 Balmoral Rd
☎62353311, ☏67339041, ⓔsloane@singnet
.com.sg. As close to a Tudor house as you
get in Singapore, the *Sloane Court* is
tucked away in a prime residential area,
near Newton MRT. Rooms are cosy and
well appointed. **4**

Hotel Supreme 15 Kramat Rd ☎67378333,
☏67337404, ⓔsupremeh@starhub.net.sg. A
great-value budget hotel well placed at the
eastern end of Orchard Road, offering
laundry and room service along with many
other facilities. **4**

YMCA International House 1 Orchard Rd
☎63366000, ☏63373140, ⓦwww.ymca.org.sg.
Smack bang in the middle of town, and
looking all the jollier for a recent lick of paint,
the *Y* offers plush but overpriced rooms,
excellent sports facilities (including rooftop
pool) and free room service from the
McDonald's downstairs. Dorm beds ($25)
are the most expensive in town, though. Bus
#36 from the airport stops right outside. **4**

YWCA Fort Canning Lodge 6 Fort Canning Rd
☎63384222, ☏63374222, ⓦwww.ywcafclodge
.org.sg. Not women-only, as you might
imagine, but still a secure and friendly
place with pool and tennis courts – and
just a stone's throw from Dhoby Ghaut
MRT station. Pass up the dorm beds,
though, a rip-off at $45 a head. **5**

Little India

Little India, along with Chinatown, is fast becoming the budget hotel centre
of Singapore. What's more, the arrival of Little India and Farrer Park MRT

stations means this colourful enclave is more accessible than ever. All the hotels in this section are keyed on the map on pp.76–77.

Ali's Nest 23 Roberts Lane (no tel). Grubby, shambolic, but undeniably welcoming homestay, one minute from Farrer Park MRT, where rooms and dorm beds ($9) share common bathrooms. When they're full, new arrivals can sleep on the floor. Prices include breakfast and free flow of hot drinks. ➋

Boon Wah Hotel 43a Jalan Besar ☎62991466, ⒻⒻ62942176. This decent Chinese hotel offers clean, if slightly cramped, rooms with TV, aircon and shower. The entrance is around the corner, on Upper Dickson Road. ➌–➍

Broadway Hotel 195 Serangoon Rd ☎62924661, Ⓕ62916414, Ⓔbroadway@pacific.net.sg. Ugly-looking but affordable hotel on Little India's main drag, boasting pleasant enough rooms with aircon, bathroom and TV. ➍

Dickson Court 3 Dickson Rd ☎62977811, Ⓕ62977833, ⓌⒾwww.dicksoncourthotel.com.sg. With smart, well-furnished rooms off light courtyard corridors, the peaceful *Dickson Court* is pretty good value; most corners of central Singapore are accessible from the bus stop across the road on Jalan Besar. ➍

Fortuna Hotel 2 Owen Rd ☎62953577, Ⓕ62947738, Ⓔfortunah@singnet.com.sg. Midrange hotel offering brilliant value for money; facilities include a health centre and secretarial services. ➍–➎

Haising Hotel 37 Jalan Besar ☎62981223. Set between Dunlop and Dickson roads, the *Haising* offers plain but spotless rooms and air-con dorms ($20). Ask the friendly front-desk staff about self-service laundry ($10). ➌–➍

Inn Crowd 35 Campbell Lane ☎62969169, Ⓦwww.the-inncrowd.com. Singapore's best guesthouse, thanks to scrupulous cleanliness, peerless facilities and the warm welcome from its owners, Ping and Hui. Guests have free use of the kitchen and free Net access, and lockers are available for long-term rental. If the one double room is taken you'll have to make do with a dorm bed ($18). Recommended. ➋

Julia's Guesthouse Zaman Centre, 1-5a Roberts Lane ☎98534790. Friendly, clean, carpeted joint with ten rooms, but not a patch on the *Inn Crowd*. Dorm beds are $10. ➋

Kerbau Hotel 54/62 Kerbau Rd ☎62976668, Ⓕ62976669, Ⓔkerbauinn@pacific.net.sg. Friendly place, if rather dark, with spruce and welcoming rooms; discounts for stays of three days or more. ➍

Little India Guest House 3 Veerasamy Rd ☎62942866, Ⓕ62984866, Ⓦwww.singapore-guesthouse.com. A smart guesthouse with excellent, fresh-looking rooms and spotless communal toilets. ➌

Perak Lodge 12 Perak Rd ☎62997733, Ⓕ63920919, Ⓦwww.peraklodge.net. One of the new breed of upper-bracket guesthouses, set within a smashing blue-and-white shophouse in a back street behind the Little India arcade, and run by friendly staff. The rooms are secure (all have safes), well appointed and welcoming, and the price includes a continental breakfast. Downstairs there's an airy, residents-only living area. Recommended. ➍

Chinatown and the waterfront

The range of budget and mid-range accommodation in **Chinatown** has grown in inverse proportion to that of Bencoolen Street's. Whatever your budget, you're sure to find an address to suit you in this most charismatic of enclaves, which boasts a mass of upmarket hotels that benefit from their proximity to the business district. All the hotels in this section are keyed on the map on pp.58–59.

Backpacker Hotel 11a Mosque St ☎62246859. Unremarkable rooms ($35–40) in an equally unremarkable place that nevertheless locates you bang in the middle of Chinatown. ➋

Backpacker Cozy Corner Hotel 5 Teck Lim St,

☎62254812, Ⓕ62254813. "Cozy" may be stretching a point, but the clean rooms, off light corridors, benefit from nice touches like watercolours of Old Chinatown, TVs and iceboxes. Excellent value. ➌

Chinatown Hotel 12–16 Teck Lim Rd,

⌾62255166, ⓕ62253912, ⓦwww.chinatown-hotel.com. Intimate boutique hotel with smart rooms and a well-stocked business centre. ④

Damenlou Hotel 12 Ann Siang Rd ⌾62211900, ⓕ62258500. Given its lovingly restored 1925 facade, the twelve compact but well-appointed rooms in this friendly hotel are surprisingly modern. After a pre-dinner drink on the rooftop garden overlooking Chinatown head down to the excellent *Swee Kee* restaurant (see p.134). ⑤

Dragon Inn 18 Mosque St ⌾62227227, ⓕ62226116. Sizeable and comfortable enough double rooms in the middle of Chinatown, all with air-con, TV, fridge and bathroom, and set in attractive shop-houses. Try to avoid rooms backing onto the central airshaft, which houses many noisy air-con units. ④

Gallery Hotel 76 Robertson Quay ⌾68498686, ⓕ68366666, ⓦwww.galleryhotel.com.sg. Extravagantly lit with neon stripes at night, and boasting some striking post-modern architecture, the *Gallery* is getting listed in those trendy "hip hotel" coffee-table books. The pool is to die for, some of Singapore's coolest nightspots are on-site, and all the urban-chic rooms offer free broadband access. Recommended. ⑧

Grand Copthorne Waterfront 392 Havelock Rd ⌾67330880; ⓕ67378880, ⓦwww.copthorne.com.sg. Equidistant from the Orchard and Chinatown districts, and a short stroll along the river from the nightspots of Clarke Quay, the *Grand Copthorne* demands consideration. Its

500-plus rooms are piled up above a selection of riverfront restaurants, and *Zouk*, Singapore's best nightclub, is next door. ⑧

The Inn at Temple Street 36 Temple St ⌾62215333, ⓕ62255391, ⓦwww.theinn.com.sg. Glossy and grand inside, this boutique hotel has been sculpted out of a row of Chinatown shop-houses. Its owners have filled it to bursting with furnishings and curios from old Singapore. Recommended. ⑤–⑥

Majestic Hotel 31–37 Bukit Pasoh Rd ⌾62223377, ⓕ62230907, ⓦwww.majestic-singapore.com. Scrupulously clean, and enormously friendly hotel within strolling distance of the sights of Chinatown. Following recent renovations, all rooms have air-con and private bathroom, while those at the front boast little balconies. ④

Robertson Quay Hotel 15 Merbau Rd ⌾67353333, ⓕ67381515, ⓦwww.robertson-quayhotel.com.sg. Cylindrical riverside hotel, whose compact but inviting rooms off cir-cular corridors yield great views of the river and city skyline. There's a cute circular pool with slide and waterfall on the third-floor terrace. Can't be faulted. ⑤

Royal Peacock Hotel 55 Keong Saik Rd ⌾62233522, ⓕ62211770, ⓦwww.royalpeacock-hotel.com. Keong Saik Road was once a notorious red-light district, and the silky, sassy elegance of the *Royal Peacock* recalls those days. Sculpted from ten shophouses, it's a superb boutique hotel, with great rooms, a bar, café and business services. The current prices make it a steal. ④–⑤

The East Coast: Geylang and Katong

Geylang and **Katong**, along Singapore's southeastern coast, have traditionally both been Malay-dominated areas. If you can't face the noise and the bustle of central Singapore, this region might appeal – certainly its cool sea breezes and Malay markets are an advantage. MRT and buses connect you quickly with downtown Singapore. All the hotels in this section are keyed on the map on p.95.

Amber Hotel 42 Amber Rd ⌾63442323, ⓕ63451911, ⓔambergoh@pacific.net.sg. Comfortable rooms with TV, air-con and bathroom just a short walk from the coast. ④

Century Roxy Park Singapore 50 East Coast Rd ⌾63448000, ⓕ63448010, ⓦwww.century-hotels.com. One of the East coast's more upmarket options, located midway between the city and Changi airport. The

design theme is contemporary Asian, the rooms sophisticated, and the choice of restaurants varied. ⑦

Fragrance Hotel 219 Joo Chiat Rd ⌾63449888, ⓦwww.fragrancehotel.com. Behind its chocolate-box exterior, a bright and cheery place, whose clean rooms boast fresh sheets, sparkling bathrooms, TV, air-con and fridge. Their website lists all other *Fragrance* branches in Singapore. ④–⑤

Hotel 81 Joo Chiat 305 Joo Chiat Rd ☎63488181, ⓕ63486960, ⓦwww.hotel81.com.sg. Housed in a beautifully restored cream-and-burgundy Peranakan building, *Hotel 81* offers rooms pleasant enough for any self-respecting business person, but at a fraction of the prices of the downtown heavyweights. Great place. Check out the *Hotel 81* website for details of the chain's many other addresses. ④

Sing Hoe Hotel 759 Mountbatten Rd ☎64400602, ⓕ63465996. Beautifully kept colonial house, with attractive reliefs on its external walls, but overpriced for its unmemorable, air-con rooms. ③

Sentosa and Ubin islands

Three luxury hotels on the island of **Sentosa** allow you to bypass the bustle of downtown Singapore. If you aren't too keen to negotiate any of the more long-winded means of transport to the island, it's possible to get a taxi direct from the airport to Sentosa (though note that from 7am to 10pm a $3 surcharge is levied). All the Sentosa hotels are keyed on the map on p.108.

The Beaufort 2 Bukit Manis Rd ☎62750331, ⓕ62750228, ⓦwww.beaufort.com.sg. A swanky hotel, fitted out in varnished wood, bounded by two 18-hole golf courses and a beach. There is a $40 price increase on Friday and Saturday. The Spa Botanica makes it the perfect place for a pampering getaway. ⑧–⑨

Shangri-La's Rasa Sentosa Beach Resort ☎62750100, ⓕ62750355, ⓦwww.shangri-la.com. Opened in 1993, the *Rasa Sentosa* is the first hotel in Singapore to have its own beach front, and its situation on Sentosa makes it a good option if you've got kids to amuse. Adults might prefer to check out the spa or sea sports centre. Prices take a $50 hike on Friday and Saturday, and rooms with sea views cost extra. ⑧

Sijori Resort Sentosa 23 Beach View ☎62712002, ⓕ6274020, ⓦwww.sijoriresort.com.sg. Sentosa's latest accommodation option, the *Sijori* is slap-bang in the middle of the island, making it an ideal base for exploring. There's a lovely pool, should you tire of theme parks and adventure rides. ⑥–⑦

Ubin Lagoon Resort 1000 Pulau Ubin ☎65429590, ⓕ65429591, ⓔubinac@singnet.com.sg. Outward-bound centre, offering archery, canoeing, trampolining, and trekking, besides more passive pleasures like bingo and sandcastle-building. The more you do, the better value the place becomes. Boats leave from Ponggol Marina; call ahead for departure times. Weekday ⑥, weekend ⑦

Camping

Changi Beach Camping at Changi is free for up to three consecutive nights, but you'll need to get a permit from the National Parks Board, Parks Management Department, 150 Beach Rd, #18-00 Gateway West, ☎63916874. It's open Mon–Fri 9am–5pm, Sat 9am–1pm.

East Coast Parkway Free camping for up to three consecutive nights, once you've obtained a permit from the bicycle kiosk near car park C3 near *McDonald's* (Mon–Sat 10am–7pm, Sun 11am–2pm; ☎64487120).

Sentosa Island Palawan Beach ☎62707888. A four-person tent is $12 per night ($16 at the weekend); camp beds are $1, and barbecue pits are $3 ($10 at the weekend).

10

Eating

A
long with shopping, **eating** ranks as a national pastime for Singaporeans, and a mind-boggling number of food outlets cater for this obsession. However, eating out is not afforded the same reverence that it receives in the West: as often as not, you'll find yourself eating off plastic plates in bare, unpretentious restaurants that ring to the sound of agitated conversation (invariably about the food at table). In Singapore, it's the food, and not the surroundings, that's important. Singapore offers new arrivals in Asia the chance to sample the whole spectrum of the region's dishes. What's more, strict government regulations ensure that food outlets are consistently hygienic – you don't need to worry about food cooked at even the cheapest stall. Dining out in Southeast Asia is a family affair, so unless you're going really upmarket don't be shy of taking the kids with you. If they're not culinary adventurers, there are always burger bars or pizza joints near at hand.

The mass of establishments serving **Chinese** cuisine reflects the fact that Chinese residents account for around three-quarters of the population. Singapore's development into a thriving seaport in the nineteenth century attracted labourers from many different regions of China, and the cuisines they brought with them still dominate the restaurant scene. You're most likely to come across Cantonese, Beijing and Szechuan restaurants, though there's not a region of China whose specialities you can't sample. **North** and **south Indian** cuisines give a good account of themselves, too, as do restaurants serving **Malay**, **Indonesian**, **Korean**, **Japanese** and **Vietnamese** food. One thing you won't find, however, is a Singaporean restaurant: the closest Singapore comes to an indigenous cuisine is **Nonya**, a hybrid of Chinese and Malay food that developed following the intermarrying of nineteenth-century Chinese immigrants with Malay women. Of course, if you insist, you can eat **Western food** in Singapore – venture beyond the ubiquitous burger chains and pizza parlours, and you'll find a host of excellent restaurants cooking anything from haggis to jambalaya. These and other dishes may be enjoyed at places geared to the dishes of a particular nation, or at **international restaurants**, whose confused menus are a patchwork of Western cuisines. A more informal alternative is to opt for a plate of **British** food – fish and chips, say – at a pub or bar.

Several specialist Chinese restaurants and a number of Indian restaurants serve **vegetarian food**, but otherwise, tread very carefully: chicken and seafood will appear in a whole host of dishes unless you make it perfectly clear that you don't want them. **Halal food** is predictably easy to find, given the number of Muslims in Singapore; the Arab Street end of North Bridge Road, and Serangoon Road's Zhu Jiao Centre both have proliferations of restaurants and stalls. There are no **kosher** restaurants, but you could try the food store at the Maghain Aboth Synagogue opposite the Church of St Peter and Paul on Waterloo Street.

Buying your own food: wet markets and supermarkets

Some guesthouses do have cooking facilities, and if you want to buy your own food or fancy a bag of fresh fruit, you're most likely to go to a **wet market** – so called because of the pools of water perpetually covering the floor. If you don't know a mango from a mangosteen, vendors are usually very helpful (see also pp.128–130). Singapore also has plenty of **supermarkets**, most of which have a delicatessen counter and bakery – some offer familiar beers from back home, too.

Wet markets

Little India is served by the large wet market in the Zhujiao Centre (Little India MRT; see p.75), at the southern end of Serangoon Road; the Chinatown Complex (Chinatown MRT; see p.67) market in **Chinatown** rewards a visit, too; and you'll find other wet markets out of the city centre, in Singapore's new towns.

Supermarkets

Carrefour 01-43 Suntec City Mall, 3 Temasek Blvd. French chain, and Singapore's first hypermarket.

Cold Storage branches at Centrepoint, Orchard Road (Somerset MRT); 293 Holland Rd (Buona Vista MRT or bus #7); 31 Amber Rd, Katong (Paya Lebar MRT, then bus #135). Local chain that stocks a wide range of Western products.

Good Gifts Emporium Golden Mile Complex, 5001 Beach Rd (bus #82 or #100 from *Raffles Hotel*). A smallish supermarket with a leaning towards Thai produce.

Isetan Wisma Atria, 435 Orchard Rd. Japanese department store and supermarket.

NTUC Fairprice Branches at Rochor Centre, 1 Rochor Rd (Bugis MRT) and 131 Killiney Rd. Reasonable Singaporean supermarket chain.

Takashimaya Ngee Ann City, 391 Orchard Rd. One of the largest department stores; the supermarket has a Fortnum & Mason franchise.

By far the cheapest and most fun place to dine in Singapore is in a **hawker centre** or **food court**, where scores of stalls let you mix and match good Asian dishes at really low prices. For a few extra dollars you graduate into the realm of proper **restaurants**, ranging from no-frills, open-fronted eating houses and coffee shops to sumptuously decorated establishments – often, though not always, located in swanky hotels. Restaurant **opening hours**, on average, are 11.30am–2.30pm and 6–10.30pm daily; hawker-stall owners tend to operate to their own schedules, but are almost always open at peak eating times.

Breakfast

Guesthouses sometimes include coffee or tea and toast in the price of the room, but the chances are you'll want to head off elsewhere for breakfast. **Western breakfasts** are available, at a price, at all bigger hotels, most famously at the *Hilton* or *Raffles*; otherwise, there are a number of cafés serving continental breakfasts, while *McDonald's*, *KFC* and *Burger King* all rustle up breakfasts before reverting to chicken and burgers after 11am. For a really cheap **fry-up** you can't beat a Western food stall in a hawker centre: here, $8 will buy you enough steak, chops and sausage to challenge even the most starving carnivore. Many visitors to Singapore find the **local breakfasts** a little hard to stomach, but if you shelve your preconceptions, there are some tasty possibilities. The classic Chinese breakfast is *congee*, a watery rice porridge augmented with chopped spring onion, crispy fried onion and strips of meat, though the titbits that comprise a *dim sum* breakfast (see "Chinese: Cantonese", p.133) tend to be more palatable to occidental tastebuds. An abiding favourite among Malays is *nasi lemak*, rice cooked in coconut milk and served with *sambal ikan bilis* (tiny crisp-fried anchovies in hot chilli paste), fried peanuts and slices of fried or hard-boiled egg. Otherwise, try investigating one of the scores of Indian establishments that serve up curry and bread breakfasts.

Ann Siang 5 5 Ann Siang Rd, Chinatown ☎63230061; see map on p.61. Civilized, cheery and airy café, just off trendy Club Street, serving scrambled eggs, Spanish omelettes and squidgy homemade cakes. After you've broken fast, check out the sumptuous Chinese-style dining rooms upstairs. Open Mon–Sat 9am–11.30pm.

Breakfast With The Birds Jurong BirdPark, Jalan Ahmad Ibrahim; see map on p.100. A buffet of local and Western breakfast favourites ($12, children $10), eaten to the accompaniment of the caged songbirds hanging above you, and with further entertainment supplied by pelicans and parrots. Daily 8–10.30am.

Coffee Bean 82 Boat Quay ☎65364355; see map on p.72. One of Boat Quay's more refined addresses, though at night you'll need to sup inside to ensure the heavy metal blaring from the adjacent bar doesn't drown the chilled jazz playing here. Open Sun–Thurs 9am–midnight, Fri & Sat 9am–3am.

De Boa (HK) Restaurant 42 Smith St, Chinatown; see map on p.61. Set opposite the Chinatown Complex, a smashing little café offering *dim sum*, *pau* (Chinese dumplings) and Chinese tea. Daily 7.30am–5pm.

Delifrance Branches at 01-K3, Scotts Shopping Centre, 6 Scotts Rd (see map on pp.54–55) and 02-19 Clifford Centre, 24 Raffles Place; see map on p.72. This stylish café is one of a chain of French delis specializing in filled croissants and pastries. Recommended. Daily 7.30am–10pm.

Dôme Ground floor, UOB Plaza, Boat Quay; branch at Singapore Art Museum; see map on p.72. Slick café, part of a global chain, boasting an impressive range of coffees and teas and a superb view over the Singapore River. Muffins, toast and croissants are reasonable, and a selection of international papers is on hand for the full breakfast effect. Daily 8am–8pm.

Famous Amos 01-05 Specialists' Shopping Centre, 277 Orchard Rd; see map on pp.54–55. Sublime handmade cookies to take away. Daily 10am–9pm.

Halia Singapore Botanic Gardens, 1 Cluny Rd ☎64766711; off map on pp.54–55 The weekend buffet breakfast ($15) in this peaceful and enchanting restaurant, serenaded by the sounds of insects, birds and whispering trees, has to be one of Singapore's most relaxing experiences. Open Sat & Sun 8–10.30am.

Mr Bean's Café 30 Selegie Rd; see map on pp.76–77. Based in the same wedge-shaped colonial building as the *Selegie Arts Centre*, *Mr Bean's* draws an interesting crowd, who breakfast on muffins, croissants, toast and coffee. American/English and continental breakfasts are available (around $6) until 11am, after which the menu turns to pizzas, sandwiches and finger food. Open 24hr.

New Flavour Gourmet 76-78 Smith St, Chinatown ☎62273878; see map on p.61. No-nonsense, Hong Kong-style *dim sum* shop fronted by towers of bamboo *dim sum* baskets. Daily 6am–midnight.

Noorul Ameen Restaurant 127 Bencoolen St; see map on pp.76–77. Does a roaring trade in *roti prata* (fried bread) and curry sauce each morning. Open 24 hr.

Pacific Coffee Company B1-26 Citylink Mall, Raffles Link One ☎68210098; see map on pp.76–77. Free Net access is laid on for partakers of the fine coffee on offer in this pleasing coffee shop, whose sassy red velvet sofas provide an ideal vantage point for people-watching. Open Mon–Fri 8am–11pm, Sat & Sun 9am–11pm.

Spinelli Coffee Company 01-02 Far East Square, 45 Pekin Street, Chinatown; see map on p.61. Some say *Spinelli* brews the finest coffee in Singapore – you can make your own mind up at this tiny courtyard outlet. Daily 10am–10pm.

Starbucks Branches at 01-46 Raffles City Shopping Centre, 252 North Bridge Rd, 01-01 OCBC Centre East, 63 Chulia St; see map on p.61 & pp.76–77. Central branches of the American coffee chain that has spread like wildfire across the island. Open Mon–Fri 7.30am–10.30pm, Sat & Sun 8am–midnight.

Steeple's Deli 02-25 Tanglin Shopping Centre, 19 Tanglin Rd, off Orchard Rd ☎67370701; see map on pp.54–55. Singapore's original deli, Steeple's has been knocking out high-quality homemade sandwiches, soups, cakes and savouries for over two decades now. Open Mon–Sat 9am–7.30pm.

Tan Hock Seng Cake Shop 88 Telok Ayer St; see map on p.61. They've been baking cakes and biscuits on site for more than fifty years at this famous Hokkien shop, just next door to the Fuk Tak Chi Street Museum. Daily 10am–8pm.

Tiffin Room Raffles Hotel, 1 Beach Rd; see map on pp.76–77. Have your buffet breakfast here and you won't need to eat until dinner; $25 per person. Daily 7.30–10am.

Wild Breakfast Singapore Zoo, 80 Mandai Lake Rd, ☎62693411; see map on p.86. A bumper buffet-style spread with seasonal tropical fruits, shared with whichever orang utan is on duty; $13 (children $10.30). Daily 9–10am.

Ya Kun Kaya Toast 01-01 Far East Square, 18 China St, Chinatown ☎64383638; see map on p.61. This Hainanese joint started out as a Chinatown stall in 1944, and still offers a stirring start to the day: piping-hot, strong coffee with kayu toast – a slab of butter and a splodge of egg and coconut spread oozing from folded toast. Open Mon–Fri 7.30am–7pm, Sat & Sun 9am–5pm.

Hawker centres and food courts

To eat inexpensively in Singapore, you go to the hawker stalls, traditionally simple wooden stalls on the roadside, with a few stools to sit at. Today, tighter regulations have swept the hawkers off the streets, and corralled them in custom-made **hawker centres**, where scores of permanent stalls line wide corridors, bristling with fixed stools and chairs. Though hygienic, hawker centres are often housed in functional buildings that tend to get extremely hot and, if you're sat next to a stall cooking fried rice or noodles, extremely smoky. As a result, an increasing number of smaller, air-conditioned **food courts** are popping up; brighter and more civilized than hawker centres, these suffer from a lack of atmosphere. In both hawker stalls and food courts, it's possible to pick up different dishes from a variety of stalls.

The standard of cooking is also very high at most stalls, and politicians and pop stars crowd in with the locals to eat at a cramped hawker's table. Hawker stalls serve a range of cuisines reflecting Singapore's ethnic make-up.

Indian and Malay noodle and rice dishes are widely available, but it's Chinese food that is prevalent. In certain venues, you'll also come across Western food like burgers, and steak and eggs; or Indonesian or Korean food.

Hawker stalls don't have menus, though most have signs in English detailing their specialities; otherwise point at anything you like the look of. When you order a dish, make it clear if you want a small, medium or large portion – or else you'll get the biggest and most expensive one. You don't have to sit close to the stall you're patronizing: find a free seat, and the vendor will track you down when your food is ready. Meals are paid for when they reach your table. A hearty meal – say, curry and rice, a fruit juice and a dessert – will cost you around $8, though if your budget doesn't run that far, you can eat well for half the price.

Hawker centres and food courts are open from lunchtime through to dinner and sometimes beyond, though individual stalls tend to open and shut as they please. Most close well before midnight, one notable exception being **Newton Circus**, where the **late-night** seafood is a constant tourist draw. There are always hot and cold drinks stalls on hand, and getting a bottle of beer is rarely difficult. If you avoid the peak lunching (12.30–1.30pm) and dining (6–7pm) periods, when hungry Singaporeans funnel into their nearest hawker centre, you should have no problems in finding a seat.

China Square Food Centre see map on p.61. Three floors of spick-and-span stalls – mainly Chinese but with Japanese, Korean and Western representation.

Chinatown Complex Smith St, at end of New Bridge Rd; see map on pp.58–59. A huge range of dishes with a predictably Chinese bias.

Food Junction B1, Seiyu Department Store, Bugis Junction, 200 Victoria St; see map on pp.76–77. Happening food court whose trendy piped music provides a stirring soundtrack to your dinner. Culinary themes as diverse as Thai, Japanese, *nasi padang* and claypot are represented, and there's a choice of local desserts or Häagen Dazs ice creams.

Food Life Food Court Level 4 Wisma Atria, Orchard Rd; see map on pp.54–55. Not a great selection, but clean, welcoming and central.

Funan the IT Mall Food Court 109 North Bridge Rd; see map on p.42. Smart basement court whose stalls serve herbal soup, claypots, Hainanese chicken and local desserts.

Geylang Serai Food Centre Geylang Serai; see map on p.94. In the heart of Singapore's Malay quarter, with a corresponding range of Malay stalls. Turn left out of Paya Lebar MRT and left again onto Sims Avenue; the centre is five minutes' walk along, on your right.

Hastings Road Food Court Little India Arcade, Serangoon Rd; see map on pp.76–77. Diminutive food court whose handful of stalls are labelled by region – Keralan, Mughlai, Sri Lankan and so on.

Kopitiam Plaza by the Park, 51 Bras Basah Rd; see map on pp.76–77. Bright and brash new food court, popular among late-night revellers with the munchies. Open 24hr.

Lau Pa Sat Festival Market 18 Raffles Quay; see map on pp.58–59. The smartest selection of hawker stalls in Singapore, and now open round the clock. At lunchtime the place is full to bursting with suits from the city; at night the clubbers take over.

Maxwell Food Centre Junction of South Bridge Rd and Maxwell Rd; see map on p.68. Old-style hawker centre, a stone's throw from the centre of Chinatown.

New Bugis Street see map on p.76–77. A handful of evening hawkers dish up Asian specialities such as satay, *laksa*, *kueh* and sushi.

Newton Circus Hawker Centre North end of Scotts Rd. Prices are a little higher than at other centres because it's on the mainstream tourist trail, but it has the advantage of staying open until late. Noted for its seafood stalls.

Orchard Emerald Food Chain Basement, Orchard Emerald, 218 Orchard Rd; see map on pp.54–55. Smart food court, halfway along Orchard Road, where the Indonesian buffet is great value.

Picnic Food Court Scotts Shopping Centre, 6 Scotts Rd; see map on pp.54–55. Slap-bang in the middle of the Orchard Road district, squeaky clean, and with lots of choice.

Satay Club Clarke Quay. A Singapore institution, serving inexpensive chicken and mutton satay. Open evenings only, from around 7pm.

Sim Lim Square Food Court 1 Rochor Canal Rd; see map on pp.76–77. Convenient if you are staying on Bencoolen Street; it's even got its own jukebox.

Smith Street Chinatown; see map on pp.58–59. At night, this narrow street is made still narrower by the two rows of food stalls that open up along it.

Telok Blangah Telok Blangah Rd; see map on p.100. Opposite the World Trade Centre, and good for a snack before or after a trip to Sentosa.

Victoria Street Food Court 83 Victoria St. Open-fronted food court with around ten stalls; good for evening seafood and handy for Beach Road and Raffles City.

Zhujiao Hawker Centre Corner of Bukit Timah and Serangoon roads; see map on pp.76–77. The bulk of its stalls, naturally enough, serve Indian food.

Restaurants and coffee shops

Restaurants in Singapore range from simple coffee shops to the most sumptuous establishments you could imagine. **Coffee shops**, invariably Chinese- or Indian-run, and usually open throughout the day, serve basic noodle and rice dishes, and sometimes feature a selection of cakes and sweetmeats. The culinary standard is never spectacularly high, but you'll be hard pressed to spend more

A food and drink glossary

Many menus in Singapore are written in English, but it's worth noting that transliterated spellings are not standardized – you may well see some of the following dishes written in a variety of ways; we've used the most widely accepted spellings.

General terms

Assam	Sour	Istimewa	Special (as in
Garam	Salt		"today's special")
Goreng	Fried	Kari	Curry
Gula	Sugar	Makan	Food
		Manis	Sweet

Meat, fish and basics

Ayam	Chicken	Sayur	Vegetable
Babi	Pork	Sotong	Squid
Daging	Beef	Sup	Soup
Ikan	Fish	Tahu	Bean curd
Kambing	Mutton	Telor	Egg
Kepiting	Crab	Udang	Prawn

Noodles (mee) and noodle dishes

Bee hoon	Thin rice noodles, like vermicelli; *mee fun* is similar.
Char kuey teow	Flat noodles with any combination of prawns, Chinese sausage, fishcake, egg, vegetables and chilli.
Foochow noodles	Steamed and served in soy and oyster sauce with spring onions and dried fish.
Hokkien fried mee	Yellow noodles fried with pieces of pork, prawn and vegetables.
Kuey teow	Flat noodles, comparable to Italian tagliatelle; *hor fun* is similar.
La mien	"Pulled noodles", made by spinning dough skipping-rope-style in the air.
Laksa	Noodles, beansprouts, fishcakes and prawns in a spicy coconut soup.
Mee	Standard round yellow noodles made from wheat flour that looks like spaghetti.
Mee goreng	Indian fried noodles.
Mee suah	Noodles served dry and crispy.
Sar hor fun	Flat rice noodles served in a chicken stock soup, to which prawns, fried shallots and beansprouts are added: a Malaysian speciality.
Wan ton mee	Roast pork, noodles and vegetables in a light soup containing dumplings.

Rice (nasi) dishes

Biriyani	Saffron-flavoured rice cooked with chicken, beef or fish; a north Indian speciality.
Claypot	Rice topped with meat (as diverse as chicken and turtle), cooked in an earthenware pot over a fire to create a smoky taste.
Daun pisang	Malay term for banana-leaf curry, a south Indian meal with chutneys and curries, served on a mound of rice, and presented on a banana leaf with *poppadoms*.

Hainan chicken rice	Singapore's unofficial national dish: steamed or boiled chicken slices on rice cooked in chicken stock, served with chicken broth and chilli and ginger sauce.
Kunyit	Rice cooked in tumeric; a side dish.
Nasi campur	Rice served with an array of meat, fish and vegetable dishes.
Nasi goreng	Fried rice with diced meat and vegetables.
Nasi lemak	A Malay classic: fried anchovies, cucumber, peanuts and fried or hard-boiled egg slices served on coconut rice.
Nasi puteh	Plain boiled rice.

Other specialities

Ayam goreng	Malay-style fried chicken.
Bak kut teh	Literally "pork bone tea", a Chinese dish of pork ribs in soy sauce, herbs and spices.
Char siew pow	Cantonese steamed bun stuffed with roast pork in a sweet sauce.
Chay tow kueh	Also known as "carrot cake", this is actually an omelette made with white radish and spring onions.
Congee	Rice porridge, cooked in lots of water and eaten with slices of meat and fish.
Dim sum	Chinese titbits – dumplings, rolls, chicken's feet – steamed or fried and served in bamboo baskets.
Dosai	South Indian pancake, made from ground rice and lentils, and served with *daal* (lentils) and spicy dips.
Fish-head curry	The head of a red snapper (usually), cooked in a spicy curry sauce with tomatoes and okra; one of Singapore's most famous dishes.
Gado gado	Malay/Indonesian salad of lightly cooked vegetables, boiled egg, slices of rice cake and a crunchy peanut sauce.
Ikan bilis	Deep-fried anchovies.
Kai pow	Similar to *char siew pow*, but contains chicken and boiled egg.
Kerupuk	Crackers.
Murtabak	Thick Indian pancake, stuffed with onion, egg and chicken or mutton.
Otak-otak	Fish mashed with coconut milk and chilli paste and steamed in a banana leaf; a Nonya dish.
Popiah	Chinese spring rolls, filled with peanuts, egg, beansprouts, vegetables and a sweet sauce; sometimes known as *lumpia*.
Rendang	Dry, highly spiced coconut curry with beef, chicken or mutton.
Rojak	Indian fritters dipped in chilli and peanut sauce; the Chinese version is a salad of greens, beansprouts, pineapple and cucumber in a peanut-and-prawn paste sauce, similar to *gado gado*.
Roti canai	Light, layered Indian pancake served with a thin curry sauce or *daal*; sometimes called *roti pratha*.

Roti john	Simple Indian dish of egg, onion and tomato sauce spread on bread and heated.
Satay	Marinated pieces of meat, skewered on small sticks and cooked over charcoal; served with peanut sauce, cucumber and *ketupat* (rice cake).
Sop kambing	Spicy Indian mutton soup.
Steamboat	Chinese equivalent of the Swiss fondue: raw vegetables, meat or fish dunked into a steaming broth until cooked.

Desserts

Bubor cha cha	Sweetened coconut milk with pieces of sweet potato, yam and tapioca balls.
Cendol	Coconut milk, palm sugar syrup and pea-flour noodles poured over shaved ice.
Es kachang	Shaved ice with red beans, cubes of jelly, sweetcorn, rose syrup and evaporated milk.
Pisang goreng	Fried banana fritters.

Tropical fruit

The more familiar fruits available in Singapore include coconut, watermelon, several types of banana, seven varieties of mango and three types of pineapple.

Ciku	Looks like an apple; varies from yellow to pinkish brown when ripe, with a soft, pulpy flesh.
Durian	Singapore's most popular fruit has a greeny-yellow, spiky exterior and grows to the size of a football. It has thick, yellow-white flesh and an incredibly pungent odour likened to a mixture of mature cheese and caramel.
Guava	A green, textured skin and flesh with five times the vitamin C content of oranges.
Jackfruit	This large, pear-shaped fruit grows up to 50cm long and has a greeny-yellow exterior with sweet flesh inside.
Langsat	Together with its sister fruit, the *duku*, this looks like a small, round potato, with juicy white flesh which can be anything from sweet to sour.

than $10 for a filling meal. Indian coffee shops tend to be a bit livelier, and are sometimes decidedly theatrical. Here you can watch the Muslim *mamak* men at work, whose job it is to make the frothy *teh tarik* (tea), by pouring liquid from a height from one vessel into another, and pound and mould the *roti* into an oily, bubble-filled shape; in some Indian coffee shops, you'll also be treated to the sight of plate-sized *murtabaks* being spun and griddle-fried.

On the whole, proper **restaurants** are places you go if you want a bit of comfort, or to savour particular delicacies found nowhere else, such as fish-head curry, Chinese specialities like shark's-fin dishes and bird's-nest soup, high-quality seafood and fine international cuisine. Singapore also has a tradition of **haute cuisine**, usually available in the top-notch hotels. Many of the best hotel-restaurants in Singapore boast reputable chefs, drawing in the punters with well-received French, Thai, Italian and Japanese food as well as more local delicacies. That said, in many restaurants, the food is not necessarily superior to

Longgan	Similar to the lychee, this has juicy white flesh and brown seeds.
Mangosteen	Available from June to August and November to January, it has a sweet though slightly acidic flavour. Its smooth rind deepens to a distinctive crimson colour when ripe.
Markisa	Known in the West as passion fruit, this has purple-brown dimpled skin with a rich flavour; frequently an ingredient in drinks.
Papaya	The milky orange-coloured flesh is a rich source of vitamins A and C.
Pomelo	The pomelo, or *limau bali*, is the largest of all the citrus fruits and looks rather like a grapefruit, though it is slightly drier and has less flavour.
Rambutan	The bright red rambutan's soft, spiny exterior has given it its name – *rambut* means "hair" in Malay. Usually about the size of a golf ball, it has a white, opaque fruit of delicate flavour, similar to a lychee.
Salak	Teardrop-shaped, the *salak* has a skin like a snake's and a bitter taste.
Star fruit	Waxy, pale-green star-shaped fruit said to be good for high blood pressure; the yellower the fruit, the sweeter its flesh.
Zirzat	Inside its bumpy, muddy green skin is smooth white flesh like blancmange, hence its other name, custard apple; also known as soursop.

Drinks

Kopi	Coffee.
Kopi-o	Black coffee.
Kopi susu	Coffee with milk.
Lassi	Sweet or sour yoghurt drink of Indian origin.
Teh	Tea.
Teh-o	Black tea.
Teh susu	Tea with milk.
Teh tarik	Sweet, milky tea, poured between two cups to produce a frothy drink.

that served at a good café or hawker stall – you're just paying the (often considerable) extra for air-conditioning and tablecloths. One reason to splash out, though, is to experience a **cultural show** of music and dance, found in several of the large Chinese seafood restaurants, all of which are detailed below.

Unless you're in a Muslim restaurant, you'll be able to wash down your meal with a glass of cold **beer**; wine is less common, though smarter establishments will normally retain a modest choice. Few **desserts** feature on Southeast Asian restaurants' menus, but the region's bounty of tropical **fruit** more than compensates; the glossary on pp.130–131 lists some of the less familiar fruits you may come across.

Tipping is not expected in Singaporean restaurants, and bills arrive complete with service charge and government tax (presently fourteen percent). Making yourself understood is rarely a problem, nor is negotiating a menu, as nearly all are written in English.

Eating in Singaporean restaurants is quite different to dining out, Western-style. Singaporeans – and particularly Singapore Chinese – tend to choose as many dishes as there are people at the table, and then order a couple more for good luck, a custom which bypasses the problem of choosing badly and then slavering after your neighbour's dish. When the food arrives, everyone dips in. English menus are available in most restaurants.

Depending on the cuisine you are eating, you have a choice of utensils at your command. **Chinese food** is traditionally eaten with **chopsticks**, which look nightmarishly difficult to use, but are actually quite easily mastered. One is laid between thumb and forefinger, and supported by your fourth and little fingers; the second chopstick is held between thumb, forefinger and second finger, and manipulated to form a pincer. To make your task slightly easier, eat, not from your plate, but from the bowl provided, holding it right up to your lips. Chinese eaters are able to feed rice from bowl to mouth with such speed that they seem to be sucking it up a tube; a china spoon is always provided in case you can't get the hang of chopsticks, but don't give up just because you're making a mess, as this isn't frowned upon in the least.

In upmarket **Indian restaurants** your placing will be set with spoon and fork, but in more basic establishments, food often arrives at table minus any utensils, and sometimes on a **banana leaf** instead of a plate. Traditionally, Indians eat by affecting a scooping action with their right hands, but if you don't fancy this, it's perfectly acceptable to ask for cutlery.

A Chinese meal is typically taken with plain steamed rice; be careful not to take too much, as leaving rice is considered rude by the Chinese. In an Indian restaurant, you can either eat your main course with rice, or scoop and mop it up with hunks of Indian bread.

If possible, try to book ahead at more upmarket restaurants, particularly on Saturday nights and Sunday lunchtimes, when they are at their busiest; moreover, bear in mind that many restaurants close over Chinese New Year, and those that don't are often bursting at the seams.

Chinese

The majority of the **Chinese** restaurants in Singapore are **Cantonese**, that is, from the province of Canton (Guangdong) in southern China, though you'll also come across northern **Beijing** (or Peking) and western **Szechuan** cuisines, as well as the **Hokkien** specialities of the southeastern province of Fujian, and **Teochew** dishes from the area east of Canton. Whatever the region, it's undoubtedly the real thing – Chinese food as eaten by the Chinese – which means it won't always sound particularly appealing to foreigners: the Chinese eat all parts of an animal, from its lips to its undercarriage, and it's important to retain a sense of adventure when exploring menus. Fish and seafood are nearly always outstanding in Chinese cuisine, with prawns, crab, squid and a variety of fish on offer. Noodles, too, are ubiquitous, and come in wonderful variations (see p.128). For something a little more unusual, try a **steamboat**, a Chinese-style fondue filled with boiling stock in which you cook meat, fish, shellfish, eggs and vegetables; or a **claypot** – meat, fish or shellfish cooked over a fire in an earthenware pot.

The other thing to note is that in many Cantonese restaurants (and in other regional restaurants, too), lunch consists of **dim sum** – steamed and fried dumplings served in little bamboo baskets.

Beijing

Beijing was traditionally the seat of China's Imperial households, and the sumptuous presentation of its cuisine reflects its opulent past. Meat dominates, typically flavoured with garlic and spring onions, though the dish for which Beijing is most famous is roast duck, served in three courses: the skin is eaten in a pancake filled with spring onion and radish, and smeared with plum sauce; afterwards, the flesh is stir-fried with vegetables, and the carcass boiled to make a soup.

Lao Beijing 03-01 Plaza Singapura, 68 Orchard Rd ☎67387207; see map on pp.54–55. Charming teahouse-style restaurant. If the braised pork trotters don't appeal, try the more mainstream dishes like sweet-and-sour fish and *popiah*; the steamboat with lamb slices is exceptional. Daily 11.30am–3pm & 6–10pm.

Pine Court Restaurant 35th floor, Mandarin Hotel, 333 Orchard Rd ☎68316262; see map on pp.54–55. Three elegant pine trees dominate this beautiful restaurant, where the speciality is whole Peking duck ($70) – enough for three hungry people. Cheaper set meals are available, too. You'll need to reserve in advance. Daily noon–2.30pm & 6.30–10.30pm.

Cantonese

Cantonese cuisine is noted for its delicacy of flavour and memorable sauces. Cantonese dishes are stir-fried, steamed or roasted, and often taken with black bean, lemon, oyster or soy sauce. Fish and seafood weigh in heavily on a Cantonese menu, either fried or steamed, and other specialities include pigeon, roast meats and frogs' legs. **Dim sum** is also a classic Cantonese meal: literally translated as "to touch the heart", it's a blanket term for an array of dumplings, cakes and titbits steamed in bamboo baskets. Though you do occasionally see it on lunch menus, traditionally *dim sum* is eaten by the Chinese for breakfast, with one basket (of three or four pieces) costing as little as $3.

Bugis Village see map on pp.76–77. Touts at the several seafood restaurants here hassle you incessantly to take a seat and a menu. The furious competition ensures prices are reasonable, despite the high proportion of tourists; all restaurants have similar, mainstream menus. Daily 5pm–3am.

Capital Restaurant 44 Bukit Pasoh Rd ☎62223938; see map on p.61. The friendly staff in this spotless restaurant recommend fried deer meat with ginger; also worth a try are the fried prawns rolled in bean curd skin. A feast for two costs under $35. Daily noon–2.30pm & 6–10.30pm.

Fatty's Wing Seong Restaurant 01-31 Burlington Complex, 175 Bencoolen St ☎63381087; see map on p.80. A Singapore institution where every dish on the wide Cantonese menu is well cooked and speedily delivered. Around $20 a head. Daily noon–11pm.

Grand City Chinese Restaurant 02-18/19 Raffles City Shopping Centre, 252 North Bridge Rd ☎63383622; see map on pp.76–77. Sizeable, enduringly popular restaurant, whose tables have rotating glass tops which ensure you needn't miss out on any of the dishes ordered. Oddities like emu with black pepper and Teochew-style goose sit alongside better-known dishes on the menu here. Mon–Sat 11.30am–2.30pm & 6.30–10.30pm, Sun 10am–2.30pm & 6.30–10.30pm.

Hai Tien Lo 37th floor, Pan Pacific Hotel, 7 Raffles Blvd, Marina Square ☎68268338; see map on pp.76–77. If you have money enough for just one blow-out, come here for exquisitely presented food and stunning views of downtown Singapore. Extravagant set meals are available, while Sunday lunchtimes (11.30am–2.30pm) are set aside for *dim sum*. Daily noon–2.30pm & 6.30–10.30pm.

Hillman Restaurant 01-159, Block 1, Cantonment Rd ☎62215073; see map on p.61. Extremely popular, thanks to its famous paper-wrapped chicken, and its rich-tasting earthen pot dishes of flavoursome stews featuring various meats and seafood in a rich sauce; small pots (around $10) fill two. Daily 11.30am–2.30pm & 5.30–10.30pm.

Lei Garden 01-24 CHIJMES, 30 Victoria St ☎63393822; see map on pp.76–77. Refreshingly understated for efforty CHIJMES, *Lei Garden* lets its classy Cantonese dishes do the talking. Stunning seafood, most of which starts the day swimming in the tanks in the dining room. Four can gorge for $140, with the special promotion meals (Sat & Sun only). Daily 11.30am–2.30pm & 6–10pm.

Li Bai Sheraton Towers Hotel, 39 Scotts Rd ☎7376888; see map on pp.54–55. Named after a poet of the Tang dynasty, a suitably sophisticated place in the bowels of the *Towers*, where your best bet is the five-course luncheon, weighing in at $50; alternatively, you can opt for lighter *dim sum*. Daily noon–2.30pm & 6.30–10.30pm.

Mitzi's 24–26 Murray Terr ☎62220929; see map on p.68. The cracking Cantonese food in this simple place, situated in a row of restaurants known as "Food Alley", draws crowds, so be prepared to queue. Two can eat for $30, drinks extra. Daily 11.30am–3pm & 5.30–10pm.

Mouth Restaurant 02-01 Chinatown Point, 133 New Bridge Rd ☎65344233; see map on p.61. Beside a popular *dim sum* menu, this jam-packed restaurant offers classy Hong Kong new-wave Cantonese food, at under $20 a head. Daily 11am–4am (*dim sum* 11.30am–5pm).

Sin Lam Huat Ubin Village, Ubin Island. Offers the best dining on Ubin; the specialities are chilli crab and tasty kampong chicken. Daily noon–7pm.

Soup Restaurant 25 Smith St ☎62229923; see map on p.61. Traditional Cantonese double-boiled and simmered soups are the speciality at this steam-heat-dependent soup shop whose elegant tables and low-hung lights recall old Chinatown. The *samsui* ginger chicken comes recommended. Daily 11.30am–10.30pm.

Swee Kee Damenlou Hotel, 12 Ann Siang Rd ☎62211900; see map on p.61. A Cantonese restaurant with real pedigree: Tang Swee Kee hawked the first bowl of his trademark *ka shou* fish-head noodles more than sixty years ago, and now his son sells this and other well-cooked dishes from the attractive coffee shop on the ground floor of his Chinatown hotel. Daily 11am–2.30pm & 5.30–11pm.

Tekong Seafood 01-2100 Blk 6, Changi Village Rd ☎65428923; see map on p.94. This Cantonese/Teochew seafood joint moved over to the mainland when Pulau Tekong was earmarked as an army shooting range; but the food is as good as ever – the Teochew steamed fish with sour prunes is particularly fab. Daily 11am–2.30pm & 5.30–11pm.

Union Farm Eating House 435a Clementi Rd. Bus #154 from Clementi MRT, alight at Maju army camp ☎64662776; see map on p.100. Until thirty years ago, this used to be a poultry farm, and palms and bamboos still surround the restaurant. The house special, *Chee Pow Kai* (marinated chicken wrapped in greaseproof paper and deep fried; $15 buys enough for two), is messy and wonderful. Daily 11.30am–8.30pm.

Wang Jiang Lou Blk A, Clarke Quay ☎63383001; see map on pp.58–59. Slick Cantonese-Teochew restaurant where the ingredients of a full seafood menu eye you suspiciously from tanks on the walls. The set menu ($68 for two) yields five dishes, plus fruit. Daily 11.30am–2.30pm & 6–11pm.

Yum Cha 02-01, 20 Trengganu St ☎63721717; see map on p.61. Big, buzzing *dim sum* joint, above the bustle of Trengganu Street, with marble tables and pictures of dumplings and teapots on the walls. Great fun. Entry is via Temple Street. Daily 8am–11pm.

Hainanese

Hainanese cuisine is synonymous in Singapore with chicken rice – the country's unofficial national dish. Chicken rice is a simple but tasty platter featuring, predictably enough, slices of chicken laid on rice that has been cooked in chicken stock. A chilli and ginger sauce is always served with the meal.

Mooi Chin Palace Restaurant B1-03 Funan the IT Mall, 109 North Bridge Rd ☎63397766; see map on p.42. Hainanese immigrants often worked as domestics to colonial families, resulting in crossover dishes such as Hainanese mutton soup and Hainanese pork chop – both cooked to perfection in this 60-year-old place, where whole *pomfret sambal* ($25) is a speciality, and set menus start from around $30 for two. Daily 11.30am–3pm & 6–10pm. Open for *dim sum* daily 7.30–9am.

Yet Con Chicken Rice Restaurant 25 Purvis St ☎63376819; see map on pp.76–77. Cheap and cheerful, old-time restaurant: try "crunchy, crispy" roast pork with pickled cabbage and radish, or chicken rice, washed down with barley water; $15 for two people. Daily 10.30am–9.30pm.

Hokkien

The **Hokkien** chef relies heavily upon sauces and broths to cook his meat and (primarily) seafood. Without doubt, Hokkien fried *mee* is the most popular Hokkien dish in Singapore – you'll find it in nearly every hawker centre on the island.

Bee Heong 4th floor, Pil Building, 140 Cecil St ☎62229075; see map on p.61. Customers are pumped through at a rate of knots in this lunchtime-only, cafeteria-style place; there's no menu, but the beggar chicken and dried chilli prawn come recommended, or ask the friendly staff for advice. Daily 11am–2.30pm.

Beng Hiang Restaurant 112–115 Amoy St ☎62216695; see map on p.61. The lack of a menu makes ordering distinctly tricky, but persistence is rewarded by well-cooked food at good-value prices – you can eat heartily for under $15. Daily 11.30am–2.30pm & 6–9.30pm.

Beng Thin Hoon Kee Restaurant 05-02 OCBC Centre, 65 Chulia St ☎65332818; see map on p.61. Hidden inside the OCBC car park, this minty green restaurant is very popular at lunchtime with city slickers from the nearby business district. Big portions make it a good and filling introduction to Hokkien cuisine. Daily 11.30am–3pm & 6–10pm.

Szechuan and Hunanese

Szechuan food is hot and spicy, with chilli, pepper, garlic and ginger conspiring to piquant effect in classic dishes such as camphor-and-tea-smoked duck, and chicken with dried chilli. The food of neighbouring Hunan province is similarly fiery; popular dishes include Hunanese honey-glazed ham and minced pigeon steamed in a bamboo tube.

Cherry Garden Restaurant The Oriental, 5 Raffles Ave, Marina Square ☎68853538; see map on pp.76–77. Elegant restaurant, designed to resemble a Chinese courtyard, and serving tasty Szechuan and Hunanese dishes. Hunanese honey-glazed ham is delectable, as is the Szechuan house speciality, camphor-smoked duck and bean curd crust (both under $30); the set lunches cost $40–60 a head. Daily noon–2.30pm & 6.30–10.30pm.

House of Mao Hunan Hotpot 01-01 Far East Sq, 11 Amoy St ☎65389292; see map on p.61. Really rather a good restaurant, once you get over the shock of being served by staff in full Red Guard fatigues, and the eerie sense of being watched over by the images of Mao on the walls. All-you-can-eat hotpots are $25 (lunch) or $30 (dinner). Daily 11.30am–2.30pm & 6.30–10.30pm.

Magic of Chongqing Hotpot 4th floor, Tanglin Shopping Ctr, 19 Tanglin Rd ☎67348135; see map on pp.54–55. Established in 1995, this homely DIY restaurant has got local pundits raving over its zesty Szechuan hotpots: choose a stock, drop in ingredients, and fish them out when cooked. Two can dine well for $70. Daily noon–3pm & 6–11pm.

Min Jiang Restaurant Goodwood Park Hotel, 22 Scotts Rd ☎67375337; see map on pp.54–55. This restaurant's reputation for fine Szechuan classics makes reservations a good idea. The decor's red tones match the fieriness of the food on offer. The hot and sour soup is really challenging; or try the simpler steamed fish in black bean sauce. A meal for two costs around $70. Daily noon–2.30pm & 6.30–10.30pm.

Teochew

Steaming is the most commonly used form of cooking in the **Teochew** kitchen, producing light but flavourful dishes such as fish steamed with sour plums. Other Teochew classics are braised goose, steamed crayfish and *oh nee* – a dessert made from creamed yam. Teochew meals are traditionally washed down with strong Chinese tea.

Ban Seng Restaurant B1-44 The Riverwalk, 20 Upper Circular Rd ☎65331471; see map on p.61. Road widening caused this venerable restaurant to decamp to just around the corner not long ago, and the traditional charcoal ovens didn't survive the move. The food is still top-notch, however: try the steamed crayfish, braised goose or stuffed sea cucumber; all moderately priced. Daily noon–2pm & 6–10pm.

Teochew City Seafood Restaurant 05-16 Centrepoint, 176 Orchard Rd ☎67333338; see map on pp.54–55. Standard Teochew restaurant whose karaoke facilities are, mercifully, confined to two private rooms; $50 suffices for a meal for two, and set lunches start at around $90. Daily 11.30am–2.30pm & 6.30–11pm.

Other speciality Chinese restaurants

Chinese Opera Teahouse 5 Smith St ☎63234862; see map on p.61. The *Sights and Sounds of Chinese Opera Show* ($35), a set dinner serenaded by Chinese musicians, and followed by excerpts from Chinese operas, is a memorable cultural treat. Open Fri & Sat 7–9pm.

Doc Cheng's Raffles Hotel, 328 North Bridge Rd ☎63311612; see map on pp.76–77. East meets West in the most recent addition to *Raffles*, an ice-cool joint themed around the global travels of imagined local *bon viveur* Doc Cheng. Though the menu betrays Thai, Indian, Japanese and Pacific Rim influences, Chinese culinary ideology provides the backbone to much of the food; the decor presents a similarly eclectic blend of Oriental, Art Deco and modernist influences. Two pay around $60. Open Mon–Fri noon–2pm, daily 7–10pm.

Goldleaf Taiwan Restaurant 24–24a Tanjong Pagar Rd ☎62256001; see map on p.68. Long-established but dowdy joint that's best avoided unless you've got a taste for congee: Taiwan porridge is the speciality, augmented by such fillings as century egg, oysters and abalone. Daily 11am–3pm & 6pm–4am.

Imperial Herbal Restaurant 3rd floor, Metropole Hotel, 41 Seah St ☎63370491; see map on pp.76–77. The place to go if you are concerned about your Yin and Yang balance: after checking your pulse and tongue, a resident Chinese physician recommends either a cooling or a "heaty" dish from the menu. For migraine sufferers the drunken scorpions are, by all accounts, a must; rheumatics should opt for crispy black ants. Daily 11.30am–2.30pm & 6.30–10.30pm.

Jing 50 Eu Tong Sen St ☎65326006; see map on p.61. An ecstasy of raw silk, cushions, transparent silk drapes, elegant lighting, gilt woodwork, and conducive planting has transformed the former Thong Chai Medical Institution into a sensational dining venue. The cuisine – listed as "signature Chinese" – offers a contemporary spin on traditional Middle Kingdom fare. Daily noon–3pm & 6–10.30pm.

Kublai Khan Mongolian BBQ 04-01 Park Mall, 9 Penang Rd ☎63344888; see map on

pp.54–55. Choose from an array of meats, vegetables and sauces, which are then cooked for you on a hot griddle in the open kitchen. Then, if you are still hungry, you can go back again, and again. Two pay around $50 for unlimited visits to the food bar, including starters and desserts. Daily 11.30am–2.30pm & 6–10pm.

Moi Kong Hakka Restaurant 22 Murray St ☎62217758; see map on p.68. The food of the semi-nomadic Hakka tribe relies heavily on salted and preserved ingredients, and dishes here, in the best Hakka food outlet in Singapore, encompass abacus yam starch beads ($6) and stewed pork belly with preserved vegetables. Daily 11.30am–2.30pm & 6–9.30pm.

Old Shanghai 55 Temple St ☎63271218; see map on p.61. Drunken chicken, marinated ham hock (both $7), sauteed eel with chive shoots ($15) and many other Shanghainese favourites, served in unfussy surroundings. Daily 11.30am–3pm & 5.30–9.30pm.

Singapura Seafood Restaurant 01-31 Selegie House, Blk 9, Selegie Rd ☎63363255; see map on pp.76–77. Sure the seafood is great, but it's hard to see beyond such Foochow classics as steamed white cabbage, fish-ball soup and fried noodles. Daily 11am–2.30pm & 6–10.30pm.

Snackworld 01-12/13 Cuppage Plaza, 5 Koek Rd; see map on pp.54–55. Hectic terrace restaurant where the Chinese menu is enlivened by hotplate crocodile meat ($25) and emu. Daily 11am–midnight.

Superbowl 80 Boat Quay ☎65386066; see map on p.72. An affordable range of 47 congees, served at marble-topped tables recalling a 1950s coffee shop. Daily 11am–11pm.

Vegetarian Chinese

Though their menus often feature "mock" meat dishes, the following selection of Chinese restaurants are all strictly **vegetarian** and use ingredients like yam, bean curd, mushrooms, water chestnuts and nuts to such imaginative effect that they'll appeal even to confirmed meat eaters.

Fut Sai Kai Restaurant 147 Kitchener Rd ☎62980336; see map on pp.76–77. Behind the prayer beads and incense sticks in the window is an old-fashioned Cantonese restaurant with a strongly Oriental atmosphere and fiery red decor; $20 is sufficient for two. Bean curd forms the backbone of Chinese vegetarian cooking, though, oddly, it reaches your table shaped to resemble meat or fish. Tues–Sun 10am–9pm.

Happy Realm Vegetarian Food Centre 03-16 Pearl's Ctr, 100 Eu Tong Sen St ☏62226141; see map on p.61. "The way to good health and a sound mind", boasts the restaurant's card; tasty and reasonably priced vegetarian dishes. Daily 11am–8.30pm.

Kwan Yim Vegetarian Restaurant 190 Waterloo St ☏63382394; see map on pp.76–77. A huge display of sweet and savoury *pow* is the highlight of this unfussy establishment, sited close to Bencoolen Street. Daily 8am–8.30pm.

Lingzhi Restaurant B1-17/18 Orchard Towers, 400 Orchard Rd ☏67343788; see map on pp.54–55. A real treat, where skewers of vegetables served with satay sauce are the highlight of an imaginative menu; there's also a takeaway counter. Daily 11am–10pm.

New Generation Eating House 5 Hindoo Rd ☏63980878; see map on p.80. Offers a fine range of Singaporean staples (*rojak, Hokkien mee, mee siam*) cooked veggie-style. Daily 10am–8pm.

American, North and South

Cha Cha Cha 32 Lorong Mambong, Holland Village ☏64621650; see map on p.100. Classic Mexican dishes ($10–22) are served in this vibrantly coloured restaurant; outside are a few open-air patio tables, ideal for posing with a bottle of Dos Equis beer, but book ahead for these. Daily 11.30am–11pm.

Billy Bombers 02-52 Bugis Jtn, 200 Victoria St ☏63378018; see map on pp.76–77. Shades of Arnold's diner in *Happy Days*: reasonably priced burgers and bowls of chilli eaten in speakeasy booths upholstered in red leather. Daily 11.30am–2.30pm & 6.30–10.30pm.

Bobby Rubino's B1-03 Fountain Court, CHIJMES, 30 Victoria St ☏63375477; see map on pp.76–77. Ribs are the speciality, but

steaks, burgers and other big-boy platters are available; eschew the "wine-rack" partitions and rough-hewn, red-brick interior and make for the terrace, superbly located below CHIJMES' looming convent. Daily 11am–midnight.

Café Iguana 01-03 Riverside Point, 30 Merchant Rd ☏62361275; see map on pp.58–59. Riverfront Mexican tucker, in colourful surroundings. Tortillas, chilli, quesadillas and all the other favourites feature on the menu, plus a huge selection of tequilas. Daily noon–3pm & 5pm–midnight.

Dan Ryan's Chicago Grill B1-01 Tanglin Place, 91 Tanglin Rd ☏67382800; see map on pp.54–55. Chug back a Budweiser and get stuck into "American portions" of ribs, burgers and chicken in a dining room that's crammed with Americana; main courses cost around $15. Daily 11.30am–midnight.

Lawry's The Prime Ribs 02-30 Paragon, 290 Orchard Rd ☏68363333; see map on pp.54–55. Superior ribs, served with Yorkshire pudding, mashed potato and whipped cream horse-radish, in a room with a view onto frenetic Orchard Road. Plan on $50 a head, with wine. Daily 11.30am–2.30pm & 5–10pm.

Ponderosa 02-20 Raffles City Shopping Centre, 252 North Bridge Rd ☏63344926; see map on pp.76–77. The perfect cure for vitamin deficiency – chicken, steak and fish dishes come with baked potato, sundae, and as much salad as you can eat, all for $28.90. Daily noon–10.30pm.

Seah Street Deli Raffles Hotel, 1 Beach Rd ☏63371886; see map on pp.76–77. New York-style deli boasting mountainous sandwiches, at around $10 each. The soda and root beer signs and outsized Americana on the walls make this the most un-colonial establishment in *Raffles Hotel*. Open Sun–Thurs 11am–10pm, Fri & Sat 11am–11pm.

European

Le Beaujolais 1 Ann Siang Hill ☏62242227; see map on p.61. Charming wine bar, stacked on two floors above one of Singapore's last

Pub food

The Dubliner Irish Pub Windsland House, 165 Penang Rd. The "World Famous" Sunday roast ($18) – a combination of lamb, beef, pork and chicken – will leave you full for a week; see p.150.

Molly Mallone's 42 Circular Rd, Boat Quay. Irish stews, oysters and bar snacks; see p.150.

remaining hills, serving cold cuts and salads and featuring a strong wine list. If you can't land one of a handful of alfresco seats, head upstairs, where you might just as well be in a Parisian café. Daily 11.30am–midnight, Sat 11.30am–1am.

Broth 21 Duxton Hill ☎63233353; see map on **p.68.** Superb fusion cuisine in an old shophouse on a delightfully quiet, tree-shaded Chinatown back street. A charming oasis – recommended. Open Mon–Fri noon–2.30pm, Mon–Sat 6–10.30pm.

Gordon Grill Goodwood Park Hotel, 22 Scotts Rd ☎67301744; see map on pp.54–55. Upmarket restaurant lent a Scottish feel by the tartan decor and the haggis with tatties: excellent food – but at a price. Set lunch ($35) is your best bet. Daily noon–2.30pm & 7–10.30pm.

Ocho 01-12/13/14 CHIJMES, 30 Victoria St ☎68831508; see map on pp.76–77. Top tapas; sit inside, amid the rugs, terracotta tiles and Moorish panels, or venture out onto the terrace, where musicians play Eagles hits, Gypsy Kings-style. The wine list impresses. Open Sun–Thurs 11am–1am, Fri & Sat 11am–2am.

Original Sin 01-62 Blk 43, Jln Merah Saga ☎64755605; see map on p.100. The bank of awards over the bar bears testimony to the quality of the vegetarian Mediterranean fare

on offer in this rust-and-aquamarine-painted dining room. The mezze plate makes an engaging appetizer; after that, you could do worse than a pizza Ibizi topped with roasted pumpkin, avocado, Spanish onion, asparagus and cheese. Strong wine list. Open Tues–Fri 6–10.30pm, Sat & Sun 11.30am–3pm & 6–10.30pm.

Da Paolo 80 Club St ☎62247081; see map on **p.61.** Great homemade pasta or splash out on authentic Sicilian meat and fish dishes washed down with one of a range of Italian wines (from $40). Open Mon–Fri 11.30am–2.30pm, Sat 6.30–11.30pm.

Pasta Fresca 30 Boat Quay ☎65326283; see **map on p.72.** Match up fresh pasta (made at the owner's own factory) and a sauce from the menu, and sit out on the riverside terrace. Around $30 a head, drinks extra. Daily 11am–10pm.

Pasta Fresca Seasports Centre Seasports Ctr, 1210 East Coast Parkway ☎64418140; see map on p.94. There are peerless views out to sea from this atap hut located just above the beach, within a sailing club; the pizzas, pastas, meat and fish dishes are not at all bad, either. At night the lights of the tankers docked south of Singapore look like fairy lights strung along the horizon. Daily 11.30am–midnight.

Paulaner Bräuhaus 01-01 Millennia Walk, 9

High tea and tiffin

Many of Singapore's swisher hotels advertise that most colonial of traditions, **high tea**, in the local press; below are a few of the more permanent choices. Typically, a Singapore high tea comprises local and Western snacks, both sweet and savoury. If you really want to play the part of a Victorian settler, Singapore's most splendid food outlet at the *Raffles* still serves **tiffin** – the colonial term for a light curry meal (derived from the Hindi word for luncheon).

Alkhaff Mansion 10 Telok Blangah Green; Redhill MRT, then bus #145; or bus #124 ☎64154888. The *Verandah Bar* hosts an English afternoon tea ($15) on Saturday and Sunday only (3–5.30pm).

Café l'Espresso *Goodwood Park Hotel*, 22 Scotts Rd ☎67301743. A legendary array of English cakes, pastries and speciality coffees. Daily 2–5pm.

Halia Singapore Botanic Gardens, 1 Cluny Rd ☎64766711. High tea (daily 3–5.30pm) offers cake and coffee or tea for $7.50.

Rose Verandah *Shangri-La Hotel*, 22 Orange Grove Rd ☎67373644. Rated the best high tea in Singapore by the American Women's Association of Singapore, no less.

Tiffin Room *Raffles Hotel*, 1 Beach Rd ☎63371886. Tiffin lunch (noon–2pm) and dinner (7–10pm) both cost over $30 per person, though the spread of edibles and the charming colonial surroundings make them worth considering. Between tiffin sittings, high tea ($25) is served (3.30–5pm).

Raffles Blvd ☎68832572; see map on pp.76–77.
German-theme-restaurant-cum-brewery,
serving generous platters of *wurst, kartof-
feln* and *sauerkraut*; the Paulaner charcoal
grilled sausage sampler ($22) yields five
sausages on a bed of sauerkraut and
mash. Two pay $70, including a *stein* of
Munich lager each. Open Sun–Fri
noon–2.30pm, daily 6.30–10.30pm.

Spizza 29 Club St ☎62242525; see map on
p.61. Homely, rustic and affordable pizzeria,
whose menu boasts a tempting A-Z of
thick-crust pizzas, cooked in a traditional
wood oven. Daily noon–3pm & 6.30–11pm.

Filipino

Kabayan Filipino Restaurant 03-25 Lucky
Plaza, 304 Orchard Rd; see map on pp.54–55.
Big, dark chamber crammed with tables to
cater for the Sunday melee of Filipino
maids; dishes are laid out buffet-style, and
best washed down with San Miguel beer.
Daily 10am–9pm.

Indian and Nepali

In the same way as the Chinese,
immigrants from north and south
India brought their own cuisines with
them. Though they vary in emphasis
and ingredients, all utilize *daal*
(lentils), chutneys, yoghurts and sweet
and sour *lassis* (yoghurt drinks); neither north nor south Indians eat beef.
North Indian food tends to rely
more on meat, especially mutton and
chicken, and uses breads – *naan, chapatis, parathas* and *rotis* – rather than
rice. The most famous style of north
Indian cooking is *tandoori* – named
after the clay oven in which the food
is cooked – and you'll commonly
come across *tandoori* chicken – marinated in yoghurt and spices and then
baked.

South Indian (and **Sri Lankan**)
food tends to be spicier and more
reliant on vegetables. Its staple is the
dosai (pancake), often served at breakfast time as a *masala dosai*, stuffed with
onions, vegetables and chutney, and
washed down with *teh tarik*. Indian
Muslims serve the similar *murtabak*, a
grilled *roti* pancake with egg, onion

and minced meat. Many south Indian
cafés turn to serving *daun pisang* at
lunchtime, usually a vegetarian meal
where rice is served on banana leaves
and small, replenishable heaps of various vegetable curries are placed
alongside; in some places, meat and
fish are on offer, too.

Though Indian food outlets span
the island, you'll find the highest concentration of really good ones in
Little India. South Indian Muslim
restaurants also tend to cluster on
North Bridge Road in the Arab
Quarter, where you'll find tasty
biriyanis and *murtabaks*.

Annalakshmi Restaurant Peninsular, Excelsior
Hotel & Shopping Ctr, 5 Coleman St
☎63399993; see map on p.42. Terrific north
and south Indian vegetarian snacks, meals
and set meals in sumptuous surroundings,
with all profits going to Kala Mandhir, an
Indian cultural association next door. Many
of the staff are volunteers from the Hindu
community, so your waiter might just be a
doctor or a lawyer. All staff work on the
adage that "the guest is god". From $10 a
dish. Open Mon–Sat 11.30am–3pm &
6–9.30pm, Sun 11am–2pm.

Azmi Muslim Food Stall 168-170 Serangoon
Rd; see map on p.80. Set in the *Thye Chong
Restaurant* on the corner of Norris Road,
chapatis are hand-cooked on a griddle in
front of you. Brains, liver and goats' legs
are served, as well as more conventional
dishes (of which the best is the *keema*
curry) on the accompanying curry menu.
Daily 10am–9pm.

Banana Leaf Appolo 56–58 Race Course Rd
☎62938682; see map on p.80. Recently refur-
bished and resplendent in marble (though
eating with your hands is still the order of
the day), this is a pioneering fish-head
curry restaurant where a wide selection of
south Indian dishes are all served on
banana leaves. Fish-head curry, $30 for
two people. Daily 10am–10pm.

Bombay Woodlands Restaurant B1-01
Tanglin Shopping Ctr, 19 Tanglin Rd
☎62352712; see map on pp.54–55. The set
lunch ($10) offers a perfect introduction to
the breads and vegetarian curries of south
India. Daily 9.30am–10pm.

Gandhi Eating House 29 Chander Rd
☎62995343; see map on p.80. Many locals

△ Noodle-maker

reckon this open-fronted place at the back of the Race Course Road restaurants is knocking out the best chicken curries in Little India; meals come on banana leaves, water in metal jugs. Daily 11am–11pm.

Gorkha Grill 21 Smith St ☎62270806; see map on p.61. There are fish, mutton and chicken dishes galore at this enchanting Nepali place, but be sure to start with *momo* (minced chicken dumplings) and end with *kheer*, or Nepali rice pudding, a tasty blend of cream, rice and cardamom. The set lunch ($9) is good value. If the murals of mountains and votive flags leave you wanting to see Nepal, speak to owner Dan, who leads treks from Kathmandu, and can book ahead for you. Daily 11.30am–11.30pm.

Islamic Restaurant 791–797 North Bridge Rd ☎62987563; see map on pp.76–77. Aged Muslim restaurant manned by a gang of old men who plod solemnly up and down between the tables. It boasts the best chicken *biriyani* in Singapore, cooked in the traditional way – heated from above and below with charcoal. $15 for two. Daily except Fri 9.30am–9.30pm.

Kinara 57 Boat Quay ☎65330412; see map on p.72. Exquisite restaurant boasting antique fittings imported from the subcontinent; a marvellous view of the river from upstairs, and elegantly presented Punjabi dishes. Around $60 for two. Daily noon–2.30pm & 6.30–10.30pm.

Komala Vilas 76–78 Serangoon Rd ☎62936980; see map on p.80. A cramped, popular vegetarian establishment special-izing in fifteen varieties of *dosai*. The "South Indian Meal", served upstairs on a banana leaf, is great value at $5. Daily 7am–10.30pm.

Madras New Woodlands Restaurant 12–14 Upper Dickson Rd ☎62971594; see map on p.80. Functional, canteen-style place serving up decent vegetarian food at bar-gain prices. House specialities are the Thali set meal ($4.70) and the VIP Thali ($6.50); samosas, bahjis and other snacks are available after 3pm, and there's a big selection of sweets, too. Recommended. Daily 7.30am–11.30pm.

Moti Mahal Restaurant 18 Murray St ☎62214338; see map on p.68. Not cheap, but one of Singapore's very best Indian restau-rants, serving tasty tandoori dishes in pleasant surroundings. The special is *murg*

massalam, a whole chicken stuffed with rice ($50; order in advance). Open Mon–Fri 11am–3pm, daily 6–10.30pm.

Muthu's Curry Restaurant 76–78 Race Course Rd ☎62932389; see map on p.80. Recent renovations have greatly spruced up this south Indian restaurant with no menu, but famous for its fish-head curry ($16–25). Daily 10am–10pm.

Orchard Maharajah 25 Cuppage Terr, Cuppage Rd ☎67326331; see map on pp.54–55. Set in a wonderful old Peranakan house, this splendid north Indian restaurant has a large terrace and a tempting menu that includes the sublime fish *mumtaz* ($14) – fillet of fish stuffed with minced mutton, almonds, eggs, cashews and raisins – worth the extra few dollars. The set lunch is good value at $16. Daily 11am–3pm & 6–11pm.

Our Village 5th floor, 46 Boat Quay ☎65383092; see map on p.72. A hidden gem, with fine north Indian and Sri Lankan food, and peachy views of the river, city and colonial district from its charming, lamplit roof terrace. Try the rich *murgh makhan-wala* ($14) or the *malai kofta* ($10), and finish with a palate-cleansing masala tea. Open Mon–Fri 11.30am–1.45pm & 6–10.30pm, Sat & Sun dinner only.

Roshni 02-01 Little India Arcade, 48 Serangoon Rd ☎62924808; see map on p.80. It's best to come at night: tuck into tasty pakoras fol-lowed by spicy chicken pepper *chettinad* ($14), then enjoy the Indian disco or (Wed–Sat) live band. Great fun. Daily 11.30am–3.30pm & 6–11pm.

Samy's Singapore Civil Service Club, Blk 25 Dempsey Rd ☎64745618. Bus #7 from Orchard MTR; alight when you see Pierce Rd to the left; see map on p.100. Once you've sunk a few Tigers at the Civil Service Club next door, you'll be ready for a stonking Samy's curry, served on a banana leaf, and best enjoyed overlooking the trees at a table on the fairy-lit verandah. Two pay around $15; beers can be ordered from the club. Recommended. Daily 11am–3pm & 6–10pm.

Selera Restaurant 15 Mackenzie Rd ☎63385687; see map on p.80. The best curry puffs – curried meat and boiled egg folded into pastry – in Singapore; 70c each. Daily 10.30am–10.30pm.

Sri Vijayah 229 Selegie Rd ☎63361748; see map on p.80. Hole-in-the-wall vegetarian joint offering unbeatable value for money:

$4 buys a replenishable mountain of rice and vegetable curries, and there's a mouthwatering display of sweetmeats at the front door. Daily 6am–10pm.

Indonesian

Similar to Malay cuisine (see below), **Indonesian** cookery is characterized by its use of fragrant, aromatic spices and sweet, peanut-based sauces. Specialities to look out for are *nasi padang* – a hot, dry style of cooking that hails from Sumatra – and *rijstaffel*, a Dutch-influenced concept that works along the same lines as a buffet, except that in this case the buffet comes to your table.

Alkaff Mansion 10 Telok Blangah Grn ☎64154888. Redhill MRT, then bus #145; or bus #124; see map on p.100. Built in the 1920s as a weekend retreat for the Alkaff family, this splendidly restored mansion offers a superb *rijstaffel* ($70): ten dishes served by a line of ten women in traditional *kebayas*. Or just have a beer in the bar, worth the exorbitant price for an hour or two of colonial grandeur. Daily noon–10.30pm.

Bumbu 44 Kandahar St ☎63928628; see map on pp.76–77. Crammed with Singaporean antiques amassed by owner, Robert Tan, *Bumbu* is as much a social history museum as a restaurant. Happily, the furnishings don't outshine the fine Indonesian/Thai cuisine on offer. The signature dish, crispy fish pillow – fish meat mixed with spices and deep-fried – is worth the journey alone. Daily 11am–2pm & 6–10pm.

Cumi Bali 20 Duxton Rd ☎90050260; see map on p.68. Slender and jolly *nasi padang* joint whose walls are strung with Indonesian fishing nets, puppets, instruments and batiks. The beef *rendang* and *ikan bakar* (BBQ fish) both hit the spot; or try one of the generous set lunches ($6). Daily noon–9pm.

House of Sundanese Food 55 Boat Quay ☎65343775; see map on p.72. Spicy salads and barbecued seafood characterize the cuisine of Sunda (West Java), served here in simple yet tasteful surroundings. Try the tasty *ikan sunda* (grilled Javanese fish) – an $18 fish feeds two to three people. Open Mon–Fri 11am–2.30pm & 5–10pm, Sat & Sun 5–10pm.

Rendezvous Restaurant 02-02 Hotel Rendezvous, 9 Bras Basah Rd ☎63397508; see map on pp.76–77. Revered *nasi padang* joint that still turns out lip-smacking curries, *rendangs* and *sambals*; the weighing machine in the corner is an unusual touch. Daily 11am–9pm.

Rumah Makan Minang 18a Kandahar St; see map on pp.76–77. Fiery *nasi padang* – highly spiced Sumatran cuisine – in the heart of the Arab Quarter; $4 ensures a good feed, while the popular barbecued fish costs $3. Daily noon–2.30pm & 6–10.30pm.

Sanur Restaurant 04-17/18 Centrepoint, 176 Orchard Rd ☎67342192; see map on pp.54–55. Hearty, reasonably priced food served by waitresses in traditional batik dress; the beef *rendang* is terrific. It's best to book ahead. Daily 11.30am–2.45pm & 5.45–10pm.

Tambuah Mas Indonesian Restaurant 04-10, Tanglin Shopping Ctr, 19 Tanglin Rd ☎67333333; see map on pp.54–55. Friendly restaurant, approached through a Minangkabau-style entrance, which offers *padang* food and a smattering of Chinese dishes. Daily 11am–10pm.

Warung M Nasir 01-05/06 1 Liang Seah St ☎63395935; see map on pp.76–77. This charming, open-fronted *nasi padang* café is a welcome addition to the Liang Seah's burgeoning dining scene. *Rendangs* and curries are taken, either at streetside tables or in the kopitiam-style dining room. Open Mon–Sat 10am–10pm.

International

Blu Shangri-La Hotel, Orange Grove Road ☎67302598; see map on pp.54–55. One of Singapore's most exquisite dining experiences: modern fusion cuisine of the highest quality, overlooking downtown Singapore from the *Shangri-La*'s 24th floor. Recommended. Daily 7–11pm.

Colours by the Bay Esplanade Mall, 8 Raffles Ave; see map on pp.58–59. Restaurant collective, offering a full palate of global cuisines, overlooking the bay beside Singapore's new theatre. With luck, your meal will coincide with an alfresco cultural performance.

Don Noodle Bistro 01-16 Tanglin Mall, 163 Tanglin Rd ☎67383188; see map on pp.54–55. Minimalist yet chic, *Don* is something of a paradox – a Western-style take on the noodle bar, imported back to the East. The menu is not country-specific, meaning that you can enjoy Indonesian *kway teow goreng* while your dining companion tucks into Japanese *ramen* noodles. Daily 11.30am–10.30pm.

The Gapz 03-09/10 Pacific Plaza, 9 Scotts Rd ☎67379336; see map on pp.54–55. Self-styled "young and trendy Asian *dim sum* and noodles bar", where the *dim sum* appear on a conveyor belt, not a trolley, and there's MTV on a huge screen. If grazing on dumplings does not appeal, you could opt for a bento set – or try designing your own noodle dish from a palette of ingredients. Mon–Sat 11.30am–10pm, Sun 7am–7pm.

Halia Singapore Botanic Gardens, 1 Cluny Rd ☎64766711. Moonlit and candlelit after dusk, *Halia*'s magical garden-verandah setting whisks you a world away from downtown Singapore. The East-meets-West lunch menu spans sandwiches, pasta and laksa, plus set lunches; at night, there are more substantial dishes such as rack of lamb and seafood stew (both $36). The high-tea deal (daily 3–5.30pm) offers cake and coffee or tea for $7.50 – or take along the papers and tuck into the weekend buffet breakfast ($15). Recommended. Daily 11am–11pm, also Sat & Sun 8–10.30am for breakfast.

Hot Stones 53 Boat Quay ☎65345188; see map on p.72. A healthy and novel twist on dining: steaks, chicken and seafood grilled at table on non-porous Alpine rock heated to 200° – no oil or fat, but bags of flavour. Daily noon–2.30pm & 6–10.30pm.

Louis' Oyster Bar 36 Boat Quay ☎65330534; see map on p.72. The Louis in question is Louis Armstrong, who beams down from all the walls. Oysters cost around $18 per half-dozen, but the "High Society Platter" (crayfish, crab, mussels, oysters and prawns on ice; $55 for two) is hard to resist. Open Mon–Fri 11am–1am, Sat & Sun 5pm–1am.

Nooch 02-16 Wheelock Pl, 501 Orchard Rd ☎62350880; see map on pp.54–55. The blurb on its menu calls this cool and popular, crescent-shaped joint overlooking Orchard Boulevard a "nondestinational" restaurant – meaning that the idea is to order and scoff your MSG-free Thai or Japanese noodles on the double, and be on your way. The *tub tim krob*, or chestnuts in syrup and coconut milk, is a good way to douse the

fires after a Thai *tom yam* soup. Recommended. Open Mon–Fri noon–3pm & 6–10.30pm, Sat & Sun noon–11pm.

Supernature 03-04/5/5 Wheelock Pl, 501 Orchard Rd ☎67371768; see map on pp.54–55. The very place to come when the toxins need flushing: salads, soy, lentil and felafel burgers, and a range of global rice and noodle dishes washed down with organic wines and lagers. Right on! Open Mon–Sat 11am–10pm, Sun 10am–8pm.

Top of the M 39th floor, Mandarin Hotel, 333 Orchard Rd ☎68316258; see map on pp.54–55. Singapore's highest revolving restaurant, and a great place to pop that question, over pan-fried goose liver and grilled rock lobster; at night, the lights of the city below are pure *Blade Runner*. Book ahead at the weekend. Daily noon–3pm & 6.30–10.30pm.

Town The Fullerton Singapore, 1 Fullerton Sq ☎67338388; see map on p.72. Despite the eclectic range of Asian and Western cuisines on the menu, your best bet is to head out onto the terrace overlooking the Singapore River, and munch away on one of the BBQ set meals ($35–65; free flow of beer $7 extra). There's also an international high tea on Saturday (11.30am–5pm, $25). Open Sun–Thurs 6.30am–midnight, Fri & Sat 6.30am–1am.

Japanese

Elegantly presented and subtly flavoured, **Japanese** cuisine is dominated by fish, which crops up in classic dishes such as sushi (raw fish wrapped in rice and seaweed) and *sashimi* (sliced or cubed raw fish). Other dishes that merit a try include *teriyaki* (chicken in a sweet sauce) and *teppanyaki* (grilled slices of meat or seafood), but bear in mind that Japanese food doesn't come cheap.

Akashi Japanese Restaurant B1-9, Tanglin Shopping Ctr, 19 Tanglin Rd ☎67324438; branch at B1-23 City Link Mall, 1 Raffles Link ☎62387767; see map on pp.54–55. Chain of understated, classical Japanese restaurants, where the sake *teriyaki* and the tempura are both good and there's a fine range of sakes with names as long as your arm. Daily noon–3pm & 6.30–10pm.

Beppu Menkan 01-01 Far East Sq, 134 Amoy St ☎64380328; see map on p.61. Choose from grilled eel, ramen noodle soup, *gyoza* dumplings and other Japanese favourites, taken amid Japanese lanterns and cartoons of avid noodle-slurpers. Should the mains leave you hungry, you could call in at the Japanese dessert stall next door. Open Mon–Fri 11am–2.30pm & 6–10pm, Sat noon–10.30pm, Sun 12.30–9pm.

Inagiku 3rd floor, Westin Plaza Hotel, 2 Stamford Rd ☎64316156; see map on pp.76–77. More of a maze than a restaurant, with four sections serving expensive, quality tempura, *teppanyaki*, sushi, and an à la carte menu – the latter the cheapest alternative. Daily noon–3pm & 6.30–11pm.

Japanese stalls Food Jctn, B1, Seiyu Department Store, Bugis Jctn, 200 Victoria St; see map on pp.76–77. *Sumo* has *sashimi*, tempura and *teriyaki* sets around $10, while nearby *Express-Teppanyaki*'s "big value meal" ($7) offers a choice of meats and vegetables flash-fried on the U-shaped hot bar. Daily 10am–9pm.

Sakae Sushi 02-13 Wheelock Pl, 501 Orchard Rd ☎67376281; see map on pp.54–55. Cheery sushi and *sashimi* bar, bang in the centre of Orchard Road, where set lunches start from $12. Diners choose to sit up at the conveyor-belt bar, or at diner-style booths around the restaurant's outer walls. Daily noon–10pm.

Senbazuru Hotel New Otani, 177a River Valley Rd ☎64338693; see map on pp.58–59. If the extensive menu proves too mind-boggling, choose from the selection of *kaiseki*, or traditional set dinners, which can run to ten courses, and will leave a sizeable hole in your pocket. Daily 11.30am–2.30pm & 6.30–10.30pm.

Shima Yakiniku 2 Murray Terr, Murray St ☎62235159; see map on p.68. A DIY delight: all the meat, salmon, prawns, frogs' legs you can eat, cooked on a hot stone at your table, for just $18 a head. Daily noon–2.30pm & 6.30–9.30pm.

Sushi Tei 20 Lorong Mambong, Holland Village ☎64632310; see map on p.100. A cross-fertilization of Tokyo sushi bar and airport baggage reclaim: diners snatch sushi ($1.50–4) from the conveyor belt looping the bar. Daily 11.30am–10pm.

Tatsu Sushi 01-16, CHIJMES, 30 Victoria St ☎63325868; see map on pp.76–77. *Tatsu* is a veteran of the notoriously fluid CHIJMES restaurant scene. Owner Ronny Chia's culinary expertise, and the high quality of

ingredients used (all fish is flown in from Japan), have resulted in a clientele that's around 75 percent Japanese. Open Mon–Sat noon–3pm & 6.30–10.30pm.

Korean

Newcomers to **Korean** food will find it both robust and exciting – perhaps this has something to do with the amount of ginseng in every dish. Meat features prominently on a Korean menu, and is often cooked by diners themselves on a table barbecue, or *bulgogi*. Another speciality is *kim chi*, or spicy pickled cabbage. For liquid refreshment, try the OB beer.

Haebok's Korean Restaurant 44–46 Tanjong Pagar Rd ☎62239003; see map on p.68. All the standard dishes, served by lukewarm staff in a plain dining room. If you aren't acquainted with Korean food, plastic models of the meals available displayed in the front window lend a few pointers. Daily 11.30am–3pm & 5.30–10.30pm.

Korean Restaurant Pte Ltd 05-35 Specialists' Ctr, 277 Orchard Rd ☎62350018; see map on pp.54–55. Singapore's first Korean restaurant, beautifully furnished and serving up a wide range of dependably good dishes at $16–20 each. Daily 11am–11pm.

Seoul Garden Korean Restaurant 03-119 Marina Sq, 6 Raffles Blvd ☎63391339; see map on pp.76–77. Entertaining, busy restaurant with daily set lunches from $7.90; best value is the all-you-can-eat Korean barbecue – a buffet of twenty seasoned meats, seafoods and vegetables cooked by customers at their tables. Open Mon–Fri 11am–3pm & 5.30–10.30pm, Sat & Sun 11am–10.30pm.

Malay and Nonya

Malay cuisine is based on rice, often enriched with coconut milk, which is served with a dizzying variety of curries and *sambal*, a condiment comprising pounded chillies blended with *belacan* (shrimp paste), onions and garlic. Other spices which characterize Malay cuisine include ginger and *galangal* (a root similar to ginger), coriander, lemon grass and lime leaves. Malaysia's most famous dish is satay, but the classic way to sample

Malay food is to eat *nasi campur*, a buffet of steamed rice served with an array of accompanying dishes; other popular dishes include *nasi goreng* (mixed fried rice with meat, seafood and vegetables); and *rendang* (slow-cooked beef, chicken or mutton in lemon grass and coconut).

Pork, of course, is taboo to all Muslims, but it has been married with Malay cooking in **Nonya** cuisine, which evolved as a result of the intermarriage of early Chinese immigrants and local Malays. Typical Nonya dishes incorporate elements and ingredients from Chinese, Malay and Thai cooking, the end product tending to be spicier than Chinese food. Chicken, fish and seafood forms the backbone of the cuisine, along with pork. Noodles (*mee*) flavoured with chillies, and rich curries made from rice flour and coconut cream, are common. A popular dish is *laksa*, noodles in spicy coconut soup served with seafood and chopped beansprouts. Other popular dishes include *ayam buah keluak*, chicken cooked with "black" nuts; and *otak-otak*, fish mashed with coconut milk and chilli paste and steamed in a banana leaf.

Bayview Café City Bayview Hotel, 30 Bencoolen St ☎63372882; see map on pp.76–77. This faceless hotel café's "Asian Hi Tea" offers a good, affordable introduction to Nonya cuisine. Sat & Sun noon–4pm.

Belachan 10 Smith St ☎ 62219810; see map on p.61. Friendly, refined Belachan (the name is Malay for shrimp paste) offers sanctuary from Smith Street's throng. The *itek manis*, duck stewed in ginger and black beans ($8), is sensational, though the set lunch (main course, veg, rice and achar; $5) offers best value. Open Tues–Sun 11.30am–3pm & 6.30–10.30pm, Mon lunch only.

Bengawan Solo Centrepoint, 176 Orchard Rd also at Clifford Ctr, 24 Raffles Pl; see map on pp.54–55. Superior Asian cake shops, specializing in Malay *kueh* (cakes). Daily 10am–8pm.

Blue Ginger 97 Tanjong Pagar Rd ☎62223928; see map on p.68. Housed in a renovated shophouse, this trendy Peranakan restaurant is proving a yuppy favourite, thanks to

dishes such as *ikan masal assam gulai* (mackerel simmered in a tamarind and lemon-grass gravy), and that benchmark of Nonya cuisine, *ayam buah keluak* – braised chicken with Indonesian black nuts. Daily 11.30am–3pm & 6.30–11pm.

Chilli Padi 11 Joo Chiat Pl ☎62479531; see map on p.94. Red batik ceiling drapes and tablecloths bring homely warmth to this family-run restaurant, whose Nonya dishes, like spicy chilli fish and *popiah*, have justly won it plaudits galore. The jars of kaya and curry pastes on sale make unusual gifts to take home. Daily 11am–2.30pm & 5.30–10pm.

Guan Hoe Soon 214 Joo Chiat Rd ☎63442761; see map on p.94. Fifty years old, and still turning out fine Nonya cuisine; try the *chen dool* (coconut milk, red beans, sugar, green jelly and ice), a refreshing end to a meal. Around $40 for two, with beer. Daily except Tues 1am–3pm & 6–9.30pm.

Mum's Kitchen 02-06, 3015 Bedok North St 5 ☎63460969; see map on p.94. The emphasis here, as you'd imagine, is on home-cooked food, Nonya-based, though with other

---

Cookery schools

Should the fine dining that Singapore offers leave you wanting to replicate some of it back home, you could give yourself a head start by attending a cookery school. Classes tend to last from two to four hours and cost $65–100.

Academy at Sunrice Fort Canning Ctr, Fort Canning Pk ☎63363307. Hosts (expensive) week-long culinary adventure holidays.

Coriander Leaf Cookery School 02-01 The Gallery Hotel, 76 Robertson Quay ☎67323354. Southeast Asian, European and Middle Eastern courses.

Raffles Culinary Academy 02-17 Raffles Hotel Arcade, 328 North Bridge Rd ☎64121256. Classes include making traditional Indian pickles and chutneys, French Cambodian fare and Nonya cuisine.

Asian incursions. House speciality Mum's Curry is wonderful, and best chased down by homemade barley water; special business lunches (Mon–Fri) offer three courses at $18 for two. Daily 11am–10pm.

Peranakan Inn 210 East Coast Rd ☎64406195; see map on p.94. As much effort goes into the food as went into the renovation of this immaculate, bright-green shophouse restaurant, which offers authentic Nonya favourites at reasonable prices; around $8 a dish. Daily 11am–3pm & 6–10.30pm.

Thai and Indochinese

You'll be thankful for a cooling bottle of Singha beer after you've done battle with a fiery **Thai** meal. Popular dishes include *tom yam* (a challengingly spicy prawn soup), green curry, fishcakes, chicken feet salad, and pineapple fried rice – which isn't fried rice with pineapple in it, but whole pineapple with fried rice inside. **Vietnamese** cuisine betrays Chinese, Thai, and French influences. Soups, *chao tom* (prawn paste barbecued on sugar cane) and spring rolls are perennial favourites, and are best washed down with Saigon's own "33" beer.

Cuppage Thai Food Restaurant 49 Cuppage Terr ☎67341116; see map on pp.54–55. Nondescript inside, but boasting a great outdoor terrace, this cheap and cheerful restaurant offers quality Thai dishes for around $8. Daily 11am–3pm & 6–11pm.

Golden Mile Complex 5001 Beach Rd; see map on pp.76–77. Known locally as "Thai Village", the *Golden Mile* is always full of Thais waiting to catch buses home. Drop by any one of its countless Thai cafés and you're sure of authentic, affordable Thai cuisine, amid an atmosphere that's pure Bangkok.

Indochine 49 Club St ☎63230503; see map on p.61. Owned by a Laos-born Australian, *Indochine* is one of Singapore's most elegant restaurants, its beautiful fixtures complemented by a truly great menu embracing Vietnamese, Laotian and Cambodian cuisine. Try the Laotian *Larb Kai* (spicy chicken salad) or *NhaTrang* roast duck and mango salad. The *chao tom* (minced prawn wrapped round sugarcane) is also mouthwatering. Mon–Sat noon–2.30pm & 6–10pm.

Indochine Waterfront Asian Civilization Museum, 1 Empress Pl ☎63391720; see map on p.72. A class apart: exquisite Southeast Asian dining on the more civilized side of the river. Start with a sharpener next door at *Bar Opiume* (p.149), and then tuck into Cambodian chilli and basil chicken ($20), or perhaps the sesame lamb tenderloin with lemon grass ($32). For dessert, give the more exotic fare a miss, and order the melt-in-the-mouth banana fritters. Open

Net cafés

As you'd expect of a nation so enamoured with cutting-edge technology, Singapore boasts numerous cafés offering email and Internet access. The emphasis is on the Internet, rather than the café side of the business, so don't expect to be spoilt for choice on the eating and drinking front. Most have nothing more than a fridge-full of soft drinks and a modest selection of pastries on display. Web access typically costs around $5 per hour, or $3 per half-hour. For more details, see p.34.

Chills Café 01-07 Stamford House, 39 Stamford Rd ☎68831016. Sedate place, focusing on email checkers, rather than gamers. Daily 9.30am–midnight.

i-surf 02-14 Far East Plaza, 14 Scotts Rd ☎67343225. Slap-bang in the middle of Orchard Road, and handy for checking prices online in mid-shopping spree. Open Mon–Fri 9am–10pm, Sat & Sun 9am–9pm.

Netzspiel 01-01, 44a Prinsep St. Central cybercafé where surfing sets you back $3 an hour. Mon–Sat 11am–11.30pm, Sun noon–11.30pm.

Singapore Computer Society 53 Neil Rd. Hushed email checking, on the outskirts of Chinatown. Mon–Fri 8.30am–5.30pm.

Travel Café 02-01, 44 Prinsep St. Backpacker-oriented café, with snacks, finger-food and soft and alcoholic drinks. Sun–Thurs 11am–11pm, Fri & Sat 11am–2am.

Mon–Fri noon–3pm & 6.30–10.30pm, Sat & Sun no lunch.

Madam Saigon 30 Liang Seah St ☎63339798. Affordable, if unremarkably appointed, restaurant whose Vietnamese chef knocks out convincing *pho* and *com tam* (broken rice with chicken), both around the $8 mark. Daily 11.30am–2.30pm & 6–10.30pm.

Patara 03-14 Tanglin Mall, Orchard Rd ☎67370818; see map on pp.54–55. Refined dining room, where the tasting menus (around $40) are a good way of acquainting yourself with Thai flavours. Daily noon–3pm & 6–10pm.

Pho Hoa 18 Lorong Mambong ☎64662737; see map on p.100. Part of a global noodle franchise, Pho Hoa knocks out decent *pho*, or Vietnamese rice noodle soup, and *com suon* (grilled pork chop, rice and salad, $9.50). The menu explains the fundamentals of *pho*, allowing you to sample a beginner's *pho*, create your own, or try the Adventurer's choice, with steak, meatballs, tripe and brisket ($10.50). Daily 11am–10pm.

Shingthai Palace 36 Purvis St ☎63371161; see map on pp.76–77. Good but characterless restaurant off Beach Road serving reasonably priced Thai dishes; try the *peek kai sord sai* (chicken wings with asparagus, prawns, mushrooms and meat). Around $20 a head. Daily 11.30am–2pm & 6–10pm.

Sukhothai 47 Boat Quay ☎65382422; see map on p.72. Chef's recommendations include fried cotton fish topped with sliced green mangoes, but you can't go far wrong whatever you plump for; the dining room is rather understated, so take advantage of the riverside tables. Daily 6.30–10.30pm, also Mon–Fri noon–3pm.

Thanying Restaurant Blk D, Clarke Quay ☎63361821; see map on pp.58–59. One of the few Clarke Quay ventures really to take off, thanks to friendly staff, a large menu and generous portions. Daily 11.30am–2.30pm & 6.30–10.30pm.

Viet Cafe 01-76 UE Sq, Unity St ☎63336453; see map on pp.58–59. The heady aromas of Vietnamese *pho* (soup) – mint, basil and citrus – hang heavy in the air at the sleek *Viet Cafe*. Follow the pebble path which leads up to the balcony or, better still, sit out on the forecourt and enjoy the night air. Handy for a late-night snack after a beer along Mohamed Sultan Road. Daily noon–3am.

Viet Lang Blk A, 01-26/27 CHIJMES, 30 Victoria St ☎63373379; see map on pp.76–77. The main dining room is dominated by a vast painting of Vietnamese ladies borne on a sea of flowers, and there's a similar textured lushness to the food. Start with a zingy pomelo salad, and then move on to the grilled pork chop with lemon grass ($13), washed down with a scented 333 beer. Daily 11.30am–10.30pm.

Nightlife

Singapore's **nightlife** has gone from strength to strength over the past decade. The island's well-developed bar and pub scene means there is now a vast range of drinking holes to choose from, with the Colonial District, riverside and Orchard Road areas offering particularly good **pub-crawl** potential. With competition so hot, more and more bars are turning to **live music** to woo punters, though this is usually no more than cover versions performed by local bands. That said, big-name groups do occasionally make forays into Southeast Asia, playing Bangkok, Kuala Lumpur and Jakarta as well as Singapore. **Clubs** also do increasingly brisk business. Glitzy and vibrant, they feature the latest imported pop, rock and **dance music**, and attract the world's best DJs.

Bars and pubs

With the **bars** and **pubs** of Singapore ranging from slick cocktail joints, through elegant colonial chambers to boozy dives, you're bound to find a place that suits you. Establishments open either in the late morning (to catch the lunchtime dining trade) or in the early evening, closing anywhere between midnight and 3am. On Friday and Saturday, opening hours almost invariably extend by an hour or two. Most serve snacks throughout the day, and many offer more substantial dishes. It's possible to buy a small glass of beer in most places for around $8, but **prices** can be double that amount in swankier joints. A glass of wine usually costs much the same as a beer, and spirits a dollar or two more. One way of cutting costs is to arrive in time for **happy hour** in the early evening, when bars offer local beers and house wine either at half price, or "one for one" – you get two of whatever you order, but one is held back for later.

Singaporeans adore **rock music**, and a plethora of bars pander to this, presenting nightly performances by local or Filipino cover bands. These are listed below, but for more details, see p.154. Also hugely popular is **karaoke**, which almost reaches an art form in some Singapore bars.

The Colonial District

Balaclava 01-01b Suntec City Convention Ctr, 1 Raffles Blvd ☎ 63391600. A homage to G-Plan or a nod to 1960s James Bond movies? Both could be said of this retro jazz bar, whose leather chairs, sassy red lamps and dark-wood veneers may make the ambience too oppressive for some tastes. There's live jazz from 8.30pm, and happy hour is 3–9pm. Mon–Thurs 3pm–1am, Fri & Sat 3pm–2am.

Bar and Billiards Room Raffles Hotel, 1 Beach Rd. A Singapore Sling ($18.50), in the colonial elegance of the hotel where the drink was invented by Ngiam Tong Boon in 1915, is a must on a visit to Singapore. Snacks are available through the afternoon, and playing billiards costs another $15 an hour. Daily 11.30am–midnight.

Bar Opiume Asian Civilizations Museum, 1 Empress Place ☎63392876. Cool-as-ice cocktail bar, ideal for a pre-dinner sharpener at adjacent *Indochine Waterfront*, where the barmen mix a mean Singapore Sling. Outside, are drop-dead gorgeous views of the waterfront; inside is a bar of mature sophistication, graced by huge crystal chandeliers, modish, square-cut leather furniture and a lordly standing Buddha statue. Recommended. Sun–Thurs 5pm–1am, Fri & Sat 5pm–2am.

City Space 70th floor, Swissôtel The Stamford, 2 Stamford Road ☎68373875. Exquisitely appointed lounge bar – but decor be hanged: you come to *City Space* to drink in the peerless, seventy-storey views across Singapore to southern Malaysia. The cocktails aren't cheap, but the warmed chilli cashews that come with your drink are to die for. Sun–Thurs 5pm–1am, Fri & Sat 5pm–2am.

Divine Parkview Sq, 600 North Bridge Rd ☎63964466. All the decadence and excess of 1920s café society comes outrageously to life at *Divine*, a big, bonkers bar whose adoption of a wine angel (a waitress, kitted out in wings and harness, who is winched up and down the 40ft wine rack) might just be the most politically incorrect thing you'll ever see. Elsewhere, Art Deco murals of prancing deer line the walls, vast brass lamps hang from the lofty ceiling, and there are life-sized mannequins of Duke Ellington, Billie Holliday and Louis Armstrong. Mon–Sat noon–midnight.

Fat Frog Café The Substation, 45 Armenian St ☎63386201. Relaxed courtyard café, sited within the Substation arts centre, where Singapore's culture vultures come to sip coffees and cold drinks and deconstruct the latest arts sensation under the shade of the whispering trees. Sun–Thurs 11.20am–11.30pm, Fri & Sat 11.30am–2am.

Liberte 01-19/20 CHIJMES, 30 Victoria St ☎63388481. *Liberte* holds centre stage on CHIJMES' main square – and rightly so. Its artsy wall hangings, flickering tea lights, mellow, Middle Eastern influenced sounds and excellent cocktails make it one of the few CHIJMES addresses where you actu-ally want to stay inside, rather than head out onto the terrace. Better still, there are free drinks for ladies from 9pm to midnight on Thursdays. Mon–Wed 5pm–2am, Thurs–Sat 5pm–3am, Sun 4pm–1am.

Lot, Stock and Barrel Pub 29 Seah St. Frequented by an early office crowd and a late backpacker crowd (the guesthouses of Beach and North Bridge roads are just around the corner), who come for the rock classics on the jukebox; happy hour 4–8pm. Daily 4pm–midnight.

Paulaner Bräuhaus 01-01 Millennia Walk, 9 Raffles Blvd. Wurst and sauerkraut might be a priority upstairs, but down amid the copper brewing vats in the bar of this themed microbrewery, lager is very much in the forefront of the punters' minds; pre-dictably busy around Oktoberfest-time. Mon–Thurs 11.30am–1am, Fri & Sat 11.30am–2am, Sun 11.30am–midnight.

The Quays

BQ Bar 39 Boat Quay ☎65369722. Arguably Boat Quay's coolest venue, thanks to its chilled dance music, comfy sofas and friendly staff. The second level affords memorable views of the river. Tues–Sat 11am–1am, Sun & Mon 11am–midnight.

Crazy Elephant 01-07 Trader's Market, Clarke Quay. The only bar with any real clout along Clarke Quay, playing decent rock music on the turntable between live sessions by the house band; decor comprises wood pan-elling and graffiti, but regulars prefer the tables out by the water's edge. Happy hour is daily 5–9pm. Mon–Thurs & Sun 5pm–1am, Fri & Sat 5pm–2am.

Harry's Quayside 28 Boat Quay ☎65383029. There's live jazz and R&B Tuesday to Saturday in this upmarket place, and a blues jam every Sunday evening. Light lunches are served and prices are lower in the early evening. Daily 11am–1am.

Home Beach Bar 15 Merbau Rd ☎68352413. Deckchairs, lanterns, reggae sounds – close your eyes and you'll swear there's sand, not concrete, underfoot at this mellow riverfront venue, where happy hour lasts from 11am to 8pm. Avoid the bar food, which will only disappoint. Daily 11am–1am.

Jazz @ Southbridge 82b Boat Quay ☎63274671. The crowd here can be rather self-consciously jazzy, but there's no faulting the quality of the nightly live music sessions. Sun–Thurs 11am–1am, Fri & Sat 11am–2am.

Mambo No. 5 60 Boat Quay. Cramped and sweaty bar, rocking over the weekend. The DJ's catholic tastes embrace soul, Motown, funk, hip-hop, reggae and R&B; not the place for a quiet chat. Daily 3pm–2am.

Milk Bar 01-09 The Gallery Hotel, Robertson Quay ☎668364431. Singapore's hippest hotel is also home to one of its coolest bars. *Milk*'s split-levels allow punters to chill out downstairs and get down, upstairs.

Molly Malone's 42 Circular Rd ☎65362029. With Kilkenny and Guinness ($12 a pint) on tap, sounds courtesy of Van Morrison and the Pogues, and a menu offering Connemara oysters and Irish stew, hardly your quintessential Singaporean boozer, but a good crack nonetheless, when full. Happy hour (11am–8pm) knocks a couple of bucks off a pint. Sun–Thurs 11am–1am, Fri & Sat 11am–2am.

Little India and around

Dravider Wines 42 Campbell Lane. Located in the heart of Little India, a local bar for local boozers, and therefore a great place to take a slice of the more spit-and-sawdust side of Singapore life. Daily noon–11.30pm.

Leisure Pub B1-01 Selegie Ctr, 189 Selegie Rd. Tame but endearing darts-oriented establishment that's ideal for a quiet chat and handy for Bencoolen Street; happy hour 4–9pm. Daily 5pm–midnight.

Roshni 02-01 Little India Shopping Arcade, 48 Serangoon Rd. Once the plates and cutlery have been cleared away, there's swinging Hindi and Tamil dance music into the night. Daily 11.30am–midnight.

Orchard Road

Alley Bar 2 Emerald Hill Rd ☎67388818. Stand up at the bar counter and you'll swear you are imbibing under the stars, such is the ingenuity of the decor in this slightly pricey joint, off Orchard Road. The candlelit seated area behind the bar is cosier. Sun–Thurs 5pm–2am, Fri & Sat 5pm–3am.

Anywhere 04-08/09 Tanglin Shopping Ctr, 19 Tanglin Rd ☎67348233. Tania, Singapore's most famous covers band, plays nightly to a boozy roomful of expats that's at its row-diest on Friday nights; happy hour Mon–Fri 6–8pm. Mon–Sat 6pm–2am.

Dubliner Windsland House, 165 Penang Rd ☎67352220. You know the formula by now: Guinness on tap, Irish memorabilia on the walls and the Pogues on the stereo. That said, the World Famous Sunday Roast ($18), a pig-boy pile of roasted meats, sausages and Yorkshire pudding, beats grazing on nuts and crisps; and all major sporting events are broadcast live. Sun–Thurs 11.30am–1am, Fri & Sat 11.30am–2am.

Excalibur Pub B1-06 Tanglin Shopping Ctr, 19 Tanglin Rd ☎67388682. Cluttered and cramped British-style pub, full of weather-beaten expats; the Whitesnake, Def Leppard and Scorpions posters on the walls give a true indication of the music that hogs the turntable. Sun–Thurs 4pm–midnight, Sat & Sun 4pm–1am.

Ice Cold Beer 9 Emerald Hill Rd ☎67359929. Noisy, hectic and happening place where the beers are kept on ice under the glass-topped bar; there are regular promotions, and there's a pool table upstairs. Happy hour is 5–9pm. Sun–Thurs 5pm–2am, Fri & Sat 5pm–3am.

No. 5 Emerald Hill 5 Emerald Hill Rd ☎67320818. Quite a pleasant Peranakan-style bar-restaurant, if you can stomach the posing bar staff, and the constant crunch of monkey nuts under foot. There's nightly live jazz in the upstairs bar. Happy hours noon–9pm & 1–2am. Daily noon–2am.

Observation Lounge 38th floor, Mandarin Hotel, 333 Orchard Rd. Swanky cocktail bar offering awesome views over downtown Singapore. Mon–Thurs & Sun 11am–1am, Fri & Sat 11am–2am.

The Sportsman 02-01 Far East Shopping Ctr. One for homesick British footie fans, this: the walls are plastered with pictures of the likes of Gazza and Beckham, big matches are screened live, and Tiger beer is $5 a mug. Daily 11am–midnight.

Snackworld Cuppage Terr, Cuppage Road. Buy a bottle of Tiger from *Snackworld* and watch the world drifting by – a great place to hang out. Daily 11am–midnight.

Swing 43a/45a Cuppage Terr, Cuppage Road ☎67347669. Late-night drinking is the main draw of this otherwise unremarkable bar, just off Orchard Road. Daily 5pm–4am.

Vintage Rock Café 01-23 Orchard Plaza, 150 Orchard Rd ☎62355768. Friendly staff and locals, great rock and R&B music on the speakers and cheapish beer make this joint. Posters of 1960s psychedelic gigs at the Fillmore and the Winterland plaster the joint. Happy hour is 4–8pm. Daily 4–11pm.

Why? Pub 04-06 Far East Plaza, 14 Scotts Rd. The budget prices in this tiny, lively pub – in a corner of Far East Plaza dominated by tattoo parlours – attract big drinkers. Daily 2pm–midnight.

River Valley Road and around

Next Page Pub 17–18 Mohamed Sultan Rd. Cool, popular pub that's the elder statesman of Mohamed Sultan Road. Decor is a mixture of Chinese wooden screens, lanterns and rough brick wall, and there's a pool table out back. The adjacent *Front Page* annexe, with its squidgy leather armchairs, is quieter and more chilled out. Daily 3pm–1am.

Siam Supper Club 01-53/55 UE Square, River Valley Rd ☎67350938. Semicircular red leather booths, a circular bar and lustrous red oval lamps lend the *Supper Club* a soothing fluidity; Buddha effigies in wall niches add an Asian twist. Cocktails are $12; bar snacks range from chicken wings to sashimi. Happy hour is 5–9pm. Mon–Sat 5pm–3am.

The Yard 294 River Valley Rd. This busy English pub was attracting a loyal crowd way back when Mohamed Sultan Road was nothing more than a row of dilapidated shophouses, and is still a great place for a beer. Bar snacks are available, and happy hour is 3–8pm. Mon–Thurs 3pm–1am, Fri & Sat 3pm–2am, Sun 5pm–1am.

Chinatown and around

Backstage Bar 13a Trengganu St ☎62271712. See review on p.153.

Bar Sa Vanh 49 Club St ☎63230145. You know a bar means business when it counts a six-metre waterfall and a Koi carp pond among its fixtures and fittings. Candle-lit, and crammed with Buddha effigies, scatter cushions and plants, the *Sa Vanh* (the name means "Heaven" in Lao) is a chilled-out bar, if ever there was one. The cool acid-jazz sounds round things off nicely. Happy hour 5–8pm. Upstairs is sister establishment the *Indochine* restaurant (p.146). Mon–Thurs 5pm–2am, Fri & Sat 5pm–3am, Sun 5pm–1am.

Carnegie's 01-01 Far East Sq, 44–45 Pekin St ☎65340850. Good-time, "let-your-hair-down" pub-disco, where Dutch courage sees to it that there's always a clutch of revellers dancing on the bar. All standard drinks are $6 during Crazy Hour (6–7pm). Sun & Mon 11am–midnight, Tues–Thurs 11am–2am, Fri & Sat 11am–3am.

Embargo 01-06 One Fullerton, 1 Fullerton Rd ☎62206556. Pre-clubbing cocktails with views over the bay are the order of the day at *Embargo*, so don't come along in jeans and pumps and expect to blend in with the beautiful people that frequent the place. Daily 5pm–2am.

Jing 50 Eu Tong Sen St ☎65326006. Sumptuous Chinoiserie defines this extraordinary drinking and dining (see p.69) experience, sculpted from the shell of a traditional Chinese building.

Post The Fullerton Singapore, 1 Fullerton Sq ☎67338388. The "refrigeration shelf" running around the island bar in this slick hotel boozer ensures icy booze from first swig to last. The Merlion cocktail, with passion fruit liquor and vodka, hits the spot. Mon–Fri noon–2am, Sat & Sun 5pm–2am.

Around Singapore

Diana Bar Civil Service Club, Blk 25 Dempsey Rd ☎64722080. There's something of the Officers' Mess about this quaint bar, located in an ex-army barracks on the road to Holland Village. High ceilings, clapboard walls and bamboo chairs make it a welcome change from the Buddhas, neon and black leather that define most Singaporean bars. Should the hunger pangs strike, there's a Chinese menu on hand – and *Samy's Indian Restaurant* (see p.141) is just next door. Daily 10.30am–10.30pm.

Full Moon Beach Bar & Grill 01-01 Costa Sands Resort, 1110 East Coast Parkway ☎64444644. The South China Sea is just a stone's skim away from this breezy, open-fronted beachfront bar. Sun–Thurs noon–2am, Fri & Sat noon–3am.

Wala Wala 31 Lorong Mambong, Holland Village ☎64624288. Rocking Holland Village joint, now into its second decade, serving Boddington's, Stella and Hoegaarden and featuring a generous happy hour (4–9pm). A live band plays upstairs in the *Bar Above*. Sun–Thurs 4pm–1am, Fri & Sat 4pm–2am.

Discos and nightclubs

Singapore's **nightclub** scene has transformed itself over the last few years. Clubs are far more self-aware, and the dance music they feature is far more cutting-edge than previously, and the cult of the celebrity DJ has taken a firm hold. Happily, Singaporean clubbers themselves remain, on the whole, more intent on having fun than on posing. European and American dance music dominates (though some play Cantonese pop songs, too), and many feature live bands playing cover versions of current hits and pop classics.

Clubs tend to open around 9pm, though some start earlier in the evening with a happy hour. Indeed, the difference between bars and discos has recently begun to blur, and some now include bars or restaurants that kick off at lunchtime. Most have a **cover charge**, at least on busy Friday and Saturday nights, which fluctuates between $10 and $30, depending on what day it is and what sex you are; it almost invariably entitles you to a drink or two. It's worth checking the local press to see which venues are currently in favour; a scan through *8 Days*, *IS* or *Juice* magazines will bring you up to date. Singapore also has a plethora of extremely seedy **hostess clubs**, in which Chinese hostesses working on commission try to hassle you into buying them an extortionately expensive drink. Fortunately, they are easy to spot: even if you get beyond the heavy wooden front door flanked by brandy adverts, the pitch darkness inside gives the game away.

Bar None Marriott Hotel 320 Orchard Rd ☎68314656. Popular *Bar None*'s house band Energy are a Singapore institution; when they aren't playing their polished rock covers sets, the DJs veer from Latino to alternative, and from R&B to top 40 hits; happy hour 7–9pm. Daily 6pm–3am.

Boom Boom Room Far East Sq, 130-2 Amoy St ☎64350030. The nightly comedy and dance show laid on by drag artist Kumar and his flamboyant friends is tame by the standards of the old Bugis Street nightspots it recalls, though still well attended and enjoyed by locals and tourists. Current pop hits fill the space between shows; $20 cover charge applies. Daily 8.30pm–2am.

Brix 10–12 Scotts Rd ☎67307107. Formerly known as *Brannigan's*, this large basement bar has shed its pick-up joint reputation, roughed up its decor a bit, and moved up into the premier league of Singapore clubs. On Mondays, the usual R&B and jazz-funk sounds give way to salsa lessons. A cover charge of $20 applies Thurs–Sat. Sun–Tues 7pm–2am, Wed–Sat 7pm–3am.

Centro 02-02 One Fullerton, 1 Fullerton Rd ☎62202288. Should you tire of ogling the glamorous clubbers, there are great views out to the Singapore harbour from sophisticated *Centro*. The intimate dance floor moves house and garage sounds; recent guest DJs have included Judge Jules and

Roger Sanchez. A $28 cover charge applies except on Wed, when ladies get free entry, champagne and house spirits. Wed–Sun 9pm–3am.

China Black 12th floor Pacific Plaza, 9 Scotts Rd ☎67347677. *China Black*'s emphasis upon chart hits and R&B makes it a safe haven for occasional clubbers who don't know their trance from their handbag house. Fri 5pm–3am, Sat 7pm–3am, Sun 9pm–3am.

DBL-O 01-24 Robertson Walk, 11 Unity St ☎67352008. With its massive dance floor, sassy *DBL-O* really can pack in the punters. House, garage and R&B are the favoured musical styles. Wed night is free for ladies; on other nights, cover charges range from $10 to $20. Wed–Sat 8pm–3am.

Liquid Room 01/05 The Gallery Hotel, 76 Robertson Quay ☎63338117. Bring your dancing shoes – *Liquid Room* is a dark, cramped, pumping place majoring on trance and techno, and the dance floor is a sea of bodies. Daily 7pm–3am.

Madam Wong's 28/29 Jalan Mohamed Sultan ☎68340107. Vast warren of a pub-cum-disco in a former rice warehouse, where scruffy red walls, weathered Chinese signage, opium beds and scatter cushions evoke an enticing retro-Asian chic. Early-evening acid jazz gives way to higher-octane dance music later on. Happy hour is

5–10pm; cover charge of $15 after 9pm, Fri & Sat. Daily 5pm–3am.

Milieu 2nd floor, Peranakan Place, 180 Orchard Rd ☎67381000. There's a Peranakan theme at play in the design of this central joint, where ex-*Zouk* DJs play house to enthusiastic regulars; happy hour is 7–10pm. Daily 7pm–3am.

Phuture 17 Jiak Kim St ☎67382988. Dark, smoky joint, with harder hip-hop, break beat and drum and bass sounds than the other *Zouk* venues and therefore a more youthful crowd. Cover charge is $15 before 9pm, then $25. Wed–Sat 7pm–3am.

Velvet Underground 17 Jiak Kim St ☎67382988. Less thumping than *Phuture*

and *Zouk*, and therefore favoured by a slightly older, more chilled-out crowd. Lava lamps create a suitably dreamy and chilled ambience. The cover charge ($25 for ladies, $35 for men) affords access to *Zouk* and *Phuture*. Tues–Sat 9am–3pm.

Zouk 17 Jiak Kim St ☎67382988. Singapore's trendiest club, fitted out with palm trees and Moorish tiles to create a Mediterranean feel. As well as *Zouk* itself, the warehouse it occupies also hosts *Phuture* and *Velvet Underground* (above). Famous DJs like Paul Oakenfold guest regularly. Cover charge is $15 before 9pm, then $25. Wed–Sat 7pm–3am.

Gay and lesbian nightlife

Singapore's **gay and lesbian scene**, while understated, is far more upfront than it was in the Nineties. That said, discretion is still advisable, as practising homosexuality is illegal in prudish Singapore. Until recently, venues promoting or even tolerating homosexuality came under close scrutiny, and were subjected to regular spot checks. Happily, the authorities' attitudes have relaxed in the last few years, and openly gay venues, including saunas and massage parlours, are now tolerated. There have even been gay and lesbian **Mardi Gras parties** held on Sentosa – the first of which, Nation01, was viewed as the coming out party for the local gay and lesbian community.

At night, the Singapore scene centres on Chinatown and Tanjong Pagar, where there are a fair number of **bars**. In addition, **clubs** are now targeting the pink dollar by laying on gay nights.

The best way to keep abreast of the current hotspots is to go **online**. ⓦ www.sgboy.com, a portal for gay men in Singapore, details all the best bars and clubs of the moment, as well as cruising hotspots, including MRT stations, shopping centres and swimming pools. Another invaluable resource for gays in Singapore is ⓦ dragoncastle.net/singapore.html, while ⓦ www.fridae.com is a pan-Asian portal targeting lesbians as well as gays.

Actor's Bar 13–15 South Bridge Rd ☎65332436. Lesbian-friendly bar, just around the corner from Boat Quay, where the emphasis is on chilling out on big sofas. Daily 5pm–2am.

Backstage Bar 13a Trengganu St ☎62271712. Gay-friendly bar plastered with posters of The *Sound of Music* and other musicals, and with a small balcony over the hustle and bustle of Chinatown. Daily 7pm–2am.

Boom Boom Room (see p.152). Risqué nightclub, famed for its drag shows; the second Wednesday of every month is a lesbian night.

Centro (see p.152). Sunday night is *Centro* Boyz night; and there is a girls' night on

every first Tuesday of the month.

East West Bar 77 Neil Rd ☎62275537. As the name suggests, this place is geared up as a meeting point for visitors to Singapore and locals. There is an appealing sophistication at play, both in the decor and the tunes on the turntable – all in all, a grown-up option. Daily 6pm–2am.

Fat Frog Café (see p.149). Draws a regular gay crowd, though not exclusively gay.

Taboo 21 Tanjong Pagar Rd ☎62256256. Currently Singapore's steamiest, most flirtatious gay bar – so much so that it received a warning about its crowd control policy a while back. Expect a full-on dance attack. Daily 5pm–2am.

Vincent's Lounge 15 Duxton Rd ☏62231126. Singapore's pioneering gay bar, and still going strong in its second decade. Don't expect lavish decor or a young, clubby scene, though: *Vincent's* is a mellow hangout that draws a mature clientele. Happy hour daily 7–9pm. Open Sun–Thurs 5pm–1am, Fri & Sat 5pm–2am.

Why Not? 56 Tras St ☏63233010. Pumping gay club, especially on Fridays and Saturdays, when the dance floor and podiums are awash with young revellers. Daily 9pm–2am.

Xpose Café 49 Cuppage Terrace. Gay bar just off Orchard Road, serving decent Thai food, but best avoided on Wed, Fri and Sat unless you are prepared to take the karaoke mike. Daily 4pm–midnight.

Velvet Undergound (see p.153). Popular with both the gay and lesbian communities of Singapore. There's a lesbian party on the first Sunday of every month.

Live music

Singapore is too far off the European and North American tour trail to attract many big-name **Western performers**, but there are occasional forays to rally the troops – Eric Clapton, Deep Purple, Michael Jackson, Alanis Morissette, Mariah Carey and the Stones have all visited in recent years. Concerts of this calibre are usually staged at the Singapore Indoor Stadium, and exhaustively covered by the local press for weeks beforehand. **Local bands** do exist and some aren't at all bad, but these are more likely to perform in community centres, rather than decent venues. Rivalling Western music in terms of popularity in Singapore is **Canto-pop**, a bland hybrid of Cantonese lyrics and Western disco beats whose origins lie in the soundtracks of 1950s Cantonese movie musicals; Hong Kong Canto-pop superstars visit periodically, and the rapturous welcome they receive make their shows quite an experience.

No matter who else is in town, you can always catch a set of cover versions at one of Singapore's bars and clubs; the main venues are picked out below. If you like middle-of-the-road **rock** music, you'll be in your element, as scores of local and Filipino bands nightly belt out Bryan Adams and Eagles hits. **Jazz** and **blues** ensembles are also popular. For more low-key musical accompaniment, go to any of the swankier hotels in town, and you're bound to find a resident pianist crooning Sinatra standards.

The most exhaustive lists of what's on are to be found in the weekly magazine, *8 Days*, the fortnightly *IS* and monthly *Where Singapore,* though the "Life!" section of the *Straits Times* is also worth a scan.

Anywhere See p.150. Good-time rock music by local favourites Tania.

Balaclava See p.148. Live torch song and jazz sets nightly.

Crazy Elephant See p.149. Live blues and rock throughout the week.

Harry's Quayside See p.149. Live jazz Wed–Sat, and a blues jam Sun evening.

Jazz @ Southbridge See p.149. Mellow jazz played live.

Molly Malone's See p.150. Two guitar'n'-fiddle sets nightly.

No. 5 Emerald Hill See p.150. Live jazz upstairs nightly.

Singapore Indoor Stadium Stadium Road ☏63442660. The usual venue for big-name bands in town; tickets are available through Sistic or Ticketcharge (see p.156).

Theatres on the Bay 1 Esplanade Drive ☏68288222. Western and Asian stars take the stage, between musicals.

World Trade Centre 1 Maritime Sq ☏63212187. Hosts international acts from time to time, as well as presenting free local gigs in its amphitheatre (check press for details).

Entertainment and the arts

The opening of Singapore's iconic integrated national arts centre, the Esplanade – Theatres on the Bay centre, in October 2002, has transformed Singapore's **performing arts** scene, and given the island a cultural focal point. But there is a plethora of venues away from the Esplanade that also serve up notable performances. Of all the performing arts, **drama** gets the best showing in Singapore, the island's theatres staging productions that range from English farces to contemporary productions by local writers. **Classical music** also gets a good airing, thanks to the busy schedule of the Singapore Symphony Orchestra. Western and Asian **dance** events crop up periodically; you are sure to see some if you time your trip to coincide with the annual **Singapore Festival of the Arts** in June. **Asian culture** is showcased in Singapore's major venues from time to time, but tends to appear more often on the street than in the auditorium, particularly around the time of the bigger festivals. **Cinema** is big business in Singapore, with up-to-the-minute Asian and Western movies all drawing big crowds, and the annual **Singapore International Film Festival** in April.

Information, listings and tickets

For **information** on cultural events and performances, pick up a copy of either the *Singapore Straits Times* (whose daily "Life!" supplement has a good "what's on" section), *8 Days* magazine, the fortnightly – and free – *IS* magazine, or *Where Singapore*, which is monthly, and also free. Alternatively, phone the venue's box office – all the relevant numbers are given below. **Sistic** and **CalendarONE TicketCharge** are Singapore's central ticketing agencies; see box on p.156 for details. The cost of a ticket to a cultural performance in Singapore usually starts at around $10, though international acts command substantially higher prices.

Classical music

At the epicentre of the **Western** classical music scene in Singapore is the **Singapore Symphony Orchestra**. Performances by the national orchestra take place at Esplanade – Theatres on the Bay and often feature guest soloists,

Ticketing agencies

Singapore has two ticketing agencies, Sistic and CalendarONE TicketCharge. Their booking lines and outlets are open Mon–Sat 10am–8pm, Sun noon–6pm.

Sistic

Booking hotline ☎63485555,
  ⓦwww.sistic.com.sg.
Bhaskar's Arts Academy, 19
  Kerbau Rd.
Chinese Opera Teahouse, 5
  Smith St.
Far East Square, 43 Pekin St.
Parco Bugis Junction, 200
  Victoria St.
Raffles City Shopping Centre.
Scotts Shopping Centre, 6
  Scotts Rd.
Specialists' Shopping Centre, 277
  Orchard Rd.

Victoria Concert Hall,
  Parliament Lane.
Wisma Atria, 435 Orchard Rd.

CalendarONE TicketCharge

Booking hotline ☎62962929,
  ⓦwww.ticketcharge.com.sg.
Centrepoint, 176 Orchard Rd.
Forum the Shopping Mall, 583 Orchard
  Rd.
Funan the IT Mall, 109 North
  Bridge Rd.
Substation, 45 Armenian St.
Tanglin Mall, 163 Tanglin Rd.

conductors and choirs from around the world; occasional **Chinese** classical music shows are included in the programme. From time to time, ensembles from the orchestra also give **lunchtime concerts**. In addition, the Singapore Symphony Orchestra gives occasional free performances in Singapore's parks, while Sentosa Island also hosts regular Sunday concerts – the shows are free, but the usual Sentosa entry fee applies.

Chinese Opera Teahouse 5 Smith St
☎63234862. $35 buys you Chinese dinner and an opera performance. See p.136 for more details.
Nanyang Academy of Fine Arts Chinese Orchestra 111 Middle Rd ☎63376636.
Chinese classical and folk music.
Singapore Chinese Orchestra Singapore

Conference Hall, 7 Shenton Way ☎64403839,
ⓦwww.sco.com.sg. Performances of traditional Chinese music throughout the year, plus occasional free concerts.
Singapore Symphony Orchestra Esplanade –
Theatres on the Bay ☎63381230,
ⓦwww.sso.org.sg. Performances throughout the year.

Film

With over fifty **cinemas** on the island, you should have no trouble finding a movie that appeals to you, and at a price ($5–8) that compares favourably with Europe and America. As well as Hollywood's latest blockbusters, a wide range of **Chinese**, **Malay** and **Indian movies**, all with English subtitles, are screened. Chinese productions tend to be a raucous blend of slapstick and martial arts, while Malay and Indian movies are characterized by exuberant song-and-dance routines. Cinema-going is a popular pastime so, if you plan to catch a newly released film, turn up early – and take a jumper along, as air-con units are perpetually on full blast. Be prepared, also, for a lot of noise during shows: Singaporeans tend to talk all the way through subtitled movies, and the rustling of a bag of popcorn pales next to the sound of melon seeds being cracked and crunched. The most central cinemas are listed below, but check the local press for a full rundown of any special events or one-offs that might be taking place.

Cultural performances

If you walk around Singapore's streets for long enough, you're likely to come across some sort of streetside **cultural event**, most commonly a **wayang**, or Chinese opera, played out on tumbledown outdoor stages that spring up overnight next to temples and markets, or just at the side of the road. Wayangs are highly dramatic and stylized affairs, in which garishly made-up and costumed characters enact popular Chinese legends to the accompaniment of the crashes of cymbals and gongs. Wayangs take place throughout the year, but the best time to catch one is during the Festival of the Hungry Ghosts, when they are held to entertain passing spooks, or during the Festival of the Nine Emperor Gods (see p.161). The STB may also be able to help you track down a wayang, and as usual the local press is worth checking.

Another fascinating traditional performance, **lion dancing**, takes to the streets during Chinese New Year, and **puppet theatres** appear around then, too.

For **Western films** in their original language, the Alliance Française, 1 Sarkies Rd (℡67378422), screens French films every Tuesday at 9pm and holds an annual film festival in November. There are also regular presentations at the British Council (see "Directory" on p.178 for address) and the Goethe Institute, 05-01 Winsland House II, 163 Penang Rd (℡67354555).

The **Singapore International Film Festival** (Ⓦwww.filmfest.org.sg) takes place in April. Now an annual event, it screens over 150 films and shorts – mostly by Asian directors – over two weeks. Smaller festivals are mounted throughout the year by the Singapore Film Society (Ⓦwww.sfs.org.sg).

Golden Village GV Grand 03-29 Great World City, 1 Kim Seng Promenade ℡67358484. Singapore's poshest cinema, with state-of-the-art digital sound, fully reclinable seats. Pricey at $25 a ticket.

Lido Level 5, Shaw House, 350 Orchard Rd ℡67380555. Five screens, including the luxurious Lido Classic.

Omni-Theatre Singapore Science Centre, 15 Science Centre Rd ℡64252500. 3D movies; see p.103 for details.

Orchard Cineplex 8 Grange Rd ℡62351155. Central and recently renovated cinema, with a swish new shopping centre constructed around it.

Suntec Cineplex 03-51 Suntec City Mall, 3 Temasek Blvd ℡68369074. Latest releases and Asian blockbusters.

UA Beach Road 4th floor, Shaw Leisure Gallery, 100 Beach Rd ℡63912550. Screens slightly more cerebral movies than most.

UA Bugis Junction Level 4, Parco Bugis Junction, 200 Victoria St ℡63912550. Shows Western and Chinese blockbusters.

Yangtse Pearl's Centre, 100 Eu Tong Sen Rd ℡62237529. Located in the heart of Chinatown, this place shows Western and Oriental films.

Theatre and the performing arts

Singapore boasts a thriving **drama** and performance scene, encompassing lavish musicals like *Singin' in the Rain* and the tiniest of repertory companies. Prices of tickets range from around $15 upwards. Foreign companies visit regularly, and usually perform at Esplanade – Theatres by the Bay or the Victoria or Kallang theatres. Performances of **dance** are also common – notably by the Singapore Dance Theatre (℡63380611, Ⓦwww.singaporedancetheatre.com), which performs contemporary and classical works at various venues, and sometimes by moonlight, at Fort Canning Park.

Singapore's annual **Festival of the Arts** attracts class acts from all over the world. A schedule of events is published in May, a month before the festival begins so, unless you are in Singapore for quite a while, you'll probably have trouble getting tickets for the more popular events. However, an accompanying **fringe festival** takes place concurrently, and its programme always includes free street and park performances. In addition, Singapore hosts a biennial Festival of Asian Performing Arts in odd years, which showcases the cultures of neighbouring nations.

Action Theatre 42 Waterloo St ☎ 68370842. Showcases contemporary works by Singaporean playwrights.

Drama Centre Canning Rise, Fort Canning Park ☎ 63360005. Drama by local companies.

Esplanade – Theatres on the Bay 1 Esplanade Drive ☎ 68288222. Sucks up all the biggest events to hit Singapore's shores.

Jubilee Hall Raffles Hotel, 1 Beach Rd ☎ 63371886. Occasionally stages retro plays.

Kala Mandhir Cultural Association Peninsula, Excelsior Hotel, 5 Coleman St ☎ 63390492. Dedicated to perpetuating traditional Indian art, music and dance.

Kallang Theatre 1 Stadium Walk ☎ 63458488. Has played host to visiting companies such as the Bolshoi Ballet, and touring musicals like *Chicago*.

Singapore Repertory Theatre DBS Drama centre, 20 Merbau Rd, Robertson Quay ☎ 67338166. Engligh-language theatre, showcasing western plays with Asian actors.

Substation 45 Armenian St ☎ 63377800. Self-styled "home for the arts" with a multi-purpose hall that presents drama and dance, as well as art, sculpture and photography exhibitions.

Victoria Concert Hall and Theatre 11 Empress Place ☎ 63396120. Visiting performers and successful local performances that graduate here from lesser venues.

Festivals

With so many ethnic groups and religions present in Singapore, you'll be unlucky if your trip doesn't coincide with some sort of **festival**, either secular or religious. Religious celebrations range from exuberant, family-oriented pageants to blood-curdlingly gory displays of devotion; secular events tend to comprise a carnival with a cast of thousands. Below is a chronological round-up of Singapore's major festivals, with suggestions of where best to enjoy them. Most have no fixed **dates**, but change annually according to the lunar calendar. We've listed rough timings, but for specific dates each year it's a good idea to check with the STB, which produces a monthly round-up of festivals in Singapore.

Some, but by no means all, festivals are also **public holidays**, when many shops and restaurants may close. For a full list of public holidays, see p.33.

January–March

Thaiponggal

Mid-Jan A Tamil thanksgiving festival marking the end of the rainy season and the onset of spring. In Hindu homes, rice is cooked in a new pot and allowed to boil over, to symbolize prosperity. At the Sri Srinivasa Perumal Temple on Serangoon Road, food is prepared against a cacophony of drums, bells, conch shells and chanting, offered up to the gods, and then eaten by devotees as a symbol of cleansing.

Chinese New Year

Jan–Feb Singapore's Chinese community springs spectacularly to life to welcome in the new lunar year. The festival's origins lie in a Chinese legend telling of a horned monster that was awoken by the onset of spring, terrorizing nearby villagers until they discovered it could be held at bay by noise, light and the colour red. Essentially, Chinese New Year is a family affair – old debts are settled, friends and relatives visited, mandarin oranges exchanged, red envelopes

(*hong bao*) containing money given to children, and red scrolls and papers bearing the character *fu* pasted to front doors as a sign of good fortune. Even so, there's still plenty to see in Chinatown, whose streets are ablaze with lanterns and fairy lights. Chinese opera and lion and dragon dance troupes perform in the streets, while ad hoc markets sell sausages and waxed ducks, pussy willow, chrysanthemums, lanterns and mandarin oranges; particularly splendid is the flower market that sets up on open ground at the junction of Neil and Kreta Ayer roads. On and along the Singapore River, the Hong Bao Special takes place, an extravaganza of floats, fireworks, music, dance and stalls that lasts for a couple of weeks. SBC's annual televised Lunar New Year Countdown is broadcast live from an outdoor location in Chinatown, and is well worth looking out for in the press. Colourful parades of stilt-walkers, lion dancers and floats along Orchard Road celebrate the Chingay (literally, "gaily decorated float") holiday, part of the New Year festivities, though nowadays a multicultural affair.

Thaipusam

Jan/Feb Not for the faint-hearted, this Hindu festival sees entranced penitents walking the three kilometres from Little India's Sri Perumal Srinivasa Temple to the Chettiar Temple on Tank Road, carrying kavadis – elaborate steel arches decorated with peacock feathers and attached to their skin by hooks and prongs – and with skewers spiked through their cheeks and tongues, to honour the Lord Murugan. Some join the procession to pray for assistance, others to give thanks for heavenly aid already granted. Coconuts are smashed at the feet of the penitents for good luck as they set off, and friends and relatives jig around them en route, singing and chanting to spur them on.

Hari Raya Haji

Feb/March An auspicious day for **Singapore's** Muslims, who gather at mosques to honour those who have completed the Haj, or pilgrimage to Mecca (birthplace of Muhammad); goats are sacrificed, and their meat given to the needy.

April–August

Qing Ming

April Ancestral graves are cleaned and restored, and prayers and offerings of joss sticks, incense papers and food made by Chinese families at the beginning of the third lunar month, to signal the onset of spring and a new farming year.

Singapore Film Festival

April Movies, shorts, animations, documentaries, with due focus given to local and Southeast Asian moviemakers. ⓦwww.filmfest.org.sg

Vesak Day

May Saffron-robed monks chant sacred scriptures at packed Buddhist temples, and devotees release caged birds to commemorate the Buddha's birth (May), enlightenment and the attainment of Nirvana; in the evening, candle-lit processions are held at temples. Race Course Road's Temple of a Thousand Lights is a good place to view the proceedings.

Birthday of the Third Prince

May Entranced mediums cut themselves with swords to honour the birthday of the Buddhist child god Ne Zha, who is said to carry a magic bracelet and a spear, and to ride the wind; their blood is wiped on much sought-after paper charms at temples around the state.

Dumpling Festival

May/June Stalls along Albert Mall sell traditional pyramid-shaped Chinese dumplings in the run-up to the Dumpling Festival, celebrated on the fifth day of the fifth lunar month. The festival commemorates Qu Yuan, a Chinese scholar who drowned himself in protest against political corruption. Local people, it is said, tried to save him from sea creatures by beating drums, disturbing the waters with their oars, and throwing in rice dumplings to feed them, but to no avail.

Singapore Arts Festival

June Annual celebration of world dance, music, drama and art, utilizing venues around the state, with events lasting several weeks.

Dragon Boat Festival

June/July Rowing boats, bearing a dragon's head and tail, their crews spurred on by the pounding of a great drum in the prow, race across Marina Bay to commemorate Qu Yuan (see above).

Singapore National Day

August 9 Singapore's gaining of independence in 1965 is celebrated with a national holiday and a huge show at either the Padang or the National Stadium, featuring military parades and fireworks.

Festival of the Hungry Ghosts

August/September Sometimes called *Yue Lan*, this festival is held to appease the souls of the dead released from Purgatory during the thirty days of the seventh lunar month, and so forestall unlucky events. Chinese street operas are held, and joss sticks – some the size of a man – red candles and paper money are burnt outside Chinese homes. Paper effigies of worldly goods such as houses, cars and servants are sometimes burnt, too. Elsewhere, marquees are set up in the street to hold festive banquets, followed by auctions of pieces of charcoal, cake and flowers – all thought to be auspicious.

WOMAD

Aug/Sept Four-day celebration of international music, arts and culture on the lawns of Fort Canning Park.
ⓦwww.womad.org/Singapore

September–December

Birthday of the Monkey God

Sept (also Feb) To celebrate the birthday of one of the most popular deities in the Chinese pantheon, mediums possessed by the Monkey God's spirit pierce themselves with skewers and dispense charms written in their own blood at the Monkey God Temple on Seng Poh Road, while a sedan chair possessed by the god himself is carried by worshippers. Elsewhere street operas and puppet shows are performed – look out for ad hoc canopies erected near Chinese temples.

Moon Cake Festival

Sept Also known as the Mid-Autumn Festival (held on the fifteenth day of the eighth lunar month), when Chinese people eat and exchange moon cakes (made from sesame and lotus seeds and stuffed with red bean paste or a duck egg) to honour the fall of the Mongol Empire – plotted, so legend has it, by means of messages secreted in cakes. Another, simpler explanation is that the cakes represent the full moon, at its brightest at this time of year. Moon cake stalls spring up across Singapore two weeks before the festival, but particularly in Chinatown.

Lantern Festival

Sept Strictly speaking a subset of the Moon Cake Festival (above), the Lantern Festival is celebrated over two weeks in the Chinese Gardens (see p.104), where children parade with gaily coloured lanterns and cultural shows; lion and dragon dances are a common sight.

Navarathiri

Sept–Oct Hindu temples such as the Chettiar Temple on Tank Road, and Chinatown's Sri Mariamman Temple, devote nine nights to classical dance and music in honour of Dhurga, Lakshmi and Saraswathi, the consorts of the Hindu gods Shiva, Vishnu and Brahma. Visitors are welcome at the nightly performances that take place at temples across the island. On the tenth night, a silver horse is carried at the head of a procession from Tank Road, taking in River Valley, Killiney and Orchard roads and Clemenceau Avenue.

Thimithi

Sept–Nov Another dramatic Hindu ceremony, this one sees devotees proving the strength of their faith by running across a four-metre-long pit of hot coals at the Sri Mariamman Temple in Chinatown. Outside the temple, devotees in their hundreds line up awaiting their turn, and building up their courage by dancing, shouting and singing.

Festival of the Nine Emperor Gods

Oct The nine-day sojourn on earth of the Nine Emperor Gods, thought to cure ailments and bring good health and longevity, is celebrated at the Kiu Ong Yiah Temple on Upper Serangoon Road by Chinese opera and mediums cavorting in the streets. Capping the festival is a procession, during which effigies of the nine gods are carried in sedan chairs.

Pilgrimage to Kusu Island

Oct Locals visit Kusu Island (see p.111) in their thousands to pray for good luck and fertility at the Tua Pekong Temple and the island's Muslim shrine. The pilgrimage commemorates the ancient tale of a turtle that turned itself into an island to save two shipwrecked sailors.

Deepavali (Diwali)

Oct/Nov Serangoon Road is festooned with fairy lights during this, the most auspicious of Hindu festivals, celebrating the victory of the Lord Krishna over Narakasura, and thus of light over dark. Oil lamps are lit outside homes to attract Lakshmi, the goddess of prosperity, and prayers are offered at all temples.

Ramadan Sept–Nov

Muslims spend the ninth month of the Islamic calendar fasting in the daytime in order to intensify awareness of the plight of the poor and to identify with the hungry. Many also abstain from drinking, smoking and sex. The fast is broken nightly with delicious Malay sweetmeats served at stalls outside mosques. The biggest collection of stalls sets up along Bussorah and Kandahar streets, outside the Arab Quarter's Sultan Mosque, though the lights, bustling bazaar and Malay Village of Geylang (see p.93) also warrant a visit. Muslims mark Hari Raya Puasa, the end of Ramadan, by feasting, donning their best traditional clothes and visiting family and friends.

Christmas

December 25 Singapore's central shopping centres vie annually for the best decorations in town, making Christmas a particularly colourful and atmospheric time for shopping.

Shopping

For many stopover visitors, Singapore is synonymous with **shopping**, though – contrary to popular belief – prices are not rock bottom across the board, owing to the consistently strong Singaporean dollar and a rising cost of living. Good deals can be found on watches, cameras, electrical and computer equipment, fabrics and antiques, and cut-price imitations (Rolexes, Lacoste polo shirts, and so on) are rife, but many other articles offer no substantial saving. Choice and convenience, though, make the Singapore shopping experience a rewarding one, with scores of shopping centres and department stores meaning that you're rarely more than an air-conditioned escalator ride away from what you want to buy. What's more, come during the annual **Great Singapore Sale** (from late May to early July), and you'll find seriously marked-down prices in many outlets across the island.

The art of shopping in Singapore

Unless you're in a department store, prices are negotiable, so be prepared to **haggle**. If you're planning to buy something pricey – a camera, say, or a stereo – it's a good idea to pay a visit to a reputable department store and arm yourself with the correct retail price, so you'll know if you're being ripped off. Asking for the "best price" is always a good start to negotiations; from there, it's a question of technique, but be realistic – shopkeepers will soon lose interest if you offer an unreasonably low price. Moving towards the door of the shop often pays dividends: it's surprising how often you'll be called back. And don't be hurried into a purchase, but shop around until you're content with the deal you've secured.

Usual **shopping hours** are daily 10am–9pm, though some shopping centres, especially along Orchard Road, stay open until 10pm. The only exception to this is the Christian-owned C. K. Tang's, which closes on Sunday.

Deposits, guarantees and refunds

Deposits shouldn't be required unless you're having clothes made up by a tailor – don't trust any other shops if they ask you to part with cash before you receive your purchase. If you buy any electrical goods, make sure you get an international, not a national, **guarantee**, and that it's dated and endorsed by the shop. Guarantees should detail the model and serial number of your purchase. It's also important to check that the product's **voltage** and cycle is compatible with that of your home country – especially if you're from Canada or the USA. Even if you are not buying something that warrants a guarantee, make sure you leave with a receipt – larger stores will produce one as a matter of course, though in small outlets you may have to ask for itemized proof of purchase. **Refunds**, while often possible in department stores for faulty goods, are unusual in small shops, but if you wish to make an official complaint, a receipt will be required.

Singapore's goods and services **tax** (GST) adds a five percent sales tax to all goods and services, but tourists can claim a refund on purchases of $300 or over (receipts of $100 or more can be pooled) at retailers displaying a blue and grey **Tax Free Shopping** sticker. Ask retailers to draft you a Global Refund Cheque, which you can then redeem subsequently at the airport. For more information, call the Global Refund Hotline on ☎62256238.

Should you have a complaint that you can't resolve with a particular store, contact the Retail Promotions Centre on ☎64502114. Or you can go to Singapore's Small Claims Tribunal, Subordinate Courts, 5th floor, Apollo Centre, 2 Havelock Road ☎64355946, ⓦwww.small-claims.gov.sg, which has a fast-track system for tourists; it costs $10 to have your case heard.

Customs, shipping and insurance

If you are buying in bulk, or purchasing products made of materials such as crocodile skin or ivory, be aware of **customs** regulations back home – your nation's consulate should be able to tell you what you can and can't import. Any weapons (including the *kris*, or Malay ceremonial sword) going through Singapore customs must have an export permit issued by the Arms and Explosives Licensing Division, 02-701 Police Cantonment Complex, 391 New Bridge Road (☎68350000). Larger stores will usually pack and ship items home for you, or you can go to the General Post Office (see p.33); either way, be sure to arrange **insurance**.

Antiques and crafts

Singapore bulges with stores selling Asian antiques and crafts, ranging from Bornean wooden effigies to Korean chests, and from Chinese snuff bottles to Malaysian pewterware. If it's **antiques** you're after, trawling through Tanglin Shopping Centre and Tudor Court at the western end of Orchard Road, or Holland Road Shopping Centre in Holland Village (see p.103), is your best bet.

Crafts can be found everywhere, but again there are specific areas worth heading for. Chinatown boasts a glut of souvenir stores stocking interesting goods beside the usual tack, and is home to the Singapore Handicraft Centre (see below). Little India's shops stock all manner of Indian bangles, bindis, and music. At Marina Square there are daily demonstrations of traditional crafts while Arab Street is good for robust basketware and leatherware.

Amida 219 South Bridge Rd. Burmese drums, gongs, offering vessels, pots and Buddhas.
Antiques of the Orient 02-40 Tanglin Shopping Ctr, 19 Tanglin Rd. Specialists in antiquarian books, maps and prints.
China Mec 03-31/32 Raffles City Shopping Ctr, 250 North Bridge Rd. Vast selection of Beijing cloisonné goods – patterned bowls, statues and other articles decorated with copper inlays and enamel.
Cho Lon 43 Jln Merah Saga, Holland Village. Crammed with Pan-Asian delights such as framed Burmese Bible translations, busts of Ho Chi Minh and Mao, and Jaipur palace costumes.
Eng Tiang Huat 284 River Valley Rd. Oriental musical instrument shop whose owners like nothing better than to demonstrate their

△ Orchard Road

stock; also wayang (opera) costumes and props.

Far East Inspirations 33 Pagoda St. The classiest of several antique shops along Pagoda Street, carrying Asian furniture, porcelain-based lamps, prints and watercolours.

Funan Stamp and Coin Agency 03-03 Funan the IT Mall, 109 North Bridge Rd. As you'd expect, a wealth of old coins and stamps.

House of Zhen 252 South Bridge Rd. This expansive store at South Bridge's junction with Temple Street, matches the famous Katong Antiques House (below), in its range of antiques, collectables and furniture. Members of staff are friendly and knowledgeable.

Katong Antiques House 208 East Coast Rd. Dark, cluttered Aladdin's cave of Asian collectables; through its swing doors are tiffin carriers, Peranakan slippers and clothes, and Chinese porcelain. Keeps rather erratic hours.

Lajeunesse Asian Art 94 Club St. Stock in this beguiling outlet spans all corners of Southeast Asia and beyond; Buddhist statuary a speciality.

Lim's Arts & Living 02-01 Holland Rd Shopping Ctr, 221 Holland Ave, Holland Village. A sort of Asian Conran shop, packed with bamboo pipes, dainty teapots, cherrywood furniture, bird cages, box pillows and lamps crafted from old tea jars. Recommended.

Lopburi 01-04 Tanglin Place, 91 Tanglin Rd. Seriously fine – and seriously expensive – antique Buddhas and Khmer sculptures, as well as some old silk textiles.

National Museum Shop 53 Armenian St (the Substation); 71 Bras Basah Rd (the Singapore Art Museum). A potpourri of books, prints, souvenirs and artefacts homing in on Singapore's cultural heritage.

Ming Village 32 Pandan Rd. Jurong East MRT, then bus #78; free shuttle from Orchard Hotel daily 9.20am. Ming and Qing dynasty porcelain reproductions made by hand, according to traditional methods – most fascinating is the painstaking work of the painters. This is not a place to come unless you are dead set on buying some porcelain.

One Price Store 3 Emerald Hill Rd. This venerable old shop, fronted by a jungle of potted plants, carries everything from carved camphorwood chests to

Chinese snuff bottles.

Poh Hwa Stamp Maker 02-50 Hong Lim Complex, Blk 531 Upper Cross St. Handmade yet inexpensive rubber stamps.

Polar Arts of Asia 02-16 Far East Shopping Ctr. Thousands of Buddha statues of all shapes, sizes, poses and nationalities.

Red Peach Gallery 68 Pagoda St. A fragrant shop, thanks to its soaps, candles, aromatherapy oils and incense; there are also contemporary Asian arts, tea sets, fabrics and chopsticks.

Rishi Handicrafts 58 Arab St. Leather sandals, necklaces, briefcases, belts and knick-knacks.

Selangor Pewter 32 Pandan Rd; outlet at 03-33 Raffles City Shopping Ctr, 252 North Bridge Rd. The Pandan Road HQ (Jurong East MRT, then bus #78) is a store masquerading as something more cultural, with its "museum" of pewterware and free demonstrations all increasing the pressure to buy; unless you have an abiding interest in pewter, best stick with the downtown branch.

Sin Huat Hin Wine Merchant 6 lg Mambong, Holland Village. There's no wine here but ceramic elephant, dragon pots and Chinese porcelain ware is stacked high.

Sin Chew Chinese Cultural Products Supermarket 01-00 Skyline Bldg, 192 Waterloo St. Sells effigies, trinkets, necklaces, books and other Buddhist-related goods.

Singapore Handicraft Centre Chinatown Point, 133 New Bridge Rd. This place gathers around fifty souvenir shops under one roof, making it a handy one-stop shopping point.

The Tatami Shop 02-10 Esplanade Mall, 8 Raffles Ave. Charming shop within the Theatres by the Bay, specializing in Japanese tatami mats, rugs and miscellanea.

Teajoy Shop 01-05 North Bridge Centre, 420 North Bridge Rd. A dandy collection of Chinese tea sets and glazed porcelain ware.

Tong Mern Sern Antiques Blk D Clarke Quay. A potpourri of ancient bits and bobs – postcards, abacuses, lamps – from Singapore's past.

Zhen Lacquer Gallery 1a/b Trengganu St. Boxes, bowls, trays and paintings, whose exquisite polished finish is crafted from the resin of the lacquer tree.

Fine art

Sophisticated Singapore has become something of a sales hub for contemporary **Asian art** works, of late, and a thriving number of galleries exist to feed off this fact. As elsewhere in the world, high-quality art doesn't come cheap here – but if your wallet can run to a classy painting or sculptor on a regional theme, you'll have yourself an Asian memento to last you a lifetime.

Artfolio 02-12/25 Raffles Hotel Arcade, 328 North Bridge Rd. Contemporary Southeast Asian pieces are the speciality here – look out for the works of Malaysian sculptor and painter Eng Tay and Singaporean artist Ong Kim Seng.

Galerie Dauphin 80 Cairnhill Rd. Located in an immaculately restored conservation building close to Scotts Road, Galerie Dauphin brings together paintings and sculpture by regional and global artists.

Jasmine Fine Arts 04-14 Orchard Point, 160 Orchard Rd. Appealing art works from China; next door is the Orchard Point Exhibition Hall, and there are many other outlets on the same floor.

Kwok Gallery 03-01 Far East Shopping Ctr, 545 Orchard Rd. The Kwoks have been amassing and selling antique Chinese art works for nearing a century; their inventory is accordingly broad and impressive.

MITA Building 140 Hill St. As good a selection of art galleries as you'll find in Singapore. Cape of Good Hope and Gajah galleries both carry a lot of Asian works, while Art-2 specializes in contemporary Burmese artists.

Singapore Tyler Print Institute 41 Robertson Quay. Housed in a nineteenth-century riverside godown, the STPI is a state-of-the-art print- and paper-making workshop cum art exhibition space cum print shop.

Sun Craft 02-08 Tanglin Shopping Ctr, 19 Tanglin Rd. Work by well-known local artists, using a range of different media.

Bookshops

MPH bookshops stock a wide choice of titles, and crop up all over town, with branches at B1-26a Citylink Mall, 1 Raffles Link, and 02-24 Raffles City Shopping Centre, 252 North Bridge Road. **Times** shops are also well stocked; you'll find a central branch at 04-08/15 Centrepoint, 175 Orchard Road.

Most bookshops carry selections of Western magazines and newspapers of varying breadth – as do the newsagents you find in every hotel foyer.

Books Kinokuniya 03-10/15 Ngee Ann City, 391 Orchard Rd. Singapore's largest bookstore by a long way, with an excellent selection of novels and magazines; branch at Sogo Department Store, 3rd floor, Raffles City Shopping Centre, 250 North Bridge Rd.

Borders 01-00 Wheelock Place, 501 Orchard Rd. All-conquering US bookstore chain, with an in-house café.

Madam Joe Holland Ave, Holland Village. Superb selection of magazines from around the world, at a street-side stall outside the Holland Road Shopping Centre.

Popular 04-23 Bras Basah Complex, Blk 231 Bain St; B1-02 Orchard MRT, 437 Orchard Rd. Cannot boast the stock of the bigger names, but still a safe bet for current bestsellers and local interest books.

Pro Saint Book Store 02-77 Bras Basah Complex, 231–233 Bain St. Books bought, sold and exchanged.

Select Books 03-15 Tanglin Shopping Ctr, 19 Tanglin Rd. A huge array of specialist books on Southeast Asia.

Sunny Bookshop 03-02 Far East Plaza, 14 Scotts Rd. New and secondhand English- and Chinese-language books.

Electronic equipment

Electronic equipment remains reasonably priced in the duty-free city of Singapore, but don't expect miracles. What's more impressive than Singapore's prices is its range of goods – whether you want to buy an MP3 player, a laptop, a camera or even a karaoke machine, some or other store is bound to stock the model you're after. Singaporeans love all things high-tech, and entire shopping centres specialize in electronics, making comparing prices and models a breeze. Orchard Road's Lucky Plaza is the focal point for **cameras**, with nearby Orchard Plaza and Far East Plaza also crammed with stores. You'll find the galleries of Sim Lim Tower and Sim Lim Square, around the intersection of Bencoolen Street and Rochor Road, teeming with stores selling **electronic goods** galore, from transistor radios to state-of-the-art TVs, DVDs and handhelds. For **computers** and **software**, Funan the IT Mall, 109 North Bridge Road, boasts a choice second to none, though nearby Peninsula Plaza specializes in this field too. Haggling is the norm in electrical goods shops, and all the rules laid out on p.163 apply – as do the warnings about checking compatibility and ensuring you get an international guarantee.

Jewellery

Singapore's glut of stores selling precious stones and gold means that **jewellery** prices remain competitive. Goldsmiths, in particular, are abundant, and their **gold** is of a consistently high quality – usually 22 or 24 carat. Prices of gold jewellery are affected, to some extent, by the craftsmanship involved, though primarily it's the weight and current market rate that dictate cost. Goldsmiths aplenty are to be found in Chinatown's People's Park Complex, and at the Pidemco Centre, 95 South Bridge Road, where the entire first floor is a jewellery mart. Little India's Serangoon Road has a wide choice, too, while in Orchard Road you'll find gold worked by international designers. Orchard Road is also the place to find high-quality **pearls**, **precious stones** and **jade**, or try Arab Street and Chinatown. As ever, bargaining is essential.

Chu's Jade Centre 01-53/54 Chinatown Point, 133 New Bridge Rd. Semiprecious stones, huge clusters of freshwater pearl necklaces, and exquisite jade sculptures.
CT Hoo 01-22 Tanglin Shopping Centre, 19 Tanglin Rd. Pearl specialists up at the western end of Orchard Road.
Famous Goldsmith 91 Serangoon Rd. Large range of gold chains and jewellery, on Little India's main drag.
Je T'aime 120 Oxley Rise. International designs in gold.
Larry's 'B' Tower 01-17 Ngee Ann City, 391

Orchard Rd. Hong Kong-designed gold, and precious gems – or have something tailor-made.
Png Watch dealer 02-206 Golden Mile Food Centre, 505 Beach Rd. Buys and sells antique watches.
Richard Hung Jewellers 01-24 Lucky Plaza, 304 Orchard Rd. Well-regarded jewellers, based in central Orchard Road, where staff are all qualified gemologists.
Risis Botanic Gardens, Cluny Rd. Specializes in jewellery made by gold-plating real orchids.

Music

CDs and tapes of all the latest mainstream and classical Western releases are universally available, as well as a surprising number of independent ones. In addition, most music stores stock a wide library of **Canto-pop** releases, though to check out some **Indian sounds** you'll have to go to Serangoon Road, and for Malay artists you'll want to make for the Joo Chiat Complex. **Thai pop** – often very good – is available at stores in the Golden Mile Complex on Beach Road. CDs cost around $20–25, but one or two smaller stores slash prices considerably.

Disc Planet 03-123 Far East Plaza, 14 Scotts Rd. Electronic music specialists.

HMV Singapore 01-11 The Heeren Shops, 260 Orchard Rd. Global music chain, now in Singapore, and offering good deals on latest releases.

Roxy Records 03-36 Funan the IT Mall, 109 North Bridge Rd. Discerning CD store with a good collection of indie and dance sounds, plus Singaporean artists.

Sembawang 03-04 Raffles City Shopping Ctr, 252 North Bridge Rd. A modest selection of CDs, but at prices that are consistently a dollar or two below those in the major chains.

Supreme Record Centre 03-28 Centrepoint, 175 Orchard Rd. One of the widest pop music selections in Singapore, plus a selection of imports from England and the USA.

That CD Shop 01-17 Tanglin Mall, 163 Tanglin Rd. Excellent collection of new age, Acid jazz and classical CDs that draws discerning musos in droves.

Tower Records 2nd floor Suntec City Mall, 3 Temasek Blvd. Wide choice of CDs and DVDs.

Fashion and textiles

There is a vibrant **fashion scene** in Singapore, and several of the city's eminent designers have their own boutiques. Inevitably, their works lean heavily upon Asian textiles and motifs. Up-and-coming local designers' collections are best witnessed during Singapore Fashion Week (Ⓦ www.singaporefashion-week.com.sg), when there are daily shows in central shopping malls.

Having a suit made up at one of the scores of **tailors** operating in Singapore, while not as cheap as in Bangkok, is still a money-saving exercise. The trick is to have a very clear idea of the style you want, and several days in hand for having alterations made. At the measuring stage, ensure the tailor knows exactly what design you want – it helps if you have a photo or catalogue clipping of the sort of suit you have in mind. A **deposit** is required at this stage, but don't be persuaded into paying the full cost until you've had as many fitting sessions as are necessary for the suit to be tailored to your satisfaction. Orchard Road's shopping centres boast the greatest number of tailors – try Far East Plaza, Far East Shopping Centre, Lucky Plaza or Orchard Plaza; otherwise, Peninsula Plaza has several options, or check out the pricier hotel-arcade tailors.

For something a little more ethnic, you'll find Singapore is exactly the hotbed of Asian **fabrics** you'd expect it to be. The streets of the Arab Quarter, and the markets of Geylang Serai stock the greatest choice of fabrics, including vast selections of Malaysian and Indonesian **batik**. Batik is produced by applying hot wax to a piece of cloth with either a pen or cotton stamp; when the cloth is dyed, the wax resists the dye and a pattern appears, a process that can be repeated many times to build up colours. The traditional way to wear batik is as a **sarong** – a rectangular length of cloth wrapped around the waist and legs to form a sort of skirt, worn by both males and females. The exquisite style of fabric known as **songket** is a step up in price from batik. Made by handweaving gold and silver thread into plain cloth, songket is used to make sarongs, headscarves and the like. Silk, too, is abundant: Chinese, Japanese and Thai silks are all available, or there are the primary-coloured silk **sarees** of Little India's fabric stores.

As well as ethnic fabrics, Singapore is also a great place to stock up on cheap and cheerful **travelling gear** such as T-shirts and shorts. Finally, **carpets** – both new and antique – from all over the world are competitively priced in Singapore.

Aljunied Brothers 91 Arab St; 04-75 Lucky Plaza, 304 Orchard Rd. Batik lengths as well as ready-made clothes.

Amir & Sons 03-01/7 Lucky Plaza, 304 Orchard Rd. Fine carpets from Persia, Pakistan, Turkey and China.

Dakshaini Silks 164 Serangoon Rd. Premier Indian embroidered silks.

Far East Plaza 14 Scotts Rd. The basement level yields alley after alley of tiny local boutique outlets, such as Series, Barcode and Red 2, catering for Singapore's young urban fashionistas.

Goodwill Trading Co **56 Arab St.** Indonesian batik sarongs heaped on varnished wood shelves.

Heeren: Annex 4th floor, The Heeren, 260 Orchard Rd. A whole floor of street and club wear by local designers such as Solid Fuel, Cloud Nine and Forward Statement.

House of Etiquette 86 Tanjong Pagar Rd. Breathtaking, sumptuous traditional Chinese wedding robes to buy or rent.

Jim Thompson Silk Shop 01-07 Raffles Hotel Arcade, 328 North Bridge Rd. Though businessman Jim Thompson disappeared under mysterious circumstances in Malaysia's Cameron Highlands in 1967, his name is still a byword for quality silk.

Little India Footwear 48 Serangoon Rd. Spangly, strappy shoes straight off the set of a Bollywood musical.

Marks and Spencer B1/B2 Wheelock Place, 501 Orchard Rd. Fashions and underwear for men and women, as well as toiletries and food.

Milkboy 02-205 Golden Mile Food Centre, 505 Beach Rd. One of a cluster of stalls selling Kangol, Stussy, Adidas and other urbanwear.

M)phosis B1-09 Ngee Ann City, 391 Orchard Rd. Chic, glamorous women's eveningwear and shoes by Singaporean designer, Colin Koh.

The Orientalist 10 Tanglin Rd. Imposing address at western end of Orchard Road, offering absolutely vast range of carpets from Persia, Pakistan, India and Turkey.

Projectshopbloodbros 01-42 Wisma Atria, 435 Orchard Rd. Laid-back, cocktail-bar chic for women.

Shanghai Tang 02-09 Ngee Ann City, 391 Orchard Rd. Exotic silk tunics and other high-fashion Chinoiserie by a Hong Kong designer.

Sithi Vinayagar Co 69 Serangoon Rd. Raw Thai and embroidered silks and sarees.

Song+Kelly21 1st floor, Forum Shopping Mall, 583 Orchard Rd. Understated men's and women's casual wear in muted colours.

S.S. Bobby Traders 57 Arab St. Indian, Chinese and Thai silks, linen and lace.

15

Sports

Singapore may be the gastronomic capital of Southeast Asia, but its range of affordable **sports facilities** means there is no excuse for running to fat during your stay. Whether your recreational leaning is towards racquet sports, watersports, golf, or less energetic pastimes such as snooker and darts, you'll find ample opportunities. We've listed alphabetically the main possibilities below, along with advice on whom to contact. Armchair sports fans will find some scope, too, for **spectator sports**, but don't expect your fixture list to be as congested as it is back home. Should sporting activities not be your idea of a holiday, you might consider a day's pampering at one of Singapore's many **spas**.

International events do crop up periodically, some even attracting the odd household name, but on the whole, you'll have a simple choice between horse racing and soccer. The listings magazine, *8 Days*, details all forthcoming events, big and small, while the STB will fill you in on all major events in the Singaporean sporting calendar. Online, the best resources are ⓦwww.singaporesport.com.sg and the Singapore Sports Council's site ⓦwww.ssc.gov.sg.

Bowling

A game of **tenpin bowling** in one of the centres listed below costs around $3.50 before 6pm on a weekday, and around $4 after 6pm and through the weekend. For up-to-the-minute details of bowling halls in Singapore check out ⓦwww.tenpinbowling.com.sg.
Cathay Bowl Leisure Court, 1018 East Coast Parkway ☏64440118.
Orchard Bowl Level 9, Cathay Cineleisure Orchard, 8 Grange Rd ☏62382088.
Plaza Bowl 08-11 Textile Centre, 200 Jalan Sultan ☏62924821.
Super Bowl 03-200 Marina Square, 6 Raffles Boulevard ☏63346334.

Cricket

The Singapore Cricket Club hosts **cricket** matches, from March through October, on Saturday after-

noons and Sunday mornings; spectators are welcome to watch from the Padang (see p.43), though entry into the club itself is restricted to members only.

Cycling and rollerblading

For cycling opportunities and bike rental in Singapore, see "Getting around", p.31. It's also possible to try rollerblading along the tracks of the East Coast Park. Again, see "Getting around", p.31, for rental outlets.

Golf

Singapore boasts a number of **golf** courses quite disproportionate to its size, and several of them are truly world-class. All the clubs listed below allow non-members to play upon payment of a green fee, though all will be bulging with members at the weekend. Green fees start from around $80 for eighteen holes, but you'll pay far more than this at the island's poshest country clubs; caddies' fees are around the $25 mark. Most clubs have their own driving range, but a cheaper option is the Parkland Golf Driving Range, 920 East Coast Parkway (℡64406726), where a good, long session won't run to more than $10.

If you just want to watch golf, the **Singapore Open Golf Championship** is an annual event that usually attracts some big names. The Johnnie Walker Classic, Southeast Asia's most prestigious golf tournament, was staged here in 1996, and is likely to return in the future.

Changi Golf Club 20 Netheravon Rd ℡65455133.

Jurong Country Club 9 Science Centre Rd ℡65685188.

Keppel Club 10 Bukit Chermin Rd ℡62735522.

Raffles Country Club 450 Jalan Ahmad Ibrahim ℡68617655.

Seletar Country Club 101 Seletar Club Rd ℡64860801.

Sentosa Golf Club 27 Bukit Manis Rd, Sentosa Island ℡62750022.

Horse racing, riding and polo

On-course **horse racing** features on the card at Singapore Turf Club, 1 Turf Club Avenue, only eighteen days a year, but the live coverage of Malaysian meetings that are shown on a giant screen at other times ensures you need never lose track of current form. For more information, see p.92, call ℡68791000 or visit ⓦwww.turfclub.com.sg. Otherwise, the Singapore Polo Club, 80 Mount Pleasant Road (℡62564530), hosts regular **polo** matches; call ahead for a current fixture list.

When the urge to saddle up becomes too great, there are several organizations offering **horse-riding** sessions. One is the Singapore Polo Club (see above), another, the **Bukit Timah Saddle Club**, 51 Fairway Drive (℡64662782). Sessions at these two places will set you back around $150.

Indoor sports: snooker, pool and darts

Snooker and **pool** are hugely popular in Singapore, and there are heaps of clubs from which to choose; all are listed in Singapore's Yellow Pages.

The Billiard Rooms, 03-01 20 Trengganu Street (℡62242997), is centrally located in the heart of Chinatown. At **Monstercue**, 02-42 Meridien Shopping Centre, 100 Orchard Road (℡62381689), there are twelve pool tables. **Pool Room**, attached to *DBL-O* nightclub at 02-20 Robertson Walk, 11 Unity Street (℡67352008), is another central option. Clubs typically open between 10am and 2am, and an hour's play costs around $10, with rates increasing in the evening. While their dress code doesn't run to bow ties and waistcoats, you may find you are stopped at the door unless you are wearing long trousers, a collar and closed footwear.

As is only proper, a game of **darts** entails a trip to a pub – locals at both the *Leisure Pub* (p.150) and the *Yard* (p.151) take the game very seriously.

Martial arts

Martial arts are not as evident as you would imagine in a country of such predominantly Chinese stock as Singapore. The best chance of catching any sort of performance is to watch locals practising **T'ai chi** – a series of slow, balletic exercises designed to stimulate mind and body – early in the morning at the Singapore Botanic Gardens. You'll find details of Singaporean T'ai chi schools and instructors at ⓦwww .singapore-taiji.com.

Skiing

Strange though it may sound, **skiing** – along with snowman-building and snowball fighting, is possible at *Snow City*, an indoor snow centre in western Singapore. See p.104 for more details.

Soccer

The number of column inches set aside for **soccer**, both local and international, in the *Straits Times* and *New Paper* testifies to the huge interest taken in the sport over here. English and European league and cup matches are shown weekly on TV, and there are occasional visits from world-famous teams such as Liverpool and Arsenal. Many pubs and bars (see p.148) advertise live sports screenings via satellite – those based on traditional British and Irish pubs are your best bet.

Singapore's national side draws crowds large enough to fill the 55,000-capacity National Stadium in Kallang. Until 1995, the team played in the Malaysia Premier League and the Malaysia Cup, but in 1995, the Football Association of Singapore (FAS) pulled out of both, possibly motivated by a desire to disassociate itself from the bribes scandal that rocked Malaysian soccer in 1994. Since then, the FAS has set up the S.League, Singapore's first ever professional league, which features twelve teams, including Chinese club Sinchi FC, and the Singaporean national under-23 team. The S.League season runs from February to October, and a game is shown live on Singaporean TV's Channel i, every Saturday night. In addition, the league's twelve teams battle for the Singapore Cup every year. For a current fixture list and ticketing details, check out the local press or go to Ⓦwww.sleague.com.

Tickets for **national fixtures** normally go on sale in the week before match days, at the National Stadium's FAS box office (Ⓣ63457111). Again, check the local press or Ⓦwww.fas.org.sg for details.

Spas

Singaporeans have gone health-treatment-crazy over the last few years, and a raft of luxury **spas** have opened up to cater for them. All offer a combination of whirlpools, pools, aromatherapy and beauty treatments, massages, saunas and body scrubs – but at a price. In Amrita Spa, for instance, treatments range from $45 to $170.

Amrita Spa 06-01 Raffles City Convention Centre, 2 Stamford Rd Ⓣ63364477.
Essence Vale 02-07 Orchard Emerald, 218 Orchard Rd Ⓣ67358082.
Esthetica 04-17 Takashimaya Shopping Centre, 291a Orchard Rd Ⓣ67337000.
Spacare 02-10 Paradiz Centre, 1 Selegie Rd Ⓣ63399118.

Swimming

All hotels of a certain size in Singapore have **swimming** pools, but if you're in budget accommodation, you will have to opt either for the beach or for a public pool. The island's longest stretch of beach lies along the East Coast Park, but you'll find the waters off Sentosa's sands much cleaner. Singapore's twenty or so **public pools** are listed in the Yellow Pages. The most central of these is the River Valley Swimming Complex across the road from Clarke Quay, on River Valley Road. Out east, there's the Katong Swimming Complex at 111 Wilkinson Road; while in the west of the island in Holland Village, there's the Buona Vista Swimming Complex, at 76 Holland Drive.

Tennis, squash and badminton

Though a number of venues across Singapore offer facilities for racket sports, their popularity means it pays to book well in advance. On average, halls are open daily 7am–10pm, and an hour's **badminton**, **squash** or **tennis** in them costs between $7 and $10. Many will rent out rackets for two or three dollars, but phone ahead to check first.

Kallang Squash & Tennis Centre 52 Stadium Rd ☎64406839.

Singapore Badminton Hall 100 Guillemard Rd ☎63457554 or ☎63441773.

Singapore Tennis Centre 1020 East Coast Parkway ☎64499034.

Watersports

Sea-locked Singapore Island offers extensive scope for **watersports**. The **Pasta Fresca Sea Sports Centre** offers affordable introductory courses for newcomers to **windsurfing** and **sailing**, while proficient non-members can rent windsurfing boards and lasers by the two-hourly session for $22 and $24 respectively.

    Canoeing is possible at Changi Point, East Coast Park and Sentosa Island, and costs around $10 an hour, and a couple of dollars more for a double-seater. For **waterskiing**, head for the Kallang River, northeast of the downtown area, or for either Sembawang or Ponngol, in the north of the island. You can expect to pay upwards of $70 an hour. Finally, several **scuba** outfits operate out of Singapore; however, for one of their trips into local, Indonesian or Malaysian waters, you'll pay several hundred dollars.

Cowabunga Ski Centre Kallang Stadium Lane ☎63348813. Offers a course of four water-skiing lessons for beginners ($150).

Living Seas 01-36 The Riverwalk, 20 Upper Circular Rd ☎64350436. Arranges PADI courses and regional diving trips, as well as renting and selling equipment.

Pasta Fresca Sea Sports Centre 1210 East Coast Parkway ☎64495118. A range of water-sports for all levels. Also has a good beach-front Italian restaurant.

Ponngol Sea-Sports Ponngol Marina, 600 Ponngol 17th Ave ☎63864736. Wakeboarding and waterskiing in the far north of the island.

ProAir Watersports SAF Yacht Club, 43 Admiralty Rd West, Sembawang Camp ☎67568012. Wakeboarding specialists, with a Jacuzzi in which to relax, after a strenuous day's boarding.

William Water Sports Centre 35 Ponngol 24th Ave, Ponngol Point ☎62575859. Waterskiing and wakeboarding courses and sessions.

16

Kids' Singapore

Y ou needn't have any reservations about bringing your **children** to Singapore. Just walking around the streets unearths enough of interest to keep even the most active imagination on the boil for a while, and when the prospect of traipsing through the umpteenth camera shop induces murmurings of rebellion among your kids, you'll find plenty of **activities** to amuse them. Singapore's efforts to craft itself into a fully fledged holiday destination have resulted in an array of theme parks and attractions, some geared specifically to children, others with more general family appeal; otherwise, beaches and open spaces abound. You'll find there are significant reductions on **admission prices** for children to Singapore's various attractions, often more than fifty percent. The suggestions below should give you some ideas for whiling away time; most places have been covered in the text, so you'll find further information by turning to the relevant page.

Taking in the spectacle of one of Singapore's many local **festivals** (see p.159) is another sure-fire way of keeping kids entertained, but be selective: some are wholesome – Chinese New Year, with its puppet shows, street operas and dragon and lion dances is one – but others, such as Thaipusam, could prove disturbing for children. For details of watching and playing **sport**, see Chapter 15.

Eating needn't be a problem with children in tow. The listings in Chapter 10 cover a wide range of cuisines, ranging from the exotic to the familiar, so if your children aren't great culinary adventurers, you'll can always track down a burger bar or pizza joint nearby. In Southeast Asia, dining out is a family affair and shown little of the reverence it enjoys in the West, so unless you're going really upmarket, don't be shy of taking the kids with you.

Most mid-range and upmarket **hotels** in Singapore make no charge for children under 12 if they are occupying existing spare beds in hotel rooms. However, if you require an extra bed to be put in your room, ten to fifteen percent of the room rate is usually charged. Cots are almost invariably provided free. When you need time to yourself, **babysitting** is easy to arrange, either through a hotel or a private agency (see the *Singapore Buying Guide*, Singapore's telephone directory).

Parks, gardens and outings

The following parks, attractions and activities should all carry particular appeal for kids. Some – but by no means all – require payment of an entry fee.

Bukit Timah Nature Reserve Hiking and biking tracks through primary rainforest, under the watchful eyes of inquisitive

macaques. See p.85.
Cable cars These whisk you from the World Trade Centre (see p.99) to Mount Faber,

which affords tremendous views of Keppel Harbour and the city.

Dizzee World 01-01/2 The Foundry, Clarke Quay. Loud, cavernous arcade, full of video games and other amusements.

East Coast Parkway Kilometres of clean sand, biking and rollerblading tracks and barbecue pits. Camping is also possible See p.122.

Fort Canning Park Pleasant strolls, plus underground bunkers dating from World War II to explore in the park; and the River Valley Swimming Complex on the southern slope. See p.51.

Jurong BirdPark Residents, which include penguins, birds of prey and hornbills, are accessed by hopping on a sci-fi panorail. Kids will love the simulated tropical storm, daily at noon. See p.104.

Marina South Spacious park featuring an imaginative playground, kite-flying locals and great views of the city. See p.73.

Pan Pacific Hotel lifts Running up and down the outside of the hotel; the most exhilarating way to take in a bird's-eye view of the city.

Pulau Ubin (see p.97) and **southern isles** (see p.107). Biking, beaches and boats there and back.

Sea and river cruises (see p.32). Cruises around the Singapore River and the southern isles. Best of all for kids is the Wacky Duck tour (see p.31), taken on a Vietnam War-era amphibious craft that drives around the city before launching into Singapore Harbour.

Singapore Botanic Gardens Beautifully peaceful gardens, with oodles of space for kids to explore. See p.56.

Singapore Zoological Gardens (see p.90). Singapore's zoo, acclaimed for its humane conditions, complete with tram, animal shows and interactive children's zone, besides opportunities for breakfast with assorted animals (see p.126). For a late-night treat, the post-dusk **Night Safari** (see p.90), adjoining the zoo, opens a window on the animals' nocturnal habits.

Sungei Buloh Wetland Reserve A charming reserve, home to kingfishers, mudskippers, herons and eagles. See p.92.

Museums and theme parks

When your kids tire of rampaging around parks, gardens and islands, you may want to introduce them to some of the rather more cerebral attractions Singapore has to offer. All the listings below will provide them with plenty of historical or cultural food for thought.

Asian Civilization museums The Singapore River Interpretive Gallery (featuring oral history accounts of river life) and Peranakan Gallery have much to interest youngsters. See pp.42 and 50.

Chinatown Heritage Centre If any museum is capable of grabbing kids' attention, it is this, with its faithful reconstruction of the appalling conditions endured by early Chinese settlers in Singapore. See p.67.

Escape Theme Park No Disneyland, but still a selection of enjoyable rides. See p.98.

Haw Par Villa Hundreds of lurid statues, murals and dioramas offering imaginative retellings of Chinese myths – some of which are rather gory and risqué. See p.101.

Sentosa Island Extensive pleasure island with enough attractions to fill a whole day, as well as beaches and wildlife. See p.106.

Singapore History Museum Hit-and-miss, though the dioramas telling Singapore's history may well appeal to children, as might the 3D glasses you don before viewing the story of Singapore in the "theatrette". See p.51.

Singapore Discovery Centre Motion simulators and virtual reality rides. See p.105.

Singapore Science Centre Scores of hands-on science exhibits targeted at children, as well as an omni-theatre screening educative films on a wraparound screen. See p.103.

Snow City Skiing, tobogganing and snowman making. See p.104.

Temples

All of the temples listed below are colourful, arresting and eventful enough to interest an open-minded child. Some feature fortune-tellers, turtle ponds and caged snakes.

Shops

The shops and shopping centres below all cater for children. For nappies and other toiletries, see "Pharmacies" in the Directory (p.179).

Comics World B1-22 Parklane Shopping Mall, 35 Selegie Rd ☎63396413. Stocks current American titles, figurines and collectables, from Batman to the X-Men.

Computer Games are sold in the Funan Centre and Peninsula Plaza, both on North Bridge Road. For **electrical goods**, make for either Sim Lim Tower or nearby Sim Lim Square, at the junction of Bencoolen Street and Jalan Besar.

Mothercare 01-34/39 Centrepoint, 176 Orchard Rd ☎67327566. Worldwide chain stocking everything your child could ever need, from romper suits to buggies.

My Little Wardrobe 01-18/19 Forum the Shopping Mall, 583 Orchard Rd ☎67326167. Boutique carrying colourful and fashionable kiddies' wear from pre-eminent designers, including Oshkosh B'Gosh, Boboli and Mickey for Kids. One of numerous kids' clothes stores in this shopping centre.

Borders 01-00 Wheelock Place, 501 Orchard Rd ☎62357146. A healthy selection of books for the young, and a laissez-faire attitude that allows kids to plonk themselves down on the ground and have a good browse before buying.

Toys "R" Us 03-04 Forum the Shopping Mall, 583 Orchard Rd ☎662354322. Kids will think they have died and gone to heaven in this, Singapore's largest toy shop.

16

Kuan Yim Temple Waterloo St. See p.49.
Phor Kark See Temple Bright Hill Drive. See p.90.
Lian Shan Shuang Lin Temple Jalan Toa Payoh. See p.89.
Sakaya Muni Budha Gaya Temple Race Course Rd. See p.79.

Sasanaramsi Burmese Buddhist Temple Tai Gin Rd. See p.89.
Sri Mariamman Temple South Bridge Rd. See p.79.
Sri Srinivasa Perumal Temple Serangoon Rd. See p.79.
Thian Hock Keng Temple Telok Ayer St. See p.80.

KIDS' SINGAPORE | Shops

Directory

Airlines The main airlines are listed below. You'll find any others in the phone directory. Aeroflot 01-02/02-00 Tan Chong Tower, 15 Queen St ☎63361757; Air Canada Singapore, 101 Thomson Rd, 01-08 United Square ☎62561198; Air India, B1-10/12 UIC Building, 5 Shenton Way ☎62205277; Air New Zealand, 24-08 Ocean Building, 10 Collyer Quay ☎65358266; American Airlines, 06-05 Cairnhill Place, 15 Cairnhill Rd ☎67370900; Berjaya Air, 67 Tanjong Pagar Rd ☎62276698; British Airways, 06-05 Cairnhill Place, 15 Cairnhill Rd ☎65897000; Cathay Pacific, 16-01 Ocean Building, 10 Collyer Quay ☎65331333; Garuda, 12-03 United Square, 101 Thomson Rd ☎62505666; KLM, 12-06 Ngee Ann City Tower A, 391a Orchard Rd ☎67377622; Lufthansa, 05-07 Palais Renaissance, 390 Orchard Rd ☎62455600; MAS, 02-09 Singapore Shopping Centre, 190 Clemenceau Ave ☎63366777; Philippine Airlines, 01-10 Parklane Shopping Mall, 35 Selegie Rd ☎63361611; Qantas, Unit 06-05/08 The Promenade, 300 Orchard Rd ☎65687000; Royal Brunei 03-11 UE Shopping Mall, 81 Clemenceau Ave ☎62354672; Royal Nepal Airlines, 03-09 Peninsula Shopping Centre, 3 Coleman St ☎3395535; Silkair, 08-01 Temasek Tower, 8 Shenton Way ☎62238888; Singapore Airlines, 02-26 The Paragon, 290 Orchard Rd ☎62238888; SriLankan Airlines, 13-02 Keck Seng Tower, 133 Cecil St ☎62236026; Thai Airways, 02-00 The Globe, 100 Cecil St ☎62249977; United Airlines, 44-02 Hong Leong Building, 16 Raffles Quay ☎68733533.

Airport enquiries The toll-free Changi airport flight information number is ☎1-800/5424422.

British Council West of Orchard Rd at 30 Napier Rd ☎64731111.

Car rental Avis, 01-01 Concorde Hotel Shopping Centre, 317 Outram Rd ☎67371668 and Terminal 2, Changi airport ☎65428855; Hertz, 01-01 Thong Teck Building, 15 Scotts Rd ☎1800-734 4646 and Terminal 2 Changi airport, ☎65425300; Sintat, 8 Kim Keat Lane ☎62952211 and Terminal 1, Changi airport ☎65427288.

Credit card helplines American Express ☎1800-299 1997; Diners Club ☎62944222; Mastercard ☎65332888; Visa ☎64375800.

Dentists Listed in the *Singapore Buying Guide* (equivalent to the Yellow Pages) under "Dental Surgeons" and "Dentist Emergency Service".

Departure tax A $15 tax is levied on all flights out of Singapore.

Doctors There are clinics in most shopping centres – there are scores in both the Tanglin Shopping Centre and the Specialists Shopping Centre; for A&E listings, see "Hospitals" below.

Electricity Singapore's mains electricity is 220–240 volts, 50 Hertz.

Embassies and consulates Australia ☎68364100; Brunei ☎67339055; Canada ☎62253240; France ☎68807800; Germany ☎67371355; India ☎67376777; Indonesia ☎67377422; Ireland ☎62387616; Malaysia ☎62350111; New Zealand ☎62359966; Philippines ☎67373977; Sri Lanka ☎62544595; Thailand ☎67372644; UK ☎64739333; USA ☎64769100; Vietnam ☎64625938.

Emergencies Police ☎999; Ambulance and Fire Brigade ☎995 (all toll-free); larger hotels have doctors on call at all times.

Hospitals Singapore General, Outram Rd ☎62223322, Alexandra Hospital, Alexandra Rd ☎64722000, and National University Hospital, Kent Ridge ☎67795555 are all state hospitals and all have outpatient/A&E departments. Raffles Hospital ☎63111555 is private, but very central.

Immigration department For visa extension enquiries, contact the Singapore Immigration and Registration Department, 10 Kallang Rd (Mon–Fri 9am–5pm; ☎63916100).

Laundry DryClean Express offers a pick-up and delivery service, ☎68615933/ ☎62860811; Washy Washy, 01-18 Cuppage Plaza, 5 Koek Rd (Mon–Sat 10am–7pm).

Left luggage A 24-hr luggage storage service is available in both terminals at Changi airport. Charges range from a dollar upwards, depending on size. Call ☎62140628 or 62141683.

Library Until the new library currently under construction at the junction of Middle and North Bridge roads is complete, Singapore National Library is beside the National Museum on Stamford Road (Mon 11am–8pm, Tues–Fri 9am–8pm, Sat 9am–5pm, Sun 1–5pm).

Pharmacies Guardian pharmacy has over forty outlets, including ones at Centrepoint, 176 Orchard Rd; Raffles City Shopping Centre, 252 North Bridge Rd; and Clifford Centre, 24 Raffles Place. Usual hours are 9am–6pm, but some stay open until 10pm.

There are also around fifty outlets of Watson's pharmacy. For out-of-hours medication, you will need to go to one of the hospitals listed above.

Police In an emergency, dial ☎999; otherwise call the freephone police hotline, ☎1800-255 0000.

Taxis CityCab ☎64-520220 or 65522222; Comfort ☎65521111.

Time Singapore is eight hours ahead of GMT, sixteen hours ahead of US Pacific Standard Time, thirteen hours ahead of Eastern Standard Time, and two hours behind Sydney.

Tipping Tipping is not customary in Singapore. Restaurants, however, automatically add a service charge and government tax (around fifteen percent) to bills.

Travel agents All the following are good for discounted air fares and buying bus tickets to Malaysia and Thailand: Airpower Travel, 131a Bencoolen St ☎63346571; E & O Services (for the Eastern & Oriental Express), 32-01 Shaw Tower, 100 Beach Rd ☎63923500; Harharah Travel, 1st floor, 171a Bencoolen St ☎63372633; STA Travel, 33a Cuppage Terrace ☎67377188, ⊛www.statravel.com.sg; Sunny Holidays, 01-70 Parco Bugis Junction, 200 Victoria St ☎63345545.

Vaccinations Travellers' Health & Vaccination Clinic, Tan Tock Seng Hospital Medical Centre, 11 Jalan Tan Tock Seng ☎63572222.

Women's helpline Women's helpline

Contexts

Contexts

A brief history of Singapore 183

Religion 190

Chinese astrology 194

Singaporean recipes 198

Singapore in literature..202

Books 210

Glossary 214

A brief history of Singapore

What little is known of Singapore's **ancient history** relies heavily upon legend and supposition. Third-century Chinese sailors could have been referring to Singapore in their account of a place called Pu-Luo-Chung, or "island at the end of a peninsula". In the late thirteenth century, **Marco Polo** reported seeing a place called Chiamassie, which could also have been Singapore: by then the island was known locally as Temasek – "sea town" – and was a minor trading outpost of the Sumatran Srivijaya empire. The island's present name comes from the Sanskrit *Singapura*, meaning "Lion City", and was first recorded in the sixteenth century. A legend narrated in the Malay annals (the *Sejarah Melayu*) told how a Sumatran prince saw a lion while sheltering on the island from a storm; the annals reported that the name had been in common use since the end of the fourteenth century.

Throughout the fourteenth century, Singapura felt the squeeze as the Ayuthaya and Majapahit empires of Thailand and Java struggled for control of the Malay peninsula. Around 1390, a Sumatran prince called **Paramesvara** threw off his allegiance to the Javanese Majapahit empire and fled from Palembang to present-day Singapore. There, he murdered his host and ruled the island until a Javanese offensive forced him to flee north, up the peninsula, where he and his son, **Iskandar Shah,** subsequently founded the Melaka sultanate. A grave on Fort Canning Hill (see p.51) is said to be that of Iskandar Shah, though its authenticity is doubtful. With the rise of the Melaka sultanate, Singapore devolved into an inconsequential fishing settlement; a century or so later, the arrival of the Portuguese in Melaka forced Malay leaders to flee southwards to modern-day Johor Bahru for sanctuary, and a Portuguese account, in 1613, of the razing of an unnamed Malay outpost at the mouth of Sungei Johor marked the beginning of two centuries of historical limbo for Singapore.

Sir Stamford Raffles and the founding of Singapore

By the late eighteenth century, with China opening up for trade with the West, the **British East India Company** felt the need to establish outposts along the Straits of Melaka to protect its interests. Penang was secured in 1786, but with the Dutch expanding their rule in the East Indies (Indonesia), a port was needed further south. Enter visionary colonial administrator **Thomas Stamford Raffles** (see p.44 full biography). In 1818, the governor-general of India authorized Raffles, then lieutenant-governor of Bencoolen (in Sumatra), to establish a British colony at the southern tip of the Malay Peninsula; early the next year, he stepped ashore on the northern bank of the Singapore River, accompanied by Colonel William Farquhar, who was a former Resident of Melaka and was fluent in Malay.

At the time, inhospitable swampland and tiger-infested jungle covered Singapore, and its population is generally thought to have numbered around

150, although some historians suggest it could have been as high as a thousand. Raffles recognized the island's potential as a deep-water harbour, and immediately struck a treaty with **Abdul Rahman**, *temenggong* (chieftain) of Singapore, establishing a British trading station there. The Dutch were furious at this British invasion of what they considered was their territory, but Raffles – who still needed the approval of the sultan of Riau-Johor for his outpost, as Abdul Rahman was only an underling – disregarded Dutch sensibilities. Realizing that the sultan's loyalties to the Dutch would make such approval impossible, Raffles approached the sultan's brother, Hussein, recognizing him as the true sultan, and concluded a second treaty with both the *temenggong* and His Highness the **sultan Hussein Mohammed Shah**. The Union Jack was raised, and Singapore's future as a free trading post was set.

Strategically positioned at the foot of the Straits of Melaka, and with no customs duties levied on imported or exported goods, Singapore's expansion was meteoric. The population had reached ten thousand by the time of the first census in 1824, with Malays, Chinese, Indians and Europeans arriving in search of work as coolies and merchants. In 1822, Raffles set about drawing up the demarcation lines that divide present-day Singapore. The area south of the Singapore River was earmarked for the Chinese; a swamp at the mouth of the river was filled and the commercial district established there, while Muslims were settled around the Sultan's Palace in today's Arab Quarter. The Singapore of those times was a far cry from the pristine city of the late twentieth century. "There were thousands of rats all over the district," wrote Abdullah bin Kadir, scribe to Stamford Raffles, "some almost as large as cats. They were so big that they used to attack us if we went out walking at night and many people were knocked over."

The early boom years

In 1824, Sultan Hussein and the *temenggong* were bought out, and Singapore ceded outright to the British. Three years later, the fledgling state united with Penang and Melaka (by now under British rule) to form the Straits Settlements, which became a British crown colony in 1867. For forty years the laissez-faire economy boomed, though life was chaotic and disease was rife. More and more immigrants poured onto the island and by 1860 the population had reached eighty thousand, with each arriving ethnic community bringing its attendant cuisines, languages and architecture. **Arabs, Indians, Javanese** and **Bugis** (from Sulawesi) all came, but most populous of all were the **Chinese**, who arrived in numbers from the southern provinces of China and settled quickly, helped by the clan societies (*kongsis*) already establishing footholds on the island. The British, for their part, erected impressive Neoclassical theatres, courts and assembly halls, and in 1887 Singapore's most quintessentially British establishment – the **Raffles Hotel** – opened for business.

By the end of the nineteenth century, the opening of the Suez Canal and the advent of steamships had consolidated Singapore's position at the hub of international trade in the region, with the port becoming a major staging post on the Europe–East Asia route. In 1877, **Henry Ridley** began his one-man crusade to introduce the rubber plant into Southeast Asia, a move which further bolstered Singapore's importance: the island soon became the world centre of rubber exporting. This status was further enhanced by the slow but steady drawing of the Malay Peninsula under British control – a process begun with the Treaty of Pangkor in 1874 and completed in 1914 – which meant that Singapore gained further still from the mainland's tin- and rubber-based economy. Between 1873 and 1913, trade increased eightfold, a trend which continued well into the twentieth century.

Singapore's Asian communities found their political voice in the 1920s: in 1926, the **Singapore Malay Union** was established, and four years later, the Chinese-supported **Malayan Communist Party (MCP)** appeared. But pro-independence activity had still not achieved its goal when the spectre of war reared its head in 1942.

The Japanese invasion and occupation

In 1942, the bubble burst. In December 1941, the **Japanese** had bombed Pearl Harbor and invaded the Malay Peninsula. Less than two months later they were at the top of the causeway, safe from the guns of "Fortress Singapore", which pointed south from what is now Sentosa Island. The inhabitants of Singapore had not been prepared for an attack from this direction and on February 15, 1942, the fall of Singapore (which the Japanese then renamed Syonan, or "Light of the South") was complete.

Three and a half years of brutal Japanese rule ensued, during which thousands of civilians were executed in vicious anti-Chinese purges, and Europeans were either herded into **Changi Prison**, or marched up the peninsula to work on Thailand's infamous "Death Railway". Less well known is the vicious campaign, known as **Operation Sook Ching**, mounted by the military police force, or *Kempeitai*, during which upwards of twenty-five thousand Chinese males between 18 and 50 years of age were shot dead at Punggol and Changi beaches as enemies of the Japanese.

The postwar years

In 1945, Singapore passed back into British hands, but things were never to be the same. Singaporeans now wanted a say in the governing of their island. A year later, the Straits Settlements were dissolved, and Singapore became a crown colony in its own right. Island politics, though, remained closely linked with those of the Peninsula for the next nineteen years.

Across the causeway, Malay nationalists set up the **United Malays National Organization (UNMO)** in 1946, whose main tenet was that Malays should retain special privileges over Chinese and Indians in Malaya. The pressure they brought to bear on the British government resulted, in February 1948, in the establishment of the Federation of Malaya, which brought together all the states of Peninsular Malaya, but not Singapore, whose inclusion would have led to ethnic Malays being in a minority. Protests erupted in Singapore at this exclusion, with the **Malayan Democratic Union (MDU)** calling for integration with Malaya – a position that commanded little support among the Chinese population. Singapore's first ever elections, a month later, were boycotted by the MDU.

The possibility of Singapore having no landward defences no more entered my mind than that of a battleship being launched without a bottom.

Sir Winston Churchill.

The hills and jungles of northern and western Singapore were the setting of the battle for "the strongest British bastion east of Suez". Popular wisdom had it that a Japanese attack could come only from the sea: the view of one British intelligence officer, that "the Japanese are very small and short-sighted and thus totally unsuited physically to tropical warfare", embodied the complacency and self-delusion of the Allied Command under **Lieutenant-General Arthur Percival**.

Events were to prove the British wrong. On December 8, 1941, Japanese forces led by **General Tomoyuki Yamashita** – the "Tiger of Malaya" – landed on Malaya's northeastern coast at Kota Bahru. By the end of January they had reached Johor Bahru, a kilometre away from Singapore. Judging that the Japanese attack would focus on the northeast coast of Singapore, Percival deployed what few defences were at his disposal there, leaving the scant Australian presence guarding the northwest stretched to breaking point.

From his command room in JB's istana, Yamashita oversaw a week's bombing of Singapore. Then, on February 7, 1942, the **invasion** began, with Japanese Imperial Guards mounting an attack on Pulau Ubin, northeast of Singapore. On the following day, Yamashita ordered intensive bombing of the coastline west of the causeway. Having softened up their point of invasion, the Japanese used collapsible launches and the cover of darkness to attack the area west of what is now Sungei Buloh Reserve. Allied troops quickly withdrew in disarray, and by the following morning the Japanese had probed eight kilometres inland. After another landing a day later, this time at the mouth of the Kranji River, the Imperial Army began its two-pronged offensive.

Tengah Airfield (then 5km north of Jurong Lake) fell on February 9, and the following day saw Yamashita take his first steps on Singaporean soil and **establish command** near the airfield, as his troops pushed towards MacRitchie and Peirce reservoirs, the city's only sources of water.

Between February 11 and 14, **decisive victories** were won by the Japanese at Bukit Timah Hill and a few hundred metres from today's Haw Par Villa at Pasir Panjang Village, where a brigade of Malays made a heroic 48-hour stand before being all but wiped out. By February 14, Singapore was as good as lost – a fact that made the massacre of two hundred patients and staff at the Alexandra Hospital (northwest of Mount Faber) all the more appalling. Faced with further loss of life – and unaware to what extent Japanese supplies were stretched – Percival travelled up Dunearn Road to the Ford Motor Factory at Bukit Timah Village, where Yamashita was now based, and **surrendered** on Sunday, February 15. Winston Churchill called the British surrender "the worst disaster and the largest capitulation in British history"; it later transpired that the Japanese forces had been outnumbered and their supplies hopelessly stretched immediately prior to the surrender.

Chinese opposition to the Federation of Malaya on the mainland ignited the **Communist Emergency**, an MCP-led guerrilla struggle lasting from 1948 until 1960, whose aim was to turn Singapore and Malaysia into a republic; in Singapore, the MCP was outlawed, and a state of emergency declared.

In the 1950s Singapore's progress towards independence slowly gathered momentum. In 1953 the British government appointed a commission to review the island's constitution, and though still flawed (only 25 of a legislative assembly of 32 were voted in), the elections of April 1955 were the most representative seen so far on the island. **David Marshall**, leader of the victorious **Labour Front**, became chief minister.

By 1957, the Federation of Malaya had achieved independence, and that same year, the British government agreed to the establishment of an elected, 51-member legislative assembly in Singapore. Full internal self-government was achieved in May 1959, when the **People's Action Party (PAP)**, led by Cambridge law graduate **Lee Kuan Yew**, won 43 of the 51 seats. Lee became Singapore's first prime minister, and quickly looked for the security of a merger with neighbouring Malaya. For its part – and despite reservations about aligning itself with Singapore's predominantly Chinese population – anti-Communist Malaya feared that extremists within the PAP would turn Singapore into a Communist base, and accordingly preferred to have the state under its wing.

In 1963, Singapore combined with Malaya, Sarawak and British North Borneo (modern-day Sabah), to form the **Federation of Malaysia**. The alliance, though, was an uneasy one. Differences soon developed between Lee Kuan Yew and the mainland's Malay-dominated **Alliance Party** over the lack of egalitarian policies. Although the PAP had dominated recent elections, many Chinese were concerned that Malays exercised too great a control over the federation. Tensions rose on the island and ugly racial incidents developed into full-scale riots, in which several people were killed. Within two years Singapore was asked to leave the federation, in the face of outrage in Kuala Lumpur at the PAP's attempts to break into Peninsular politics in 1964.

Hours after announcing Singapore's full independence, on August 9, 1965, a tearful Lee Kuan Yew described the event, on national TV, as "a moment of anguish". One hundred and forty-six years after Sir Stamford Raffles had set Singapore on the world map, the tiny island, with no natural resources of its own, faced the prospect of being consigned to history's bottom drawer of crumbling colonial ports.

Independence

Against all the odds, Lee's personal vision and drive transformed Singapore into an Asian economic heavyweight. Political alignments were made to maximize business opportunities, and the economy grew fast: per capita income increased an astonishing fourfold between 1965 and 1977, with huge profits being made in financial services, high-tech manufacture, information technology and the petroleum industry. The high taxes these boom areas produced were used to bolster the island's infrastructure and housing, and by 1980, the impossible had been achieved: Singapore stood on the verge of becoming a **Newly Industrialized Economy (NIE)**, along with Hong Kong, Taiwan and South Korea.

But these developments were achieved at a price. Heavy-handed **censorship of the media** was introduced, and offences such as dropping litter were punished in a draconian style, with offenders submitted to the public humiliation of forced litter duty. Most disturbing of all was the government's attitude towards political opposition. When the opposition **Worker's Party** won a by-election in 1981, the candidate, J.B. Jeyaretnam, found himself charged with several criminal offences, and chased through the Singaporean law courts for the next decade. The archaic **Internal Security Act** still grants the power to detain without trial anyone the government deems a threat to the nation – a law which kept political prisoner **Chia Thye Poh** under lock and key from

1966 until 1998 for allegedly advocating violence. Population policies, too, have brought criticism from abroad. These began in the early 1970s, with a **birth control campaign** which proved so successful that it had to be reversed: the 1980s saw the introduction of the "Go For Three" project, which offered tax incentives for those having more than two children in an attempt to boost the national – and, some say, more specifically the Chinese Singaporean – birth rate. Lee Kuan Yew also made clear his conviction that Singapore's educated elite should intermarry, thereby breeding the sort of babies that would serve the country well in the future.

At times, Singapore tries so hard to reshape itself that it falls into self-parody. "We have to pursue this subject of fun very seriously if we want to stay competitive in the twenty-first century", was the reaction of government minister, George Yeo, when challenged on the fact that some foreigners found Singapore dull. Whether Singaporeans will continue to suffer their government's foibles remains to be seen. Adults beyond a certain age remember how things were before independence, and, more importantly, before the existence of the MRT system, housing projects and savings schemes. Their children and grandchildren have no such perspective, however, and telltale signs – presently nothing more extreme than feet up on MRT seats, or jaywalking – suggest that the government can expect more dissent in future years. Already a substantial brain drain is afflicting the country, as Singaporeans with skills to offer choose to move abroad in the pursuit of a more liberal environment.

Singapore today

The man who has led Singapore into the new millennium is **Goh Chok Tong**, who became prime minister upon Lee's retirement from that post in 1990. Goh made it clear, at the beginning of his tenure, that he favoured a more open form of government. In April 2001, he even allowed an unprecedented anti-government rally to take place, which raised funds for veteran opposition leader, J.B. Jeyaretnam. But Lee still looms over the political scene in his role as senior minister, and his son, deputy prime minister **Brigadier-General Lee Hsien Loong**, is waiting in the wings to succeed to the top spot, once Goh retires.

The events of the past decade do suggest that, until he does retire, Goh has a mandate for change. In the 1991 elections he suffered the relative setback of seeing an unprecedented four opposition members voted into parliament. However, in the elections of January 1997 (which the PAP had won even before the polling stations opened, as opposition candidates contested fewer than half of the seats), he clawed back two of these seats, partly thanks to insinuations that constituencies failing to return their PAP candidate would drop down the waiting list for housing estate renovations. In the **November 2001 elections**, he again won all but two of the 84 seats being contested.

Politics apart, recent years have been as tough on Singapore economically as its residents can remember in decades. The state was able to weather the **financial crisis** that struck first Thailand, and then the rest of Southeast Asia in the late 1990s. Though the economy slowed – and unemployment rose – it emerged from the crisis dented but intact. However, the global downturn that followed the events of September 11, 2001 has taken a further economic toll. After achieving ten percent growth in 2000, the economy had contracted two percent by the end of 2001; and by late 2002, the *Straits Times* was warning of a possible recession if GDP growth continued to contract. The impact of 9/11 has not been confined to economics. In September 2002, the authorities arrested 21 suspected terrorists. And in early 2003, a report from the Ministry of Home Affairs detailed a series of alleged plots by Jemaah Islamiah, a regional group of radical Muslims, to attack Western interests in Singapore.

In February 2003, Singapore's first cases of Severe Acute Respiratory Syndrome, or **SARS**, came to light, adding another problem to those of the economy and terrorism. Within weeks, the island was one of the global hotspots for SARS, with an official death toll that had risen to 31 by the end of May 2003. The Singaporean government moved decisively to counter the threat posed by SARS to its population and its tourism trade, earning praise from the World Health Organization for surpassing the WHO's recommended measures. For more practical information on Singapore's current SARS status, turn to "Health", on p.24.

Religion

otal **freedom of worship** is enjoyed in Singapore, whose multicultural society is reflected in the wide range of creeds that it supports. Over half of the population of 3.87 million follow Chinese religions – mostly Buddhism, but with elements of Taoism and Confucianism. Malays, who make up fourteen percent of the population, are predominantly Muslim, while the nation's Indians are either Hindu, Muslim or Sikh. In addition, one in ten Singaporeans are Christians: most are Protestants, though all denominations are represented, and there's a large enough Jewish community to support two synagogues.

Below are overviews of the three main strands of belief in Singapore today: Chinese religions, Islam and Hinduism.

Chinese religions

Singaporean Chinese are mainly either **Buddhist**, **Taoist** or **Confucianist**, although in practice they are often a mixture of all three. These different strands of Chinese religion ostensibly lean in very different directions, but in practice the combination of the three comprises a system of belief which is first and foremost pragmatic. The Chinese use religion to ease their passage through life, whether in the spheres of work or family, while temples double as social centres, where people meet and exchange views.

Buddhism

Buddhism states that the suffering of the world can only be achieved by attaining a state of personal enlightenment, or nirvana, through meditation. The founder of Buddhism, **Siddhartha Gautama**, was born a prince in Lumbini in present-day Nepal, around 500 BC. Shielded from knowledge of suffering and death for the first decades of his life, he subsequently renounced his pampered life and spent years in meditation, before finding enlightenment under a bodhi tree. At this point he became the Buddha or "Awakened One". (In Singapore and Southeast Asia he is called *Sakyamuni*, or "Holy Man of the Sakya tribe".) In his first sermon, Buddha taught the four noble truths: that suffering exists; that its source should be recognized; that one should strive for a cessation of suffering; and that this can be achieved by following the **Eightfold Path** – practising right views, intentions, speech, action, livelihood, effort, mindfulness and concentration. The Buddhist faith is split into two schisms: **Hinayana** (Lesser Vehicle) Buddhism, which teaches individuals how to attain enlightenment for themselves, and **Mahayana** (Greater Vehicle) Buddhism – favoured in Singapore – which teaches that, having reached enlightenment, followers should help others to do the same.

Taoism

Unity with nature is the chief tenet of Taoism, a philosophical movement dating from the sixth century BC, and propounded by the Chinese scholar **Lao Tze**. Taoism advocates that people follow a central path or truth, known as *Tao* or "The Way", and cultivate an understanding of the nature of things. This search for truth has often expressed itself in Taoism by way of superstition on the part of its devotees, who engage in fortune-telling and the like. The Taoist gods are mainly legendary figures – warriors, statesmen, scholars – with specific powers that can generally be determined by their form; others represent incarnations of the forces of nature.

Confucianism

Confucianism began as a philosophy based on piety, loyalty, humanitarianism and familial devotion. In the 2500 years since **Confucius**, its founder, died, it has transmuted into a set of principles that permeate every aspect of Chinese life. A blueprint for social and moral harmony, the Confucian ideology stresses one's obligation to family, community and the state, hinging on the individual's need to recognize his or her position in the social hierarchy and act accordingly – son must obey father, student must obey teacher, subject must obey ruler. Little wonder that Lee Kuan Yew has long advocated Confucian values in Singapore.

Chinese temples

The rules of **geomancy**, or **feng shui** (wind and water), are rigorously applied to the construction of **Chinese temples**, so that the buildings are placed to render them free from evil influences. Visitors wishing to cross the threshold of a temple have to step over a kerb that's intended to trip up evil spirits, and walk through doors painted with fearsome door gods; fronting the doors are two stone lions, providing yet another defence. Larger temples typically consist of a front entrance hall opening onto a walled-in courtyard, beyond which is the hall of worship, where joss (luck) sticks are burned below images of the deities. The most important and striking element of a Chinese temple is its roof. They are grand, multi-tiered affairs, with low, overhanging eaves, the ridges alive with auspicious creatures such as dragons and phoenixes and, less often, with miniature scenes from traditional Chinese life and legend. Temples are also normally constructed around a framework of huge, lacquered timber beams, adorned with intricately carved warriors, animals and flowers. More figures are moulded onto outer walls, which are dotted with octagonal, hexagonal or round grille-worked windows. Feng shui comes into play again inside the temple, with auspicious room numbers and sizes, colour and sequence of construction. Elsewhere in the temple grounds, you'll see sizeable ovens stuffed constantly with slowly burning fake money, prayer books and other offerings. Pagodas – tall, thin towers thought to keep out evil spirits – are common too.

Chinese temples play an important part in Chinese community life, and some hold occasional musical and theatrical performances, which can be enjoyed by visitors as well as locals. Temples are open from early morning to early evening and devotees go in when they like, to make offerings or to pray; there are no set prayer times. Visitors are welcome and larger temples have janitors who will show you round, although few speak good English.

Islam

Islam ("submission to God") was founded in Mecca in present-day Saudi Arabia by **Muhammad** (570–632 AD), the last in a long line of prophets that included Abraham, Moses and Jesus. Muhammad transmitted Allah's final and perfected revelation to mankind through the writings of the divinely revealed "recitation", the **Koran**. The official beginning of Islam is dated as 622 AD, when Muhammad and his followers, exiled from Mecca, made the **hijra**, or migration, north to Yathrib, later known as Medina, "City of the Prophet". The *hijra* marks the start of the Islamic calendar, 1 AH (Anno Hijra). All the central tenets of Islam are embodied in the Koran, with the most important known as the **Five Pillars of Islam**. The first pillar is *shahada* – the confession of faith, "There is no god but God, and Muhammad is his messenger." The *shahada* is recited at the *salat*, the second pillar, which enjoins the faithful to kneel five times daily and pray in the direction of Mecca. The other three tenets are: alms-giving to the local Muslim community (*zakat*); fasting during the ninth month of the Muslim lunar calendar, **Ramadan** (*saum* – see p.162); and the pilgrimage (**haj**) to Mecca, money and health allowing.

The first firm foothold made by Islam in Southeast Asia was the conversion of the court of Melaka, in modern-day Malaysia, in the early fifteenth century. One after another, the powerful Malay court rulers took to Islam, adopting the title sultan (ruler); nearby Singapore couldn't help but feel its influence. Today, almost all of Singapore's Malays are Muslims, as well as a proportion of its Indian population. The form of Islam practised is fairly liberal. Some, but not all, women wear long dress and headscarves, and certain taboos – like not drinking alcohol – are ignored by a growing number of Muslims.

Mosques

While only a small proportion attend the mosque every day, all Muslims converge on their nearest **mosque** on Friday – the day of prayer. Once there, the men wash their hands, feet and faces three times in the outer chambers, before entering the prayer hall to recite sections of the Koran. After this initial period, an **Imam** will lead prayers and, on occasions, deliver a sermon, in which the teachings of Muhammad will be applied to a contemporary context. Women cannot enter the main prayer hall during prayers and must congregate in a chamber to the side of the hall.

Visitors are welcome at certain times, provided that their shoulders and legs are covered. No non-Muslim is allowed to enter a mosque during prayer time or go into the prayer hall at any time, although it's possible to stand just outside and look in.

Hinduism

Hinduism reached the Malay Peninsula and Singapore long before Islam, brought by Indian traders more than a thousand years ago. Its base of support grew in the nineteenth century, when large numbers of indentured workers and convicts arrived from the subcontinent to labour on rubber estates and in construction.

Hinduism had no founder, but grew slowly over thousands of years. Its central tenet is the belief that life is a series of rebirths and reincarnations (*samsara*) that eventually leads to spiritual release (*moksha*). An individual's progress is determined by his or her *karma*, very much a law of cause and effect, in which negative decisions and actions slow up the process of upward reincarnation and positive ones accelerate it.

A whole variety of deities are worshipped, which on the surface makes Hinduism appear complex, but with only a loose understanding of the **Vedas** (the religion's holy books) the characters and roles of the main gods quickly become apparent. The deities you'll come across most often are the three manifestations of the faith's Supreme Divine Being: **Brahma the Creator**, **Vishnu the Preserver** and **Shiva the Destroyer**. Other enduring favourites among Hindus include: elephant-headed Ganesh, the son of Shiva, who is evoked before every undertaking except funerals; Vishnu's consort, the comely Lakshmi, worshipped as goddess of prosperity and wealth; and Saraswati, wife to Brahma, and seen as a goddess of purification, fertility and learning.

Hindu temples

Visitors are welcome to explore **Hindu temples**, but are expected to remove their shoes before entering. Step over the threshold and you enter a veritable Disneyland of colourful gods and fanciful creatures. The style is typically **Dravidian** (South Indian), as befits the largely Tamil population, with a soaring *gopuram*, or entrance tower, teeming with sculptures, and a central courtyard leading to an inner sanctum (off-limits to tourists) dedicated to the presiding deity. In the temple precinct, there are always busy scenes – incense burning, the application of sandalwood paste, and the *puja* (ritual act of worship).

Chinese astrology

Most people are interested to find out what sign they are in the Chinese zodiac system, particularly since – like the Western system – each person is supposed to have characteristics similar to those of the sign that related to their birth date.

There are twelve Chinese zodiac signs, corresponding to twelve types of animals, whose characteristics you'll find listed below. These animal signs have existed in Chinese folk tradition since the sixth century BC, though it wasn't until the third century BC that they were incorporated into a formal study of astrology and astronomy, based around the lunar calendar. Quite why animals emerged as the vehicle for Chinese horoscopy is unclear: one story has it that the animals used are the twelve that appeared before the command of Buddha, who named the years in the order in which the animals arrived.

Each lunar year (which starts in late January/early February) is represented by one of the twelve animal symbols. Your sign depends on the year you were born – check the calendar chart below – rather than the month as in Western systems.

The details below will tell you the basic facts about your character and personality, though it's only a rough guide: to explore your real Chinese astrological self, you need to be equipped with your precise date and time of birth as well as a specialist textbook that can cast light on all your horoscopical idiosyncrasies. The animals always appear in the same order so that if you know the current year you can always work out which one is to influence the coming Chinese New Year.

The Rat

Characteristics: usually generous, intelligent and hard-working, but can be petty and idle; has lots of friends but few close ones; may be successful, like challenges and be good at business, but is insecure; generally diplomatic; tends to get into emotional entanglements.

Partners: best suited to Dragon, Monkey and Ox; doesn't get on with Horse and Goat.

Famous Rats: Wolfgang Amadeus Mozart, William Shakespeare, Marlon Brando, Doris Day, Yves St Laurent, Leo Tolstoy, Jimmy Carter, Prince Charles, Ozzy Osbourne, Gwyneth Paltrow, Ben Affleck, Eminem, Prince Harry, Bono.

The Ox

Characteristics: healthy; obstinate; independent; usually calm and cool, but can get stroppy at times; shy and conservative; likes the outdoors and old-fashioned things; always finishes a task.

Partners: best suited to Snake, Rat or Rooster; doesn't get on with Tiger, Goat or Monkey.

Famous Oxen: Walt Disney, Adolf Hitler, Napoleon Bonaparte, Richard Nixon, Vincent Van Gogh, Peter Sellers, Dustin Hoffman, Robert Redford, Margaret Thatcher, Shirley Bassey, Jane Fonda, Jack Nicholson, George Clooney, Saddam Hussein.

Calendar Chart

Date of Birth

1/2/1900	–	18/2/1901 Rat	14/2/1953	–	2/2/1954 Snake
19/2/1901	–	7/2/1902 Ox	3/2/1954	–	23/1/1955 Horse
8/2/1902	–	28/1/1903 Tiger	26/1/1955	–	11/2/1956 Goat
29/1/1903	–	15/2/1904 Rabbit	12/2/1956	–	30/1/1957 Monkey
16/2/1904	–	3/2/1905 Dragon	31/1/1957	–	17/2/1958 Rooster
4/2/1905	–	24/1/1906 Snake	18/2/1958	–	7/2/1959 Dog
25/1/1906	–	12/2/1907 Horse	8/2/1959	–	27/1/1960 Pig
13/2/1907	–	1/2/1908 Goat	28/1/1960	–	14/2/1961 Rat
2/2/1908	–	21/1/1909 Monkey	15/2/1961	–	4/2/1962 Ox
22/1/1909	–	9/2/1910 Rooster	5/2/1962	–	24/1/1963 Tiger
10/2/1910	–	29/1/1911 Dog	25/1/1963	–	12/2/1964 Rabbit
30/1/1911	–	17/2/1912 Pig	13/2/1964	–	1/2/1965 Dragon
18/2/1912	–	5/2/1913 Rat	2/2/1965	–	20/1/1966 Snake
6/2/1913	–	25/1/1914 Ox	21/1/1966	–	8/2/1967 Horse
26/1/1914	–	13/2/1915 Tiger	9/2/1967	–	29/1/1968 Goat
14/2/1915	–	13/2/1916 Rabbit	30/1/1968	–	16/2/1969 Monkey
14/2/1916	–	22/1/1917 Dragon	17/2/1969	–	5/2/1970 Rooster
23/1/1917	–	10/2/1918 Snake	6/2/1970	–	26/1/1971 Dog
11/2/1918	–	31/1/1919 Horse	27/1/1971	–	14/2/1972 Pig
1/2/1919	–	19/2/1920 Goat	15/2/1972	–	2/2/1973 Rat
20/2/1920	–	7/2/1921 Monkey	3/2/1973	–	22/1/1974 Ox
8/2/1921	–	27/1/1922 Rooster	23/1/1974	–	10/2/1975 Tiger
28/1/1922	–	15/2/1923 Dog	11/2/1975	–	30/1/1976 Rabbit
16/2/1923	–	4/2/1924 Pig	31/1/1976	–	17/2/1977 Dragon
5/2/1924	–	23/1/1925 Rat	18/2/1977	–	6/2/1978 Snake
24/1/1925	–	12/2/1926 Ox	7/2/1978	–	27/1/1979 Horse
13/2/1926	–	1/2/1927 Tiger	28/1/1979	–	15/2/1980 Goat
2/2/1927	–	22/1/1928 Rabbit	16/2/1980	–	4/2/1981 Monkey
23/1/1928	–	9/2/1929 Dragon	5/2/1981	–	24/1/1982 Rooster
10/2/1929	–	29/1/1930 Snake	25/1/1982	–	12/2/1983 Dog
30/1/1930	–	16/2/1931 Horse	13/2/1983	–	1/2/1984 Pig
17/2/1931	–	5/2/1932 Goat	2/2/1984	–	19/2/1985 Rat
6/2/1932	–	25/1/1933 Monkey	20/2/1985	–	8/2/1986 Ox
26/1/1933	–	13/2/1934 Rooster	9/2/1986	–	28/1/1987 Tiger
14/2/1934	–	3/2/1935 Dog	29/1/1987	–	16/2/1988 Rabbit
4/2/1935	–	23/1/1936 Pig	17/2/1988	–	5/2/1989 Dragon
24/1/1936	–	10/2/1937 Rat	6/2/1989	–	26/1/1990 Snake
11/2/1937	–	30/1/1938 Ox	27/1/1990	–	14/2/1991 Horse
31/1/1938	–	18/2/1939 Tiger	15/2/1991	–	3/2/1992 Goat
19/2/1939	–	7/2/1940 Rabbit	4/2/1992	–	22/1/1993 Monkey
8/2/1940	–	26/1/1941 Dragon	23/1/1993	–	9/2/1994 Rooster
27/1/1941	–	14/2/1942 Snake	10/2/1994	–	30/1/1995 Dog
15/2/1942	–	4/2/1943 Horse	31/1/1995	–	18/2/1996 Pig
5/2/1943	–	24/1/1944 Goat	19/2/1996	–	6/2/1997 Rat
25/1/1944	–	12/2/1945 Monkey	7/2/1997	–	27/1/1998 Ox
13/2/1945	–	1/2/1946 Rooster	28/1/1998	–	15/2/1999 Tiger
2/2/1946	–	21/1/1947 Dog	16/2/1999	–	4/2/2000 Rabbit
22/1/1947	–	9/2/1948 Pig	5/2/2000	–	23/1/2001 Dragon
10/2/1948	–	28/1/1949 Rat	24/1/2001	–	11/2/2002 Snake
29/1/1949	–	16/2/1950 Ox	12/2/2002	–	31/1/2003 Horse
17/2/1950	–	5/2/1951 Tiger	1/2/2003	–	21/1/2004 Goat
6/2/1951	–	26/1/1952 Rabbit	22/1/2004	–	8/2/2005 Monkey
27/1/1952	–	13/2/1953 Dragon			

The Tiger

Characteristics: adventurous; creative and idealistic; confident and enthusiastic; can be diplomatic and practical; fearless and forward, aiming at impossible goals, though a realist with a forceful personality.

Partners: best suited to Horse for marriage; gets on with Dragon, Pig and Dog; should avoid Snake, Monkey and Ox.

Famous Tigers: Karl Marx, Queen Elizabeth II, Alec Guinness, Stevie Wonder, Ludvig Van Beethoven, Marilyn Monroe, Princess Anne, Charles de Gaulle, Rudolf Nureyev, John Coltrane, Tom Cruise.

The Rabbit

Characteristics: peace-loving; sociable but quiet; devoted to family and friends; timid but can be good at business; needs reassurance and affection to avoid being upset; can be vain; long-lived.

Partners: best suited to Pig, Dog and Goat; not friendly with Tiger and Rooster.

Famous Rabbits: Fidel Castro, Bob Hope, Harry Belafonte, David Frost, Martin Luther King, Josef Stalin, Queen Victoria, Albert Einstein, Brad Pitt, Tiger Woods.

The Dragon

Characteristics: strong, commanding, a leader; popular; athletic; bright, chivalrous and idealistic, though not always consistent; likely to be a believer in equality.

Partners: best suited to Snake, Rat, Monkey, Tiger and Rooster; should avoid Dog.

Famous Dragons: Joan of Arc, Ringo Starr, Mae West, John Lennon, Frank Sinatra, Salvador Dali, Kirk Douglas, Che Guevara, Yehudi Menuhin, Maya Angelou, Pierce Brosnan, Russell Crowe.

The Snake

Characteristics: charming, but possessive and selfish; private and secretive; strange sense of humour; mysterious and inquisitive; ruthless; likes the fine things in life; a thoughtful person, but superstitious.

Partners: best suited for marriage to Dragon, Rooster and Ox; avoid Snake, Pig and Tiger.

Famous Snakes: J.F. Kennedy, Abraham Lincoln, Edgar Allan Poe, Mao Zedong, Pablo Picasso, Johannes Brahms, Franz Schubert, Lennox Lewis, J.K. Rowling, Tony Blair, Bob Dylan, Stephen Hawking.

The Horse

Characteristics: nice appearance and deft; ambitious and quick-witted; favours bold colours; popular, with a sense of humour; gracious and gentle; can be good at business; fickle and emotional.

Partners: best suited to Tiger, Dog and Goat; doesn't get on with Rabbit and Rat.

Famous Horses: Neil Armstrong, Babara Streisand, Paul McCartney, Theodore Roosevelt, Rembrandt, Raquel Welch, Leonid Brezhnev and Igor Stravinsky.

The Goat

Characteristics: a charmer and a lucky person who likes money; unpunctual and hesitant; too fond of complaining; interested in the supernatural.

Partners: best suited to Horse, Pig and Rabbit; should avoid Ox and Dog.

Famous Goats: Andy Warhol, Liberace, Michelangelo, Laurence Olivier, James Michener, Diana Dors, Nicole Kidman, John Major, Michael Owen, Keith Richards, Pamela Anderson, Robert De Niro, Noel Gallagher, Bill Gates, Mick Jagger.

The Monkey

Characteristics: very intelligent and sharp, an opportunist; daring and confident, but unstable and egoistic; entertaining and very attractive to others; inventive; has a sense of humour but with little respect for reputations.

Partners: best suited to Dragon and Rat; doesn't get on with Tiger and Ox.

Famous Monkeys: Leonardo da Vinci, Mick Jagger, Bette Davis, Charles Dickens, Julius Caesar, Paul Gauguin, Rene Descartes, Kylie Minogue, Michael Schumacher, Christine Aguilera, Halle Berry.

The Rooster

Characteristics: frank and reckless, and can be tactless; free with advice; punctual and a hard worker; imaginative to the point of dreaming; likes to be noticed; emotional.

Partners: best suited to Snake, Dragon and Ox; doesn't get on with Pig, Rabbit and Rooster.

Famous Roosters: Michael Caine, Prince Philip, Charles Darwin, Peter Ustinov, Elton John, Katharine Hepburn, Peter O'Toole, Anna Kournikova, Renee Zellweger, Osama bin Laden.

The Dog

Characteristics: alert, watchful and defensive; can be generous and is patient; very responsible and has good organizational skills; spiritual, home-loving and non-materialistic.

Partners: best suited to Rabbit, Pig, Tiger and Horse; should avoid Dragon and Goat.

Famous Dogs: David Niven, Henry Moore, Brigitte Bardot, Liza Minnelli, Zsa Zsa Gabor, Winston Churchill, Elvis Presley, Sophia Loren, Voltaire, Madonna, George W. Bush, Naomi Campbell, Bill Clinton, Michael Jackson.

The Pig

Characteristics: honest; vulnerable and not good at business, but still materialistic and ambitious; outgoing and outspoken, but naïve; kind and helpful to the point of being taken advantage of; calm and genial.

Partners: best suited to Dog, Goat, Tiger and Rabbit; should avoid Snake and Rooster.

Famous Pigs: Alfred Hitchcock, Ronald Reagan, Maria Callas, Henry Kissinger, Woody Allen, Julie Andrews, Humphrey Bogart, Al Capone, Ernest Hemingway, Ewan McGregor, Iggy Pop.

Singaporean recipes

The most profound pleasures of a stay in Singapore revolve around meal times; eating is a national mania, and locals have some fifty thousand establishments from which to choose. Of course, swanky restaurants abound for gourmands intent on exploring the exclusive end of Asian cooking, but it's far more rewarding to visit a hawker stall, eating house or coffee shop, and sample everyday food as eaten by the Singaporeans.

We can't re-create for you the sensory overload of a busy hawker centre, but **recipes** for three of the island's most popular dishes are given below, representing Singapore's major ethnic groups, the Chinese, Malays and Indians. For the vast majority of visitors, these are a much better reflection of local food than bird's nests and shark's fins.

None of the **ingredients** used should be difficult to find in your local stores, and they don't require specialist equipment to cook.

Hainanese Chicken Rice

You can't walk far in Singapore without stumbling across a coffee shop or stall that serves **Hainanese Chicken Rice**, a deceptively unassuming dish of succulent **boiled chicken** laid on **aromatic rice** that's regarded by many as Singapore's unofficial national dish. The first giveaway is the row of ghostly pale chickens hanging on butcher's hooks along the shop front, the second the ringing noise of metal on butcher's block as the overalled Chinese cook hacks away unceremoniously with his meat cleaver at the chicken carcasses.

Part of the appeal of the dish (which was imported by immigrants from the Chinese island of Hainan, south of China off the north coast of Vietnam) lies in its simplicity and its completeness. Nothing is wasted, with the stock created by boiling the chicken being used to cook rice before finally ending up as a light broth. Hainanese Chicken Rice is traditionally served with chilli and ginger sauce, soya sauce and minced garlic.

Serves 4 people

1.7l or 3 pints chicken stock
Whole 1.5kg or 3lb chicken, giblets removed
1 red chilli, finely sliced
2 cloves garlic, crushed
1cm or half inch piece ginger, finely grated
1 teaspoon salt
Half teaspoon freshly ground black pepper
400g or 13oz long grain rice
Half cucumber, sliced
3 tomatoes, sliced
2 tablespoons soya sauce

For the chilli and ginger sauce:
8 fresh red chillies, chopped
4cm or 1.5 inch piece ginger, grated
2 cloves garlic, chopped
1 tablespoon vinegar
Sugar and salt to taste

Bring the stock to the boil in a large pan, add the whole chicken, along with the chilli, garlic, ginger, salt and pepper. Cover the pan, and boil the chicken for 45 minutes or until tender. Remove the chicken form the stock and set to one side, reserving the stock. While the chicken is cooling, rinse the rice thoroughly, and cook in the chicken stock. Meanwhile, make the sauce. Pound together the chillies, ginger and garlic in a pestle and mortar. Transfer to a bowl and add the vinegar.

When the rice is cooked, drain, reserving the stock. Pack the rice into cups, and upturn them onto individual plates to form domes.

Cut the chicken into slices, lightly baste them with soya sauce, and lay them around the rice. Garnish with cucumber and tomato. Finally, bring the remaining stock to the boil, season to taste, and serve as a soup.

Satay

If any one Malaysian dish has caught the world's culinary imagination it's surely **satay**, an aromatic snack comprising marinated strips of meat skewered on small sticks, grilled and dipped in a spicy peanut sauce. The sight of the Muslim Malay satay man, sporting a *songkok* and fanning the flames of his charcoal barbecue pit with a woven fan, is a reassuringly traditional one in today's high-tech Singapore. **Beef** and **chicken** are the two classic ingredients for Malay satay, though oddities such as fish, seafood and vegetarian satays often crop up on Singaporean menus. The pork satay of the Nonya cook is a variation of the traditional Malay satay, reflecting the Chinese predilection for pork.

There are two styles of satay: **satay terkan**, for which the meat is finely minced and wrapped around a skewer, and the far tastier **satay chochok**, for which whole pieces of meat are used. Nowadays, satay is sold in bunches of five or ten; in days gone by, customers would accumulate skewers during an evening, and the satay man would tally the bill by counting these up at the end of the night.

Makes approximately 20–30 sticks of satay

400g or 13oz beef or chicken, cut into thin strips
Oil for basting

For the marinade:
1 lemon grass stalk, sliced and crushed
8 shallots, finely sliced
2 cloves garlic, chopped
1 teaspoon cumin
1 teaspoon coriander
1 teaspoon turmeric
1 teaspoon sugar
Pinch of salt
2 tablespoons peanut oil

For the sauce:
1 lemon grass stalk, finely grated
2.5cm or 1 inch piece ginger, finely grated
1 onion, finely sliced
10 dried red chillies, soaked and finely chopped
2 cloves garlic
3 tablespoons tamarind juice

250g or 8oz unsalted peanuts, finely chopped
2 tablespoons sugar
Salt to taste
Oil for frying

To make the marinade, mix the lemon grass, shallots, garlic, cumin, coriander, turmeric, sugar and salt in the oil. Mix the strips of meat into the paste and leave for a couple of hours.

Meanwhile, prepare the sauce. Pound the lemon grass and ginger in a pestle and mortar. Fry the onion over a moderate heat for five minutes or until soft, stirring occasionally. Add the lemon grass, ginger, chillies and garlic and mix. Cook for a further two minutes. Now add the tamarind juice, peanuts, sugar, salt and 200ml or 7fl oz water, and simmer for 15 minutes or until thickened.

Skewer the strips of marinated meat onto small skewers and grill on a barbecue or under a preheated hot grill until crisp, regularly brushing the meat with oil.

Satay is best served hot, dipped in the sauce, with generous chunks of raw cucumber and onion.

Murtabak

The **murtabak** is a thick pancake stuffed with meat, fried onion and egg, and loved by Singapore's Indian population. Half the fun of ordering a murtabak is watching it being made: murtabak cooks have made an art out of spinning their dough dramatically up in the air to stretch it paper-thin, and perhaps it's this process that has earned the dish the otherwise misleading title of Singapore's answer to the pizza. The spectacle is best viewed at one of the Muslim Indian restaurants behind the Sultan Mosque, on North Bridge Road: the *Zam Zam* even boasts a champion in the field. Murtabaks can be made out of chicken or beef, but more often, they feature **minced mutton**. In Singapore, they are cooked on wide griddles, but a frying pan will do. A saucer of curry sauce or **daal** perfectly complements the dish.

Makes 6 murtabaks

For the dough:
300g or 10oz plain flour
Half teaspoon salt
1 tablespoon ghee (or butter)
Oil to coat dough balls
Flour for rolling

For the filling:
2 tablespoons ghee (or vegetable oil)
2 medium-sized onions, finely sliced
4 green chillies, finely sliced
3 garlic cloves, crushed
5 eggs
400g or 13oz minced meat
1 teaspoon garam masala
Salt and pepper to taste

To make the dough, place the flour, salt and ghee in a mixing bowl and slowly add approximately 8 tablespoons of warm water, mixing together until a stiff dough is formed. Knead until soft. Divide the dough into six balls and leave standing in a covered dish for at least an hour, turning once or twice.

Next, make the filling. Heat the ghee in a pan over moderate heat, add the onion, chilli and garlic, and fry for 5 minutes stirring occasionally. Meanwhile, beat the eggs in a bowl. When the onions are soft, add the meat and garam masala and season. Cook for 20 minutes or until cooked through.

To assemble a murtabak, lift a ball of dough out of the oil and roll out as thinly as possible on a floured surface. Transfer the dough to a greased and pre-heated griddle, or frying pan.

As the dough begins to cook, baste it with beaten egg, and then heap a mound of filling in the middle. Fold in the four corners of the dough to form a parcel, and cook for a couple of minutes on each side, basting with egg to secure the flaps. Serve at once.

Singapore in literature

S ince its foundation in 1819, Singapore has provided rich pickings for travel writers, novelists and historians. However, due to the scarcity of indigenous written material, we have to rely almost exclusively on writings by foreign visitors for early depictions of the island.

The one notable exception is the historian **Abdullah bin Kadir**, born in Melaka in 1797 of Malay and Tamil stock, and later employed as a scribe by Sir Stamford Raffles. The first excerpt below comes from his autobiography, the *Hikayat Abdullah*. Published in Malay in 1849, it remains, despite factual inaccuracies, a fascinating social and historic document. It is interesting to contrast Abdullah's squalid portrayal of early Singapore with the altogether more civilized picture painted by spunky English traveller **Isabella Bird** thirty years later. By the time of her five-week tour of Singapore and the Malay states in 1879, recorded in *The Golden Chersonese*, Bird had already seen Amenca, Canada, Hawaii, Australia and New Zealand. Subsequent travels took her to Armenia, Persia, Kurdistan, Kashmir and Tibet and saw her honoured as the first woman fellow of the Royal Geographical Sociey in 1892.

Singapore's contemporary writers are represented first by Lee Tzu Pheng, a lecturer at the National University of Singapore, whose poem *My Country and My People* reflects the cultural disorientation inherent in the establishment of a new nationhood. Finally, R. Rajaram's short story *Hurry* is played out against a Singapore completely remoulded since the days of Abdullah, though the nineteenth-century scribe would surely have recognized the hustle and bustle that Rajaram evokes in his story.

Hikayat Abdullah

It was Colonel Farquhar's habit to go for a walk every morning looking round the district. It was all covered with thick scrub. Only in the middle of the open space already mentioned were there no thick bushes, but only myrtle, rhododendron and eugenia trees. On the side nearest the shore were many kinds of trees, *ambong-ambong*, *melpari*, *bulangan* and scattered tree trunks. On the opposite side of the river there was nothing to be seen except mangrove trees, *bakau*, *api-api*, *buta-buta*, *jeruju* and strewn branches. There was no good piece of ground even as much as sixty yards wide, the whole place being covered in deep mud, except only on the hills where the soil was clay. There was a large rise, of moderate elevation, near the point of the headland at the estuary of Singapore River.

In the Singapore River estuary there were many large rocks, with little rivulets running between the fissures, moving like a snake that has been struck. Among these many rocks there was a sharp-pointed one shaped like the snout of a swordfish. The Sea Gypsies used to call it the Swordfish's Head and believed it to be the abode of spirits. To this rock they all made propitiatory offerings in their fear of it, placing bunting on it and treating it with reverence. "If we do not pay our respects to it," they said, "when we go in and out of the shallows it will send us to destruction." Every day they brought offerings and placed them on the rock. All along the shore there were hundreds of human skulls rolling about on the sand; some old, some new, some with hair still sticking to them, some with the teeth filed and others without. News of these skulls was brought to Colonel Farquhar and when he had seen them he ordered them to be gathered up and cast into the sea. So the people collected them in sacks and threw them into the sea. The Sea Gypsies were asked, "Whose are all these skulls?" and they replied, "These are the skulls of men who were robbed at sea. They were slaughtered here. Wherever a fleet of boats or a ship is plundered it is brought to this place for a division of the spoils. Sometimes there is wholesale slaughter among the crews when the cargo is grabbed. Sometimes the pirates tie people up and try out their weapons here along the sea shore." Here-too-was the place where they went in for cockfighting and gambling.

One day Colonel Farquhar wanted to ascend the Forbidden Hill, as it was called by the *temenggong*. The *temenggong*'s men said, "None of us has the courage to go up the hill because there are many ghosts on it. Every day one can hear on it sounds as of hundreds of men. Sometimes one hears the sound of heavy drums and of people shouting." Colonel Farquhar laughed and said, "I should like to see your ghosts," and turning to his Malacca men, "Draw this gun to the top of the hill." Among them there were several who were frightened, but having no option they pulled the gun up. All who went up were Malacca men, none of the Singapore men daring to approach the hill. On the hill there was not much forest and not many large trees, only a few shrubs here and there. Although the men were frightened they were shamed by the presence of Colonel Farquhar and went up whether they wanted to or not. When they reached the top Colonel Farquhar ordered the gun to be loaded and then he himself fired twelve rounds in succession over the top of the hill in front of them. Then he ordered a pole to be erected on which he hoisted the English flag. He said, "Cut down all these bushes." He also ordered them to make a path for people to go up and down the hill. Every day there was this work being done, the undergrowth being slashed down and a pathway cleared.

At that time there were few animals, wild or tame on the Island of Singapore, except rats. There were thousands of rats all over the district, some almost as large as cats. They were so big that they used to attack us if we went out walking at night and many people were knocked over. In the house where I was living we used to keep a cat. One night at about midnight we heard the cat mewing and my friend went out carrying a light to see why the cat was making such a noise. He saw six or seven rats crowding round and biting the cat; some bit its ears, some its paws, some its nose so that it could no longer move but only utter cry after cry. When my companion saw what was happening he shouted to me and I ran out at the back to have a look. Six or seven men came pressing round to watch but did nothing to release the cat which only cried the louder at the sight of so many men, like a person beseeching help. Then someone fetched a stick and struck at the rats, killing the two which were biting the cat's ears. Its ears freed, the cat then pounced on another rat and killed it. Another was hit by the man with a stick and the rest ran away. The cat's face and nose were lacerated and covered with blood. This was the state of affairs in all the houses, which were full of rats. They could hardly be kept under control, and the time had come when they took notice of people. Colonel Farquhar's place was also in the same state and he made an order saying, "To anyone who kills a rat I will give one *wang*." When people heard of this they devised all manner of instruments for killing rats. Some made springtraps, some pincer traps, some cage-traps, some traps with running nooses, some traps with closing doors, others laid poison or put down lime. I had never in my life before seen rats caught by liming; only now for the first time. Some searched for rat-holes, some speared the rats or killed them in various other ways. Every day crowds of people brought the dead bodies to Colonel Farquhar's place, some having fifty or sixty, others only six or seven. At first the rats brought in every morning were counted almost in thousands, and Colonel Farquhar paid out according to his promise. After six or seven days a multitude of rats were still to be seen, and he promised five *duit* for each rat caught. They were still brought in in thousands and Colonel Farquhar ordered a very deep trench to be dug and the dead bodies to be buried. So the numbers began to dwindle, until people were bringing in only some ten or twenty a day. Finally the uproar and the campaign against the rats in Singapore came to an end, the infestation having completely subsided.

Some time later a great many centipedes appeared, people being bitten by them all over the place. In every dwelling, if one sat for any length of time, two or three centipedes would drop from the attap roof. Rising in the morning from a night's sleep one would be sure to find two or three very large centipedes under one's mat and they caused people much annoyance. When the news reached Colonel Farquhar he made an order saying that to anyone who killed a centipede he would give one *wang*. Hearing this, people searched high and low for centipedes, and every day they brought in hundreds which they had caught by methods of their own devising. So the numbers dwindled until once in two or three days some twenty or thirty centipedes were brought in. Finally the campaign and furore caused by the centipedes came to an end, and people no longer cried out because of the pain when they got bitten.

The above extract is taken from the *Hikayat Abdullah*, by Abdullah bin Kadir, translated by A.H. Hill (1969), with kind permission of Oxford University Press/Penerbit Fajar Bakti.

The Golden Chersonese

Singapore, January 19, 1879.

It is hot – so hot! – but not stifling and all the rich-flavoured, coloured fruits of the tropics are here – fruits whose generous juices are drawn from the moist and heated earth, and whose flavours are the imprisoned rays of the fierce sun of the tropics. Such cartloads and piles of bananas and pineapples, such heaps of gold and green giving off fragrance! Here, too, are treasures of the heated crystal seas – things that one has dreamed of after reading Jules Verne's romances. Big canoes, manned by dark-skinned men in white turbans and loin-cloths, floated round our ship, or lay poised on the clear depths of aquamarine water, with fairy freights – forests of coral white as snow, or red, pink, violet, in massive branches or fernlike sprays, fresh from their warm homes beneath the clear warm waves, where fish as bright-tinted as themselves flash through them "living light". There were displays of wonderful shells, too, of pale rose-pink, and others with rainbow tints which, like rainbows, came and went – nothing scanty, feeble, or pale!

It is a drive of two miles from the pier to Singapore, and to eyes which have only seen the yellow skins and non-vividness of the Far East, a world of wonders opens at every step. It is intensely tropical; there are mangrove swamps, and fringes of coco-palms, and banana groves, date, sago and travellers' palms, tree ferns, india-rubber, mango, custard-apple, jack-fruit, durian, lime, pomegranate, pineapples, and orchids, and all kinds of strangling and parrot-blossomed trailers. Vegetation rich, profuse, endless, rapid, smothering in all shades of vivid green, from the pea-green of spring and the dark velvety green of endless summer to the yellow-green of the plumage of the palm, riots in a heavy shower every night and the heat of a perennial sunblaze every day, while monkeys of various kinds and bright-winged birds skip and flit through the jungle shades. There is a perpetual battle between man and the jungle, and the latter, in fact, is only brought to bay within a short distance of Singapore.

I had scarcely finished breakfast at the hotel, a shady, straggling building much infested by ants, when Mr Cecil Smith, the Colonial Secretary, and his wife called, full of kind thoughts and plans of furtherance; and a little later a resident, to whom I had not even a letter of introduction, took me and my luggage to his bungalow. All the European houses seem to have very deep verandahs, large, lofty rooms, punkahs everywhere, windows without glass, brick floors, and jalousies and "tatties" (blinds made of grass or finely split bamboo) to keep out the light and the flies. This equatorial heat is neither as exhausting or depressing as the damp summer heat of Japan, though one does long "to take off one's flesh and sit in one's bones…"

It is all fascinating. Here is none of the indolence and apathy which one associates with Oriental life, and which I have seen in Polynesia. These yellow, brown, tawny, swarthy, olive-tinted men are all intent on gain; busy, industrious, frugal, striving and, no matter what their creed is, all paying homage to Daikoku. In spite of the activity, rapidity, and earnestness, the movements of all but the Chinese are graceful, gliding stealthy, the swarthy faces have no expression that I can read, and the dark liquid eyes are no more intelligible to me than the eyes of oxen. It is the "Asian mystery" all over.

It is only the European part of Singapore which is dull and sleepy looking. No life and movement congregate round the shops. The merchants, hidden away behind jalousies in their offices, or dashing down the streets in covered buggies, make but a poor show. Their houses are mostly pale, roomy, detached bungalows, almost altogether hidden by the bountiful vegetation of the climate. In these their wives, growing paler every week, lead half-expiring lives, kept alive by the efforts of ubiquitous "punkah-wallahs"; writing for the mail, the one active occupation. At a given hour they emerge, and drive in given directions, specially round the esplanade, where for two hours at a time a double row of handsome and showy equipages moves continuously in opposite directions. The number of carriages and the style of dress of their occupants are surprising, and yet people say that large fortunes are not made nowadays in Singapore! Besides the daily drive, the ladies, the officers, and any men who may be described as of "no occupation", divert themselves with kettle-drums, dances, lawn tennis, and various other devices for killing time, and this with the mercury at 80°! Just now the Maharajah of Johore, sovereign of a small state on the nearest part of the mainland, a man much petted and decorated by the British Government for unswerving fidelity to British interests, has a house here, and his receptions and dinner parties vary the monotonous round of gaieties.

The native streets monopolise the picturesqueness of Singapore with their bizarre crowds, but more interesting still are the bazaars or continuous rows of open shops which create for themselves a perpetual twilight by hanging tatties or other screens outside the side walks, forming long shady alleys, in which crowds of buyers and sellers chaffer over their goods, the Chinese shopkeepers asking a little more than they mean to take, and the Kings always asking double. The bustle and noise of this quarter are considerable, and the vociferation mingles with the ringing of bells and the rapid beating of drums and tom-toms, an intensely heathenish sound. And heathenish this great city is. Chinese josshouses, Hindu temples, and Mohammedan mosques almost jostle each other, and the indescribable clamour of the temples and the din of the joss-houses are faintly pierced by the shrill cry from the minarets calling the faithful to prayer, and proclaiming the divine unity and the mission of Mahomet in one breath.

How I wish I could convey an idea, however faint, of this huge, mingled, coloured, busy, Oriental population; of the old King and Chinese bazaars; of the itinerant sellers of seaweed jelly, water, vegetables, soup, fruit and cooked fish, whose unintelligible street cries are heard above the din of the crowds of coolies, boatmen and gharriemen waiting for hire; of the far-stretching suburbs of Malay and Chinese cottages; of the sheet of water, by no means clean, round which hundreds of Bengalis are to be seen at all hours of daylight unmercifully beating on great stones the delicate laces, gauzy silks, and elaborate flouncings of the European ladies; of the ceaseless rush and hum of industry, and of the resistless, overpowering, astonishing Chinese element, which is gradually turning Singapore into a Chinese city! I must conclude abruptly, or lose the mail.

I.L.B.

Letter VII (Beauties of the Tropics), extracted from *The Golden Chersonese*, by Isabella Bird.

My Country and My People

My country and my people
are neither here nor there, nor
in the comfort of my preferences,
if I could even choose.
At any rate, to fancy is to cheat;
and worse than being alien, or
subversive without cause,
is being a patriot
of the will.

I came in the boom of babies, not guns,
a 'daughter of a better age';
I held a pencil in a school
while the 'age' was quelling riots
in the street, or cutting down
those foreign 'devils',
(whose books I was being taught to read).
Thus privileged I entered early
the Lion City's jaws.
But they sent me back as fast
to my shy, forbearing family.

So I stayed in my parents' house,
and had only household cares.
The city remained a distant way,
but I had no land to till;
only a duck that would not lay,
and a runt of a papaya tree,
(which also turned out to be male).

Then I learnt to drive instead
and praise the highways till
I saw them chop the great trees down,
and plant the little ones;

impound the hungry buffalo
(the big ones and the little ones)
because the cars could not be curbed.
Nor could the population.
They built milli-mini-flats
for a multi-mini-society.
The chiselled profile in the sky
took on a lofty attitude,
but modestly, at any rate
it made the tourist feel 'at home'.

My country and my people
I never understood.
I grew up in China's mighty shadow,
with my gentle, brown-skinned neighbours;
but I keep diaries in English.
I sought to grow
in humanity's rich soil,
and started digging on the banks, then saw
life carrying my friends downstream.

Yet, careful tending of the human heart
may make a hundred flowers bloom;
and perhaps, fence-sitting neighbour,
I claim citizenship in your recognition
of our kind,
my people, and my country,
are you, and you my home.

My Country and My People by Lee Tzu Pheng,
reprinted by kind permission of Heinemann

Hurry

I was running. In the centre of the road. True, I wasn't running like the wind, but my speed was fast enough for beads of perspiration to run down my body and my breath to come in short gasps.

Cars and lorries flashed past me either way. Still I kept running. Somehow it seemed appropriate that I should be running on the white centre line separating the dual carriageway.

Where were the vehicles heading to? I didn't know. Did the drivers in them know where I was running to? No, but there was a possibility that they would think I was a lunatic. So I should not continue to run in this manner.

I would have to cross the road, walk or run the short distance to the MRT station to board a train to Orchard Road. Then I would have to disembark and cross the road to Dynasty Hotel to meet my friend Kamal staying there.

The train would arrive at the station in two minutes' time and I must be in it. I was running in this wild manner all for this. I had crossed half the road. Now running along the white line, I tried desperately to find a way through the thick of the moving traffic to find an opening to make my dash across. Suddenly I spied an opening and lashed across, leaving behind two drivers screeching to a halt as they tried to avoid the collision. One driver even made an obscene gesture with his hands.

I felt a sense of regret. Not at his gesture, but that I had cut his speed of travel. Anyway, there was no time to apologise to him. I had to catch that train or I would really be late.

I must buy a car, I thought to myself. It would be so convenient considering the amount of travelling I have to do. The convenience was more than that. A motorist dares to use foul language and rude gestures because he knows he is safe from the poor pedestrian out on the road. Yes, a car is definitely a convenience in more ways than one.

Miraculously I arrived at the Jurong Station with thirty seconds to spare. From the third level of the station, I could see the sun had half-disappeared in the horizon. When I had left my home in the morning, he had also been half-hidden, but that was the dawn.

Passengers on the platform suddenly moved forward with some standing in the yellow safety line. I could see the train in the distance. This wasn't a bus. There would be ample time for all to board the train before it pulled out. Then why the rush? To ensure that they could get seats? But even if one pushed his way through not everyone could get a seat. I wasn't going to be left out however. I, too, rushed with the crowd and pushed my way to the front.

As the train ground to a halt and the doors slid open we rushed in. I was lucky enough to grab the only seat in my compartment and sank down gladly.

My eyes scanned the passengers. Young, old, middle-aged, they all seemed lost in some thoughts. What were they thinking about, or were they just staring blankly, I wondered.

As the train pulled up at the next station, another human wave entered the train. I noticed my friend Ravi among them in the next compartment. Ravi is a very close friend. Well, at least during our school days. But I still considered him as one. Unfortunately, we had not had many opportunities to meet as often as we used to. As he was staying in the Jurong area, occasionally we met like this in the train.

He had not noticed me. "Hello, Ravi!" I shouted across. He turned, saw me and waved. My voice, however, had shattered the silence in the train and several dozen pairs of eyes bored into me. I turned pink with embarrassment.

Ravi could not come any nearer, the crowd was that thick. No one appeared willing to allow Ravi to walk through to me.

"How is father?" I gestured with my hands. His father had been ill for some time. Ravi answered in a similar manner, giving me the thumbs down sign. His normally cheerful face was tinged with sadness.

As the train sped on, I wondered what I could do. I attempted to convey how I felt with expressions. He was about to say something but changed his mind, pulled out a paper from his pocket and started to scribble something.

The train reached Raffles Place Interchange. Most of us, including me, had to change trains. In no time, three quarters of the train had emptied. Ravi made his way through the crowd and as I was about to disembark, thrust the paper into my hands. As he didn't need to change trains, I didn't have the time to even exchange a few words.

As the train pulled away my train pulled into the opposite tunnel. Running with the others, I crossed over the platform and boarded it.

Eagerly I opened his note. "We have finalised marriage plans for Chitra. Father insists that he wants to see the marriage before he dies. I'll phone you later."

Chitra marrying. I sat stunned. How could she marry someone when she was my girlfriend...?

Why not? No one, not even Chitra, knew of my love. That's a joke isn't it!

I had wanted to tell Ravi of my love. But the opportunity had never arisen, and being the coward I am I had kept postponing the discussion. Now it was too late. Who could I blame but myself? Anyway, where did I have the time for courtship when I never returned from work till eleven in the night every day.

I crumpled the note and threw it on the floor and looked up. The passenger opposite looked meaningfully at me and the note on the floor. I had littered. Sheepishly I picked up the note and shoved it in my shirt pocket.

Irritated, I reached for a cigarette. My eyes fell on the warning note directly opposite. "No smoking! $500 fine." My hand dropped to the side. I, more than anyone else, knew that every mistake had its penalty.

The train sped on through the tunnels. It was pitch dark outside. I wasn't aware where we were. This is the drawback in travelling by train. A minute's inattention, and one loses track completely of one's whereabouts. The speed with which one was travelling was the only consolation.

Some light pierced the darkness. Instantly the passengers came to life. Orchard Station. I would have to get out here. I glanced at my watch – 7.26pm. I was pleased. Had I come by bus I would not have made it in this short time to keep my 7.30pm appointment with Kamal at Dynasty Hotel's lobby.

I crossed glittering Orchard Road and walked briskly into the hotel. But Kamal was not there. Maybe he was still up in the room. Reception should be able to help.

"Can you give me Kamal's room number?"

"Mr Kamal just vacated his room. His flight was brought forward and he's left for the airport."

If he had just left, he must be waiting for a cab outside the hotel. In my hurry, I must have missed him outside. Maybe, just maybe, I could catch him before he caught a cab, I thought as I dashed out.

Hurry, by R. Rajaram, translated by K. Sulosana.

Books

The majority of books about Singapore tend to be penned by Western visitors to the region, rather than by local writers. Only in the last few decades has writing about Singapore by Singaporeans themselves begun to gather momentum.

The best selection of local writing is available on the island itself, though Skoob Books of London is doing much to introduce Singaporean literature to the West. Some of the titles below are ostensibly concerned with Malaya or Malaysia, but all cast some light on Singapore, as the island's fortunes have always been closely linked with those of the Peninsula.

In the reviews below, books marked ⬚ are particularly recommended; o/p signifies out of print.

Travel writing and exploration

⭐ **John Bastin** (ed) *Travellers' Singapore*. Singapore-related vignettes from as early as 1819 and as late as the Japanese conquest of 1942.

Isabella Bird *The Golden Chersonese*. Delightful epistolary romp through old Southeast Asia, penned by the intrepid Bird, whose adventures in the Malay states in 1879 ranged from strolls through Singapore's streets to elephant-back rides and encounters with alligators.

G.M. Gullick *They Came To Malaya*. A cornucopia of accounts of people, places and events, written by the governors, planters and explorers who tamed Malaya and Singapore.

Rev G.M. Reith *1907 Handbook to Singapore* (o/p). Intriguing period piece which illuminates early-twen-tieth-century colonial attitudes in Singapore: drill hall, gaol and docks are detailed, while the list of useful Malay phrases includes such essentials as "harness the horse" and "off with you".

⭐ **Michael Wise** (ed) *Travellers' Tales of Old Singapore*. Identical in theme to Bastin's *Travellers' Singapore* (above), though Wise's selection of tales is the more catholic and engrossing of the two.

Gavin Young *In Search of Conrad*. Young plays detective and historian, tracing Joseph Conrad's footsteps around Southeast Asia in search of the stories and locations that inspired him. Young's time in Singapore takes him from the National Library to Bidadari cemetery in search of A.P. Williams – Conrad's Lord Jim.

History and politics

Abdullah bin Kadir *The Hikayat Abdullah* (o/p). Raffles' one-time clerk, Melakan-born Abdullah later turned diarist of some of the most formative years of Southeast Asian history; his first-hand account is crammed with illuminating vignettes and character portraits.

Barbara Watson Andaya and Leonard Andaya *The History of Malaysia*. Unlike more paternalistic histories, written by former colonists, this standard text on the region takes a more even-handed view, and finds time for cultural coverage.

David Brazil *Street Smart Singapore*. An Aladdin's cave of Singaporean history and trivia that remains fascinating throughout. Published by Times Editions, Singapore.

Maurice Collis *Raffles* (o/p). The most accessible and enjoyable biography of Sir Stamford Raffles: very readable.

Images of Asia series: Maya Jayapal's *Old Singapore*. Concise volume which charts the growth of the city-state, drawing on contemporary maps, sketches and photographs to engrossing effect.

Lee Kuan Yew *The Singapore Story*. Spanning the 42 years from his birth to Singapore's separation from Malaysia in 1965, the Granddaddy of contemporary Singapore's first volume of memoirs has drawn plaudits from the likes of Thatcher and Chirac, Keating and Kissinger. Essential reading for anyone wanting the inside track on Singapore's huge expansion over the past fifty years.

Nick Leeson *Rogue Trader*. Leeson's own account of his beginnings, his ambitions and of the whirlpool of deceit in which he floundered as the result of his covert trading in Singapore. The inadequacies of Barings' systems and controls are revealed as contributing factors, though Leeson's apparent lack of penitence wins him little sympathy.

James Minchin *No Man Is An Island*. A well-researched and at times critical study of Lee Kuan Yew, which refuses to kowtow to Singapore's ex-PM and is hence unavailable in Singapore itself, but gleefully sold in shops throughout Malaysia.

C. Mary Turnbull *A Short History of Malaysia, Singapore and Brunei* Published by Graham Brash in Singapore, this is an informed introduction to the region, touching on the major issues that have shaped it. Its big brother, Turnbull's *History of Singapore 1819–1988* (o/p), is, in contrast, as scholarly an approach to Singapore as you could wish for.

C.E. Wurtzburg *Raffles of the Eastern Isles*. A weighty and learned tome that's the definitive study of the man who founded modern Singapore; not for the marginally interested.

WWII and the Japanese Occupation

Noel Barber *Sinister Twilight*. Documents the fall of Singapore to the Japanese, by re-imagining the crucial events of the period.

Russell Braddon *The Naked Island*. Southeast Asia under the Japanese: Braddon's disturbing and moving first-hand account of the POW camps of Malaya, Singapore and Siam displays courage in the face of appalling conditions and treatment. Worth scouring second-hand stores for.

Peter Elphick *Singapore: The Pregnable Fortress*. Drawing on documents made available only in 1993, Elphick has produced the definitive history of the fall of Singapore, showing the gaffes, low morale and desertion that led to it; a scholarly *tour de force*.

Culture and society

Culture Shock! Singapore. Cultural dos and don'ts for the leisure and business traveller to the region, spanning subjects as diverse as handing over business cards and belching after a fine meal.

Leslie Layton *Songbirds in Singapore* (o/p). A delightful examination of songbird-keeping in Singapore, detailing all facets of the pastime, from its growth in the nineteenth century to its most popular birds.

Tan Kok Seng *Son of Singapore* (o/p). Tan Kok Seng's candid and sobering autobiography unearths the underside of the Singaporean success story, telling of hard times spent as a coolie.

Literature

Charles Allen *Tales from the South China Seas*. Memoirs of the last gen-eration of British colonists, in which predictable Raj attitudes prevail, though some of the drama of every-day lives, often in inhospitable con-ditions, is evinced with considerable pathos.

Noel Barber *Tanamera*. Romantic saga based in mid-twentieth-century Singapore.

Gopal Baratham *Moonrise; Sunset*. When How Kum Menon's fiancée is murdered while sleeping by his side in Singapore's East Coast Park, it seems everyone he knows has a motive. How Kum turns detective, and an engaging whodunnit emerges. In *A Candle or the Sun*, Baratham swallows hard and tackles the thorny issue of political corruption.

★ **Anthony Burgess** *The Long Day Wanes*. Burgess's Malayan trilogy – *Time for a Tiger, The Enemy in the Blanket* and *Beds in the East* – published in one volume, provides a witty and acutely observed vision of 1950s Malaya, underscoring the racial prejudices of the period. *Time for a Tiger*, the first novel, is worth reading for the Falstaffian Nabby Adams alone.

★ **James Clavell** *King Rat*. Set in Japanese-occupied Singapore, a gripping tale of survival in the noto-rious Changi Prison.

Joseph Conrad *Lord Jim*. Southeast Asia provides the backdrop to the story of Jim's desertion of an appar-ently sinking ship and subsequent efforts to redeem himself; modelled upon the sailor A.P. Williams, who lived and died in Singapore.

Alastair Dingwall (ed) *Southeast Asia Traveller's Literary Companion*. Among the bite-sized essays in this gem of a book are enlightening seg-ments on Malaysia and Singapore, into which are crammed biogra-phies, a recommended reading list, historical, linguistic and literary backgrounds. Excerpts range from classical Malayan literature to the nations' leading contemporary lights.

★ **J.G. Farrell** *The Singapore Grip*. Lengthy novel – Farrell's last – of World War II Singapore in which real and fictitious characters flit from tennis to dinner party as the count-down to the Japanese occupation begins.

Skoob Pacifica Anthology No. 1 and No. 2. These two thorough compendia of writings from the Pacific Rim together comprise an invaluable introduction to the con-temporary literatures of Singapore and Malaysia.

W. Somerset Maugham *Short Stories Volume 4*. Peopled by hoary sailors, bored plantation-dwellers and colonials with mutton-chop whiskers and topees, Maugham's short stories resuscitate the Malaya of a century ago; quintessential colonial literature graced by an easy style and a steady eye for a story.

Southeast Asia Writes Back! Anthology. A thorough compendium of writings from the Pacific Rim, published by Skoob, that provides a useful introduction to the contemporary literature of Singapore.

Paul Theroux *Saint Jack.* The compulsively bawdy tale of Jack Flowers, an ageing American who supplements his earnings at a Singapore ship's chandlers by pimping for Westerners; Jack's jaundiced eye and Theroux's rich prose open windows on Singapore's past.

Wildlife

G.W.H. Davison and Chew Yen Fook *A Photographic Guide to Birds of Peninsular Malaysia and Singapore.* Well-keyed and user-friendly, these slender volumes carry oodles of glossy plates that make positive identifying a breeze.

Chua Ee Kiam *Chek Jawa:* *Discovering Singapore's Biodiversity.* The shallow tidal flats of Chek Jawa, on Pula Ubin's east coast, were saved from the redevelopers in 2001. This beautiful book, published by Select Books, traces its salvation, and features stunning photography of its rich wildlife.

Glossary

Baba Straits-born Chinese (male).

Bukit Hill.

Bumboat Small cargo boat.

Cheongsam Chinese dress with long slit up the side.

Chunan Plaster made from eggs, lime, sugar and coconut husks.

Expressway Motorway/freeway.

Five-foot way Covered verandah outside a shophouse.

Godown Riverside warehouse.

Gopuram Bank of sculpted deities over entrance to a Hindu temple.

Haj Trip to Mecca.

Halal Something that's permissible by Islam.

Hawker centre A cluster of food stalls gathered under one roof and sharing common tables.

Istana Palace.

Jalan Road.

Kampung Village.

Kavadi Steel frames hung from the bodies of Hindu devotees during Thaipusam.

Keramat Auspicious Malay site.

Kongsi Chinese clan association.

Kris Wavy-bladed dagger.

Lorong Lane.

Mahjong A Chinese game with similarities to dominoes.

Mandi Asian method of bathing by dousing with water from a tank using a small bucket.

Masjid Mosque.

Nonya Straits-born Chinese (female); sometimes *Nyonya*.

Padang Field or square.

Peranakan Straits-born Chinese.

Pulau Island.

Ramadan Muslim fasting month.

Rotan Rattan cane; used in the infliction of corporal punishment.

Saree Traditional Indian woman's garment, worn in conjunction with a *choli* (short-sleeved blouse).

Singlish Singaporean English.

Shophouse Shuttered building with living space upstairs and shop space on ground floor.

Songkok Hat worn by Muslim males.

Sultan Ruler.

T'ai chi Chinese martial art; commonly performed as an early-morning exercise.

Temenggong Chieftain.

Tiffin Lunch.

Tongkang Chinese sailing boat.

Trishaw Three-wheeled bicycles with a carriage for passengers.

Wayang Chinese opera.

Acronyms

CBD Central Business District.

JB Johor Bahru.

KL Kuala Lumpur.

MCP Malayan Communist Party.

MDU Malayan Democratic Union.

MRT Mass Rapid Transit system.

PAP People's Action Party.

SIA Singapore International Airline.

STB Singapore Tourist Board.

UNMO Malaysia's United Malays National Organization.

WTC World Trade Centre.

Index

and small print

Index

Entries in colour indicate a map

A

Abdul Gaffoor Mosque ...78
accommodation 115
addresses 27
airlines 178
  in Australia and New
    Zealand 14
  in the UK and Ireland 10
  in the US and Canada 13
airport 26, 178
Amoy Street 62
antiques and crafts 164
Arab Quarter, The 81
Arab Street 81
Armenian Church
  of Saint Gregory the
  Illuminator 50
arrival 26
Asian Civilization
  Museum 50
ATMs 21

B

badminton 173
banks 20
Barings Bank 70
bars 148
batik 169
Battle Box 52
beaches 111
Bencoolen Street,
  hotels around 79
bike rental 31
boat cruises 32
Boat Quay 71
Boat Quay, restaurants
  and cafés 72
books 202
bookshops 167
bowling 171
Bras Basah Road 48
Bugis Village 49
Bukit Batok 87
Bukit Timah Nature
  Reserve 85
bus terminals 27
buses 30
Butterfly Park and Insect
  Kingdom Museum 111

C

car rental 31, 178
carpets 169
Change Alley Aerial
  Plaza 71
Changi Prison 95
Changi Village 96
Chettiar Hindu
  Temple 53
CHIJMES complex 48
children's Singapore 175
China Street 63
Chinatown 57
Chinatown and the
  Financial District ...58–59
Chinatown Complex 67
Chinatown Heritage
  Centre 67
Chinatown restaurants ...61
Chinese and Japanese
  Gardens 104
Chinese astrology 194
Chinese Chamber of
  Commerce 50
Chinese New Year 159
Chinese opera 157
Chinese tea 66
Cinemania 109
City Hall 46
city transport 29
Clarke Quay 52
classical music 155
Clifford Pier 71
climate ix
clothes shopping 169
Club Street 63
clubs 152
Colonial District 41
Colonial District 42
cookery schools 145
costs 20
credit cards 21
cricket 171
crime 36
cultural performances ...157
currency 20
customs 18, 164
cycling 171

D

darts 172
Deepavali 78, 162
dentists 178
departure 28
departure tax 178
Dhoby Ghaut 55
disabled travellers 37
discos 152
doctors 178
drugs 36
Duxton Hill 68

E

East Coast hotels 95
East Coast Park 93
East India Company 44
Eastern and Oriental
  Express 17
Eastern Singapore 94
eating 123
electrical goods 167
embassies
  foreign 178
  Singaporean 18
Emerald Hill Road 56
emergencies 36, 178
Empress Place
  Building 42
Escape Theme
  Park 98
Esplanade – Theatres
  on the Bay 47
Eu Tong Sen Street 69
Eu Yan Sang
  Medical Hall 63

F

Far East Square 62
ferry terminals 27
festivals 32, 159
film 156
Financial District, The 70
flights
  from Australia and New
    Zealand 14

from Southeast Asia 16
from the UK and Ireland 10
from the US and Canada....12
food and drink
glossary........................128
food courts 126
food markets.................124
Fort Canning Park...........51
Fort Siloso....................109
Fuk Tak Ch'i Street
Museum 62
Fullerton Building............71
gay and lesbian
Singapore...................152

G

Geylang...........................93
ginseng 64
glossary 214
golf 171
Goodwood Hotel 56

H

Hajjah Fatimah
Mosque 83
Haw Par Villa................101
hawker centres 126
health 24
high tea 138
history of Singapore 183
Holland Village 103
horse riding...................172
hospitals 179

I

Images of Singapore
Exhibition 109
immigration 179
information..............19, 155
inoculations....................25
insurance 23
Internet cafés...............146
ISIC 21
Istana Kampong Glam....83
Istana Negara
Singapura....................55

J

jewellery 168
Joo Chiat Complex.........95
Joo Chiat Road...............95
Jurong BirdPark............104
Jurong Lake 103

K

Katong 93
Kranji War Cemetery
and Memorial 91
Kuan Yim Temple............49
Kusu Island 112

L

Lau Pa Sat Festival
Market........................71
laundry 179
Lazarus Island..............112
left luggage 179
Lian Shan Shuang Lin
Temple.........................89
Little India 74
Little India and the
Arab Quarter..........76–77
Little India
Conservation Area 75
Little India restaurants...80
live music 154

M

Madrasah Al Junid
Al-Islamiah 83
Malay Village.................93
Mandai Orchid
Gardens 91
maps 19
Marina South 73
martial arts....................172
medical centres 25
meditation 98
Merlion 111
Merlion Park...................71
money.............................20
Mount Faber 99
MRT system...................29
Musical Fountain 111

N

National Orchid Garden...56
New Bridge Road 69
newspapers 35
Night Safari 91
nightlife 148
North Bridge Road.........81
Northern Singapore 86

O

online information 19
opening hours................32
Orchard Road 54
Orchard Road..........54–55
organized tours..............31
overland from
Southeast Asia.............16

P

package tours
in Australia and New
Zealand....................15
in the UK and Ireland.........11
in the US and Canada 13
Padang, The 43
Parliament House 43
Peranakans 56, 80
pharmacies 179
Phor Kark See
Temple.........................90
Pink Street 78
police 36, 179
polo 172
pool 172
Port of Singapore 73
post................................33
pub food 137
public holidays...............33
pubs 148
Pulau Hantu 112
Pulau Seking................112
Pulau Ubin 97

R

radio...............................35
Raffles City.....................47
Raffles Hotel 47
Raffles Place.................70
Raffles, Sir
Stamford 44,183
Rafflesia arnoldii 45

Ramadan 152
recipes, Singaporean....198
Reflections at Bukit
  Chandu 103
religion 190
restaurants 127
rollerblading 171
rubber plantations...........56

S

safety 35
Sago Street.....................67
Sakaya Muni Buddha
  Gaya Temple 79
SARS 24
Sasanaramsi Burmese
  Buddhist Temple 89
Sentosa.........................107
Sentosa Island 108
Sentosa Orchid
  Gardens 111
Sepoy Mutiny...................46
Serangoon Road.............75
shopping...........54, 69, 163
Singapore Art
  Museum 49
Singapore Botanic
  Gardens 56
Singapore Cricket
  Club..............................44
Singapore Discovery
  Centre 105
Singapore History
  Museum 51
Singapore Recreation
  Club..............................45
Singapore River 41
Singapore Science
  Centre 103
Singapore Sling 48
Singapore Turf Club........92
Singapore Zoological
  Gardens 90
Sister's Islands.............112
skiing.............................172
snooker 172
Snow City 104
soccer 173
songbirds 60
songket 169
Southeast Asia..............16
spas 173
sports............................171
squash 173

Sri Mariamman Hindu
  Temple..........................64
Sri Srinivasa Perumal
  Temple..........................79
Sri Veeramakaliamman
  Temple..........................78
St Andrew's Cathedral....46
St John's Island 112
State of Johor
  Mosque 101
STB offices 19
student cards.................21
Substation......................50
Sultan Mosque................83
Sun Yat Sen Villa............87
Sungei Buloh Nature
  Park 92
supermarkets 124
Supreme Court 46
swimming......................173

T

T'ai chi 172
tailors 169
Tan Yeok Nee Mansion ...56
Tanjong Pagar 66
taxis 31
telephones 33
television 35
Telok Ayer Street............60
Telok Blangah 99
temperature 000
tennis 173
Thai Buddhist Temple 97
Thai village 84
theatre..........................157
Theatres by the Bay
  project 47
Thian Hock Keng
  Temple..........................60
Thimithi 64
Thong Chai Medical
  Institute 69
tiffin 138
Tiger Brewery................105
time difference 179
tipping 179
tour operators
  in Australia and New
    Zealand..........................15
  in the UK and Ireland..........11
  in the US and Canada 13
tourist offices, overseas..19
tours..............................31

train station.....................27
trains, Eastern and
  Oriental Express...........17
travel agents
  in Australia and New
    Zealand............................15
  in the UK and Ireland..........11
  in the US and Canada 13
  online 9
travellers' cheques.........21
trishaws.........................32
Turtle Island 112

U

Ubin Village....................97
Underwater World.........109
URA Gallery 64

V

Victoria Concert Hall.......43
Victoria Theatre..............43
visas................................18
Volcanoland 109

W

Wak Hai Cheng Bio
  Temple..........................62
Waterloo Street..............49
watersports...................174
weather 000
websites.........................19
Western Singapore 100
wiring money 22
Wondergolf....................109
World Trade Centre.........99

Y

youth cards.....................21

Z

Zhujiao Centre 75

A rough guide to Rough Guides

In the summer of 1981, Mark Ellingham, a recent graduate from Bristol University, was travelling round Greece and couldn't find a guidebook that really met his needs. On the one hand there were the student guides, insistent on saving every last cent, and on the other the heavyweight cultural tomes whose authors seemed to have spent more time in a research library than lounging away the afternoon at a taverna or on the beach.

In a bid to avoid getting a job, Mark and a small group of writers set about creating their own guidebook. It was a guide to Greece that aimed to combine a journalistic approach to description with a thoroughly practical approach to travellers' needs – a guide that would incorporate culture, history and contemporary insights with a critical edge, together with up-to-date, value-for-money listings. Back in London, Mark and the team finished their Rough Guide, as they called it, and talked Routledge into publishing the book.

That first *Rough Guide to Greece*, published in 1982, was a student scheme that became a publishing phenomenon. The immediate success of the book – with numerous reprints and a Thomas Cook Prize shortlisting – spawned a series that rapidly covered dozens of destinations. Rough Guides had a ready market among low-budget backpackers, but soon also acquired a much broader and older readership that relished Rough Guides' wit and inquisitiveness as much as their enthusiastic, critical approach. Everyone wants value for money, but not at any price.

Rough Guides soon began supplementing the "rougher" information about hostels and low-budget listings with the kind of detail on restaurants and quality hotels that independent-minded visitors on any budget might expect, whether on business in New York or trekking in Thailand.

These days the guides – distributed worldwide by the Penguin Group – offer recommendations from shoestring to luxury and cover more than 200 destinations around the globe, including almost every country in the Americas and Europe, more than half of Africa, and most of Asia and Australasia. Our ever-growing team of authors and photographers is spread all over the world, particularly in Europe, the USA and Australia.

In 1994, we published the *Rough Guide to World Music* and *Rough Guide to Classical Music*, and a year later the *Rough Guide to the Internet*. All three books have become benchmark titles in their fields – which encouraged us to expand into other areas of publishing, mainly around popular culture. Rough Guides now publishes:

- Travel guides to more than 200 destinations worldwide
- Dictionary phrasebooks to 22 major languages
- History guides ranging from Ireland to Islam
- Maps printed on rip-proof and waterproof Polyart™ paper
- Music guides running the gamut from Opera to Elvis
- Restaurant guides to London, New York and San Francisco
- Reference books on topics as diverse as the Weather and Shakespeare
- Sports guides from Formula 1 to Man Utd
- Pop culture books from Lord of the Rings to Cult TV
- World Music CDs in association with World Music Network.

Visit **www.roughguides.com** to see our latest publications.

SMALL PRINT

Rough Guide credits

Text editor: Ruth Blackmore
Managing director: Kevin Fitzgerald
Series editor: Mark Ellingham
Editorial: Martin Dunford, Jonathan Buckley, Kate Berens, Ann-Marie Shaw, Helena Smith, Olivia Swift, Ruth Blackmore, Geoff Howard, Claire Saunders, Gavin Thomas, Clifton Wilkinson, Alexander Mark Rogers, Polly Thomas, Joe Staines, Richard Lim, Duncan Clark, Peter Buckley, Lucy Ratcliffe, Alison Murchie, Matthew Teller, Andrew Dickson, Fran Sandham, Sally Schafer, Matthew Milton, Karoline Densley, Ella O'Donnell, Andy Turner (UK); Andrew Rosenberg, Yuki Takagaki, Richard Koss, Hunter Slaton (US).
Design & Layout: Link Hall, Helen Prior, Julia Bovis, Katie Pringle, Rachel Holmes, Andy Turner, Dan May, Tanya Hall, John McKay, Sophie Hewat (UK); Madhulita Mohapatra,

Umesh Aggarwal, Sunil Sharma (India)
Cartography: Maxine Repath, Ed Wright, Katie Lloyd-Jones (UK); Manish Chandra, Rajesh Chhibber, Jai Prakash Mishra (India)
Cover art direction: Louise Boulton
Picture research: Sharon Martins, Mark Thomas
Online: Kelly Martinez, Anja Mutic-Blessing, Jennifer Gold, Audra Epstein, Suzanne Welles, Cree Lawson (US); Manik Chauhan, Amarjyoti Dutta, Narender Kumar (India)
Finance: Gary Singh
Marketing & Publicity: Richard Trillo, Niki Smith, David Wearn, Chloë Roberts, Demelza Dallow, Claire Southern (UK); Geoff Colquitt, David Wechsler, Megan Kennedy (US)
Administration: Julie Sanderson
RG India: Punita Singh

Publishing information

This fourth edition published November 2003 by **Rough Guides Ltd**,
80 Strand, London WC2R 0RL
345 Hudson St, 4th Floor,
New York, NY 10014, USA.
Distributed by the Penguin Group
Penguin Books Ltd,
80 Strand, London WC2R 0RL
Penguin Putnam, Inc.
375 Hudson St, NY 10014, USA
Penguin Books Australia Ltd,
487 Maroondah Highway, PO Box 257,
Ringwood, Victoria 3134, Australia
Penguin Books Canada Ltd,
10 Alcorn Avenue, Toronto ON,
M4V 1E4 Canada
Penguin Books (NZ) Ltd,
182–190 Wairau Road, Auckland 10,
New Zealand
Typeset in Bembo and Helvetica to an original design by Henry Iles.
Printed in Italy by LegoPrint S.p.A.

220pp includes index.
A catalogue record for this book is available from the British Library.

ISBN 1843530759

The publishers and authors have done their best to ensure the accuracy and currency of all the information in **The Rough Guide to Singapore**; however, they can accept no responsibility for any loss, injury or inconvenience sustained by any traveller as a result of information or advice contained in the guide.

1   3   5   7   9   8   6   4   2

Help us update

We've gone to a lot of effort to ensure that the fourth edition of **The Rough Guide to Singapore** is accurate and up-to-date. However, things change – places get "discovered", opening hours are notoriously fickle, restaurants and rooms raise prices or lower standards. If you feel we've got it wrong or left something out, we'd like to know, and if you can remember the address, the price, the time, the phone number, so much the better.

We'll credit all contributions, and send a copy of the next edition (or any other Rough

Guide if you prefer) for the best letters. Everyone who writes to us and isn't already a subscriber will receive a copy of our full-colour thrice-yearly newsletter. Please mark letters: **"Rough Guide Singapore Update"** and send to: Rough Guides, 80 Strand, London WC2R 0RL, or Rough Guides, 4th Floor, 345 Hudson St, New York, NY 10014. Or send an email to **mail@roughguides.com**.

Have your questions answered and tell others about your trip at **www.roughguides.atinfopop.com**.

Acknowledgements

Mark would like to thank Susie his wife for love and patience beyond the call, and his parents and entire family for their continuing love and support.

The editor would like to thank Carole Mansur for proofreading, Edward Wright for maps, Umesh Aggarwal and Sunil Sharma for typesetting, Mark Thomas for picture research and Karoline Densley for the index.

Readers' letters

Thanks to all the readers who took the trouble to write in with their comments and suggestions (and apologies to anyone whose name we've misspelt or omitted):

Stephanie Higgins, Rae McDonald, Siobhan Edwards, Deborah Brownson, Peter & Lucie Wise, Ellen Otty, Clive Walker, Roy & Audrey Bradford, Kerry Watson and Mary Mann.

SMALL PRINT

Photo credits

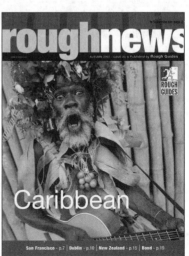

TRAVEL • MUSIC • REFERENCE • PHRASEBOOKS •

Europe

Algarve
Amsterdam 🌐
Andalucia 🌐
Austria
Barcelona 🌐
Belgium
 & Luxembourg
Berlin 🌐
Britain
Brittany
 & Normandy
Bruges & Ghent
Brussels 🌐
Budapest
Bulgaria
Copenhagen
Corfu
Corsica
Costa Brava
Crete
Croatia
Cyprus 🌐
Czech & Slovak
 Republics 🔲
Devon &
 Cornwall
Dodecanese
 & East Aegean
Dordogne
 & the Lot
Dublin 🌐
Edinburgh
England
Europe
First-Time
 Around the
 World
First-Time

Europe 🔲
Florence 🌐
France 🔲 ⊙
French Hotels
 & Restaurants
Germany 🔲
Greece 🔲 🌐 ⊙
Greek Islands
Hungary 🔲 ⊙
Ibiza &
 Formentera
Iceland
Ionian Islands
Ireland ⊙
Italy 🔲 ⊙
Lake District
Languedoc
 & Roussillon
Lisbon
London 🌐
London Mini
 Guide
London
 Restaurants
Walks around
 London
Madeira
Madrid
Mallorca
Malta & Gozo
Menorca
Moscow
Netherlands
Norway
Paris 🌐 ⊙
Paris Mini Guide
Poland 🔲
Portugal 🔲 ⊙
Prague 🌐

Provence & the
 Côte d'Azur
Pyrenees
Romania
Rome 🌐
Sardinia
Scandinavia
Scotland ⊙
Scottish
 Highlands &
 Islands
Sicily
Spain 🔲 ⊙
St Petersburg
Sweden
Switzerland
Tenerife &
 La Gomera 🌐
Turkey 🔲 ⊙
Tuscany &
 Umbria
Venice &
 The Veneto 🌐
Vienna
Wales ⊙

Asia

Bali & Lombok
Bangkok
Beijing
Cambodia
China 🔲
First-Time Asia
Goa
Hong Kong &
 Macau
India 🔲 ⊙
Indonesia 🔲
Japan 🔲 ⊙

Laos
Malaysia,
 Singapore
 & Brunei
Nepal
Philippines
Singapore
South India
Southeast Asia
Thailand 🔲 🌐
Thailand
 Beaches &
 Islands
Tokyo
Vietnam 🔲

Australasia

Australia 🌐 ⊙
Gay & Lesbian
 Australia
Melbourne
New Zealand
 🌐
Sydney

North America

Alaska
Baltic States
Big Island
 of Hawaii ⊙
Boston 🌐
California 🌐
Canada
Chicago
Florida
Grand Canyon
Hawaii
Honolulu

🌐 map   🔲 phrasebook   ⊙ cd

Rough Guides publishes new books every month.

TRAVEL ∘ MUSIC ∘ REFERENCE ∘ PHRASEBOOKS

TRAVEL

Las Vegas
Los Angele0s 🌐
Maui
Miami & the
   Florida Keys 🌐
Montréal
New England
New Orleans
New York City 🌐
New York City
   Mini Guide
New York
   Restaurants
Pacific
   Northwest
Rocky
   Mountains
San Francisco 🌐
San Francisco
   Restaurants
Seattle
Skiing and
   Snowboarding
   in North
   America
Southwest USA
Toronto
USA
Vancouver
Washington DC 🌐
Yosemite

**Caribbean
& Latin
America**

Antigua &
   Barbuda

Argentina 🌐 ⊙
Bahamas
Barbados
Belize
Bolivia
Brazil
Caribbean
Central America
Chile
Costa Rica
Cuba 🌐 ⊙
Dominican
   Republic 🌐
Ecuador
First-Time Latin
   America
Guatemala 🌐
Jamaica ⊙
Maya World
Mexico 🗺 🌐 ⊙
Peru ⊙
St Lucia
Trinidad &
   Tobago 🌐

**Africa &
Middle East**

Cape Town
Egypt 🗺 🌐 ⊙
Gambia ⊙
Israel &
   Palestinian
   Territories
Jerusalem
Jordan
Kenya 🗺 ⊙
Morocco 🌐
South Africa,
   Lesotho
   & Swaziland
   🗺 🌐

Syria
Tanzania ⊙
Tunisia
West Africa ⊙
Zanzibar
Zimbabwe ⊙

**Reference
Music**

Acoustic Guitar
Classical Music
Country Music
Country: 100
   Essential CDs
Cuban Music
Drum'n'bass
Flute
House
Irish Music
Jazz
Latin: 100
   Essential CDs
Music USA
Opera
Reggae
Rock
Rock: 100
   Essential CDs
Soul: 100
   Essential CDs
Techno
World Music
   Vol1
World Music
   Vol2

Reference

The Beatles
Books for
   Teenagers
Children's

Books, 0–5
Children's
   Books, 5–11
Cult Football
Cult Movies
Cult Pop
Cult TV
Digital Stuff
Elvis
Formula 1
History of China
History of Egypt
History of
   England
History of
   France
History of India
History of Islam
History of Italy
History of Spain
History of USA
The Internet
Internet Radio
James Bond
Man Utd
Personal
   Computers
Pregnancy &
   Birth
Shopping Online
Travel Health
Travel Online
Unexplained
   Phenomena
The Universe
Videogaming
Weather
Website
   Directory
Women Travel

Rough Guides music & reference

THE MRT SYSTEM

Legend:
- East-West line
- North-South line
- North-East line
- ○ Interchange station

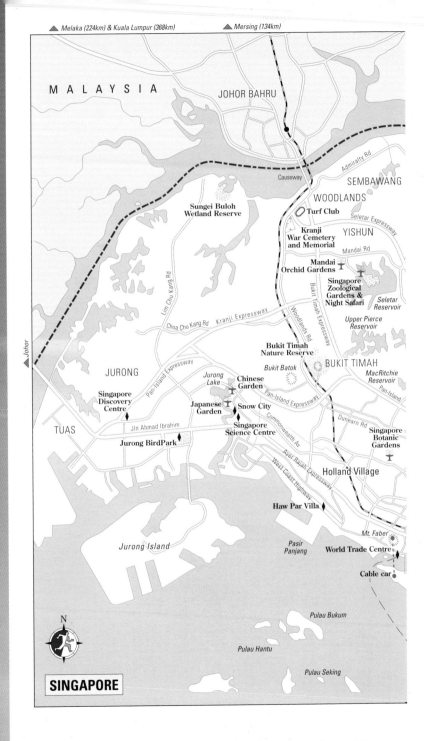